进出口贸易结算 （双语版）（第二版）

Settlement for Imports and Exports

主编 ● 傅泳

西南财经大学出版社
Southwestern University of Finance & Economics Press
中国·成都

图书在版编目(CIP)数据

进出口贸易结算=Settlement for Imports and Exports:汉英对照 / 傅泳主编.—2 版.—成都:西南财经大学出版社,2024.2
ISBN 978-7-5504-6115-4

Ⅰ.①进… Ⅱ.①傅… Ⅲ.①进出口贸易—国际结算—汉、英 Ⅳ.①F746②F830.73

中国国家版本馆 CIP 数据核字(2024)第 043933 号

进出口贸易结算/Settlement for Imports and Exports(双语版)(第二版)
JINCHUKOU MAOYI JIESUAN(SHUANGYU BAN)

主 编 傅 泳

策划编辑:李晓嵩
责任编辑:李晓嵩
责任校对:王 琳
封面设计:何东琳设计工作室
责任印制:朱曼丽

出版发行	西南财经大学出版社(四川省成都市光华村街 55 号)
网 址	http://cbs.swufe.edu.cn
电子邮件	bookcj@ swufe.edu.cn
邮政编码	610074
电 话	028-87353785
照 排	四川胜翔数码印务设计有限公司
印 刷	四川五洲彩印有限责任公司
成品尺寸	185mm×260mm
印 张	26.875
字 数	740 千字
版 次	2024 年 2 月第 2 版
印 次	2024 年 2 月第 1 次印刷
印 数	1— 2000 册
书 号	ISBN 978-7-5504-6115-4
定 价	59.80 元

第二版前言

本书是 2013 年西南财经大学出版社出版的中英文双语教材《进出口贸易结算》的修订版。此次修订，笔者在保留原书的基本框架、编写体例、编写特色、基本内容以及中英文对照的基础上，依据国际商会的《2010 年国际贸易术语解释通则》和《跟单信用证统一惯例》（UCP 600）等一系列有关国际贸易的规则、惯例进行了修订，对部分内容做了增补、调整和更新，并针对近年来电子商务的迅猛发展，将国际结算与国际贸易和跨境电子商务进行了宏观对比，使读者能够及时了解和掌握新知识、适应和判断新变化。

本书以马克思列宁主义、毛泽东思想、邓小平理论、"三个代表"重要思想、科学发展观和习近平新时代中国特色社会主义思想为指导，坚持以立德树人为根本任务，致力于将党的二十大精神与教材内容相衔接，并对标新文科背景下"英语+商务"的复合型要求，力求以规范、简练的语言对知识点进行系统、全面的梳理，使读者掌握进出口贸易结算业务的专业知识，熟悉规范的中英文表述，并提高运用英语处理进出口贸易结算业务的能力。

进出口贸易结算这门学科具有系统性、实务性和可操作性的特点，本书增加了练习题并附参考答案。一方面，本书通过选择题、填空题、案例分析题、实务操作题等不同形式的知识类练习题，方便读者对照检查对重要知识点的掌握情况，熟悉相关单据的缮制要求，了解结算业务的实际状况；另一方面，本书通过思政类练习题，着力挖掘知识点中所蕴含的思政元素，传播中华优秀传统文化，弘扬社会主义核心价值观。

本书可以作为高等院校商务英语专业及商务类专业国际商务方向、国际贸易方向、国际结算方向的本科生、研究生相关课程的配套教材。西南财经大学商务英语专业为国家级一流本科专业建设点，本书是该专业建设点的专业教材之一。本书也可以作为国际贸易、国际商务从业者的辅助资料。

笔者主持了西南财经大学中央高校教育教学改革在线开放课程"国际支付与结算（英）"，与西南财经大学另外两位教师共同完成了该门课程的慕课项目。该课程已在学堂在线（http://www.xuetangx.com）上线，本书可以作为该在线课程的参考书。

本书在编写过程中参阅了大量的文献资料，笔者在此对这些文献资料的提供者和编者以及单据样例涉及的相关公司表示深深的谢意和敬意。限于笔者的实际业务经验和学识水平，书中难免出现疏漏和不足，敬请专家学者和广大读者批评指正。

傅泳

2024 年 1 月

前言

改革开放以来，随着中国加入世界贸易组织和外贸经营权的放开，我国的对外进出口贸易发展突飞猛进。在此背景下，可以预见，我国企业的业务将日益国际化，更多的经营主体将会加入进出口贸易的行列中来，更多的企业将会更加需要既具备娴熟的英语语言技能，又具备经贸专业知识的复合型、应用型人才。本书是一本"以复合型为背景"的中英文对照经贸类专业教材，旨在使读者掌握对外进出口贸易结算业务的专业知识，获得相关标准的、规范的专业理论及专业术语，提高运用英语处理进出口贸易结算业务的能力。为实现此目的，本书的编写具有以下几个特色：

第一，中英对照，深层复合。结算业务是进出口贸易中非常重要的核心业务，涉及货物的出运和货款的收付，对进出口贸易的顺畅运作至关重要。本书强调专业性和系统性，读者可以通过本书的英文部分对相关理论进行系统学习。本书的中文翻译部分能方便读者进行中英文对照和比较，更好地理解相关的专业内容，帮助读者将英语和结算业务专业知识进行深层次复合。

第二，注重实务，编排合理。本书分为引入篇、票据篇、结算篇和单据篇共4篇、12章。引入篇介绍结算业务与对外进出口贸易的关系，帮助读者从宏观角度对结算业务在对外进出口贸易领域以及在整个国际商务领域的位置进行准确定位。票据篇、结算篇和单据篇按结算业务的构成分别成篇，使初学者能一目了然地了解结算业务的构成情况，进而一步步掌握各部分的具体内容、相互关系以及在实务操作中的整体配合，从而避免出现只见树木不见林，不能将理论知识运用于实际操作的情况。

第三，图文并茂，形象直观。本书把许多复杂的概念与结算步骤用实务样例和流程图表勾画出来，形象直观地阐释了概念的意义、概念与概念之间的逻辑关系以及结算业务的操作过程。

第四，单据标准，格式规范。结算业务的核心是单据业务，整个流程涉及纷繁复杂的单据。因此，缮制格式规范、内容正确和组合正确的单据是顺利完成一笔进出口贸易业务的保证。基于此，本书对重要的单据样例逐条进行了阐释，并选取了一些编者在实际结算业务操作过程中处理运作过的单据实例。

本书可以作为高等院校商务英语专业以及商务类专业国际商务、国际贸易、国际结算的本科、研究生课程教材，也可以作为国际贸易、国际商务从业者的辅助工具。

本书在编写过程中参阅了大量的文献资料，笔者对这些文献资料的提供者和编者以及单据样例涉及的相关公司表示深深的谢意和敬意。由于笔者水平有限，敬请国内外专家学者和广大读者批评指正。

傅泳

2013 年 7 月

CONTENTS

Part 1   Introduction

Part 2　Instruments

Part 3　Settlement

Part 4   Documents

(Key to Exercises)

目录

第一部分　引入篇

第二部分　票据篇

第三部分　结算篇

第四部分　单据篇

Part 1
Introduction

Chapter 1　General Introduction to International Settlement

Objectives

◇Get an overview of the major items in a Sales Contract for an international trade transaction.

◇Learn the concept and major types of international settlement.

◇Learn the documents used in international settlement.

◇Consider the connection among international trade, international settlement and cross-border e-commerce.

Section 1　International Trade and Sales Contract

International trade is the exchange of goods and services across national boundaries. On the one hand, it concerns trade transactions of both import and export. On the other hand, it includes the purchase and sale of both tangible goods and intangible services. Exports are the merchandise individuals, companies or nations sells whereas imports are the goods and services individuals, companies or nations purchase.

Starting with enquiry and through a negotiating process of offer and counter-offer, the next step in any international trade arrangement is to reach an agreement with the overseas trade partner. This agreement can be called a contract or a confirmation and can be prepared by either the exporter or the importer. When the agreement is made by the exporter, it is to be called the sales contract or sales confirmation; when it is produced by the importer, then it gets another version of purchase contract or purchase confirmation. No matter which way to call it, this agreement is a legal document and creates a legal binding upon the contractual parties.

As shown in Figure 1.1, a sales contract consists of such major items as description of commodities, quantity, unit price and amount, price terms, packing, shipment, payment and insurance. It also contains such major clauses as quality/quantity discrepancy and claim, force majeure and arbitration.

售　货　合　同

SALES CONTRACRT

卖方：SINOCHEM GUANGDONG IMPORT& EXPORT
Sellers：CORPORATION, CHINA

Contract No.：98SGQ468001
Date：APR. 28, 2023
Signed at：GUANGZHOU

地址：
Address：97,ZHANQIAN ROAD, GUANGZHOU, CHINA

Telex：　0925
Fax：　83556600

Buyers：METCH THAI ELECTRICAL APPLANCES COMPANY
Address：124 MAITRICHITR RD., BANGKOK,THAILAND

Telex：
Fax：

This Sales Contract is made by and between the Sellers and the Buyers, whereby the Sellers agree to sell and the Buyers agree to buy the under-mentioned goods according to the terms and conditions stipulated below：

(1)货号、品名及规格 Name of Commodity and Specification	(2)数量 Quantity	(3)单位 Unit	(4)单价 Unit Price	(5)金额 Amount
TRIANGLE BRANDREFERIGERATOR ACD-150W ACD-150G ACD-150Y 5% more or less both in amount and quantity allowed	200 200 200	SET SET SET	CIF BANGKOK USD 180.00 USD 180.00 USD 180.00	USD 36 000.00 USD 36 000.00 USD 36 000.00
	Total Amount			USD108 000.00

(6) Packing：　CARTON　　　　(7) Delivery Form GUANGZHOU to BANGKOK

(8) Shipping Marks：　N/M

(9)Time of Shipment：within　30　days after receipt of L/C. transshipment allowed.

(10)Terms of Payment：By 100% Confirmed Irrevocable Letter of Credit in favor of the Seller to be available by sight draft to be opened and to reach China before MAY 20, 2023 and to remain valid for negotiation in China until the 15th days after the foresaid Time of Shipment. L/C must mention this contract number. L/C advised by BANK OF CHINA GUANGZHOU BRANCH. TLX：444U4K GZBC.CN. ALL banking Charges outside China (the mainland of China) are for the account of the Buyer.

(11) Insurance：To be effected by Seller for 110% of full invoice value covering <u>WA</u> up to <u>BANGKOK</u>

~~To be effected by the buyer.~~

(12) Quality/Quantity Discrepancy and Claim：

Incase the quality or quantity/weight are found by buyer to be not in conformity with the Contract after arrival of the goods at the port of destination, the Buyers may lodge claim with the Seller supported by survey report issued by an inspection organization agreed upon by both parties, with the exception, however, of those claims for which the insurance company and the shipping company are to be held responsible, claim for quality discrepancy should be filed by the Buyer within 30 days after arrival of the goods at the port of destination, while for quantity/weight discrepancy claim should be filed by the buyer within 15 days after arrival of the goods at the port of destination. The Seller shall, within 30 days after receipt of the notification of the claim, send reply to the Buyer.

(13) Force Majeure：In case of Force Majeure, the Seller shall not be held responsible for late delivery or non-delivery of the goods but shall notify the Buyer by cable.The Seller shall deliver to the Buyer by registered mail, if so requested by the Buyer, a certificate issued by the China Council for the Promotion of International Trade or competent authorities.

(14) All disputes arising from the execution of or in connection with this contract shall be settled amicably by negotiation.In case of settlement can be reached through negotiation the case shall then be submit to China International Economic & Trade Arbitration Commission. In Shenzhen(or in Beijing)for arbitration in act with its sure of procedures. The arbitral award is final and binding upon both parties for setting the Dispute. The fee for arbitration shall be borne by the losing party unless otherwise awarded.

The Seller _____   The Buyer _____

Figure 1. 1　**Sales Contract**

Price terms in the contract refer to INCOTERMS, the English initials for the International Rules for the Interpretation of Trade Terms, published by International Chamber of Commerce in Paris, France. Price in a sales contract must be quoted in price terms.

Every trade transaction, whether it is a business of export or import, is to fulfill the sales contract with the merchandise delivered and the payments settled. The item "terms of payment" in a sales contract refers to the payment methods. In the sample contract, the payment method chosen for this transaction is letter of credit.

Section 2   International Settlement

International settlement refers to the money transfer via banks to settle accounts, debts and claims among different countries.

International settlement is originated from international tangible and intangible trade transactions as well as international non–trade transactions such as international lending and investment, international aids and grants, cross–border personal remittance, etc. For this reason, International settlement is divided into two types: international commercial settlement, which is created for the settlement of international trade, and international non–commercial settlement, which is made for non–trade transactions. While international non–commercial settlement is of equal importance in international business, international commercial settlement will constitute the core part in this book and it will be the major focus.

International settlement centers around payment methods. In a sales contract, payment methods can also be called "payment terms" or simply as "payment". There are five payment methods: remittance, collection, factoring, letter of credit and letter of guarantee, each with its own subdivisions. Among them, remittance, collection and letter of credit are the three most popular ones in international trade. Traders must make proper choice of payment methods for a transaction.

Section 3   Documents

There are two important ingredients in a payment method: financial documents and commercial documents. Without them, payment methods are not operational.

1. Financial documents

The word "financial" implies that these instruments are made for making payment. Financial documents can also be called "financial instruments" "credit instruments", or simply "instruments". They mainly refer to bills of exchange, promissory notes and checks. They are made to facilitate the settlement of payment.

As international trade involves traders from different countries and goods are transferred across national boundaries, cash–payment is both inconvenient and dangerous for the traders. In the modern era, financial instrument has taken the place of cash and become the medium of exchange to settle payments.

Financial instruments can be simply understood as "orders" given to make or collect payments. When such "orders" are performed, payments are settled. With the involvement of financial instruments, international settlement has moved into the era of non-cash settlement. As a result, it is the instrument, not the cash, that moves throughout the settlement process in international trade.

2. Commercial documents

Commercial documents are to provide documentary evidence that goods are produced, packed and insured properly and are delivered of correct quantity and quality and in timely fashion. They are made to facilitate the delivery of goods.

Commercial documents are varied and they signify whether the responsibilities in a transaction regarding the production, packing, shipment, or insurance, etc. of the goods have been fulfilled by the traders. Popular types of commercial documents are commercial invoice, packing list, bills of lading, insurance policy, inspection certificate and certificate of origin, etc. When one type of commercial document is produced, it is considered that the related obligations are taken up.

In conclusion, the realization of payment methods calls for the participation financial instruments or commercial documents. In other words, payment methods, financial instruments and commercial documents are closely related and they constitute the framework of international settlement.

3. Title documents

The word "title" signifies the right of ownership. With the development of shipping and insurance industries, two kinds of commercial documents, bills of lading and the insurance policy, have become the title documents.

In the case of bills of lading, the holder of them becomes the owner of the goods. As a result, when the seller surrenders the bills of lading, it means that he has delivered the goods and when the buyer receives these documents, it means that he has received the goods. The delivery based on title documents is called constructive delivery which is in contrast to actual delivery in early international settlement. In actual delivery, goods are delivered only when they are physically in the hands of the buyer.

When goods have been documented, they have changed the landscape of the international settlement greatly because firstly, it is possible for both the delivery and the payment to be made against documents rather than against the actual goods, and secondly, documents have become the center of international settlement.

Section 4   Connection among International Trade, International Settlement and Cross-Border E-Commerce

1. Connection between international trade and international settlement

International settlement is vital for the successful fulfillment of a sales contract in an international trade transaction. The relationship between international trade and international settlement can be further illustrated in the following points:

(1) Accounts, debts and claims arising from international trade are to be settled through international settlement.

(2) Proper choosing and execution of payment methods is essential in the establishment and fulfillment of any sales contract.

(3) Payment methods of international settlement perform the task of delivery for the importer through commercial documents and the task of payment for the exporter through financial instruments. Consequently, funds are transferred against the movement of the documents (goods) to complete an export/import transaction.

(4) Different payment method leads to different procedure of a given trade transaction.

(5) Different payment method decides the particulars of the financial documents drawn and the commercial documents made in a given trade transaction.

2. Connection between cross-border e-commerce and international settlement

The growth of the Internet and the development of international logistics as well as online payment have provided the customers from all over the world the ability to buy and sell products or services from internet-based platforms. This is known as cross-border e-commerce (CBEC). In recent years, the rapid growth of CBEC has accelerated online consumption all over the world and it has gradually become an important driving force of international trade.

According to the type of interaction, the main modes of CBEC can be divided into B2B (business to business), B2C (business to consumer), C2C (consumer to consumer) and so on. At present in China, B2B trading volume accounts for nearly 90% of the total CBEC market size. It is being increasingly realized that the B2B holds the most potential and the enterprise is in the dominant position in the CBEC market world over.

The major CBEC platforms are Amazon, eBay, Alibaba, DHgate, AliExpress, Wish, and Shopee. Among them, Amazon is the largest e-commerce company in the United States and one of the first companies to start operating e-commerce. Alibaba is a very big CBEC platform from China. eBay is a multinational e-commerce corporation, facilitating online consumer-to-consumer and business-to-consumer sales.

CBEC, as a new mode of operation, is different from the traditional foreign trading. The major differences are listed in Table 1.1.

Table 1.1　Differences between Traditional International Trade and CBEC

Items	Traditional International Trade	CBEC
Trading mode	mainly B2B trading with large quantity, fewer batches and large amount	mainly B2B, B2C or C2C trading with small quantity, more batches and small amount
Parties involved in the trading process	manufacturer - exporter - importer - wholesaler - retailer - consumer	manufacturer - retailer - consumer, or manufacturer - consumer
Payment	traditional payment methods: remittance, collection, letter of credit, etc.	third-party online payment platform (e. g., PayPal, Alipay), international credit card, remittance, letter of credit
Shipment	More than 70% shipment is by sea and container transport. Transport costs is small in proportion to the total trading amount	Mainly shipped by aviation packets and international express delivery (e. g., EMS, DHL, FedEx, UPS, TNT). Transport costs account for 30% ~ 40% or more
Customs	Customs release shall come after commodity declaration, inspection and paying the customs taxes and fees. Qualified export goods can enjoy export tax rebates	Entrust the transportation company of centralized declaration and inspection. As from 1st Jan. 2019, customs duty will be exempted for a single CBEC trading volume below RMB 5 000 or for an individual annual CBEC trading volume below RMB 26 000, to which export tax rebates are not applicable

Compared to traditional international trade, the advantages of CBEC is that any company, manufacturer or trader, large or small, or individuals can participate in foreign trade via the internet-based platforms. The CBEC sellers can put their products or services in front of, literally, hundreds of millions of new potential overseas buyers. As the trading process in CBEC is more shortened and flat-tened than traditional international trading mode, the CBEC consumers can get products or services that may be unavailable or expensive in the home markets.

Cross-border payment and settlement refers to the behavior of the parties in-volved in international economic activities to pay off international creditor's claims and accounts by the debtors with certain payment instruments and methods, and generate funds transfer and exchange. Cross - border payment and settlement methods can be divided into traditional payment methods and CBEC payment meth-ods. Traditional payment methods are mainly used for B2B transactions and they include remittance, collection and letter of credit. CBEC payment methods refer to the payment settled through bank cards, bank transfers, or online third-party pay-ment platforms, such as PayPal, Alipay, Western Union, etc.

Traditional payment methods have a long history. Methods such as letters of credit are still widely used in CBEC, especially when the trading volume and a-mount are large. In recent years, with the popularity of the Internet and people's continuous recognition of cross-border online shopping, CBEC payment methods have developed rapidly. In the market, as traditional international trade and CBEC will supplement each other, traditional payment methods and CBEC payment meth-ods will complement each other and coexist together.

Exercises for Chapter 1

I. Answer the Following Questions

1. What are the components of international settlement?

2. What are title documents and their effects on the operation of international settlement?

3. Fill in the Table 1.2, put a "√" when you think payment is to be made and "×" when payment is not to be made.

Note:

"√" in the 2nd row means physical goods are delivered by the exporter to the importer while the opposite is marked as "×".

"√" in the 3rd row means title documents have reached the importer while the opposite is marked as "×" and "NA" means not applicable.

Table 1.2 Actual Delivery or Constructive Delivery

Items	Actual Delivery		Constructive Delivery			
Physical goods	√	×	√	×	√	×
Title documents	NA	NA	√	×	×	√
Payment						

Ⅱ. Case Analysis

Situation A: Wang Hua wants to buy one keyboard from an American seller.

Situation B: XYZ Company, Chengdu wants to buy 10 000 sets of keyboards from an American seller.

1. What trading mode is recommended to Wang Hua and XYZ Company, Chengdu respectively?

2. What transportation mode will be appropriate for the commodity to be shipped to Wang Hua and XYZ Company, Chengdu respectively?

3. What payment methods will be appropriate for Wang Hua and XYZ Company, Chengdu to make payment respectively?

Ⅲ. Extended Discussions

Look at the part of a sales contract about payment methods below and consider the following questions:

> Seller shall submit invoice for payment in accordance with the following payment methods, given as a percentage of the total contract value:
> a) 40% shall be sent to the seller by telegraphic transfer upon the signing of the contract and against the receipt of the seller's invoice of the foresaid amount.
> b) 50% shall be paid by a Confirmed Irrevocable Letter of Credit in favor of the seller to be available by sight draft and to reach China before May 20,2020 and to remain valid in negotiation in China no later than 21 days after the issuing date of the Bills of Lading.
> c) 10 % shall be sent to the seller by telegraphic transfer within 6 months after the issuing date of the Sales Contract against the seller's invoice of the foresaid amount and by the buyer's inspection certificate indicating that the equipment is fully operational in accordance with specifications.
> d) The seller shall give the buyer a bank guarantee at 40% of the total contract value to cover the advance payment with the expiry date not before the actual date of arrival of the foresaid equipment.

1. Point out the payment methods used in this sales contract.

2. What are the underlying reasons behind the selection of different payment methods for one trade transaction?

3. What should we fall back on towards the creation of a 100% risk-free payment method?

Chapter 2 Popular Price Terms

Objectives

◇Learn the definition and classification of price terms.

◇Learn in detail the 6 popular price terms.

◇Get to know the other price terms.

◇Learn the factors in choosing proper price term for a transaction.

Section 1 Introduction to Price Terms

In international trade, price for each transaction should be quoted in price terms. A price term is a three-English-letter initials stipulating the obligations of the seller and those of the buyer. Generally speaking, price terms set out the obligations of the seller. Hence, by a process of elimination, the buyers' responsibilities are implied because any obligation which does not appear in a particular price term may become the responsibility of the buyer.

The International Chamber of Commerce (ICC) has, over time, developed a set of rules: *International Rules for the Interpretation of the Trade Terms* (INCOTERMS), which are also referred to as price terms, trade terms or delivery terms. From the first publication in 1936, ICC has successively updated Incoterms several times. The most recent version is INCOTERMS 2000, effective on Jan. 1, 2000.

For reasons such as business habits and individual preferences, Incoterms 2000 will not be completely replaced by Incoterms 2010 in a short time. They will coexist for some years with the latter gradually gaining dominance. In practice, it is recommended that the traders shall specify that the price quoted in a sales contract is subject to Incoterms 2000 or Incoterms 2010.

Price terms quite simply define the geographic point in the transit of goods where the risks and costs (obligations) of the exporter and importer begin and end.

When drawing up the contract, both buyer/importer and seller/exporter specially refer to INCOTERMS to clearly define their respective obligations right at the beginning of the transaction in order to eliminate any possibility of misunderstanding and subsequent disputes in the operation.

Obligations for the goods to be transported from the seller's premises to the buyer's premises mainly include the costs of production and packing, the inland transportation within the exporting and importing country, the expenses for clearing the export and import customs, the loading and unloading charges and the main carriage from the port/place of shipment to the port/place of the destination and the insurance for the goods. These obligations are illustrated in Figure 2.1.

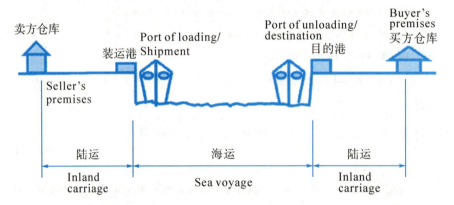

Figure 2.1 **Major Obligations in the Transit of Goods in International Trade**

1. Incoterms 2000

There are 13 different price terms in INCOTERMS 2000, organized into four groups: E, F, C and D groups as shown in Table 2.1.

Table 2.1 **Incoterms** 2000

Group E	EXW Ex Works (... named place)	Departure
Group F	FCA Free Carrier (... named place)	Main Carriage unpaid
	FAS Free Alongside Ship (... named port of shipment)	
	FOB Free on Board (... named port of shipment)	
Group C	CFR Cost and Freight (... named port of destination)	Main Carriage Paid
	CIF Cost, Insurance and Freight (... named port of destination)	
	CPT Carriage Paid to (... named place of destination)	
	CIP Carriage and Insurance Paid to (... named place of destination)	

Table2. 1(continue)

Group D	DAF Delivered at Frontier (... named place)	Arrival
	DES Delivered Ex Ship (... named port of destination)	
	DEQ Delivered EX Quay (Duty Paid) (... named port of destination)	
	DDU Delivered Duty Unpaid (... named place of destination)	
	DDP Delivered Duty Paid (... named place of destination)	

　　E group is for "Ex works" whereby the seller only makes the goods available to the buyer at the seller's own premises. From that point on all other costs are the buyer's responsibility; F group is for FCA, FAS and FOB. Under these terms, the seller is required to deliver the goods to a carrier appointed by the buyer; CFR, CIF, CPT and CIP are in C group whereby the seller has to contract for carriage to deliver the goods at the port/place of destination, but without assuming the risk of loss or damage to the goods; Finally, D group for terms in which the seller has to bear all costs and risks to bring goods to the place of destination (DAF, DES, DEQ, DDU and DDP). When price term moves from EXW to DDP, the responsibilities of the seller run from the minimum to the maximum and the opposite holds true for the buyer.

　　Figure 2. 2 is a simple way to understand this classification from the dividing points where the obligations of carriage of the exporter and importer begin and end. It is also important to note that the port/place of shipment in a price term is not always the exporter's premises where goods are produced and similarly, the port/place of destination in a price term does not always refer to the final destination of the transaction, the importer's premises.

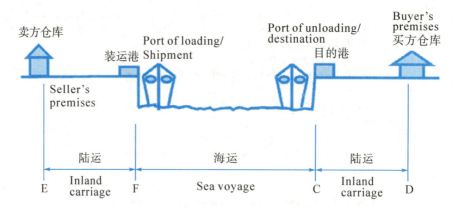

Figure 2.2　**Carriage Dividing Points**

2. Incoterms 2010

In Incoterms 2010, the number of trade terms has been reduced from 13 to 11. The change is mainly in D terms. Except DDP remains unchanged, Incoterms 2010 has added DAP and DAT to integrate and replace DAF, DES, DEQ and DDU in Incoterms 2000.

According to Incoterms 2010, 7 price terms, namely EXW, FCA, CPT, CIP, DAP, DAT, DDP, are applicable to any mode of transportation, while the other 4 price terms, namely FAS, FOB, CFR, CIF, are applicable only to sea and inland waterway transportation, as is shown in Table 2.2.

Table 2.2　**Incoterms** 2010

	Applicable for Any Mode of Transportation	
EXW	**Ex Works（named place of delivery）**	
FCA	**Free Carrier（named place of delivery）**	
CPT	**Carriage Paid to（named place of destination）**	
CIP	**Carriage and Insurance Paid to（named place of destination）**	
DAT	**Delivered at Terminal（named terminal at port or place of destination）**	
DAP	**Delivered at Place（named place of destination）**	
DDP	**Delivered Duty Paid（named place of destination）**	
	Applicable Only for Sea and Inland Waterway Transportation	
FAS	**Free Alongside Ship（named port of shipment）**	
FOB	**Free on Board（named port of shipment）**	
CFR	**Cost and Freight（named port of destination）**	
CIF	**Cost, Insurance and Freight（named port of destination）**	

Among all the 11 price terms, six terms are most commonly used — FOB,

CFR and CIF for the sea transportation, and FCA, CPT and CIP for the land transportation and multi-modes transportation where there is a combination of at least two modes of transportation by land, sea, air, rail, road or inland waterway.

Section 2   FOB, CFR and CIF

1. FOB: Free on Board (named port of shipment)

According to INCOTERMS 2010, FOB means that the seller delivers the goods on board the vessel nominated by the buyer at the named port of shipment. The risk of loss of goods of or damage to the goods passes when the goods are on board the vessel, and the buyer bears all costs and risks of loss of or damage to the goods from that point onward.

(1) The seller's main obligations under FOB:

①Deliver the goods on board the ship nominated by the buyer at the named port of shipment on the agreed dated or within the agreed period.

②Bear the risks of loss of or damage to the goods as well as all costs to the goods before the delivery.

③Pay for any export license or other official authorization and carry out applicable customs formalities for the export of the goods.

④Give the buyer sufficient notice about the delivery of the goods.

⑤Provide the buyer at the seller's expense with usual proof of delivery.

(2) The buyer's main obligations under FOB:

①Contract the carriage at its own expense for the carriage from the port of shipment and pay the freight.

②Give the seller sufficient notice of the vessel, name, loading point and the selected delivery time within the agreed period.

③Take delivery of the goods when they are shipped on board the vessel at the port of shipment.

④Bear all the risks of loss or damage to the goods as well as costs relating to the goods after delivery.

⑤Pay for any import license or other official authorization and carry out applicable customs formalities for the import of the goods.

The buyer, at the same time, may choose to arrange the marine cargo insurance and pay for the insurance premium from the port of shipment. Figure 2.3 illustrates the obligations divisions under FOB between the seller and the buyer.

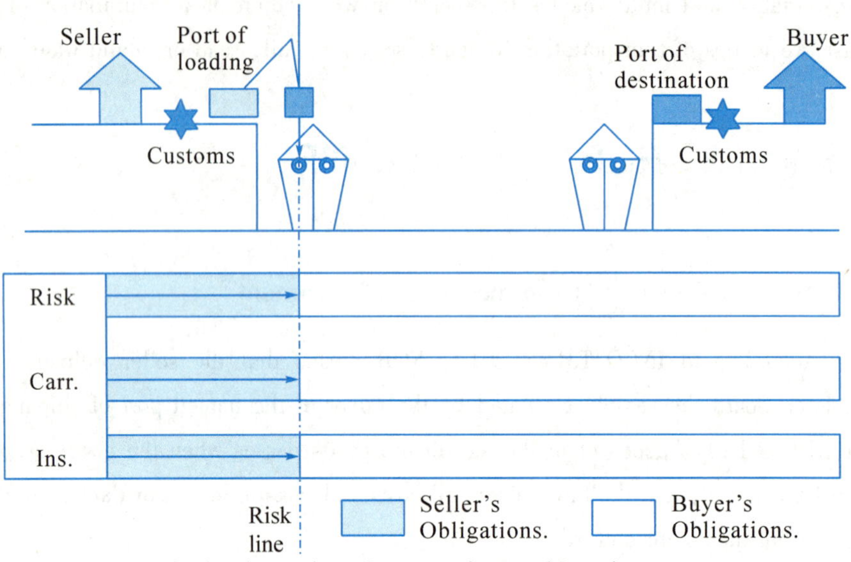

In the above chart, Carr. = carriage and Ins. = insurance cover

Figure 2.3   **FOB**

In order to further specify the responsibility of loading charges and to avoid any dispute in this regard, FOB takes the following varied terms:

(1) FOB liner terms. It means that loading and unloading expenses are included in the freight paid by the buyer to the liner company and that the seller does not have to pay for the loading.

(2) FOB under tackle. This term requires the seller to place the goods on the wharf within the reach of the ship's tackle. Loading expenses incurred thereafter will be borne by the buyer.

(3) FOB stowed. This term requires the seller to load the goods into the ship's hold and pays the loading charges including stowing expenses. Stowing refers to make proper placement and arrangement of the cargo in the hold. In practice, this term is expressed as FOBS.

(4) FOB trimmed. The seller pays all the loading expenses including the trimming expenses. Trimming means to place the bulk cargo neatly in a ship's hold and it actually involves stowing. In practice, this term is expressed as FOBT.

FOB varied terms were made before the introduction of Incoterms 2010. Although they are not established in Incoterms 2010, Incoterms 2010 do not object their application if they are chosen and specified by the contracting parties in a sales contract.

2. CFR: Cost and Freight (named port of destination)

According to INCOTERMS 2010, CFR means that the seller delivers the goods on board the vessel. The risk of loss of or damage to the goods passes when the goods are on board the vessel. The seller must contract for and pay the costs and freight necessary to bring the goods to the named port of destination.

(1) The seller's main obligations under CFR:

①Contract for the carriage of the goods and pay the freight.

②Deliver the goods on board the ship at the named port of shipment on the agreed dated or within the agreed period.

③Bear the risks of loss of or damage to the goods as well as all costs to the goods before the delivery.

④Pay for any export license or other official authorization and carry out applicable customs formalities for the export of the goods.

⑤Give the buyer sufficient notice about the delivery of the goods.

⑥Provide the buyer at the seller's expense with usual proof of delivery.

(2) The buyer's main obligations under CFR:

①Take delivery of the goods when they are shipped on board the vessel at the port of shipment.

②Bear all the risks of loss or damage to the goods as well as costs relating to the goods after delivery.

③Pay for any import license or other official authorization and carry out applicable customs formalities for the import of the goods.

The buyer, at the same time, may choose to arrange the marine cargo insurance and pay for the insurance premium from the port of shipment. It should be noted that the seller must send shipping advice sufficient both in detail and in time to enable the buyer to insure the goods on time. Otherwise, the seller is to held responsible for any losses thus incurred. Figure 2.4 illustrates the obligations divisions under CFR between the seller and the buyer.

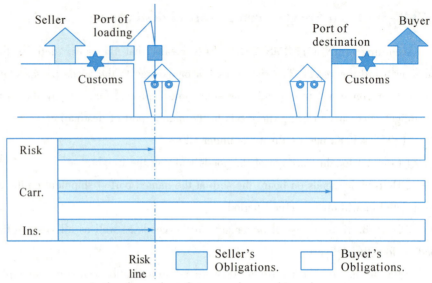

In the above chart, Carr.=carriage and Ins.=insurance cover

Figure 2.4 **CFR**

In order to further specify the responsibility of unloading charges and to avoid any disputes in this regard, CFR takes the following varied terms:

(1) CFR liner terms. The ship is responsible for the discharge of goods. The unloading charges are included in the freight that is paid by the seller.

(2) CFR landed. The goods must be unloaded onto the dock. The seller is responsible for the discharge of the goods and pays the costs, including the lighterage and wharfage charges.

(3) CFR ex tackle. This term requires the seller to lift the goods from the ship's hold onto the wharf or lighter within the reach of tackle. The buyer must pay for the lighterage when the ship is not able to reach the shore.

(4) CFR ex-ship's hold. The seller fulfills his obligations when he has made the goods available to the buyer for unloading. The buyer pays the cost for discharging the goods from the ship's hold.

CFR varied terms were made before the introduction of Incoterms 2010. Although they are not established in Incoterms 2010, Incoterms 2010 do not object their application if they are chosen and specified by the contracting parties in a sales contract.

3. CIF: Cost, Insurance and Freight (named port of destination)

According to INCOTERMS 2010, CIF means that the seller delivers the goods on board the vessel. The risk of loss of or damage to the goods passes when the goods are on board the vessel. The seller must contract for and pay for the costs and freight necessary to bring the goods to the named port of destination. The seller also contracts for insurance cover against the buyer's risk of loss of or damage to the goods during the carriage.

(1) The seller's main obligations under CIF:

①Contract for the carriage of the goods and pay the freight.

②Contract for the insurance of the goods and pay the premium.

③Deliver the goods on board the ship at the named port of shipment on the agreed dated or within the agreed period.

④Bear the risks of loss of or damage to the goods as well as all costs to the goods before the delivery.

⑤Pay for any export license or other official authorization and carry out applicable customs formalities for the export of the goods.

⑥Provide the buyer at the seller's expense with usual proof of delivery.

(2) The buyer's main obligations under CIF:

①Take delivery of the goods when they are shipped on board the vessel at the port of shipment.

②Bear all the risks of loss or damage to the goods as well as costs relating to the goods after delivery.

③Pay for any import license or other official authorization and carry out applicable customs formalities for the import of the goods.

The buyer should note that under CIF term, the seller is required to obtain insurance only on minimum cover. Should the buyer wish to have the protection of greater cover, he would either need to agree as such expressly with the seller or to make his own extra insurance arrangements. Figure 2.5 illustrates the obligations divisions under CIF between the seller and the buyer.

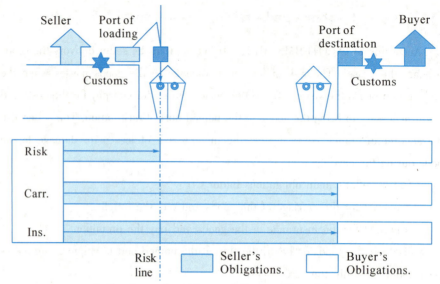

In the above chart, Carr.=carriage and Ins.=insurance cover

Figure 2.5 **CIF**

In order to further specify the responsibility of unloading charges and to avoid any disputes in this regard, CIF takes the following varied terms:

(1) CIF liner terms. The ship is responsible for the discharge of goods. The unloading charges are included in the freight that is paid by the seller.

(2) CIF landed. The goods must be unloaded onto the dock. The seller is responsible for the discharge of the goods and pays the costs, including the lighterage and wharfage charges.

(3) CIF ex tackle. This term requires the seller to lift the goods from the ship's hold onto the wharf or lighter within the reach of tackle. The buyer must pay for the lighterage when the ship is not able to reach the shore.

(4) CIF ex-ship's hold. The seller fulfills his obligations when he has made the goods available to the buyer for unloading. The buyer pays the cost for discharging the goods from the ship's hold.

FOB, CFR and CIF differ in price structure where FOB represents the basic costs in an export business, CFR the cost plus freight and CIF the cost plus freight plus insurance. However, these three terms share the same risk dividing line and the risk of loss of or damage to the goods is transferred from the seller to the buyer when goods are shipped on board the vessel at the port of shipment. Under these terms, the seller makes delivery when he makes shipment at the port of shipment and surrenders the title documents stipulated in the contract to the buyer and he is not responsible for the physical goods to reach the buyer. This kind of delivery is called the constructive delivery where delivery is made against title documents rather than the physical goods.

Section 3   FCA, CPT and CIP

These three terms are applicable to any mode of transport and multi-modal transport where the transportation of goods involves at least two modes of transportation by rail, road, air, sea and inland waterway.

1. FCA: Free Carrier (named place of delivery)

According to INCOTERMS 2010, FCA means that the seller delivers the goods to the carrier or another person nominated by the buyer at the seller's premises or another named place. The parties are well advised to specify as clearly as possible the point within the named place of delivery, as the risk passes to the buyer at that point.

(1) The seller's main obligations under FCA:

①Deliver the goods to the carrier or another person nominated by the buyer at the agreed time and place.

②Bear the risks of loss of or damage to the goods as well as all costs to the goods before the delivery.

③Pay for any export license or other official authorization and carry out applicable customs formalities for the export of the goods.

④Give the buyer sufficient notice about the delivery of the goods and the conditions of the carrying carrier.

⑤Provide the buyer at the seller's expense with usual proof of delivery.

(2) The buyer's main obligations under FCA:

①Contract at its own expense for the carriage of the goods and pay the carriage.

②Notify the seller within sufficient time the name of the carrier, the mode of transport and the point of taking delivery within the named place to enable the seller to deliver the goods.

③Take delivery of the goods when they are delivered to the carrier.

④Bear all the risks of loss or damage to the goods as well as costs relating to the goods after delivery.

⑤Pay for any import license or other official authorization and carry out applicable customs formalities for the import of the goods.

The buyer, at the same time, may choose to arrange the cargo insurance and pay for the insurance premium from the place of delivery.

2. CPT: Carriage Paid to（named place of destination）

According to INCOTERMS 2010, CPT means that the seller delivers the goods to the carrier or another person nominated by the seller at an agreed place and that the seller must contract for and pay the costs of carriage necessary to bring the goods to the named place of destination.

（1）The seller's main obligations under CPT:

①Contract for the carriage of the goods and pay the carriage.

②Deliver the goods to the carrier or another person nominated by the seller at the agreed time and place.

③Bear the risks of loss of or damage to the goods as well as all costs to the goods before the delivery.

④Pay for any export license or other official authorization and carry out applicable customs formalities for the export of the goods.

⑤Give the buyer sufficient notice to enable the buyer to take the goods.

⑥Provide the buyer at the seller's expense with usual proof of delivery.

（2）The buyer's main obligations under CPT:

①Take delivery of the goods when they are delivered to the carrier or another person nominated by the seller at the agreed time and place.

②Bear all the risks of loss or damage to the goods as well as costs relating to the goods after delivery.

③Pay for any import license or other official authorization and carry out applicable customs formalities for the import of the goods.

The buyer, at the same time, may choose to arrange the cargo insurance and pay for the insurance premium from the place of delivery.

3. CIP: Carriage and Insurance Paid to（named place of destination）

According to INCOTERMS 2010, CIP means that the seller delivers the goods to the carrier or another person nominated by the seller at an agreed place. The seller must contract for and pay the costs of carriage necessary to bring the goods to the named place of destination. The seller must contract for insurance cover against the buyer's risk of loss of or damage to the goods during the carriage.

(1) The seller's main obligations under CIP:

①Contract for the carriage of the goods and pay the carriage.

②Contract for the insurance of the goods and pay the premium.

③Deliver the goods to the carrier or another person nominated by the seller at an agreed time and place.

④Bear the risks of loss of or damage to the goods as well as all costs to the goods before the delivery.

⑤Pay for any export license or other official authorization and carry out applicable customs formalities for the export of the goods.

⑥Give the buyer sufficient notice to enable the buyer to take delivery.

⑦Provide the buyer at the seller's expense with usual proof of delivery.

(2) The buyer's main obligations under CIP:

①Take delivery of the goods when they are delivered to the carrier or another person nominated by the seller at an agreed time and place.

②Bear all the risks of loss or damage to the goods as well as costs relating to the goods after delivery.

③Pay for any import license or other official authorization and carry out applicable customs formalities for the import of the goods.

The buyer should note that under CIP term, the seller is required to obtain insurance only on minimum cover. Should the buyer wish to have the protection of greater cover, he would either need to agree as such expressly with the seller or to make his own extra insurance arrangements.

4. Comparison between FOB, CFR, CIF and FCA, CPT, CIP

As FOB, CFR and CIF are applicable only for the transport by sea and inland waterway, FCA, CPT and CIP are introduced as the counterparts to be used for goods to be transported by air, road, rail as well as multi-modal transport where the transportation of goods involves at least two modes of transportation. The introduction of FCA, CPT and CIP are made to meet the demands arising from the rapid development of modern logistics characterized by container transport and multi-modal transport.

The obligations of the seller and the buyer under FCA, CPT and CIP correspond to those under FOB, CFR and CIF. Under FCA, CPT and CIP, the risk of loss of or damage to the goods is transferred from the seller to the buyer at the time the nominated carrier accepts them at the named place. The buyer must bear all the cost and risk of the goods from the time they have been delivered to the carrier to the final destination. Their obligations concerning cost, carriage and insurance can be made clear in comparison with FOB, CFR and CIF in Figure 2.6.

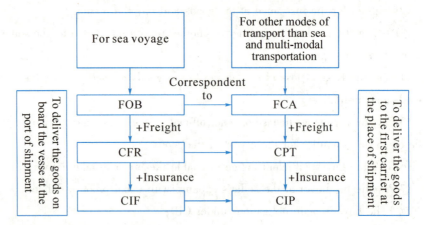

Figure 2.6 **Comparison between FOB, CFR, CIF and FCA, CPT, CIP**

Section 4　Other Price Terms

Other price terms here refer to EXW, FAS, DAT, DAP and DDP stipulated in INCOTERMS 2010. In practice, these five price terms are less popular than FOB, CFR, CIF, FCA, CPT and CIP.

1. EXW: Ex Works (named place of delivery)

According to INCOTERMS 2010, EXW means that the seller delivers when it places the goods at the disposal of the buyer at the seller's premises or another named place (i.e. works, factory, warehouse, etc.). The seller does not need to load the goods on any collecting vehicle, nor does it need to clear the goods for export, where such clearance is applicable.

(1)The seller's main obligations under EXW:

①Deliver the goods by placing them at the disposal of the buyer at the named place of delivery, not loaded on any collecting vehicle.

②Bear the risks of loss of or damage to the goods as well as all costs to the goods before the delivery.

③Provide the buyer at the seller's expense with usual proof of delivery.

(2)The buyer's main obligations under EXW:

①Take delivery of the goods at an agreed time and place.

②Bear all the risks of loss or damage to the goods as well as costs relating to the goods after delivery.

③Pay for any export and import license or other official authorization and carry out applicable customs formalities for the export and import of the goods.

EXW represents the minimum obligations for the seller but the maximum obligations for the buyer. It is advised that the buyer does not use EXW if they cannot directly or indirectly obtain export clearance.

2. FAS: Free Alongside Ship (named port of shipment)

According to INCOTERMS 2010, FAS means that the seller delivers when the goods are placed alongside the vessel (e.g., on a quay or a barge) nominated by the buyer at the named port of shipment. The risk of loss of or damage to the goods passes when the goods are alongside the ship, and the buyer bears all the costs from that moment onwards.

(1)The seller's main obligations under FAS:

①Deliver the goods at an agreed time by placing them alongside the ship nominated by the buyer at the loading point.

②Bear the risks of loss of or damage to the goods as well as all costs to the goods before the delivery.

③Pay for any export license or other official authorization and carry out applicable customs formalities for the export of the goods.

④ Give the buyer sufficient notice about the delivery of goods and the condition of the carrying vessel.

⑤Provide the buyer at the seller's expense with usual proof of delivery.

(2)The buyer's main obligations under FAS:

①Contract for the carriage of the goods and pay the freight.

②Give the seller sufficient notice of the name of the vessel, loading point and the selected delivery time within the agreed period.

③Take delivery of the goods when they are placed alongside the ship nominated by the buyer at the loading point.

④Bear all the risks of loss or damage to the goods as well as costs relating to the goods after delivery.

⑤Pay for any import license or other official authorization and carry out applicable customs formalities for the import of the goods.

FAS is applicable only for the transport by sea and inland waterway. The buyer, at the same time, may choose to arrange the marine cargo insurance and pay for the insurance premium from the port of shipment.

3. DAT: Delivered at Terminal (named terminal at port or place of destination)

According to INCOTERMS 2010, DAT means that the seller delivers the goods, once unloaded from the arriving means of transport, are placed at the disposal of the buyer at a named terminal at the named port or place of determination. "Terminal" includes any place, whether covered or not, such as quay, warehouse, container yard or road, rail or air cargo terminal. The seller bears all the risks involved in bringing the goods to and unloading them at the terminal at the named port or place of destination.

(1) The seller's main obligations under DAT:

①Contract at its own expense for the carriage of the goods to the named place at the named port or place of destination.

②Unload the goods from the arriving means of transport and deliver them by placing them at the disposal of the buyer at the named terminal at the named port or place of destination at the agreed time.

③Bear the risks of loss of or damage to the goods as well as all costs to the goods before the delivery.

④Pay for any export license or other official authorization and carry out applicable customs formalities for the export of the goods.

⑤Provide the buyer at the seller's expense with usual proof of delivery.

(2) The buyer's main obligations under DAT:

①Take delivery of the goods when they are delivered and receive them from the carrier at the named terminal at the named port or place of destination.

②Bear all the risks of loss or damage to the goods as well as costs relating to the goods after delivery.

③Pay for any import license or other official authorization and carry out applicable customs formalities for the import of the goods.

4. DAP: Delivered at Place (named place of destination)

According to INCOTERMS 2010, DAP means that the seller delivers the goods when they are placed at the disposal of the buyer on the arrival means of transport ready for unloading at the named place of destination. The seller bears all the risks involved in bringing the goods to the named place of destination.

(1) The seller's main obligations under DAP:

①Contract at its own expense for the carriage of the goods to the named terminal at the named port or place of destination.

②Deliver the goods by placing them at the disposal of the buyer on the arriving means of transport ready for unloading at the named place of destination at the agreed time.

③Bear the risks of loss of or damage to the goods as well as all costs to the goods before the delivery.

④Pay for any export license or other official authorization and carry out applicable customs formalities for the export of the goods.

⑤Provide the buyer at the seller's expense with usual proof of delivery.

(2)The buyer's main obligations under DAP:

①Take delivery of the goods when they are delivered and receive them from the carrier at the named place of destination.

②Bear all the risks of loss or damage to the goods as well as costs relating to the goods after delivery.

③Pay for any import license or other official authorization and carry out applicable customs formalities for the import of the goods.

DAP is very similar to DAT except that the place of delivery under DAT is a transport terminal in the country of destination, while under DAP, it is the final destination, either at the buyer's premises or a place nearby. DAP is often used for transactions when the importing and the exporting countries are in the same economic zone where there is no need to clear the goods as there are no customs houses between the two countries. For these transactions, the buyers would prefer to have the goods delivered at their own premises.

5. DDP: Delivered Duty Paid (named place of destination)

According to INCOTERMS 2010, DDP means that the seller delivers the goods when they are placed at the disposal of the buyer, cleared for import on the arriving means of transport ready for unloading at the named place of destination. The seller bears all the costs and risks involved in bringing the goods to the place of destination and has an obligation to clear the goods not only for export but also for import, to pay any duty for both export and import and to carry out all customs formalities.

(1)The seller's main obligations under DDP:

①Contract at its own expense for the carriage of the goods to the named place at the named port or place of destination.

②Pay for any export and import license or other official authorization and carry out applicable customs formalities for the export and import of the goods.

③Deliver the goods by placing them at the disposal of the buyer on the arriving means of transport ready for unloading at the named place of destination at the agreed time.

④Bear the risks of loss of or damage to the goods as well as all costs to the goods before the delivery.

⑤Provide the buyer at the seller's expense with usual proof of delivery.

(2) The buyer's main obligations under DDP:

①Take delivery of the goods when they are delivered and receive them from the carrier at the named place of destination.

②Bear all the risks of loss or damage to the goods as well as costs relating to the goods after delivery.

DDP represents the maximum obligations for the seller but minimum obligations for the buyer. It is advised that the seller does not use DDP if they cannot directly or indirectly obtain import clearance.

Section 5   Conclusion

Of the price terms illustrated above, it can be concluded that when price term moves from EXW to DDP, the responsibilities of the seller run from the minimum to the maximum and the opposite holds true for the buyer. Hence, we should also note the following points.

1. Price must be quoted in price terms

INCOTERMS indicate the conditions under which prices are made. These conditions represent the traders' obligations. As a result, three items will make a complete and correct quotation in international trade: Unit price with its currency + INCOTERMS + port/place of loading /unloading. For example:

Unit price in international trade quotation "USD 100/bag FOB Shanghai or USD 120/bag CIF Shanghai". In the first quotation, Shanghai is the port of shipment, while in the second one, Shanghai becomes the port of destination because it is used in different price terms.

In addition to this, sometimes a special term "commission" will be used together with a price term. Commission is a sum of money paid to the middleman for every sale that he or she makes. When commission is indicated in a price term, the middleman is to collect it from the buyer. For example, "CFR New York C3 USD 10. 00/CTN" means that the commission to the middleman is 3% which is to be paid by the buyer. The commission to the middleman may not be indicated in a price term. In this case, the commission, if any, is to be paid by the seller.

2. Quoted price varies on price term selected

When obligations under a certain price term fall heavily on the part of the exporter, he quotes higher. On the contrary, when the buyer assumes more responsibilities, the quoted price of the exporter will be lowered.

Figure 2. 7 shows that for one sales contract, the quoted unit price may vary according to different price terms:

EXW	FOB	CFR	CIF	DES	DDP
$98	$100	$110	$115	$120	$140

Figure 2. 7   **Price Terms and Quoted Price**

(**The figures here are just a theoretical illustration with no practical references**)

3. Goods can be covered by insurance under any price term

When dealing with price terms, it should always be understood that INCO-TERMS are a description of obligations from the seller's point of view rather than from that of the buyer. Therefore, when insurance is not shown, the price term only states that it is not the seller's responsibility and the insurance can be taken up by the buyer.

For example, goods can be protected under insurance coverage in FOB as much as under CIF. In a word, goods can be covered by insurance under any price term and the only difference lies in the fact that which trader is to contract with the insurance company and pays for the insurance premium.

4. Shipment contract and arrival contract

When a sales contract is made under the price term of FOB, FAS, FCA, CFR, CIF, CPT or CIP, it is called the shipment contract where constructive delivery is carried out. In constructive delivery, delivery is deemed to be made when the seller makes shipment to the named place/port of shipment and surrenders to the buyer commercial documents, including title documents, specified in the contract, but without being responsible for the goods to reach the place of destination.

The buyer should make payment to the exporter against the title documents. Under shipment contract, the risk of the loss and damage to the goods is transferred to the buyer when the goods are placed on board or alongside the ship at the port of shipment or when they have been delivered to the carrier at the place of shipment.

When a sales contract is made under the price term of EXW, it is also called the shipment contract but actual delivery is carried out. In actual delivery, delivery is deemed to be made when the physical goods are delivered to the buyer at the seller's premises. The risk of the loss or damage to the goods is transferred to the buyer when the goods are at his disposal at the seller's premises.

When a sales contract is made under the price term from DAT, DAP or DDP, it is called the arrival contract where actual delivery is carried out. Delivery is deemed to be made when the physical goods are delivered to the buyer at the terminal or the named place at the place of the destination. The risk of the loss or damage to the goods is transferred to the buyer when the goods are at his disposal at the terminal or named place at the place of the destination.

5. Factors to consider when choosing price term

As the price term determines the nature of the sales contract and the terms and conditions concerning the delivery of goods, the proper choice of price term is important to reflect the performance capacity of the traders and to enhance the economic effectiveness of the transaction. The following factors should always be taken into consideration:

(1) Mode of transport. As FOB, FAS, CFR and CIF are only applicable for sea and inland waterway transport, if the goods are to be transported by air, road, rail or multi-modal transport, the contacting parties should choose a price term from EXW, FCA, CPT, CIP, DAT, DAP and DDP.

(2) Compliance ability. INCOTERMS 2000 classify price terms into four groups of E, F, C and D, among which the buyer assumes maximum obligations under E group while the seller assumes maximum obligations under D group. For this reason, it is recommended that the buyer does not choose EXW and the seller does not choose price term from D group, especially when either the seller or the buyer cannot directly or indirectly obtain from the country of its trading partner the import/export license or other official authorization and carry out applicable customs formalities for the import/export of the goods.

The traders share obligations under price terms from F group and C group. Therefore, if they can obtain favorable freight charges and insurance premium, it is recommended that they choose FOB, FCA, FAS as the buyer and CFR, CIF, CPT or CIP as the seller.

(3) Freight change. When the freight charges are expected to change in the upward trend, it is recommended to choose FOB, FCA, FAS as the seller and CFR, CIF, CPT or CIP as the buyer. On the other hand, When the freight charges are shifting in the downward trend, it is recommended to choose just the opposite. If the future trend for the freight change is hard to predict, it is better for the seller to choose price terms from the F group and the buyer to choose from the C group.

(4) Payment method. Of the three popular payment methods, e. g., remittance, collection and letter of credit, when the payment method chosen is collection or letter of credit, the seller is recommended to choose a price term from F group and C group where the sales contract is the shipment contract with constructive delivery. In this way, the seller or the seller's bank can control the title to the goods through title documents. Title to the goods will be released only after the importer makes payment, either to the exporter itself or to the bank.

Generally speaking, there is no need for such consideration when the payment method chosen is remittance.

Exercises for Chapter 2

Ⅰ. Multiple-choice Questions (It is possible to make more than one choice)

1. The seller is not to bear the costs of export clearance under _____.

A. FCA

B. FAS

C. FOB

D. EXW

2. Construct delivery is made when the seller _____.

A. does not make delivery of the goods

B. makes delivery of both the goods and documents

C. makes delivery of the goods against documents

D. makes delivery of the goods

3. FCA differs from FOB in that _____.

A. FCA applies to all modes of transport while FOB applies to ocean and inland waterway transport only.

B. The place of delivery under FOB is on board the vessel at the port of shipment while under FCA the place of delivery can be any point within the export country.

C. FCA is more flexible than FOB.

D. FCA means more obligations to the seller.

4. A shipping advice should contain the following details EXCEPT _____.

A. the name of the vessel

B. description of goods

C. B/L number

D. date of arrival

5. That _____ is/are correct about the price term variations.

A. the variations do not change the costs division of the original price term

B. the variations do not change the place of delivery of the original price term

C. the variations do not change the risk dividing line of the original price term

D. the variations do not change the payment method of the original price term

Ⅱ. T/F Questions

1. According to INCORERMS 2000, contracts made under C group belong to shipment contracts.

2. DDP is the only trade term that requires the buyer to clear the goods for both export and import.

3. Under CIP term, if the types of insurance coverage are not specified in the sales contract, the seller is required to obtain insurance only on minimum cover.

4. To further specify the responsibility of unloading charges and to avoid any disputes in this regard, FOB takes varied terms.

5. Under CIF, if the goods are lost during transit, the buyer can refuse to make payment on receiving documents, even the documents submitted by the seller are completely correct and in full set.

Ⅲ. Case Analysis

1. Company XYZ, Chengdu has entered into a contract with Company HD, Thailand to export 100 sets of sterilized cupboards under CFR. The time of shipment is agreed to be made before 15, April. Company XYZ, Chengdu has placed the goods on board the ship on 8, April but failed to immediately send to the buyer the shipping advice, being the weekends that followed right after the shipment date. For this reason, Company HD, Thailand did not contract in time for the insurance of the goods. Unfortunately, the goods were destroyed due to a fire on the night of 8, April. Questions:

(1) Who should bear the loss?

(2) Why or why not?

2. A Chinese company, Company A, Chengdu exported 20 M/T of herbs and spices to Company B in Singapore under USD 2 500/M/T FOB Shanghai, container transport with the shipment to be made in October. Company A, Chengdu received the shipping advice from Company B on 16, Oct. In order to make shipment on time, Company A, Chengdu sent the goods on 17 Oct and the goods were stored in the dock warehouse. Unfortunately, the warehouse was on fire the very night and the goods were completely burnt and lost. Company A, Chengdu had to bear all the risks and losses to the goods. Questions:

(1) Would Company A, Chengdu suffer such a loss if the chosen price term was FCA?

(2) Why or why not?

IV. Extended Discussions

Refer to Figure 2.8 below and consider the following questions:

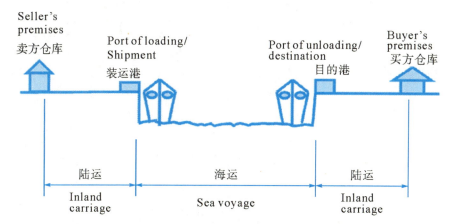

Figure 2.8   **Major Obligations in the Transit of Goods in International Trade**

1. How many parties will be involved so that the goods can be successfully transported from the exporting country to the importing country?

2. What do we learn about the importance of "team work" in trade transactions?

3. What inspiration can be drawn as to a better understanding of the Belt and Road Initiative?

Part 2
Instruments

Chapter 3   Bills of Exchange（Ⅰ）

Objectives

◇Learn the definition and major types of financial instruments.

◇Learn and analyze the definition of bills of exchange.

◇Learn the major essentials of bills of exchange.

◇Learn the concepts of value, negotiation and acceptance.

◇Learn the major parties of bills of exchange, their rights and obligations.

◇Think about the relationship between bearer and holder.

Section 1   Financial Instruments

A financial instrument, or a credit instrument, or simply an instrument, is a written or printed paper issued by one person to make unconditional payment to another person up to a certain sum of money within a certain period of time either by this person himself or by another third person designated by him.

Documents play a very important role in the modern era of international settlement. Financial instruments are made to make/collect payments. They have taken the place of cash and are devised as medium of exchange to facilitate commercial transactions by eliminating the use of money in the settlement process for import and export.

The most commonly used credit instruments in international settlement are bills of exchange, promissory notes and checks. Of the three, bills of exchange are the most popular type in the settlement process and most provisions stated in the Bills of Exchange Act are applicable to promissory notes and checks. Promissory note and checks will be introduced in Chapter 5.

Section 2　Introduction to Bills of Exchange

According to *the Bills of Exchange Act* 1882 of the United Kingdom, a bill of exchange is an unconditional order in writing, addressed by one party (drawer) to another (drawee), signed by the party giving it, requiring the party to whom it is addressed to pay on demand, or at a fixed or determinable future time, a sum certain in money, to or to the order of a specified party (payee), or to bearer.

A bill of exchange can also be called a draft or a bill. A typical bill of exchange is drawn in this manner shown in Figure 3. 1。

```
      (8)
Exchange for USD 100 000. –                    New York, June 3, 2023
                    (6)
      (7)          (1)          (9)
   At 60 days sight pay XYZ company, Hong Kong or order
                    (8)
the sum of United States Dollars One Hundred Thousand only value received.


      (3)(5)
To：BBB Bank,
    2 Hill Road
    Hong Kong                                 (2)(4)
                                   For：AAA Co., Ltd, New York
                                      (authorized signature)
```

Figure 3. 1　Sample Bill of Exchange

For better understanding, the above sample draft is indicated as the following breakdowns：

(1) An unconditional order in writing

(2) Addressed by one person (the drawer)

(3) To another (the drawee)

(4) Signed by the person giving it

(5) Requiring the person to whom it is addressed

(6) To pay

(7) On demand or at a fixed or determinable future time

(8) A sum certain in money

(9) To or to the order of a specified person or to bearer (the payee)

Figure 3. 2 shows the bills of exchange used in practice。

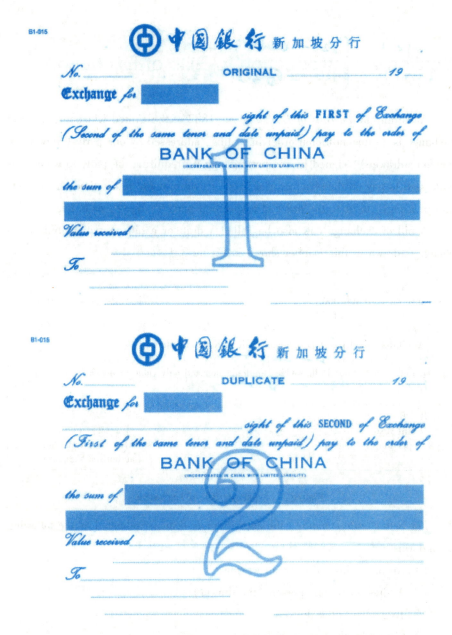

Figure 3. 2　**Bills of Exchange Used in Practice**

As is shown in Figure 3. 2, bills of exchange used in practice are often made out in a set of two which represent one liability only. When one part is paid, the other becomes void. The wording of the 1st part of the bill will read as "pay this first bill of exchange (second of the same tenor and date being unpaid) to ..." and the 2nd part will read as "pay this second bill of exchange (first of the same tenor and date being unpaid) to ..." With these wordings, double payments under one set of bills of exchange will be avoided.

"For value received" indicates that the payee obtains the bill because he has given value to the drawer. Value refers to anything that is sufficient to support a simple contract and may be given in the form of goods, services or money.

Section 3　Essentials to Bills of Exchange

Essentials refer to those prerequisite items in bills of exchange to make such bills of exchange complete and valid. All the 9 items in the breakdown list of the definition are called the essentials to a bill of exchange. The following will make a detailed explanation of 2 essentials, namely, tenor as in indicated and types of order.

1. Tenor

Tenor is stated in the definition as "on demand or at a fixed or determinable future time". Tenor means the time to effect payment by the drawee to the payee and it expresses the due date or maturity date of the draft. According to tenor, a draft is to pay on demand or at a fixed or determinable future time.

(1) Demand bill. A demand bill is also called a sight bill. A demand bill means that the drawee is required to pay at once when he is upon request, when he sees the bill or when the bill is presented to him for payment. In addition, a bill is payable on demand if it is so specified or if time for payment is not stated in a bill. For a demand bill, the date of presentment is the due date to effect payment.

Ways to express a demand bill are summarized as follows:

① "On demand pay …".

②"On presentation pay …".

③"At sight pay …".

④"Pay …".

(2)Usance bill. A usance bill is also called a time bill or a term bill. A usance bill is payable at a fixed or determinable future time. A usance bill is usually expressed in the following ways:

①Payable at a fixed future time. It should be noted that the future time means the time of the tenor is made later than the issuing date.

②Payable at a fixed time after date. For example, "pay 60 days after date …" means that the due date will be 60 days after the issuing date. "Date" refers to the issuing date of the bill.

③Payable at a fixed time after sight. "Sight" means the presentation of the bill to the drawee for acceptance. When the drawee of such a bill sees it, he should make acceptance.

Acceptance can be understood as a formal promise from the drawee to pay when the bill falls due. For this type of bill, presentment for acceptance is a must for the purpose to determine the accepting date against which the due date can be fixed.

For example, "pay one month after sight …" means one month after the accepting date is the due date to effect payment. Suppose the bill is presented on 9 Jan. 2023 and the acceptance is made on the same date, then the due date will be on 9 Feb. 2023.

④Payable at a fixed time after the occurrence of a specific event which is certain to happen. In practice, such a bill is usually made at a fixed time after the B/L date. As shipment is normally deemed as a specific event which is sure to happen, a fixed time after B/L date is a determinable future date.

For example, "pay 3 months after the B/L date …".

2. Types of order

Types of order are stated in the definition as payable "to a specified person or his order or to bearer (the payee)".

According to the different descriptions of the payee, a bill takes three corresponding types of order: restrictive order bill, demonstrative order bill and bearer order bill. Different types of order will decide the negotiability of a bill and the way of negotiation. Negotiation is the process of ownership transfer, and it signifies the right of the payee/holder to transfer the bill to another person.

①Restrictive order. A restrictive order bill is payable to a specified person only. Typical expressions are shown as follows:

Pay to A Co., Shanghai only.

Pay to A Co., Shanghai not negotiable / not transferable / not to order.

Restrictive order bill is not negotiable. This means A Co., Shanghai, the payee in the above example cannot transfer the bill to another person.

(2) Demonstrative order. A demonstrative or indicative order bill is payable to a specified person or some other person designated by him, without words prohibiting transfer or negotiation. Typical expressions are shown as follows:

Pay to A Co., Shanghai.

Pay to the order of A Co., Shanghai.

Pay to A Co. , Shanghai or order.

Pay to order.

Demonstrative order bill is negotiable. A Co. , Shanghai, the payee, in the a-
bove example can negotiate/transfer the bill to another person through endorsement
and delivery. And the negotiability is made safe by endorsement. Consequently,
demonstrative order bill has found wide application in international trade.

（3）Bearer order. A bearer order bill is a bill payable to bearer with no specified person as a payee thereon. Any person holds a bearer order bill will become
the owner of the bill. Typical expressions are shown as follows:

Pay to bearer.

Pay to A Co. , Shanghai or bearer.

Note: The word "bearer" will make the bill bearer order no matter whether a
specified party is stated with it.

A bearer order is also negotiable. It can be transferred by the bearer to another
person through mere delivery and no endorsement is required. It enjoys full negotiability but it is not safe for the absence of endorsement.

Section 4 Major Parties to Bills of Exchange

Bills of exchange take such major parties as the drawer, the drawee, the payee, the endorser, the endorsee and the holder, each with different rights and obligations respectively and acting as creditors or debtors to a draft. Among these parties, the drawer, the drawee and the payee are the immediate parties and they are
the basic parties to bills of exchange before they are transferred to another party.
The endorse, endorsee and the holder are the other parties who are created after
the negotiation of bills of exchange.

1. Drawer

The drawer is the party who draws and signs bills of exchange on the drawee
and delivers it to the payee.

The drawer is a debtor to the bills of exchange. Before a sight bill is paid and
a time bill is accepted by the drawee, the drawer is primarily liable to the payee or
holder of the instrument. In the event that the drawee dishonors the bill by non-
payment or by non-acceptance, the drawer must redeem and pay the bill. However, when a time bill is accepted, the drawer's liability becomes secondary.

2. Drawee

The drawee is the party on whom the bill is drawn and he is the party to honor the bill at the order of the drawer, i.e. to make acceptance and payment to the payee. The drawee is such named because the draft is drawn on him.

The drawee is another debtor to the bills of exchange. However, when the bill is presented to him, the drawee can make a choice whether to honor it (agree to make acceptance and payment) or dishonor it (refuse to make acceptance and payment), because he cannot prevent any party to whom he owes no debt from drawing a draft on him. This means that before the drawee agrees to honor the draft, he is not yet a debtor to the bill, and if he agrees, he acknowledges his indebtedness to the bill and in the case of a time bill, he becomes an acceptor.

An acceptor is a special drawee. When a drawee signs his name on the face of a time draft indicating his promise of payment on a due date, he becomes an acceptor. This acceptance makes the acceptor assume primary liability to the bill. As a result, the drawer holds secondary liability to the bill as mentioned above.

3. Payee

The payee is the party to receive the payment because the bill is payable to him. The payee is the first creditor to the bill and the first legal owner of the instrument. He can either claim payment against the bill or transfer (negotiate) the draft to another party. If the bill is transferred, he is called the original holder/transferer because the bill is taken away from him while the transferee, the person who takes the bill, becomes the new holder.

A bill of exchange is drawn by the drawer on the drawee payable to the payee. The basic meaning of the three immediate parties is that the drawer gives an order to the drawee, requiring it to make acceptance or payment to the payee. It should be noted that, on the one hand, it is possible for the drawer and the drawee of a bill to be the same person. On the other hand, it is also possible for the drawer and payee of a bill to be the same person.

When a bill of exchange is made out in demonstrative order or bearer order, it can be transferred from one holder to another. In doing so, the ownership of the bill is transferred from the previous holder to the subsequent party. This process of ownership transfer is called negotiation. During the course of negotiation, bills of exchange take other parties as well.

4. Endorser

It is originally the payee or the holder who signs his name on the back of a bill for the purpose of negotiation. The endorser is a debtor to the bill and the payee is the first endorser. When the payee becomes the endorser, he transforms himself from a creditor to a debtor because he obligates himself that he will be liable to the endorsee and his subsequent parties.

For example, an endorser may make a promise to his endorsee as follows: "If you, the holder of this instrument, make proper presentation for acceptance and for payment and is dishonored, I will pay the face amount of the bill upon your proper notice to me." In the process of negotiation, there may be a list of first endorser, second endorser, third endorser and so forth and the list can go on.

5. Endorsee

The endorsee is the party to whom the instrument is transferred. He is a creditor to the bills of exchange and becomes the new holder of the instrument. An endorsee can also become an endorser if he wishes to transfer the instrument to another party by signing his name on its back. And by doing so, he transforms himself into a debtor.

If the process of negotiation creates a sequence of endorsers, similarly, it will also bring about a series of endorsees. Figure 3. 3 shows a process of negotiation. When the bill is transferred from A to B and B to C and from the standpoint of C, A and B are his prior parties. If C continues to transfer the bill to D and D to E, then D and E become his subsequent parties.

Figure 3. 3   **Negotiation Process of Bills of Exchange**

6. Holder

The holder is a party who is in possession of the instrument. He is a creditor to a bill. A holder can be the payee/bearer or the endorsee. The payee will always be the original holder. A person holding a forged bill or one who has stolen a bill payable to the order of another is not a holder, but a wrongful possessor. Only the legal possessor can become the holder. Their relationship will be shown in

Figure 3.4.

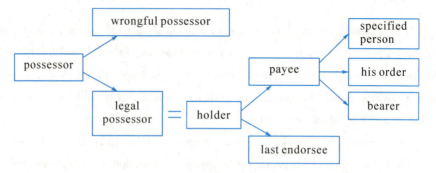

Figure 3.4　**Possessor and Holder to Bills of Exchange**

As a creditor, the holder has the following perfect title to the bill:

(1)To duly present the instrument for acceptance or payments.

(2)To transfer a bill to other persons.

(3)To endorse a bill.

(4)To give notice of dishonor to the prior party.

(5)To exercise right of recourse against the prior party.

(6)To sue in his own name.

(7)To duplicate the lost bill.

(8)To cross check or banker's demand draft, and to deliver it to a bank for collection.

In summary, the creditors to a bill are the payee/bearer, the endorsee(s) and the holder. The debtors to a bill can be the drawer, the drawee, the acceptor and endorser(s) who hold the liability to make payments. Their order of liability is as follows:

Before acceptance:①drawer;②the first endorser;③the second endorser ...

After acceptance:①acceptor;②drawer;③the first endorser;④the second endorser ...

Exercises for Chapter 3

Ⅰ. Multiple-choice Questions (It is possible to make more than one choice)

1. Financial Instruments takes _____ basic parties.

A. 2 or 3

B. 3 or 4

C. 4 or 5

D. 5 or 6

2. A draft is drawn _____ the drawee _____ the drawee _____ the payee.

A. by, payable to, to

B. on, to, payable to

C. on, payable to, by

D. by, on, payable to

3. A bill payable _____ is/are time bill.

A. two weeks after the wedding date of Susan White

B. at… sight

C. on presentation

D. one month after sight

4. A bill payable to _____ takes demonstrative order.

A. Mr. C.H. Wang or bearer

B. Bank X, Chengdu only

C. Bank Y., Shanghai or order

D. order

5. That _____ is/are correct about bills of exchange.

A. bills of exchange take 2 immediate parties

B. bills of exchange represent a payment order

C. the drawee of bills of exchange must be a bank

D. bills of exchange can be sight bills and time bills

Ⅱ. Fill in the Blanks

1. A draft is an unconditional order whereby the _____ demands the _____ to pay to the _____.

2. Complete and valid bills of exchange contain all the _____ when they are drawn.

3. When a bill issued on 30, March, 2023 is payable on 12, April 2023, it is a _____ bill according to tenor.

4. Order of liability after acceptance of a negotiated bill is as follows: the _____ takes the primary liability, the _____ takes the secondary liability and the _____ takes the third liability.

5. The _____ can be the payee or the bearer of the bill, or the endorsee who is in possession of it.

Ⅲ. Practice

Refer to the blank draft form below:

```
Exchange for ____(1)____        ____(2)____ , ____(3)____

At___(4)___ sight of this FIRST of exchange (the SECOND of the same

tenor and date being unpaid), pay to the order of ____(5)____

The sum of _____(6)_____

For value received.

To: ___(7)___                              For: ___(8)___

                                                ___(9)___
```

1. Match the number with the information given below:

(1) Issuing date: 23 July 2023.

(2) Amount: USD 35 461.50.

(3) Tenor: 90 days (after) sight.

(4) Drawer: George Anderson Inc., New York.

(5) Drawee: Irving Trust Company, New York.

(6) Payee: Brown and Thomas Inc. London or order.

2. Who is the first legal owner of the draft?

3. Can the draft be transferred? If yes, specify the endorser. If no, give your reasons.

IV. Extended Discussions

On 8 March 2023, a sight draft at USD 10 000 was issued by Hong Fa Trading Co. Ltd, Shanghai on Bank XYZ, Chengdu payable to Bo Da Trading Co. Ltd, Chengdu. On 12 March 2023, Bo Da Trading Co. Ltd, Chengdu presented the draft to Bank XYZ, Chengdu for payment and the draft was dishonored. Bo Da Trading Co. Ltd, Chengdu then immediately informed the Hong Fa Trading Co. Ltd, Shanghai of the dishonor and demanded payment from Hong Fa Trading Co. Ltd, Shanghai. However, Hong Fa Trading Co. Ltd, Shanghai refused to make payment to Bo Da Trading Co. Ltd, Chengdu on account of its being the drawer not the drawee of the draft.

Questions:

1. What responsibilities should Hong Fa Trading Co. Ltd, Shanghai take up as the drawer of the draft?

2. What can Bo Da Trading Co. Ltd, Chengdu do to make Hong Fa Trading Co. Ltd, Shanghai take up its responsibilities?

3. How to prevent the abuse of power?

Chapter 4　Bills of Exchange（Ⅱ）

Objectives

◇Learn the major types of bills of exchange acts.

◇Learn to make endorsement and acceptance.

◇Learn the movement of bills of exchange.

◇Learn the classification of bills of exchange.

◇Learn the differences between trader's bill and banker's bill, between clean bill and documentary bill.

◇Learn to calculate the net proceeds and discount interests.

Section 1　Major Acts of Bills of Exchange

Acts of a bill of exchange refer to the legal acts carried out to bear the obligations to a draft. Major acts consist of issue, endorsement, presentment, acceptance, payment, dishonor, notice of dishohor, protest, and right of recourse. Each act is initiated by different party to different party and to fulfill different purpose.

1. Issue

To issue a draft comprises two acts to be performed by the drawer. One is to draw and sign a draft, the other is to deliver it to the payee. Thus the liability of the bill is established and the bill has come into being.

When issuing a bill, the drawer must draw it in its complete form, containing all the essentials stipulated. The drawer must sign the bill as well. A bill without the drawer's signature or with a false signature is not a valid bill. The liability on a bill of exchange is by signature only: no person is liable upon a bill if he has not signed it. A bill can be made in the name of an individual or a company or by some other person under his authority. A bill so made engages the drawer under the primary liability to the bill.

To deliver means to transfer the draft from the drawer to the payee. Thus the payee is entitled to receive payments, who becomes the original holder of the bill and is the creditor to the bill.

2. Endorsement

Endorsement is made on the back of a bill of exchange. Endorsement comprises two acts: one is to sign on the back of the draft, the other is to deliver it to the endorsee/transferee.

Endorsement is an act of negotiation. A bill is negotiated when it is transferred from one person to another in such a manner as to constitute the transferee the holder of the bill. Only the holder, namely the payee/bearer and the endorsee can endorse a bill.

Endorsement is applicable when the bill is made out on the demonstrative order. The transfer of a demonstrative order bill is completed by endorsement and delivery.

Endorsement can be made in one of the following ways:

(1) Special endorsement (endorsement in full). Special endorsement consists of the name and signature of the endorser and at the same time spells out the name of the transferee. It is also called the endorsement in full.

For example:

Pay to the order of B Co., Shanghai ·········· the endorsee

For A Co., Shanghai ·········· the endorser

Signature (of the endorser)

The example shows the transfer of the bill from A Co., Shanghai to B Co., Shanghai.

A bill endorsed specially remains a demonstrative order bill. It can be further transferred by the endorsee through another endorsement and delivery. A series of consecutive special endorsements show a clear chain of endorsers and that of the endorsees.

(2) Blank endorsement (general endorsement). Blank endorsement only consists of the name and signature of the endorser/transferor and no endorsee/transferee is specified. It is also called a general endorsement.

For example:

For A Co., Shanghai ·········· the endorser

Signature (of the endorser)

When a blank endorsement is made on a bill, it will transform the original bill from demonstrative order to a bearer order. If the bill is to be further transferred, mere delivery is required. When a blank endorsement is followed by another blank one, the endorser of the subsequent endorsement will be deemed as the endorsee of the prior endorsement. Therefore, a series of blank endorsements can also be consecutive. The possessor of a bill with the last endorsement made in blank is the holder if there is no proof to indicate his title thereto is defective.

However, a blank endorsement can be changed to a special endorsement by adding above the endorser's name such wordings as "pay to" or "pay to the order" of the transferee.

(3) Restrictive endorsement. A restrictive endorsement bears such indications as "only" "not negotiable" "not transferable" "not to order" to prevent the further negotiation of the bill.

For example:

Pay to ABC Bank, Shanghai only ··········· the endorsee

For A Co., London　　　　　············ the endorser

Signature (of the endorser)

Or

Pay to ABC Bank, Shanghai not negotiable ············ the endorsee

For A Co., London　　　　　············ the endorser

Signature (of the endorser)

Restrictive endorsement will transform the demonstrative order to a restrictive order. The endorsee can only claim payment against the bill and no further transfer is allowed.

(4) Endorsement for collection. "For collection" is an instruction to the endorsee to collect the sum specified in the bill for the endorser. Endorsement for collection requests the endorsee to deal with the bill as he is instructed but the title to the bill is not transferred to him.

For example:

For collection pay to Bank A, New York ············ the endorsee

ABC Co., Shanghai　　　　　············ the endorser

Signature (of the endorser)

Or

Pay to Bank A, New York for collection ············ the endorsee

ABC Co., Shanghai　　　　　············ the endorser

Signature (of the endorser)

As the transferee is not the owner of the bill so when the bill so endorsed, the bill cannot be further transferred.

3. Presentment

Presentment of bills of exchange is also terms as presentation. Presentment is to be made by the holder to the person designated as drawee for payment in the case of a sight bill and for acceptance and payment in the case of a time bill.

The holder should present the bill within reasonable time at the proper place specified on the bill. If no place is specified, the bill should be presented at the drawee or the acceptor's business office. If no business office is specified, the bill should be presented at the drawee or the acceptor's residence.

If a bill is drawn on a bank, there are three channels for presentment:

(1) Presenting the bill at the counter of the drawee bank.

(2) Presenting the bill through clearing house exchanged to the drawee bank.

(3) Inter branches and correspondents presenting bill by airmail/courier to the drawee bank.

If the bill is duly presented and is dishonored by the drawee, the holder will obtain an immediate right of recourse against all the prior parties till the drawer.

4. Acceptance

Acceptance of a bill is the signification by the drawee of a time bill of his assent to the order of the drawer. The drawee of a time bill has no liability on the bill until he signs the bill in such a way as to signify acceptance of liability to pay the money stated in the bill.

A valid acceptance requires two acts: one is to write the word "Accepted" on the face of a bill and signed by the drawee. The mere signature of the drawee, without additional words, is sufficient. The other is to return the accepted bill to the payee for him to present the bill again on maturity date. In the case that the bill is a time bill payable at a fixed time after sight, the accepting date is deemed to be the sight date from which the maturity date is worked out.

In order to be convenient, the accepting date and the due date are stated when acceptance is made. Figure 4.1 shows such an acceptance in complete form.

```
ACCEPTED
On accepting date
to mature
On due date
For the name of the drawee
Signature
```

Figure 4.1　**Acceptance in Complete Form**

When the drawee has made acceptance, he is known as the acceptor and he becomes primary liable on the bill. When this happens, the drawer will be secondarily liable to the bill. In practice, an accepted bill can be transferred more easily than an unaccepted one because it has the definite undertaking of the acceptor to make payment on the due date.

Qualified acceptance is a variation of acceptance. Qualified acceptance means that the drawee adds a condition when he accepts the bill. Such an acceptance in express terms varies the effect of the bill as drawn, e.g. the amount payable, the time or place to effect payment, etc. can be changed. For example, a bill with a face value at USD 10 000 may be payable only at USD 9 700 when the drawee makes a qualified acceptance as shown in Figure 4.2.

```
          ACCEPTED
        1 FEB., 2023
  Payable for amount of USD 9 700 only
        For ABC Bank, London
             Signature
```

Figure 4.2　**Qualified Acceptance**

Qualified acceptance is allowed because the drawee can choose whether to assent to the order to pay by the drawer. This means he can choose to agree, to disagree or to insist on having proof that certain conditions has been fulfilled before he accepts the bill. Qualified acceptance will not make a bill invalid if the bill itself is made unconditional at the time of issue. However, the holder may refuse to take a qualified acceptance, and, if he does so, he may treat the bill as dishonored by non-acceptance.

5. Payment

Payment to a bill can be performed by any debtor to the bill to its creditor. A simple payment may not discharge a bill. Discharge is a term to indicate the end of liability of any debtor to the bill, i.e. the drawee, the acceptor, the drawer or the endorsers, if any.

A bill will be discharged only when the payment is made in due course which includes the following four conditions:

(1) Payment should be made by or on behalf of the drawee or the acceptor and not by the drawer or any endorser. The payment made by the drawer or any endorser is not a final payment because he may claim payment from the drawee or the acceptor.

(2) Payment should be made on or after the maturity date of the bill and can-

not be made in advance.

（3）Payment should be made to the holder and if the bill has been transferred. The drawee, if it is a bank, will check the endorsements or at least the sequence of the endorsements before making payment.

（4）Payment should be made in good faith, without knowing that the holder's title thereto is defective.

In short, payment in due course means payment made by the drawee or the acceptor at or after the maturity of the bill to the holder thereof in good faith. When payment is made in due course, it is the final payment and the bill is discharged. Discharge brings an end to the liability and to the movement of the bill.

6. Dishonor

Dishonor is a failure or refusal to make acceptance on or payment of a bill of exchange when presented to the drawee.

A bill of exchange may be dishonored either by non-acceptance or by non-payment. When a bill is only offered a qualified acceptance, the holder may take it or treat it as dishonored for non-acceptance. Other instances of dishonor may arise when the drawee's deliberate avoidance, his bankruptcy or even his death has made the acceptance or the payment impossible.

When a bill is dishonored, the right of recourse will be accrued to the holder at once. The holder may exercise his right of recourse against his prior endorsers and drawer for payment.

7. Notice of dishonor

When a bill is dishonored, the holder must give notice of dishonor to the drawer and all the endorsers for whom the holder may wish to make liable. The purpose of giving such notice is to inform the drawer and prior endorsers the default of acceptance or payment so that they may get ready to honor the payment.

There are two methods in which the notice of dishonor may reach the prior parties and the drawer. For the first method, the notice of dishonor must be given on the next business day after the dishonor of the draft by the holder to his direct prior party who shall do so in quick succession till the notice is given to the drawer. Any party failing to do so shall remain liable to the holder and lose his own right of recourse against all his prior endorsers and the drawer. For the second method, the holder gives the notice of dishonor to each endorser and the drawer separately to retain their liability thereon.

The first method is more convenient to the holder because he may have no knowledge of every endorser and he can be fairly certain that each endorser will pass on the notice.

If the drawer or the endorser states besides his name on the bill such wordings as "notice of dishonor excused", it means that in the event the bill is dishonored, the holder can claim compensation from him without giving him a notice of dishonor.

8. Protest

Protest is a formal certificate given by a Notary party or other authorized person to evidence that a bill of exchange has been dishonored. The protest should be done on the very day or no later than the next business day from the day of dishonor.

After a bill is dishonored and a notice of dishonor is given, the holder hands the bill to a Notary party who will present it again to the drawee to obtain a legal proof of the act of dishonor. If it is dishonored again, the Notary party then will draw a protest and return it to the holder together with the dishonored bill, against which the holder may exercise his right of recourse against the prior parties till the drawer.

The protest fee is to be borne by the drawer and will be charged to him at the time when the claim is made. However, the drawer may indicate besides his name on the bill such wording as "protest waived" or "please do not protest if dishonored" so that he will not be responsible for the protest fee. In this case, the holder may claim payment from him without protest and if the holder still wants the Notary party to draw up a protest, he himself will pay the protest fee.

9. Right of recourse

Right of recourse signifies the right of the holder to claim compensation from the drawer and the endorsers in the event that the bill has been dishonored. It is an act to the bill when the holder exercises this right. The compensation should include the amount payable on the bill with interest, the fees for giving the notice of dishonor and protest and other incurred expenses.

The holder exercises his right of recourse after he has completed the following procedures:

(1)Present the bill to the drawee for acceptance or payment and it is dishonored.

（2）Give notice of dishonor to his prior party and drawer in one business day following the day of dishonor.

（3）Make a protest for non-acceptance or non-payment in one business day following the day of dishonor.

When the drawer or any endorser writes on the bill such words as "without recourse" or "sans recourse", he will be discharged of his liability on the bill. However, such wordings will affect the negotiability of the bill.

Section 2   Movement of Bills of Exchange

A bill of exchange moves through the acts from its issue to discharge. However, the routes of the movement vary on two important factors:

Firstly, whether or not the bill is negotiated/transferred.

Secondly, whether or not the bill is dishonored.

Figure 4. 3 shows the basic movement of a bill when the bill is neither negotiated nor dishonored. The movement is simple and it only involves the 3 basic parties and 4 or 5 acts.

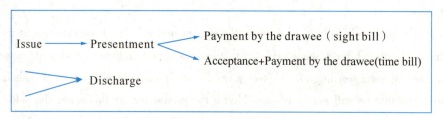

Figure 4. 3   **Basic Movement of Bills of Exchange**

Figure 4. 4 shows the movement of a bill when it is negotiated and dishonored. Therefore, this movement is more complicated than the first one. The whole process involves more parties and more acts before the bill can finally be discharged.

There can be other routes in the movement of a bill with more parties and more acts involved. It is important to note that any movement begins with the act of issue from the drawer and ends at the act of discharge from the payment of drawee or acceptor.

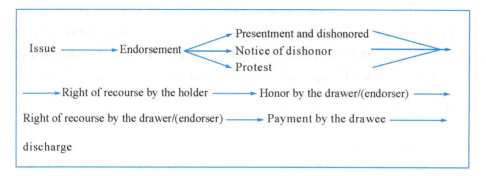

Figure 4. 4　Complicated Movement of Bills of Exchange

Section 3　Classification of Bills of Exchange

A bill of exchange is classified according to the following criteria:

1. According to the places of the three immediate parties

(1) Domestic bill or inland bill. When the three immediate parties, namely the drawer, drawee and payee reside in the same country, the bill is a domestic bill. Normally a domestic bill is drawn and payable in the same country.

(2) Foreign bill. When two of the three immediate parties reside in different countries, the bill is a foreign bill. Normally a foreign bill is drawn in one country and payable in another country.

2. According to tenor

(1) Sight bill. As its name implies, a sight bill is supposed to be paid when it is first seen by the drawee. It can be expressed as payable at sight, on demand or on presentation. When a bill specifies no time of payment, it is also considered to be a sight one.

(2) Time bill. It is a bill payable at a fixed or determinable future time. It is further classified into payable at a fixed future time, at a fixed future time after date, after sight or after the happening of a certain event which is sure to happen.

3. According to types of order

(1) Restrictive order bill. It is a bill payable to a specified person only. No negotiation is allowed.

(2) Demonstrative order bill. It is a bill payable to a specified person or his order. Negotiation is allowed and the bill is transferred by endorsement and delivery.

(3) Bearer order bill. It is a bill payable to bearer. Negotiation is allowed and the bill is transferred by mere delivery, no endorsement is required.

4. According to the drawer and the drawee

(1) Banker's draft or bank draft. It is a draft drawn by a bank on another bank or on its head/branch office. When a time banker's draft is accepted by the drawee bank, it is called a banker's acceptance bill. This kind of bill is most preferable in international settlement because it has a bank's undertaking to the bill.

(2) Commercial bill / trader's bill. It is a draft drawn by a trader on another trader or a banker. When a time bill drawn on another trader is accepted by this trader, it is called a trader's acceptance bill. If a time bill drawn on a bank is accepted by this bank, it is called a banker's acceptance bill.

5. According to whether shipping documents are attached

(1) Clean bill. Clean bill has no relevant shipping documents attached and is normally used alone in the settlement process. Shipping documents belong to commercial documents and the most popular type in international trade and settlement is bills of lading.

Clean bill may be drawn for many purposes, among which are the collection of payment for services, personal remittance and the transactions that arise in international trade but for which no shipping documents exist. However, clean bill can also be used in international goods.

(2) Documentary bill. Documentary bill should be accompanied by the relevant shipping documents in the settlement process to complete an export transaction. Documentary bill is very popular in international goods transaction.

Clean bill and documentary bill may look the same in form. The way to distinguish one from the other is to see whether it is used alone or with shipping documents attached in the settlement process.

In conclusion, it should also be noted that the classification of a bill of exchange is not clear-cut. In fact, any bill of exchange used in international trade is a combination of five types. For example, a bill can be a foreign time banker's acceptance bill payable to a specified person only, though being clean or documentary depends on the way it is used in a particular settlement process.

Section 4　Discounting

A holder can get financed through discounting the bills of exchange where he can receive payments in advance before its maturity date.

1.　The definition of discounting

Discounting a bill of exchange means that a holder of an accepted bill sells the bill to a financial institution at a price less than its face value before it reaches its maturity.

The financial institution performing discounting business is referred to as discount house. The present value the holder receives is the net proceeds. And the balance between the face value of the bill and the net proceeds is the discount interest.

The purpose of the holder to discount the bill is to obtain funds before the due date. In this way his turnover can be speeded up and he is thus financed. On the other hand, the financial institution will also make a profit by discounting bills of exchange and his profit is represented by the discount interest which is what the holder pays in order to be financed.

2.　The procedure of discounting

Figure 4.5 shows the procedure of discounting bills of exchange. When it is completed, the holder is financed and the financial institution makes a profit.

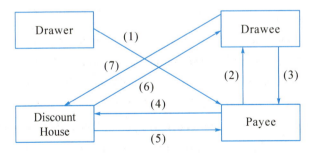

Figure 4.5　**Discounting Procedure**

（1）The drawer draws a time bill on the drawee and delivers it to the payee/ holder.

（2）The payee presents the bill to the drawee for acceptance.

(3) The drawee accepts the bill and returns it to the payee.

(4) Before due, the payee as the original holder discounts (sells) the accepted time bill to a discount house.

(5) The discount house discounts (buys) this bill and pays the net proceeds to the payee. The discount house becomes the new holder.

(6) At maturity, the discount house presents the bill for payment to the drawee.

(7) The drawee pays the face value to the discount house.

3. Calculation in discounting

The discount interest and the net proceeds will be calculated according to the following formulas:

Discount interest = (Face value × Discounting days × discounting rate) ÷ 360 (365) days

Net proceeds = Face value − Discount interest

Net proceeds = Face value × [1 − Discounting days ÷ 360 (365) days × discounting rate]

In the formulas, discounting days are the number of days from the date of discounting to the maturity date. Discounting rate is a percentage set by the financial institution for discounting.

An Example:

A bill for USD 10 000 is payable at 90 days sight. The bill is accepted on June 20, 2023 and the holder decides to discount it on June 30, 2023. If the discount rate is 10% and a year is based on 360 days, work out the discount interest and net proceeds.

The Calculation:

When the holder discounts it on June 30, the number of days left to maturity date is 90 − 10 = 80 days. So discounting days would be 80 days.

Discounting interest = (10 000 × 80 × 10%) ÷ 360 = USD 222. 22

Net proceeds = 10 000 − 222. 22 = USD 9 777. 78

The example shows that the holder will get USD 9 777. 78 when he discounts the bill on June 30, 2023. The discount house will receive USD 10 000 when he presents the bill to the drawee for payment on its due date. Therefore, the discounting house has made a profit at USD 222. 22.

4. The status of the discount house

From the point of view of negotiation of bills of exchange, the discount house acts as an endorsee who receives the bill from the endorser (the original payee/holder). However, the negotiation occurs for the special purpose of providing finance to the endorser through discounting. Normally, if no further negotiation occurs, the discount house becomes the new holder of the bill.

As a holder, the discount house bears the risk of non-payment at maturity. For this reason, the creditworthiness of the acceptor is of great concern to him. Generally speaking, the creditworthiness of a banker is more reliable than that of a trader and a big, first-class bank is better than a small one. As a result, a first-class banker's accepted bill is more preferable and acceptable than a trader's acceptance bill in the discounting market.

Again as a holder, in the event that the drawee defaults the bill by non-payment, the discount house will obtain the right of recourse against his prior endorser and the drawer. When this happens, the financed funds received by the original payee may be called back.

Exercises for Chapter 4

Ⅰ. Multiple-choice Questions (It is possible to make more than one choice)

1. After the bill is drawn, the drawer should deliver/give the bill to _____.

A. the payee

B. the drawee

C. the endorser

D. the acceptor

2. Endorsement is applicable when the bill is made out on the _____.

A. restrictive order

B. demonstrative order

C. indicative order

D. bearer order

3. When _____ is/are made, the title to the bill is not transferred to the endorsee.

A. blank endorsement

B. special endorsement

C. endorsement for collection

D. restrictive endorsement

4. Payment in due course requires that payment is made _____.

A. in good faith

B. by the drawee

C. to the holder

D. before maturity date

5. A banker's acceptance bill can be a _____ and _____ bill before acceptance.

A. sight, trader's bill

B. time, trader's bill

C. sight, banker's bill

D. time, banker's bill

Ⅱ. Fill in the Blanks

1. A sight bill must duly be presented for _____ while a time bill for _____ first and then for _____ on due date.

2. For a bill issued on 31 Jan. 2023 and accepted on 2 Feb. 2023, if the tenor is made as one month after date, the due date is _____; or, if the tenor is made as one month after sight, the due date is _____.

3. The debtors to bills of exchange are _____, _____, the acceptor, and the _____ while the creditors are _____, bearer, _____ and _____.

4. _____, _____ and _____ are to be carried out before the holder can exercises his right of recourse.

5. The present value the holder receives after the bill is discounted is termed as _____, which is equal to the face value minus _____.

Ⅲ. Practice

1. Refer to the information in Figure 4.6.

```
                    Exchange for USD 10 000        Chengdu, 1 May 2023

    _____(1)_____     At two months sight pay this first Bill of Exchange (second of
on ___(2)_____        the same tenor and date unpaid)
   to mature
on ___(3)_____        to the order of Bank of China, Chengdu ******
for ___(4)_____       the sum of US dollars ten thousand only
      (5)             value received

                    To: The Importing Co.,
                        Singapore                For: The Exporting Co., Chengdu
                                                             signature
```

Figure 4.6

(1) Make a complete acceptance on the left-hand space on 11 May 2023.

（2）If the payee wants to transfer the bill to Overseas Union Bank, Singapore in blank endorsement, make such endorsement.

（3）Having made blank endorsement, the bill is sent to Overseas Union Bank, Singapore who wants to covert the blank endorsement to a restrictive one to themselves, make such endorsement.

2. A bill for USD 100 000 is payable at 120 days sight. The bill is drawn, accepted and discounted on 6 Oct 2023. If the discounting rate is at 9% per annum and the year contains 365 basic days. Write out the formulas and calculate the discount interest and net proceeds.

Ⅳ. Case Question

Company YG, Bangkok imported 2 000 metric tons of cement from Company RD, Chengdu at USD 500 000. Upon arrival of the commodity, Company YG, Bangkok issued drafts at 2 months after sight on itself payable to the order of Company RD, Chengdu for the same contract value. The drafts were also accepted on the issuing date.

10 days later, Company RD, Chengdu imported a batch of timber at USD 455 000 from Company JX, Hanoi. In order to clear its debt, Company RD, Chengdu made endorsement and transferred the drafts to JX Company, Hanoi, with the balance of USD 45 000 settled by bank transfer.

Later, however, disputes occurred between Company YG, Bangkok and Company RD, Chengdu on the fact that Company YG, Bangkok found that 1/3 of the goods were inferior in quality.

On due date, JX Company, Hanoi presented the drafts to Company YG, Bangkok for payment, but the drafts were dishonored. The reasons of dishonor given by Company YG, Bangkok to JX Company, Hanoi were of the inferior quality of the cement the former had received from Company RD, Chengdu.

Question: Is it proper and right for Company YG, Bangkok to dishonor the drafts by non-payment? Give your reasons to support your opinion.

Ⅴ. Extended Discussions

Refer to the following sentence in the act of "discharge":

Payment should be made in good faith, without knowing that the holder's title thereto is defective.

Questions:

（1）Translate the sentence into Chinese, pointing out the translation skill applied in the translation of "good faith".

(2)Which of the following Five Ethical Norms from Confucianism, "仁、义、礼、智、信" can be used to translate "good faith"?

(3)Think deeply about the act of "discharge", do some research and offer your opinion in the understanding of and confidence in our culture.

Chapter 5   Promissory Note and Check

Objectives

◇Learn the definition of promissory note.

◇Learn the definition and classification of check.

◇Learn the process of check clearing.

◇Consider the connection of different types of financial instrument.

Section 1   Promissory Note

A promissory note is an unconditional promise in writing made by one person (the maker) to another (the payee) signed by the maker engaging to pay on demand or at a fixed or determinable future time a sum certain in money to or to the order of a specified person or bearer.

Promissory note can also be termed as note. Figure 5. 1 is an example of a promissory note.

```
                        (6)
Promissory Note for USD 40 000          Singapore, June 1, 2023
        (7)        (2)   (1)(5)                  (3)(8)
At 60 days after date we promise to pay to the order of ABC Co.
              (6)
the sum of US dollars forty thousand only.
                                        (2)
                        For XYZ International Pte. Ltd., Singapore
                                        (4)
                                Authorized Signature
```

Figure 5. 1   **Promissory Note**

1. Essentials to a promissory note

Similar to bills of exchange, the definition of promissory note stipulates the essentials which are prerequisite to validate it. The essentials can be shown in the following breakdown:

(1) An unconditional promise in writing.

(2) Made by one person (the maker).

(3) To another (the payee).

(4) Signed by the maker.

(5) Engaging to pay.

(6) A sum certain in money.

(7) On demand or a at a fixed or determinable future day.

(8) To or to the order of a specified person or bearer.

2. Comparison between promissory note and bills of exchange

As another major type of credit instruments, promissory notes, compared with bills of exchange, are equally subject to the provisions *Bills of Exchange Act* except the following differences:

(1) A promissory note is an unconditional promise, whereas a bill is an unconditional order.

(2) Immediate parties. There are only two immediate parties to a promissory note, namely the maker and the payee; whereas there are three basic parties to a bill of exchange, namely the drawer, the drawee and the payee. The maker of a note corresponds to the drawer and the drawee of a bill.

(3) Acceptance requirement. As the maker of a promissory note is the person primarily liable on it, acceptance is not applicable to it. For this reason, time note is seldom made payable at a fixed time after sight; whereas acceptance is generally required for a time bill, especially for a time bill payable at a fixed time after sight.

(4) Protest requirement. Protest is not applicable to a foreign note in the event of dishonor, whereas a dishonored foreign bill must be protested for the holder to obtain right of recourse.

(5) The drawer and the payee. The maker and the payee cannot be the same person for a note; whereas a bill of exchange allows the drawer and the payee to be the same person.

(6) Full set. A promissory note is a solo note when issued, whereas a bill of exchange is usually in a duplicate set when issued. When one part of a bill is paid,

the other part becomes void.

3. Major forms of promissory note

（1）Banker's note. The promissory note has found its wide application in banks. A banker's note made by a bank payable to a specified person can be deemed as cash.

A sight banker's note payable to bearer is a "legal tender" which is part of the currency realm. Banker's sight bearer order notes are put under special statutory basis and can be issued by the central bank or the authorized banks only.

As an uncontrolled issue of banker's sight bearer order notes by commercial banks will certainly disturb a country's monetary system. Therefore, commercial banks can only issue note payable to a specified person.

（2）Trader's note. Trader's note, also termed as commercial papers, is a time bearer order promissory note whose maker is a firm or a trader. Whoever pays the face value to the maker becomes the payee of the note.

Trader's note is not to be used as payment tool. It is issued for the drawer to raise funds from the public, so it is issued with interest to the public. When local government or big enterprise issues time note, normally with the tenor to be within a year, to the public for similar purpose to raise funds, it is called bonds.

（3）Treasury bill. Though named bill, treasury bill is a time bearer order promissory note issued by the central bank authorized by the Ministry of Finance. Treasury bills are sold on discount at a certain rate per annum to investors, mostly commercial banks with the tenor to be made at 91 days after date.

Net proceeds are the selling price of the treasury bill. The investor buys treasury bill at net proceeds and gets face value when the treasury bill falls due. The discount interest represents the investor's profit.

Similar to trader's note, treasury bill is not to be used as payment tool, either. It is issued for the central government to raise funds and the payee to make a profit, and more importantly, for the central government to regulate money surplus and deficiency in the market.

Section 2　Check

An unconditional order in writing addressed by the customer to a bank signed by that customer authorizing the bank to pay on demand a sum certain in money to or to the order of a specified person or bearer.

In simple words, a check can be understood as a bill of exchange drawn on a banker on demand. Check can also be spelt as cheque. Figure 5. 2 is an example of a check.

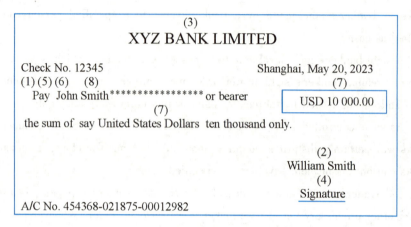

Figure 5. 2 **Check**

Checks are pre-printed by the banker for its customers. Blank check books are held by the customer who fills in (draws) a check when needed and deliver it to the payee.

1. Essentials to a check

Similar to bills of exchange and promissory note, the definition of check stipulates the essentials which are prerequisite to validate it. The essentials can be shown in the following breakdown:

(1) An unconditional order in writing.

(2) Addressed by the customer (drawer).

(3) To a bank (drawee).

(4) Signed by that customer.

(5) Authorizing the bank to pay.

(6) On demand.

(7) A sum certain in money.

(8) To or to the order of a specified person or bearer (payee).

2. The immediate parties to a check

There are three immediate parties to check:

(1) The drawer. To "draw" means writing out a check for a certain amount of

money in the account with the banker. In other words, the drawer is the person who writes the check.

Before a person can draw a check on a bank, he must first obtain an account with the bank. Secondly, when drawing a check, it is the drawer's responsibility to make sure that there is enough balance in his account to cover the check amount. Otherwise, the check will be bounced.

(2) The drawee. The drawee is a bank on whom the check is drawn and to whom the order to pay is given. He is the bank with which the drawer maintains an account.

The bank is obliged to honor a customer's check up to the amount of his credit balance or agreed overdraft. In the case when the bank wrongly dishonors a customer's check, it is to bear the full responsibility and will make the necessary compensation.

(3) The payee. The payee is a person to whom the check is expressed to be payable.

3. Check crossing and check clearing

(1) Uncrossed check. An uncrossed check refers to the one which is written on "plain" bank form, without two parallel lines drawn on the face. An uncrossed check can be exchanged for cash over the counter when the payee/holder presents it for payment to the drawee bank. Figure 5.3 is an example of an uncrossed check.

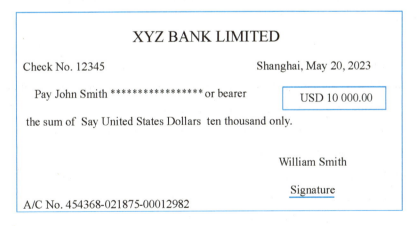

Figure 5.3   **Uncrossed Check**

(2) Crossed check. A crossed check refers to two parallel lines drawn on its face, and usually this is done on the top left corner of the check. The payee/holder

of a crossed check cannot get cash payment over the counter and the check amount should be paid into a bank account. The purpose of crossing a check is to ensure that the right holder to obtain the payment. Crossed check is further divided into two types.

①General crossing. A check is generally crossed when the check bears two parallel lines across its face, either with or without the words "and company" "& Co." "not negotiable" "A/C payee" between the lines. Figure 5.4 shows a general crossing.

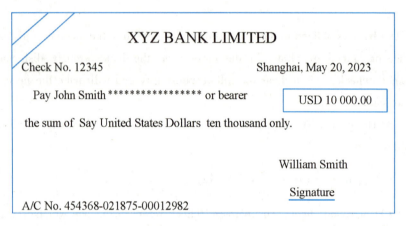

Figure 5.4   **General Crossing**

The effect of a general crossing is to make the check payable through a bank account only. General crossing does not specify the collecting bank. That is to say, the drawee bank should honor the check presented by any bank provided it is a correctly complete valid one.

②Special crossing. When a check bears across its face an addition of the name of a banker, either with or without the words "and company" "& Co." "not negotiable" "A/C payee" and the two parallel lines, that addition constitutes a special crossing. Figure 5.5 shows a special crossing.

The effect of a special crossing is to make the check payable only through the account of that specified bank (e.g. ABC Bank Limited, Chengdu) which is to act as the collecting bank. No other bank is to present the check for payment.

It should be noted that both the drawer and the payee can do the following:

Firstly, Cross an uncrossed check.

Secondly, Change a general crossing to a special one.

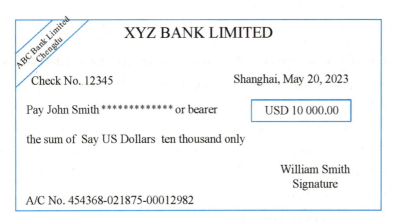

Figure 5. 5　**Special Crossing**

（3）Crossed check clearing. For the payee/holder to get the crossed check a-mount, he must first deposit the crossed check into a bank with which he maintains an account and upon which he makes a request to collect the check amount for him. This bank is called the collecting bank and may or may not be the drawee bank of the check.

The following procedure in Figure 5. 6 shows the steps to clear a crossed check, supposing that the payee/holder deposit a crossed check into a bank (the collecting bank) other than the drawee bank.

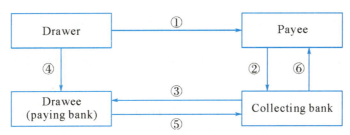

Figure 5. 6　**Crossed Check Clearing Procedure**

①The drawer draws a check and delivers it to the payee.

②Payee deposits the check to the collecting bank and asks the latter to collect the payment for him.

③After scrutiny, the collecting bank forwards the check to the drawee bank on behalf of the payee.

④After scrutiny, the drawee debits the amount from the drawer's account with him.

⑤The paying bank transfers the funds to the collecting bank.

⑥The collecting bank credits the amount to the payee's account.

4. Comparison between check and bills of exchange

As another major type of credit instruments, compared with bills of exchange, checks are equally subject to the provisions of *Bills of Exchange Act* except the following differences:

(1) A bill of exchange may be drawn by any person upon another, whereas a check can be only drawn by a customer on his banker where he maintains an account with sufficient credit balance in it.

(2) The tenor of the bill may be either sight or time whereas the check can only be made payable on demand.

(3) After the bill is accepted, the acceptor is primarily liable for payment. Acceptance is not applicable to a check and the drawer should always hold primary liability to the check.

(4) Acceptance made by the acceptor of a bill is irrevocable whereas the duty and authority of the drawee bank to pay a check may be terminated by the countermand of payment by the drawer.

(5) The rules concerning crossing are applicable to check only. In addition, it should be noted that check is not designed to be negotiated, the rules on negotiation has little significance on check.

5. Comparison of draft, promissory note and check

Table 5.1 compares the differences of the three major forms of financial instruments.

Table 5.1 Comparison of Draft, Promissory Note and Check

Items	Draft	Promissory Note	Check
Feature	Order	Promise	Order
Drawer	A/<u>A</u>/<u>A</u>	A	A/<u>A</u> (customer)
Drawee	B/<u>A</u>/B	A	B/<u>B</u> (bank)
Payee	C/<u>C</u>/<u>A</u>	C	C/<u>A</u>
Tenor	sight/ time	sight/ time	sight/
Acceptance	Applicable	NA	NA

Exercises for Chapter 5

I . Multiple-choice Questions (It is possible to make more than one choice)

1. A time note can be payable _____.

A. at a fixed time after sight

B. at a fixed time after date

C. at a fixed time after the occurrence of an event which is certain to happen

D. at a fixed future date

2. _____ can be made to be the payee of a check.

A. a trader

B. a firm

C. a bank

D. an individual

3. That _____ is/are correct about check.

A. check is a conditional payment order

B. the drawee of a check can be a bank, a firm or an individual

C. check can be sight or time

D. check is a demand draft on a bank

4. When the balance in the drawer's account is not enough to cover the check amount, the check is a/an _____.

A. uncrossed check

B. bad check

C. crossed check

D. specially-crossed check

5. For a check, the relationship between the drawer and drawee is _____.

A. importer and exporter

B. supplier and its customer

C. bank and its customer

D. debtor and creditor

II . Fill in the Blanks

1. The _____ of a promissory note is the party primarily liable on it.

2. The investor buys treasury bills at _____ and gets _____ when the bills fall due.

3. A "legal tender" is a _____, bearer order note issued by the country's _____ bank authorized by the finance department of that country.

4. Either the _____ or the _____ of a check can change a general crossing to a special one.

5. When a check bears across its face an addition the name of a _____, either with or without the words "and company" "& Co." "not nego-tiable" "A/C payee" and the _____, that addition constitutes a special crossing.

III. Answer the Following Questions

1. If GBP 5 000 000.00 treasury bills were sold on a discount at the rate of 6.5% per annum. Write out and calculate the selling price of these bills based on 365 days a year.

2. Xiao Fang, a student currently studying at a university in Chengdu, China, receives a birthday check at USD 1 000 from her uncle, Mr. Wang, in America drawn on Bank of America, New York, answer the following questions:

(1) Indicate the parties and tenor of the check.

(2) How to clear/cash the check in a feasible way?

IV. Case Question

X issued a check on Bank B payable to Y. But Y delayed for a long time be-fore he went to the bank to present the check for payment, during which time, un-fortunately, Bank B went bankrupt and Y could not cash the check. Unable to ob-tain payment from the drawee, Y went to X for payment. But the check was dishon-ored by X because X held that the check was overdue and expired.

Question: Can X dishonor the check? Did X give proper reasons for the dis-honor?

V. Extended Discussions

Answer the following questions:

1. Translate "绿色债券" into English and point out the type of instrument it belongs to.

2. Do some research about the major functions, application and significance of "绿色债券".

Part 3
Settlement

Chapter 6   Remittance

Objectives

◇Learn the classification of payment methods.

◇Learn the definition and classification of remittance.

◇Learn the procedures of M/T, T/T and D/D.

◇Learn the requirements of the drafts drawn in D/D.

◇Learn the application of remittance in international trade.

◇Learn the characteristics of remittance.

Section 1   Introduction of Payment Methods

International funds transfer is made for the purposes of:

Firstly, Settlement of debts arising from international trade

Secondly, Settlement of personal remittance from friends to relatives or friends abroad

Thirdly, Settlement of government aids to foreign countries

When international funds transfer is made to settle the debts arising from international trade, it is international commercial settlement, which is the focus of this book. When funds transfer is made for the other two purposes, it is international non-commercial settlement.

In international commercial settlement, funds are to be transferred via banks and banks transfer funds across the borders at the request of their customers (traders), or, that the traders will require the banks to transfer funds for them to their foreign counterparts to whom the payments are due. In this settlement process, customers (traders) are "principals" who give instructions to banks to transfer money to another party, known as the "beneficiary". The banks become the "intermediary" or the "agents" of their customers, the "principals". The "principal"—

"agent" relationship is significant in international settlement. Any payment method in international settlement will reflect this important relationship where two traders and their banks will be involved.

It is also important to distinguish payment methods from payment tools in international settlement. Payment tools can be either cash or credit instruments. In the non-cash settlement era, although cash is needed to calculate the amount of payments and the exporter finally gets cash payment when the whole settlement process is completed, credit instruments, mainly bills of exchange, are operating in the whole process. Payment methods, however, consist of two parts: credit instruments and commercial documents. In other words, although payment methods involve payment tools, but payment tools alone do not make payment methods.

Section 2　Classification of Payment Methods

1. According to the usage in practice

    (1) Remittance.
    (2) Collection.
    (3) Letter of credit.
    (4) Letter of factoring.
    (5) Letter of guarantee.

2. According to payment tools

    (1) Cash settlement. Cash settlement means that cash is used in the settlement process as the medium of exchange, which is the case when international settlement has not been fully developed.

    (2) Non-cash settlement. Non-cash settlement means that credit instruments, mainly bills of exchange, are used as the medium of exchange in the settlement process. Non-cash settlement is an indicator that international settlement has moved into its modern era. All five payment methods mentioned above fall into this category.

3. According to the credit standing

    (1) Trader's credit. In trader's credit, the payment undertaking to the exporter is given by the importer. Remittance and collection are payment methods based on

the trader's credit.

(2)Banker's credit. In banker's credit, the payment undertaking to the exporter is given by a bank rather than the importer. Letter of credit, factoring and letter of guarantee are payment methods based on banker's credit.

As banker's credit is deemed higher than that of a trader and the exporter enjoys higher security of payment when the payment method chosen for the transaction is based on the banker's credit, though he still relies on the credit standing of a bank to effect payment.

4. According to the direction of the movement of the instrument in relation to that of the funds flow

(1)Remittance. In remittance, the debtor (importer) gives proceeds (payments) to the bank and asks the bank to transfer the funds via certain credit instrument or certain payment instruction to the creditor (exporter). The drawer of the credit instrument or the issuer of the payment instruction is the importer's bank. The drawee of the credit instrument or the addressee of the payment instruction is the exporter's bank.

Remittance indicates that the funds flow in the same direction as the credit instruments or the payment instruction transmitted therein. The movements are shown in Figure 6.1 (The straight lines represent the movement of the funds and the dotted lines represent the directions of the instrument or the payment instruction).

Figure 6.1 **Remittance**

Of the five payment methods, only remittance falls in to the category of remittance.

(2)Reverse remittance. In reverse remittance, the creditor (exporter) draws an instrument on the debtor (the importer) or the debtor's bank, requiring the banks to collect payment for him based on the instrument.

Reverse remittance indicates that the funds flow in an opposite direction of the credit instrument transmitted thereon. Collection, letter of credit, factoring and let-

ter of guarantee fall into this category. The movements are shown in Figure 6. 2
(The straight lines represent the movement of the funds and the dotted lines represented the direction of the instruments) .

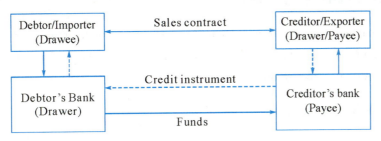

Figure 6. 2   **Reverse–remittance**

Section 3   Introduction to Remittance

As a payment method shown in Figure 6. 3, remittance refers to a bank (the
remitting bank) , at the request of its customer (the remitter) , transfers a certain
sum of money to its overseas branch or correspondent bank (the paying bank) instructing it to pay to a named person (the payee/beneficiary) domiciled in that
country.

Figure 6. 3   **Remittance as Payment Method**

The four immediate parties in remittance are:

1. Remitter

A remitter is the party who will make the payment. He is the person who requires his bank to remit funds to the beneficiary in a foreign country. In international trade, he is the buyer and the importer.

2. Remitting bank

Remitting bank is to remit funds at the request of a remitter to the paying bank and instructing the latter to pay a certain amount of money to a beneficiary. In international trade, it is the importer's bank.

3. Paying bank/Receiving bank

A paying bank or a receiving bank is to receive funds from and be instructed by the remitting bank to pay a certain sum of money to a beneficiary. In international trade, it is the exporter's bank.

4. Payee/Beneficiary

The payee or beneficiary is the person whom is to receive funds by remittance. In international trade, he is the seller or the exporter.

Section 4   Classification of Remittance

According to the different ways to give the payment instruction, remittance can be classified as remittance by airmail (M/T), remittance by telegraphic transfer (T/T) and remittance by banker's demand draft (D/D).

1. M/T: Remittance by airmail

(1) The definition of M/T. The remitting bank, at the request of the remitter, transfers the funds by means of sending/posting a payment instruction to the paying bank, asking the latter to pay a certain sum of money to the beneficiary. The definition of M/T is shown in Figure 6.4.

Figure 6.4   The Definition of M/T

M/T makes use of post service to transfer the payment instruction. A payment instruction is an authenticated order in writing addressed by the remitting bank to the paying bank. In M/T, payment instruction is given in Mail Transfer Payment Order.

Mail Transfer Payment Order is based on Application for Mail Transfer. The Application should be filled in by the remitter before he requires his bank to transfer the proceeds for him. When filled in and signed by the customer and stamped by the bank, the Application becomes a contract between the bank (remitting bank) and the customer (the remitter) whereby the bank is to transfer the funds.

The blank form is pre-printed by the bank and is made in a set with the first part being the Application for Mail Transfer, the second being the Mail Transfer Payment Order and the third being the customer's copy. Mail Transfer Payment Order must be signed by the remitting bank before sending to the paying bank.

A sample M/T application form and M/T payment order will be shown in Figure 6. 5 and Figure 6. 6.

Figure 6. 5　**Sample M/T Application Form**

Figure 6.6   Sample M/T Payment Order

(2) M/T procedure. A detailed M/T procedure is shown in Figure 6.7.

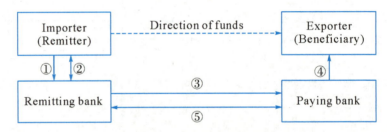

Figure 6.7   M/T Procedure

① The remitter gives his signed written application to his bank, requiring it to transfer the funds through M/T.

② The remitting bank checks the remitter's account. If it is positive, the remitting bank stamps on the application form and returns the customer's copy to the remitter for record. The remitting bank then debits the remitter's a/c with the amount to be remitted together with its commission and airmail expenses. (In the case when there is no account available, the customer will give proceeds to the remitting bank together with the application form).

③ The remitting bank issues and posts a Mail Transfer Payment Order to the paying bank.

④ The paying bank releases the funds to the beneficiary after verifies the Mail Transfer Payment Order against the sample specimen of the remitting bank's authorized signature and checks the identity of the beneficiary.

⑤ The paying bank claims reimbursement (compensation) from the remitting bank.

2. T/T: Remittance by telegraphic transfer

(1) T/T Definition. The remitting bank, at the request of the remitter, transfers funds by means of cable/telex/SWIFT message to the paying bank, asking the latter to pay a certain sum of money to the beneficiary. The definition of T/T is shown in Figure 6. 8.

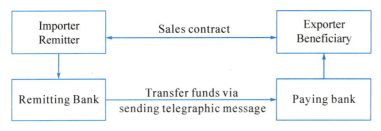

Figure 6. 8   **The Definition of T/T**

Bank pre−prints blank Application for Telegraphic Transfer for its customers. Figure 6. 9 shows a sample T/T application form.

Telegraphic message is sent by telex, cable or SWIFT. SWIFT is the English initials for Society of Worldwide Interbank Financial Telecommunications. SWIFT messages sent among its member banks of this society are telegraphic ones. When the remitting bank's authorized signature is used to validate the mail message under M/T, any telegraphic message under T/T must be authenticated by test key or SAK (SWIFT Authentic Key).

Test key or SAK is code arrangements agreed upon by two banks in advance to authenticate telegraphic message. The code of the test key consists of a series of tabulated numbers, each representing a particular month, date, amount, currency and other related item. The Indicated numbers are totaled to make the test key or SAK which must be sent together with the telegraphic message to verify it.

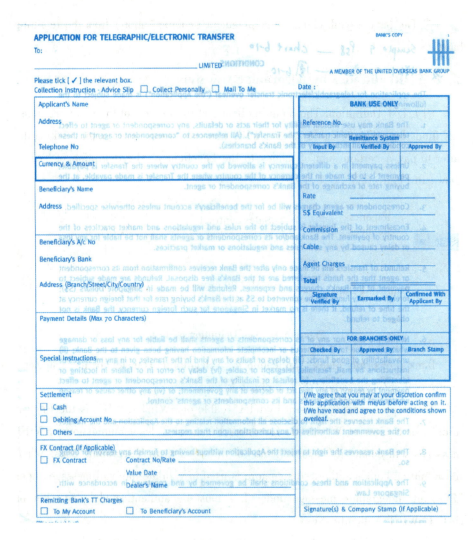

Figure 6. 9   Sample T/T Application Form

（2）T/T procedure. A detailed procedure of T/T is shown in Figure 6. 10.

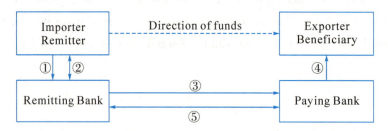

Figure 6. 10   T/T Procedure

① The remitter gives his signed written application to his bank, requiring it to transfer the funds through T/T.

② The remitting bank checks the remitter's account. If it is positive, the remitting bank stamps on the application form and returns it to the remitter for record. The remitting bank then debits the remitter's a/c with the amount to be remitted together with its commission and telegraphic transfer expenses(In the case when there is no account available, the customer will give proceeds to the remitting bank together with the application form).

③ The remitting sends the payment instruction by telex/cable/SWIFT to the paying bank.

④The paying bank releases the funds to the beneficiary after verifies the telegraphic message against the test key or SAK and checks the identity of the beneficiary.

⑤The paying bank claims reimbursement (compensation) from the remitting bank.

3. D/D：Remittance by banker's demand draft

(1)D/D Definition. The remitting bank, at the request of the remitter, draw a bill of exchange on the paying bank ordering the latter to pay on demand a certain sum of money to the beneficiary who will also be the payee of the draft. The definition of D/D is shown in Figure 6. 11.

Figure 6. 11　**The Definition of D/D**

Bank may pre－print Application for Demand Draft/Telegraphic Transfer in which the customer may choose applicable boxes to fill in when he requests D/D or T/T services from the bank. Figure 6. 12 shows such an application form.

In D/D, payment instruction is given in the form of a banker' demand draft which is drawn by the remitting bank on the paying bank payable to the exporter on demand.

Figure 6. 13 shows an example of such a draft, which can also be considered as a check with the three immediate parties as：

The drawer：The Royal Bank of Canada, Mongkok Branch, Hong Kong

The drawee：The Royal Bank of Canada, Toronto, Canada

The Payee：ABC Co., Toronto, Canada

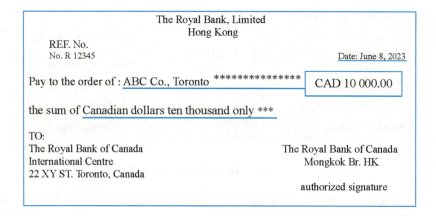

Figure 6.12　**Sample Application for Demand Draft/Telegraphic Transfer**

The Royal Bank, Limited
Hong Kong

REF. No.
No. R 12345　　　　　　　　　　　　　　　　Date: June 8, 2023

Pay to the order of : ABC Co., Toronto　＊＊＊＊＊＊＊＊＊＊＊＊＊＊　| CAD 10 000.00 |

the sum of Canadian dollars ten thousand only ＊＊＊

TO:
The Royal Bank of Canada　　　　　　　　The Royal Bank of Canada
International Centre　　　　　　　　　　　Mongkok Br. HK
22 XY ST. Toronto, Canada

　　　　　　　　　　　　　　　　　　　authorized signature

Figure 6.13　**Sample Draft Used in D/D**

（2）D/D procedure. A detailed procedure of D/D is shown in Figure 6.14.

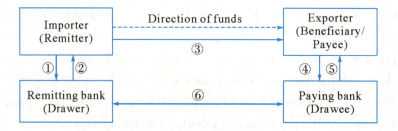

Figure 6.14　**D/D Procedure**

① The remitter gives his signed written application to his bank requiring it to transfer the funds by D/D.

② The remitting bank checks the remitter's account with him. If it is positive, the remitting bank stamps on the application form and returns it to the remitter for record. The remitting bank then debits the account with the amount to be remitted and its commissions, draws a draft on the paying bank payable to the exporter. The draft drawn is handed to the remitter(In the case of personal remittance, the customer will provide the remitted amount to the bank before the latter draws a banker's draft).

③ The remitter sends the draft to the exporter.

④ Upon receipt of the draft, the exporter/payee presents the draft for payment to the paying bank.

⑤ After authentication of the draft against authorized signature, the paying bank releases the funds to the exporter.

⑥ The paying bank claims reimbursement against the remitting bank.

When compared with M/T and D/D, T/T is the fastest and most secure form of remittance. The bank charges the highest commission under T/T. However, on account of its speed and security, T/T is often chosen by traders, especially when the remitted amount is large and the transfer of funds is subject to a time limit.

Section 5　Application of Remittance

When traders apply remittance to settling payment for an import or export transaction, in addition to the selection of M/T, T/T and D/D, they must make a further choice from payment in advance and open account.

1. Payment in advance

By its very name, payment in advance signifies that the time of payment comes before the time of the delivery of goods or the provision of services. That is, the importer first settles payment through M/T, T/T or D/D and the exporter makes delivery after the funds are transferred to him through remittance. Obviously, this method is favorable to the exporter while putting the importer at great risks.

Payment in advance is unfavorable to the importer on the following grounds:

(1) He pays in advance, tying up his capital prior to the receipt of the goods

or services.

（2）He bears the risk of non-delivery on the part of the exporter.

（3）He has no assurance that what he contracted for will be supplied, received or received within the agreed time period or received in quality or quantity ordered.

As a result, payment in advance will be used under the following conditions：

（1）When it is in the seller's market with conditions favoring the exporter. In order to secure the goods, the importer has to offer favorable terms to him.

（2）When the manufacturing process or services delivered are to be specialized or capital intensive, the importer may agree to finance the exporter by partial payment in advance and partial progress payment.

（3）The exporter may insist to settle the payment in advance when the buyer's credit standing is doubtful or when there is an unstable political economic environment in the buyer's country which will result in the delay in receipt of funds which is beyond the seller's control.

On the whole, in order to protect himself, the importer should make sure before the application of payment in advance that the credit standing of the exporter must be exceedingly good, or that he will agree to pay in advance only a certain percentage of the amount with the balance to be paid through other payment methods.

2. Open account（O/A）

Open account is just the opposite of payment in advance. Open account means that the exporter makes delivery before the importer makes payment to him through M/T, T/T or D/D. Although the time of payment is agreed to be made on a predetermined future date, the exporter is in fact selling on credit without any safeguards about the performance of the importer. The method is in the importer's favor and exposes the exporter to great risks.

Open account is unfavorable to the exporter on the following grounds：

（1）He bears the risk of non-payment on the part of the importer.

（2）He releases the title to the goods without having assurance of payment.

（3）His own capital is tied up until he receives the payment.

（4）There is possibility that political events will impose regulations which defer or block the movements of funds to him.

Open account is used under the following conditions：

（1）When it is in the buyer's market with conditions favoring the importer. In order to be competitive, the exporter may choose to offer the importer this favorable term, though O/A is not the only way to make the exporter competitive.

(2) When there is a long-standing or regular business relationship between traders.

(3) When a multi-national company ships the goods to its foreign branches or subsidiaries.

On the whole, in order to protect himself, the exporter should make sure before the application of O/A that the credit standing of the importer is exceedingly good. Otherwise, he may need to require open account to be taken under a bank guarantee or that he uses this term only for a certain percentage of the transaction.

Section 6　Characteristics of Remittance

Remittance is based on the trader's credit. That is, banks only transfer funds at the request of the remitter/importer and they assume no payment undertaking to the exporter. In addition to this, banks do not deal with documents in the settlement process of remittance. Documents, namely the commercial documents and financial instruments, if any, are sent directly by the traders themselves. In other words, banks play minimum role in remittance. Banks' low involvement in remittance brings about the following advantages and disadvantages.

Compared with collection and letter of credit, on the one hand, remittance is the simplest and the least expensive payment method on account of banks' low involvement. On the other hand, however, remittance is the most risky one to the traders for the same reasons. Under payment in advance, the importer bears the extreme risk of non-delivery from the exporter. When this happens, the importer loses payments and goods are not available. Under open account, the exporter is exposed to the greatest risk of non-payment from the importer. When this happens, the exporter loses both payments and goods. Remittance cannot reduce these risks on its own.

Exercises for Chapter 6

I. Multiple-choice Questions (It is possible to make more than one choice)

1. _____ is/are a payment method.

A. Bills of exchange

B. Promissory note

C. Letter of credit

D. Collection

2. _____ is/are reverse–remittance and _____ is/are based on trader's credit.

A. Remittance

B. Collection

C. Bills of exchange

D. Letter of credit

3. According to the different ways to give the payment instruction, remittance can be classified as _____

A. M/T, T/T, D/D

B. payment in advance and open account

C. M/T and payment in advance

D. T/T and open account

4. In D/D, the drawer, drawee and payee of the drafts are _____ respectively.

A. paying bank, importer, remitting bank

B. remitting bank, paying bank, exporter

C. importer, paying bank, exporter

D. importer, exporter, remitting bank

5. The selection from M/T, T/T or D/D for a trade transaction is up to _____.

A. the banks

B. the traders and the banks

C. the International Chamber of Commerce

D. the traders

II. Fill in the Blanks

1. _____ is used to authenticate T/T message, and if the message is sent by SWIFT, _____ is used for the authentication.

2. _____ means that the exporter makes delivery before the importer makes payment to him through M/T, T/T or D/D.

3. When the payment method _____ is chosen for a transaction, if the exporter is dishonest, the importer is exposed to the risks of losing both money and goods.

4. In M/T, the _____ is an authenticated order in writing addressed by the remitting bank to the paying bank.

5. When the demand is _____ than the supply, it is the buyer's market.

III. Case Questions

Case One

According to a sales contract, payment was to be made by a demand draft 20 days before delivery. On the next day after receiving the draft from the post office, the exporter immediately arranged shipment, sent the shipping documents to the importer and presented to draft to his bank for payment. One week later, the draft was dishonored because after scrutiny, the bank found out that the draft was a forged one. Unable to obtain payment, the exporter contacted the importer urgently but, unfortunately, the exporter could not be able to reach the importer but the goods had been taken delivery by the importer against shipping documents sent by the exporter himself.

Questions:Specify the payment method chosen and point out the lessons the exporter should learn from this transaction.

Case Two

The exporter, ABC Co., Chengdu intends to make a deal with a new customer, XYZ Co., Vietnam who wants to buy a large amount of cotton towels at USD 12 000. In the counter offer to the exporter, the importer proposes that he shall pay 15% of the sales proceeds in advance and T/T the balance to the seller no later than two weeks after the delivery.

Questions:

1. How many payment methods are proposed for the deal? What are they?

2. Should the exporter accept the payment terms under normal market condition? Give your reasons to support your opinion.

3. What suggestions can the exporter give to the importer if he wants to make the deal?

IV. Extended Discussions

Ms. Ye has rented a shop at the International Shopping Mall, Phase II in Yi Wu, Zhejiang, selling bags and suitcases. On 5 April, 2023, a purchasing agent from Da Qin International Trading Co. came to her shop and placed an order at RMB 17 700. On 22 April, she delivered the ordered goods to the buyer's place as agreed and on 5 May she went there again to collect the payment. To her surprise, the owner of Da Qin International Trading Co. disappeared so she could not get the payment.

It turned out that she was not alone in loosing payments. According to preliminary survey, more than 100 shops were cheated by Da Qin International Trading Co. and the total amount of the swindled goods exceeded RMB 1 500 000. However, the average loss suffered by each individual shop was not very big, with only one shop losing more than RMB 50 000, most shops about RMB 10 000 and one shop only at RMB 1 000. "We are always on the alert of international trade frauds when the trade volume is large. But we would tend to let down our guard when it comes to the Minimum Order Quantity," said the other shop owners. Compared with many other trade frauds that occur every year, this is a small case with the average loss at about RMB 10 000 for each shop.

Questions:

1. What payment method is chosen by the shop owners in these transactions?

2. What causes the loss for the shop owners?

3. Does it mean that those frauds will not create any serious consequences because the cheated amount is small?

4. Does it mean that dishonest trading is a good bargain because it can bring in more money than a fair trading? Give reasons to support your opinion.

Chapter 7   Collection

Objectives

◇Learn the definition and parties of collection.

◇Learn the classification of collection.

◇Learn the procedures of D/P sight, D/P after sight and D/A.

◇Learn the requirements of the drafts drawn under collection.

◇Learn the characteristics of collection.

Section 1   Definitions of Collection

1. Definition one

Collection means the handling of documents by banks in accordance with instructions received to:

(1) Obtain payment or acceptance.

(2) Deliver documents against payments or against acceptance.

The word "documents" here include both the financial documents and commercial documents.

2. Definition two

Collection means an arrangement whereby the goods are shipped and the relevant bill of exchange is drawn by the seller on the buyer, or document(s) is sent to the seller's bank with clear instruction for collection through one of its correspondent banks (head office/branches) located in the domicile of the buyer. This arrangement is shown in Figure 7.1.

Figure 7.1   Collection Definition Two

Section 2   Parties to Collection and URC

1. The principal

He is the person who entrusts the collection items (documents) to his bank. He is so called based on his principle-agent relationship with his banker. He is the exporter and the drawer of the draft. He is also the shipper because he consigns the goods to shipment.

2. The drawee

He is the drawee because the draft is drawn on him. He should honor the draft by payment or acceptance. He is the importer.

3. Remitting bank

Remitting bank is the exporter's bank. He receives the collection items (drafts or other documents) from the principal/exporter and forwards the collection items to its correspondent bank or overseas head/branch office, asking the latter to collect proceeds from the importer.

4. Collecting bank

Collecting bank is to receive the collection items from remitting bank and presents the draft to the drawee. It is the importer's bank and can be the correspondent bank or a head/branch office of the remitting bank.

When the principal specifies a collecting bank, remitting bank will forward documents to that bank. When no collecting bank is specified, remitting bank will choose a collecting bank for the principal. In practice, it is better for the choice to be left to remitting bank. Not all overseas banks can be relied upon, and it is much safer for the remitting bank to select one which it knows will carry out instructions properly.

Uniform Rules for Collection (URC) was published by International Chamber of Commerce. It is an internationally accepted code of practice covering documentary collections. It has a legal binding on all parties and all bank authorities and the collection order will state that the collection is subject to URC. URC will apply unless the collection order states otherwise or the laws in one of the countries concerned specially contradict the rules in URC. URC 522, the latest version of URC, takes effect on Jan. 1, 1996. The most recent version is URC 322, effective on 1 Jan, 1978.

Section 3   Classification of Collection

According to whether title documents (shipping documents) are attached to the financial documents when submitted to the remitting bank, collection can be divided into clean collection and documentary collection.

1. Clean collection

Clean collection is the collection on financial instruments alone without being accompanied by shipping documents. Shipping documents, if any, will be forwarded by the exporter directly to the importer. When a credit instrument is accompanied by non-shipping documents such as commercial invoice, the collection is also considered to be clean one.

Clean collection is mainly used to collect incidental expenses occurred in a transaction such as freight, insurance premium, commission or any other supplementary charges. On other occasions, clean collection is also used in the collection of down-payment or in the case of service transactions where there are no shipping documents available.

2. Documentary collection

Documentary collection is the collection on financial instruments being accompanied by shipping documents or collections on shipping documents without financial documents. When financial instruments are not included, the stamp duty, a tax on the drawer of a financial instrument, can be avoided and the amount to be collected will be indicated clearly by commercial invoice.

Compared with clean collection, documentary collection means that the banks will assume higher liability because they have the shipping documents in their hands. Documentary collection enjoys higher popularity in international tangible trade.

Documentary collection can be further divided into documents against payment (D/P) and documents against acceptance (D/A). The division is based on the different conditions against which the documents are released to the importer. Generally speaking, D/P is more favorable to the exporter while D/A is more favorable to the importer.

(1) Documents against payment (at) sight [D/P (at) sight]. D/P (at) sight means that the collecting bank releases the documents against payment of sight draft or simply against sight payment of the importer, and the exporter gets sight payment. The draft, if any, used under D/P (at) sight must be sight one. When payments are made at sight by the importer/drawee, documents are released to him immediately.

However, draft may not be a must under this method since the collecting bank can release the documents against the payment of commercial invoice, a commercial document clearly indicating the amount to be paid. Figure 7.2 shows the procedure of D/P (at) sight.

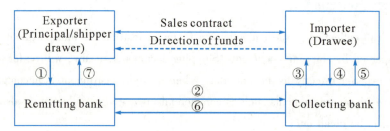

Figure 7.2 The Procedure of D/P (at) Sight

①After shipment is made and the shipping documents are obtained, the exporter draws a sight draft on the importer for the value of the goods, fills in the application form for collection indicating clearly that the documents will be released under D/P (at) sight. The exporter then submits it with the draft and the commercial documents to his banker for collection (If draft is not used, it is not drawn and not submitted).

②The remitting bank completes its own collection order based on the application form and forwards it with other collection items he receives to the collecting bank.

③Acting as an agent for the remitting bank, the collecting bank notifies the importer upon receipt of the collection order and collection items and presents the draft to him for payment (If no draft is presented, the collecting bank simply notifies the importer to make sight payment).

④The importer makes payment at sight to the collecting bank.

⑤The collecting bank releases documents to the importer against his sight payment.

⑥The collecting bank remits the proceeds to the remitting bank according to the instructions on the collection order.

⑦The remitting bank credits the payment to the exporter's account with him.

(2) Documents against payment after sight (D/P after sight). D/P after sight means that the collecting bank releases the documents against the importer's payment of time bill, and the exporter gets time payment. The draft used under this method is a time one. Documents are to be released to the importer only when he makes the payment at the due date of the draft. Figure 7.3 shows the procedure of D/P after sight.

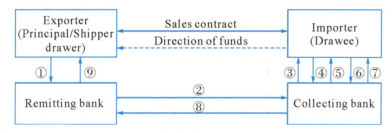

Figure 7.3　**The Procedure of D/P After Sight**

①After shipment is made and the shipping documents are obtained, the exporter draws a time draft on the importer for the value of the goods, fills in the application form for collection, indicating clearly that documents will be released under D/P after sight. The exporter then submits it with the draft and the commercial documents to his banker for collection.

②The remitting bank completes its own collection order based on the application form and forwards it with other collection items he receives to the collecting bank.

③Acting as an agent for the remitting bank, the collecting bank notifies the importer upon receipt of the collection order and the collection items and presents the draft to him for acceptance.

④The importer accepts the draft upon presentment and returns the accepted draft to the collecting bank.

⑤At maturity, the collecting bank presents the accepted draft again for payment.

⑥The importer makes payment at maturity (time payment).

⑦The collecting bank releases documents to the importer against his time payment.

⑧The collecting bank remits the proceeds to the remitting bank according to the instructions on the collection order.

⑨The remitting bank credits the payment to the exporter's account with him.

(3) Documents against acceptance (D/A). Documents against acceptance (D/A) means that the collecting bank releases the documents against the buyer's acceptance to the draft, and the exporter gets time payment. The draft required under D/A is a time one. Figure 7.4 shows the procedure of D/A.

Figure 7.4　**The Procedure of D/A**

①After shipment is made and the shipping documents are obtained, the exporter draws a time draft on the importer for the value of the goods, fills in the application form for collection, indicating clearly that the documents will be released under D/A. The exporter then submits it with the draft and the commercial documents to his banker for collection.

②The remitting bank completes its own collection order based on the application form and forwards it with other collection items he receives to the collecting bank.

③Acting as an agent for the remitting bank, the collecting bank notifies the importer upon receipt of the collection items and presents the draft to him for acceptance.

④The importer accepts the draft and returns it to the collecting bank.

⑤The collecting bank releases documents to the importer against his acceptance.

⑥Upon due date, the collecting bank presents the accepted draft again for payment.

⑦The importer makes payment on due date.

⑧The collecting bank remits the proceeds to the remitting bank according to the instructions on the collection order.

⑨The remitting bank credits the payment to the exporter's account with him.

Section 4　Collection Order

　　Collection order is a standard form of authority which enables the exporter/remitting bank to include specific instructions to his bank/the collecting bank regarding documentary collection. Collection is carried out according to the specific instructions contained in the collection order. Figure 7.5 shows a collection order drafted by International Chamber of Commerce.

Subject to uniform rules for collections (1978 Revision) International Chamber of Commerce Publication No. 322

PLEASE COLLECT THE UNDERMENITIONED FOREIGN BILL OR DOCUMENTS

Full Name and Address of Drawer/Exporter	For Bank Use Only	Date	I.S.B. Collection No.
	Drawers reference (to be quoted in all correspondence)		
	For Bank Use Only	Due Date	Correspondence Reference
Consignee–Full Name and Address	Drawee (if not Consignee)–full Name and Address		
	For Bank Use Only	Fate Dates	
TO　Barclays Bank PLC S.W.I.F.T.　ADDRESS BARC GB22	Drawers Bankers Barclays Bank Account No.	Sorting Code No. 20–	Ref. No.

PLEASE FORWARD DOCUMENTS ENUMERATED BELOW BY AIRMAIL FOLLOW SPECIAL INSTRUCTIONS AND THOSE MARKED X

Bill of Exchange	Comm'l Invoice	Cert'd /Cons Inv.	Cert.of Origin	Ins'ce Pol/ Cert.	Bill of Lading	Parcel PostRec'pt	AirWaybill

Combined Transport Doc.	Other Documents and whereabouts of any missing original Bill of Lading

Release Documents on	Acceptance	Payment	If unaccepted and advise reason by		Protest	Do Not Protest
If documents are not taken up on arrival of goods	Warehouse Goods	Do Not Warehouse			Cable	Airmail
	Insure Against File	Do Not Insure	If unpaid and advise reason by		Protest	Do Not Protest
Collect All Charges	Yes	No			Cable	Airmail
Collect Correspondent's Charges ONLY	Yes	No	Acceptance /Payment may be deferred until arrival of goods		Yes	No
Goods and carrying vessel			After final payment Remit proceeds by		Cable	Airmail

For Bank Use Only
In case of need refer to		For Guidance	Accept their Instructions

SPECIAL INSTRUCTIONS 1. Represent on arrival of goods if not honored on first presentation

Date of Bill of Exchange	Tenor		Amount of Collection
Bill of Exchangeclaused	Please apply Proceeds of this collection as indicated with an "X"	Credit us in Sterling	
		Credit our Foreign Currency Account No.	
		Apply to Forward Contract No.	
	I/We agree that you shall not be liable for any loss, damage, or delay however caused which is not directly due to the negligence of your own officers and servants Any charges and expenses not recovered from the drawees, including any costs of protecting the merchandise, may be charged to us		
For Bank use Only	Dates & Signature		

Figure 7.5　**A Collection Order**

When filled in and signed by the exporter and submitted to the remitting bank, this standard form of authority is the Application for Collection. Against this Application, the remitting bank makes collection order and forwards it to the collecting bank. When submitted by the exporter at the beginning of the procedure, this standard form serves as a covering letter to the collection items operated in the collection process. Figure 7.6 is a sample of Application for Documentary Collection.

TO: BANK OF CHINA   DATE:
    SINGAPORE

Dear Sirs

I/we enclose herewith the following draft(s) and document(s) for collection subject to the terms and conditions set out overleaf:

Bill No.	Amount	Due Date/Tenor	Drawee

Documents	Drafts	B/L	Invoice	P/W List	Ins Cert	Cert Origin	Cert of Qly /Qty	AWB	D.O.	

kindly act in accordance with my/our instructions marked "X" as indicated hereinbelow:

( )   Deliver document(s) against payment   ( )   Deliver Document(s) against acceptance
( )   All banking charges are for the account of the drawee.
( )   All collecting bank's charges are for the account of drawee and your charges are for my/our account.
( )   Protest for non-payment   ( )   Protest for non-acceptance
( )   Overdue interest to be collected from the drawee at % per annum from due date to the approximate date of return remittance in Singapore.
( )   Interest to be collected from the drawee at % per annum from first presentation to the approximate date of return remittance in Singapore.

In case of need or difficulties, please communicate with (seller's representative):
Address:

Tel:
Who will endeavor to obtain the honoring of the aforesaid draft(s), without any alteration of my/our instructions.

In case of dishonor, the goods may, in the option of your correspondent or agent, be landed, cleared through the customs, warehoused and insured at my/our costs and expenses.

It is understood and agreed that, having exercised due care in the selection of any correspondent to whom the abovementioned items any be sent for collection, you shall not be responsible for any act, omission, default, suspension, insolvency or bankruptcy of any such correspondent or sub-agent thereof, or for any delay in remittance, loss in exchange or loss of items or their proceeds during transmission or in the course of collection, but your responsibility shall be only for your own acts.

PAYMENT INSTRUCTIONS:
( )   Please advance/discount the bill.
( )   Please pay us only upon receipt of funds
( )   Please credit proceeds to our account no.:
( )   Please offset Import Bill(s) ref.:
( )   Please utilize Forward Contract no.:
( )   Hold proceeds and contact: at Tel. No.

SPECIAL INSTRUCTIONS:
Please deliver the documents through: Yours faithfully
(Drawee's Banker)

(X) Whichever is applicable.
(Subject to Uniform Rules for Collections ICC Publication No. 322)

Figure 7.6 Application for Documentary Collection

Major items of collection order will be illustrated below from the point of view of an Application for Documentary Collection, for the two are the same in terms of contents:

(1) Name and address of the drawer/exporter.

(2) Name and address of the remitting bank (the drawer's bank).

(3) Particulars of the draft where the information of the drawee/importer will be shown.

(4) Documents covered/submitted. The exporter is expected to indicate clearly the name and the number of copies of documents he submits.

(5) Documents release conditions

Documents will be released to the importer whether against D/P or against D/A. In the absence of such instructions, documents will be released against payment.

(6) Store and insurance clause. If documents are not taken up on arrival of goods, instructions are required on whether to warehouse and insure the goods. In the event that the importer does not pay or accept the draft, the collecting bank will be instructed by such a clause to warehouse and insure the goods. The cost of this operation will be borne by the exporter.

(7) Protest clause. Specific instructions are required whether to protest in the event of dishonor by either non-payment or non-acceptance. The protest fee will be borne by the collecting bank who will be reimbursed by the exporter's bank who will in turn debit his customer.

(8) The case of need. The case of need is an agent of the exporter who is resident of the importer's country. In the event of default, the collecting bank will refer to him in the settlement process.

(9) The signature of the drawer/exporter.

(10) Special instructions. This is a space where the information of the collecting bank is entered. The collecting bank may be indicated by the exporter or he may leave it up to the remitting bank to decide.

(11) Subject to URC. Normally, it is a must that the collection order should bear clearly the following statement: This collection order is subject to Uniform Rules for Collections (1978 Revision) International Chamber of Commerce publication No. 322 or its later version, URC 522, effective on 1 Jan 1996.

Section 5   Collection Draft

Drafts drawn under collection should meet the following requirements：

(1)Drawer：the exporter.

(2)Drawee：the importer.

(3)Payee：The bill can be made payable to one of the three parties.

①The beneficiary. The beneficiary, namely the exporter is the payee. When he submits the draft with documents to the remitting bank, he should endorse the bill to the collecting bank in collection endorsement.

②The remitting bank. The remitting bank can also be the payee. The drawn clause to the draft indicates that it is for collecting that the remitting bank has been made the payee. The remitting bank should endorse the bill to the collecting bank in collection endorsement before the bill is forwarded with documents.

③The collecting bank. The collecting bank can be the payee as well. And again, the drawn clause to the draft indicates that it is for collecting that the collecting bank has been made the payee. No endorsement is required for this type of bill.

(4)Tenor：sight or time.

Figure 7.7 is a sample of draft drawn under collection.

Documents are to be delivered only against payment of this bill

representing   100%value of our Invoice No.

No.TA.60153   *Exchange for* USD 19 800.00   Shanghai Dec,25 2023

At 60 days after sight sight of this *FIRST of Exchange(Second of Exchange being unpaid)*
Pay to the order of Bank of China,Shanghai
The sum of U.S.DOLLARS NINETEEN THOUSAND EIGHT HUNDRED ONLY

To:Ewing General Trading
  Post Box No.1489
  Dubai

China National Import & Export Corporation
Shanghai Branch,Shanghai,China
Authorized Signature

Figure 7.7   **Collection Draft**

Section 6　Characteristics of Collection

Collection is based on trader's credit. This means that banks assume no payment undertaking to the exporter in collection. However, banks should deal with documents in the settlement process of collection. According to URC, the banks doing collection business should act in good faith and exercise reasonable care. Banks must check that they appear to have received the documents which are specified in the collection order, though they have no obligation to exam the documents any further. As a result, banks assume greater liabilities in collection than in remittance. Banks' greater involvement in collection brings about the following advantages and disadvantages to the traders.

1. Advantages under collection

In comparison with payment in advance and open account, collection, particularly documentary collection, is a compromise in the sense that the risks to either the exporter or the importer are reduced to a certain degree.

(1) Advantages to the exporter. Once documents are passed to the bank by the exporter rather than being sent directly to the importer under open account, banks can exercise an absolute right over the goods through the title documents (shipping documents). Normally, title to the goods does not pass to the buyer until the draft is paid (D/P) or accepted (D/A). Therefore, the extreme risks of non-payment from the importer and losing goods under O/A exposed to the exporter are reduced. Under documentary collection, if the importer wants to obtain title documents for the goods, he should make payment or acceptance to the collecting bank first.

(2) Advantages to the importer. When the importer makes payment (D/P) or acceptance (D/A), he is sure that the goods have been shipped and the documents are placed with banks available to him. Therefore, the extreme risks of non-delivery from the exporter and losing money under payment in advance exposed to the importer are reduced. Under documentary collection, if the exporter wants to get payment or acceptance, he should make delivery first and place the documents with the remitting bank.

2. Risks under collection

Generally, collection is more favorable to the importer because whether under

D/P or D/A, the exporter should always make delivery first and place the documents in the hands of the banks.

(1) Risks to the exporter.

①Under D/P. The exporter is exposed to the risk of non-payment from the importer under D/P. This may happen when a buyer intentionally refuses to take delivery when, for example the market for the imported goods shrinks and the market price falls. Although the exporter does not lose the goods because the importer cannot get physical goods without payment, they are at the overseas port, in chance of being damaged, stolen or possibly incurring demurrage. Demurrage means charges levied by port authorities for goods which are not collected on time.

In such circumstances, the exporter may find himself in an unfavorable condition to find an alternative buyer or pay to ship the goods back or accept to settle the payment with the importer at a reduced price. Therefore, when a payment method is on trader's credit, the credit standing of the trading partner is very important.

②Under D/A. The exporter is exposed to the risk of non-payment from the importer with an additional risk of losing the physical goods because under D/A, documents, and therefore the goods are released on acceptance, with no guarantee that the payment will be forthcoming at maturity. Once the bill of exchange is accepted, the exporter is in no better position than under an open account term, except that he has a trader's accepted bill with him on which he can sue the importer if it is dishonored at maturity. Once the bill of exchange is accepted, the exporter is also exposed to the risk of losing both payment and goods.

As a measure of self-protection, the exporter is recommended that he only uses D/A for partial amount with the balance to be settled through other payment methods.

(2) Risks to the importer. Although collection is generally in his favor, the importer will also bear risks as follows.

①Under D/P. Although the importer is not exposed to the risk of non-delivery from the exporter, he is liable to get wrong goods, goods that are inferior or not of the contract description. Under D/P, payment is made prior to the possession of the physical goods, with no opportunity for the importer to inspect the goods. Whether the goods delivered are of the contract description will entirely depend on the exporter's credit standing.

②Under D/A. Under D/A, the importer gets goods against acceptance, which enables him to inspect the goods before payment. However, according to *Bills of Exchange Act*, the importer's credit-worthiness will be harmed if he refuses to make payment against the accepted bill in the event that the imported goods are inferior to the conditions described in the sales contract. Therefore, the importer is still exposed to the risk of getting wrong goods, though not the risk of non-delivery from the exporter. And again, when a payment method is on trader's credit, the trading partner's credit standing is of vital importance.

Exercises for Chapter 7

I . Multiple-choice Questions (It is possible to make more than one choice)

1. In collection, the exporter plays the role of _____.

A. principal

B. drawer

C. drawee

D. shipper

2. When _____ are submitted, the collection is clean collection.

A. draft

B. draft with insurance policy

C. draft with commercial invoice

D. draft with bills of lading

3. When the transaction is goods transaction, the traders can choose _____ to settle the payments.

A. clean collection only

B. documentary collection only

C. clean collection and documentary collection

D. clean collection or documentary collection

4. According to documents release conditions, collection can take its subdivision(s) as _____.

A. documentary collection

B. clean collection

C. D/P sight

D. O/A

5. Under D/A, a complete acceptance made by the drawee should include _____.

A. the word "accepted"

B. the accepting date

C. the signature of the acceptor

D. the due date

Ⅱ. Fill in the Blanks

1. In collection, the exporter is the party to give to his bank collection items, which are,_____ or commercial documents.

2. In collection, when the collecting bank is not made as the payee of the draft,_____ is needed.

3. The tenor of the draft under remittance is _____ while the tenor of the draft under collection is sight or time.

4. Under D/A, the importer's _____ will be harmed if he refuses to make payment against the accepted bills in the event that the imported goods are inferior to the conditions described in the sales contract.

5. The remitting bank completes its own _____ based on the application form and forwards it with collection items received to the collecting bank.

Ⅲ. Case Questions

Case One

In an export transaction, Trader AAA exported 50 000 boxes of frozen chicken to Trader BBB under D/A 60 days sight. The seller made shipment on 5, March 2023 and submitted collection items to his bank for collection on 8, March 2023. The buyer accepted the draft on 17, March, 2023. After the arrival of goods, the collecting bank released documents to the buyer against his acceptance and the buyer obtained the shipping documents and took delivery of the goods afterwards. Later on, the buyer sold the goods but suffered a great loss due to the shrink of the local market. When the draft reached its due date on 16, May 2023, the buyer fails to make payment. In order to collect payment, the seller asked The Case of Need to contact the buyer and pressed for the payment. After several round of difficult negotiations, the buyer finally agreed to make payment, but at a discounted price of 70% of the original price into four installments spreading a whole year starting from 1, July 2023 to 1, July 2024.

Question:

1. Should the collecting bank be responsible for Trader AAA's loss? Why or why not?

2. What lessons should Trader AAA learn from this transaction?

Case Two

Company A, Shanghai exported of a batch of peanuts at USD 45 000 and the payment term in the sales contract read as follows: "The buyers shall duly accept the documentary draft drawn by the seller at 20 days sight upon first presentation and make payment on its maturity. The shipping documents are to be delivered on acceptance." Company A, Shanghai made shipment accordingly and presented documents on March 15 to the remitting bank for collection.

On April 25, Company A, Shanghai received an e-mail from the buyer, saying: "As per your shipping notice, we have contacted the shipping company and been informed that the goods have arrived. But presently we have not received the relevant documents to take delivery. Please check and send documents to us as soon as possible."

After check with the remitting bank, Company A, Shanghai, on May 10, received a reply from the collecting bank forwarded through the remitting bank: "We acknowledge the receipt of documents No. ×××× and the Collection Order. But because the drawee's address on both the documents and the Collection Order is too general and incomplete, we tried but could not locate the drawee and make presentment of the draft. Waiting for your further instruction."

Through checking the copies of the documents, Company A, Shanghai found that due to the negligence and carelessness of its own clerk, the detailed information of the buyer's address was not given in the application form and other relevant documents. Through the remitting bank, Company A, Shanghai sent immediately the detailed information to the collecting bank.

On May 15, Company A, Shanghai received a note of dishonor from the collecting bank through the remitting bank. According to the note, the buyer dishonored the draft because of the much-delayed documents, and the goods could not be picked up in time. What's worse, part of the goods was damaged by rain and the delay in taking delivery of goods incurred demurrage at high expenses.

Company A, Shanghai tried to negotiate with the buyer but could not reach an agreement. As it is impossible and not worth to ship the goods back, Company A, Shanghai had to commit the goods to an alternative buyer on consignment and suffered a huge loss.

Questions:

1. Which type of collection is chosen for the transaction?

2. Should the collecting bank be held responsible for the loss to Company A, Shanghai? Why or why not?

3. What lessons should Company A, Shanghai take?

IV. Extended Discussions

A Chinese company, Company A, made an export transaction of 160 bags with Company B in Latin America. According to the sales contract, the payment term chosen is D/P 30 days after sight. On May 14, Company A presented full set of documents to the collecting bank for collection and the time draft was accepted with the due date to be on June 20.

On June 15, Company A received a letter of complaint from Company B by which the buyer complained that the moisture content in some bags exceeded the standard limit, which caused moldy particles. Company A was surprised at receiving the letter before the due date of the draft but after checking with the banks, it was true that Company B took the delivery on June 15. Right after the checking, Company A sent a replacement to Company B together with a letter of apology. Because of its immediate and proper handling, the incident has not made any negative impact on the creditworthiness on Company A.

Questions:

1. Why did Company A feel surprised when received the letter of complaint from Company B?

2. What lesson do we learn from this case as to improve our professional competence to ensure successful transactions with trading partners from other developing countries?

Chapter 8　Letter of Credit

Objectives

◇Learn the definition and parties of L/C.

◇Learn the procedure of documentary credit.

◇Learn the contents of and the drafts drawn under L/C.

◇Learn the classification of L/C.

◇Learn the amendment of L/C.

◇Learn the documents examination and characteristics of L/C.

Section 1　Definitions of Letter of Credit

1. Definition one

The International Chamber of Commerce (ICC) publication No.415 has defined letter of credit as follows:

A letter of credit is a written undertaking issued by a bank (the issuing bank) given to the seller (the beneficiary) at the request and in accordance with the instructions of the buyer (the applicant) to effect payment at sight or at a determinable future time up to a stated sum of money and against stipulated documents which are complied with the terms and conditions of the credit.

Letter of credit stresses a conditional undertaking of payment by a bank. The word "conditional" means that the beneficiary should submit stipulated documents within a designated time limit and against any stipulated terms and conditions. The phrase "effect payment" means that the payment under L/C can be effected by payment, acceptance or negotiation.

2. Definition two

A documentary credit is any arrangement, however named or described, whereby a bank (the issuing bank) acting at the request and on the instructions of a customer (the applicant) or on his own behalf:

(1) Is to make a payment to or to the order of a third party (the Beneficiary), or is to accept and pay bills of exchange drawn by the beneficiary.

(2) Authorizes another bank to effect such payment, or to accept and pay such bills of exchange.

(3) Authorizes another bank to negotiate, against stipulated documents provided that the terms and conditions of the credit are complied with.

Figure 8.1 shows such an arrangement.

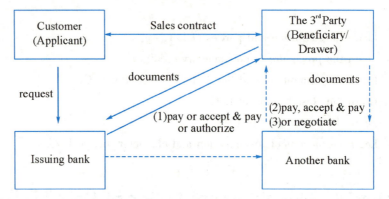

Figure 8.1　**The Definition Two of L/C**

In practice, it is more popular for the beneficiary to present documents to his bank (another bank), represented by the dotted line, rather than directly to the Issuing bank, represented by the straight line.

Letter of credit can be issued by airmail (Figure 8.2) or by SWIFT (Figure 8.3). If it is issued by airmail, it ought to be authenticated by signatures and if it is issued by SWIFT, by SAK.

Name of issuing bank: The French Issuing Bank 38 rue FrancoisLer 75008 Paris, France	Irrevocable Documentary Credit	Number 12345
Place and Date of Issue: Paris, 1 January 2023	Expiry Date and Place for Presentation of Documents Expiry Date: May 29, 2023 Place for Presentation: The American Advising Bank, Tampa	
Applicant: The French Importer Co. 89 rue du Commerce Paris, France		
	Beneficiary: The American Exporter Co. Inc. 17 Main Street Tampa, Florida	
Advising Bank:　　　　　Reference No The American Advising Bank 456 Commerce Avenue Tampa, Florida		
	Amount: US $ 100 000. – one hundred thousand U.S. Dollars	

Partial shipments ☒allowed ☐not allowed	Credit available with Nominated Bank: The American Advising Bank, Tampa
Transshipment ☒allowed ☐not allowed	☒by payment at sight ☐by deferred payment at: ☐by acceptance of drafts at: ☐by negotiation
☐ Insurance covered by buyers	
Shipment as defined in UCP 600 From: Tampa, Florida For transportation to: Paris, France Not later than: May 15, 2023	Against the documents detailed herein: ☒and Beneficiary's draft(s) drawn on: The American Advising Bank, Tampa

● Commercial Invoice, one original and 3 copies
● Multimodal Transport Document issued to the order of the French Importer Co.
  marked freight prepaid and notify XYZ Custom House Broker Inc.
● Insurance Certificate covering the Institute Cargo Clauses and the Institute War and Strike Clauses for 110% of the invoice value endorsed to The French Importer Co.
● Certificate of Origin evidencing goods to be of U.S.A. Origin
● Packing List
Covering: Machinery and spare parts as per pro-forma invoice number 657
dated December 17, 2022–CIP INCOTERMS 2010

Documents to be presented within 14 days after date of shipment but within the validity of the Credit

We hereby issue the Irrevocable Documentary Credit in your favor. It is subjected to the Uniform Customs and Practice for Documentary Credits and engages us in accordance with the terms thereof. The number and the date of the Credit and the name of our bank must be quoted on all drafts required. If the Credit is available by negotiation, each presentation must be noted on the reverse side of this advice by the bank where the Credit is available.

The document consists of 2 signed page(s)   The French Issuing Bank

Name of advising bank: The American Advising Bank 456 Commerce Avenue Tampa, Florida Reference Number of Advising Bank: 2417 Place and Date of Notifications: January 14, 2023, Tampa	Notification of Irrevocable Documentary Credit
Issuing Bank: The French Issuing Bank 38 rue FrancoisLer Paris , France	Beneficiary: The American Exporter Co. Inc. 17 Main Street Tampa, Florida
Reference Number of the Issuing Bank: 12345	Amount: US $ 100 000. – one hundred thousand U.S. Dollars

We have been informed by the above-mentioned Issuing Bank that the above-mentioned Documentary Credit has been issued in your favor
Please find enclosed the advice intended for you

Check the Credit terms and conditions carefully. In the event you do not agree with the terms and conditions, or if you feel unable to comply with any of those terms and conditions, kindly arrange an amendment of the Credit though your contracting party(the Applicant).

Other information:

☐This notification and the enclosed advice are sent to you without any engagement on our part.
☒As requested by the Issuing Bank, we hereby add our confirmation to this Credit in accordance with the stipulations under UCP 600.

                                                                    The American Advising Bank

Figure 8.2   **A Sample of Credit Issued by Airmail**

```
                                    OF SGD35.00 / SGD35.00

RECEIVED = issue of a documentary credit  FM700 ================= S-COPY 0002 =

* DESTINATION   FCBKSGSGAXXX                    SW1996110BFS000000009400
* SESS   2097                                  DATE RCVD 08-NOV-96 17:10
* SEQU 154575

* ORIGINATOR    FCBKTWTPAXXX                    FROM SWIFT
* SESS   2307   FIRST COMMERCIAL BANK           DATE SENT 08-NOV-96 17:10
* SEQU 374328   TAIPEI

---------------------------- NORMAL ----------------------------
                                                    FIRST COMMERCIAL BANK
                                                       SINGAPORE BRANCH
* :27 /sequence of total          :1 / 1            No. 6698-2116
* :40A/form of documentary credit :IRREVOCABLE
* :20 /documentary credit number  : 6NF2/00508/1163
* :31C/date of issue              :08/11/96
* :31D/date and place of expiry   :15/12/96 SINGAPORE
* :50 /applicant                  :FUSC  INDUSTRIAL CORP
                                   P.O. BOX 84-2
                                   TAIPEI TAIWAN
* :59 /beneficiary                :O  INTERNATIONAL PTE LTD.
                                   14  WOODLANDS INDUSTRIAL PARK
                                   SINGAPORE
* :32B/currency code amount       :USD 17660.00
  :ID/available with/by-name,addr :AVAILABLE WITH ANY BANK
                                   BY NEGOTIATION
* :42C/drafts at                  :DRAFTS AT SIGHT
                                   FOR FULL INVOICE VALUE
* :42D/drawee - name and addr     :DRAWN ON US
* :43P/partial shipments          :PROHIBITED
* :43T/transshipment              :PROHIBITED
* :44A/on board/disp/taking charge:SINGAPORE
* :44B/for transportation to      :KAOHSIUNG
* :44C/latest date of shipment    :30/11/96
* :45A/descr goods and/or services:FOB SINGAPORE
       BUILDING MATERIALS
       MORTAC SEALER, CEMENTITIOUS STUCCO AND STUCCO SPRAY GUN
* :46A/documents required         :
     . SIGNED COMMERCIAL INVOICE IN 6  COPIES INDICATING THIS
       CREDIT NUMBER.
     . FULL SET LESS ONE OF CLEAN ON BOARD MARINE BILLS OF LADING
       MADE OUT TO THE ORDER OF FIRST COMMERCIAL BANK
       NOTIFY APPLICANT, MARKED ''FREIGHT COLLECT'' AND INDICATING
       THIS CREDIT NUMBER.
     . PACKING LIST IN 3  COPIES SIGNED BY BENEFICIARY.
     . BENEFICIARY'S  CERTIFICATE STATING THAT ONE SET OF SHIPPING
       DOCUMENTS, INCLUDING: 1/3 CLEAN ORIGINAL ON BOARD OCEAN
       BILL OF LADING HAS BEEN SENT TO THE APPLICANT.
     . CERTIFICATE OF ORIGIN OF SINGAPORE.
* :47A/additional conditions      :
     . THE NUMBER AND THE DATE OF THE CREDIT AND THE NAME OF OUR BANK
       MUST BE QUOTED ON ALL DRAFTS.
* :71B/charges                     :ALL BANKING CHARGES INCLUDING

**= = = = = = = = = = = = = = CMT7/00024791/12-NOV-96/09:01:13 = P 1/2 =
```

RECEIVED 16 NOV 1996

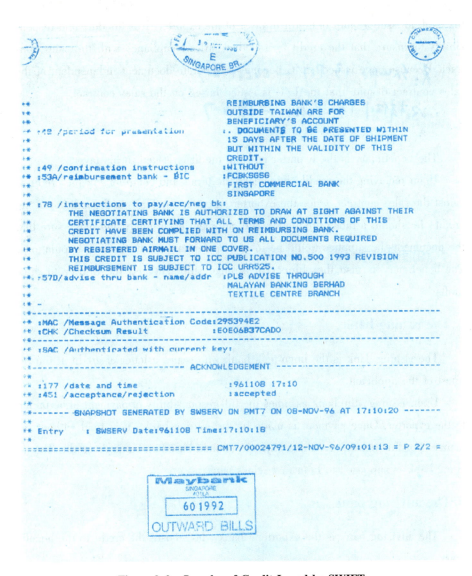

Figure 8. 3   **Samples of Credit Issued by SWIFT**

Section 2   Immediate Parties to Documentary Credit

1. Applicant

The applicant of L/C is the importer.

When the sales contract stipulates that the settlement is under L/C, the importer fills in and signs a L/C application form by which he is making a request to his bank to issue a letter of credit in favor of the exporter. It is his duty and responsibility to ensure that the credit is issued in strict compliance with the sales contract. Because once issued, L/C becomes a separate document independent of the sales contract despite that the L/C is issued based on the sales contract.

2. Beneficiary

The beneficiary is the exporter and the credit is issued in his favor.

Upon receiving the credit, he checks the terms and conditions in the credit against the sales contract. Once the exporter agrees to the terms and condition of the credit, he should arrange production and shipment accordingly and make sure that the documents he supplies would be in strict compliance with the L/C stipulations. The beneficiary is also the shipper to arrange shipment and the drawer to draw drafts.

3. The issuing bank

The issuing bank is the importer's bank who issues a letter of credit at the request of the applicant.

Upon issuing, the bank assumes the full responsibility of payment undertaking to the exporter. Once payment is made by the issuing bank, it is final without recourse. For this reason, L/C is a payment method based on banker's credit. The issuing bank is supposed to be a first-class bank.

4. The advising bank

The advising bank is the exporter's bank who advises the credit to the beneficiary.

The advising bank assumes no payment undertaking upon itself, however, it should take reasonable care to check the apparent authenticity of the credit before it advises.

It is of vital importance to have the L/C advised through a local bank before the exporter relies or acts on the "documentary credit". As in practice, unfortunately, fraudulent documentary credits issued by a foreign fictitious non-existing "bank" are a fact in real life situations. Therefore, it is necessary that the authenticity of both the issuing bank and the credit itself are checked by a local advising bank.

Section 3　Other Parties to Documentary Credit

To facilitate the operation of the documentary credit, other banks may be nominated by the issuing bank in the process. These banks mainly include the confirming bank, the paying bank, the accepting bank, the negotiating bank and the reimbursing bank. These banks are referred to as other parties to the credit.

1. The confirming bank

When an advising bank has been authorized or requested by the issuing bank to add its own confirmation and it is prepared to do so, it will state so on its advice to the beneficiary and then become a confirming bank.

Such a confirmation constitutes its commitment to pay or to accept without recourse to the beneficiary provided all the documents stipulated in the documentary credit are presented in order and that the terms and conditions of the documentary credit are complied with.

When the L/C is confirmed, the beneficiary has two independent bankers' payment undertakings against one credit, one from the issuing bank and the other from the confirming bank. The payment by the confirming bank is effected without recourse against the exporter.

2. The paying bank

In the case of a credit available by payment, the issuing bank nominates itself or another bank, usually the exporter's bank to be the paying bank.

The paying bank effects payment to the exporter without recourse provided all the documents stipulated in the documentary credit are presented in order and that the terms and conditions of the documentary credit are complied with.

3. The accepting bank

In the case of a credit available by acceptance, the issuing bank nominates itself or another bank, usually the exporter's bank to the accepting bank.

The accepting bank accepts and effects payment to the exporter without recourse at maturity provided all the documents stipulated in the documentary credit are presented in order and that the terms and conditions of the documentary credit are complied with.

4. The negotiating bank

In the case of a credit available by negotiation, the issuing bank nominates another bank, usually the exporter's bank to become the negotiating bank. A bank may become a negotiating bank either as a result of being specially nominated in the credit or as a result of simply being any bank when the credit is a freely negotiable credit. It should be noted that the issuing bank itself can never become a negotiating bank.

The negotiating bank negotiates (buys) the drafts or documents presented by the exporter, provided all the documents stipulated in the documentary credit are presented in order and that the terms and conditions of the documentary credit are complied with. After negotiation, the negotiating bank becomes the new holder of the drafts. He has the right to claim payment to the drawee and obtains the right of recourse against the exporter in the event of dishonor by non-payment. Therefore, payment to the exporter is made with recourse.

5. The reimbursing bank

Reimbursing bank is nominated by the issuing bank to honor the claim from the paying bank, the accepting bank or the negotiating bank on behalf of the issuing bank. Reimbursing bank is to facilitate funds transfer and thus is always the branch/head office of the issuing bank in the country of the exporter.

When payment is effected to the exporter, the claiming bank, i.e. the paying bank, accepting bank or negotiating bank, forwards the documents to the issuing bank while claiming reimbursement from the reimbursing bank. The reimbursement made by the reimbursing bank is not a final payment. That is to say, the issuing bank can reclaim the funds from the claiming bank, once the issuing bank finds any discrepancies between the documents and the credit.

When the issuing bank does not nominate a reimbursing bank in a credit, the reimbursement is to be made by the issuing bank itself. The issuing bank will check the compliance of the documents before making reimbursement and once the reimbursement is made by the issuing bank, it is made without recourse.

In conclusion, it should be noted that the different bank names indicate the different roles the banks play, rather than the actual number of banks involved in a L/C operation. The distinction is not a clear-cut and one bank can simultaneously assume different roles in a single process.

Section 4   UCP 600

UCP is the English initials for *the Uniform Customs and Practices for Documentary Credit* published by International Chamber of Commerce (ICC) in Paris, France.

UCP is the governing rules concerning documentary credit. The banks' obligations are conditioned on total compliance with its terms and conditions. Any issued L/C should indicate clearly that the said L/C is "subject to *the Uniform Customs and Practice for Documentary Credits.*"

UCP 600, the ICC publication No.600 effective on 1 July, 2007, is the latest version of UCP up to now, and its most recent version is UCP 500, effective on 1 Jan, 1994.

Section 5   The Procedure of Documentary Credit

Figure 8. 4 shows such a procedure.

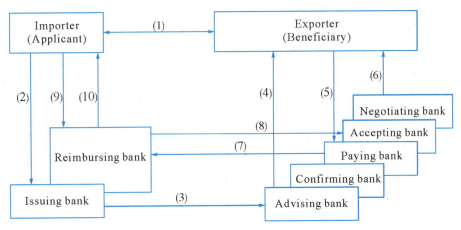

Figure 8. 4   **The Procedure of Documentary Credit**

(1) Sales contract is established between the exporter and the importer, agreeing to settle the payment by L/C.

(2) The importer (the applicant) fills in and signs an application form and requests his banker (the issuing bank) to issue a credit in favor of the exporter (the beneficiary). It is the importer's duty to make the application form consistent

with the sales contract.

（3）The importer's bank examines the creditworthiness of the buyer before it considers issuing the documentary credit. If the applicant is a new customer to the bank, he may need to pay a deposit margin up to 20% of the credit amount. Having been issued, the credit is passed on to the exporter's bank which represents the beneficiary in his country.

（4）The exporter's bank is expected to pass the documentary credit to the beneficiary after verification of the genuineness of the credit as:

① Advising bank — When the exporter's bank assumes no payment undertaking upon itself.

②Confirming bank — When the bank adds its own confirmation on the credit while advising the credit at the authorization or request of the issuing bank.

（5）The exporter checks the terms and conditions of the credit against the sales contract. If there are discrepancies, the beneficiary may have the option to accept the credit as it stands when the discrepancies are considered to be of minor importance or, to ask the applicant to have the credit amended through the issuing bank when the discrepancies are considered to be of major importance, so as to make the credit in line with the contract.

After shipment is made and shipping documents are obtained, the exporter prepares other documents according the L/C requirements. These documents are to be presented, often, to the exporter's own bank acting as:

①The paying bank — If the credit is a payment credit and the payment is to be made to the beneficiary by either sight or deferred payment.

②The accepting bank — If the credit is an accepting credit and the payment to the beneficiary is to be made by acceptance first and payment at maturity of drafts.

③The negotiating bank — If the credit is a negotiable L/C and payment to the beneficiary is to be made by negotiation of drafts and documents.

（6）The paying bank, accepting bank or the negotiating bank checks the documents against the terms and conditions of the credit. If all is proper, the above said bank is to effect payments by payment, acceptance or negotiation.

（7）The paying bank, accepting bank or negotiating bank, as the claiming bank, forwards documents to the issuing bank while claiming reimbursement from the reimbursing bank. If no reimbursing bank is nominated in the credit or the reimbursing bank fails to make the compensation, the reimbursement is made by the issuing bank.

（8）The reimbursing bank or the issuing bank makes reimbursement to the claiming bank.

(9) The importer makes payments to the issuing bank.

(10) The issuing bank releases documents to the importer against his payment.

Section 6　Documentary Credit Application Form

The blank form for documentary credit application is to be pre-printed by the bank and to be filled in and signed by the applicant / the importer. Once signed, it is a contract between the applicant and the issuing bank. When filling in the application, the importer must make it consistent with the sales contract. The major contents of documentary credit application form are shown below:

(1) The full name and address of the beneficiary.

(2) The amount and currency of the documentary credit.

(3) The type of documentary credit, a popular credit is irrevocable and documentary.

(4) The credit availability.

(5) The drawee and the tenor of the draft.

(6) A general description of the goods, indicating its price term, e.g. CIF, CFR, FOB or other INCOTERMS.

(7) Details of the documents required.

(8) The application should indicate the port/place of shipment and the port/place of destination.

(9) Whether the freight is to be prepaid or to be collected. This item should be made consistent with the given INCOTERM.

(10) Whether transshipment is allowed or not.

(11) Whether partial shipment is allowed or not.

(12) The latest date for shipment.

(13) The presentment period.

(14) The date and place of expiry of the documentary credit.

(15) Whether the documentary credit is to be a transferable one.

(16) How the documentary credit is to be advised, i.e. by mail or by tele-transmission. In practice, the bank may also hold the credit for the beneficiary's own collection if the residences are in the same city.

International Chamber of Commerce has drafted a standard form for documentary credit application as shown in Figure 8.5, against which different banks may devise its own form.

(3)Irrevocable Documentary Credit Application

Applicant:	Issuing Banks:
Date of Application:	Expiry Date and Place for Presentation of Documents
☐issue by (air) email ☐with brief advice by teletrans-mission (see UCP 600 Article 11)(16) ☐issue by teletransmission (see UCP 600 Article 11) ☐Transferable Credit-as per UCP 600 Article 48 (15)	Expiry Date: Place for Presentation: (14)
Confirmation of the Credit: (3) ☐not requested ☐requested ☐authorized if requested by Beneficiary	Beneficiary: (1)
	Amount in figures and words (please use ISO Currency Codes): (2)
Partial shipments☐allowed ☐not allowed (11)	
Transshipments ☐allowed ☐not allowed(10) Please refer to UCP 600 transport Articles for exceptions to this condition	Credit available with Nominated Bank:C☐by payment sight ☐by deferred payment at: (4) ☐by acceptance of drafts at:
☐ Insurance will be covered by us	☐by negotiation Against the documents detailed herein:
Shipment as defined in UCP 600 Article 46 From: For transportation to: (8) Not later than: (12)	☐and Beneficiary's draft(s) drawn on:(5)
Goods(Brief description without excessive details – See UCP 600 Article 5): (6)	Terms ☐ FAS ☐ CIF ☐ FOB ☐ Other terms (6) ☐ CFR ☐as per INCOTERMS

Commercial invoice☐ signed original and ☐copies

Transport Document:
☐ Multimodal Transport Document Covering at least two different modes of transport (7)
☐ Marine/Ocean Bill of Lading covering a port-port shipment
☐ Non-negotiable Sea Waybill covering a port-port shipment
☐ Air Waybill original for the consignor
☐ Other transport document
☐ to the order of
☐ endorsed on blank
☐ marked freight ☐ prepaid ☐ payable at destination(9)
☐ notify

Insurance Document:
☐ Policy ☐ Certificate   Declaration under an open cover covering the following risks

Certificates:
☐ Origin
☐ Analysis
☐ Health
☐ Other

Other Documents:
☐ Packing List
☐ Weight List

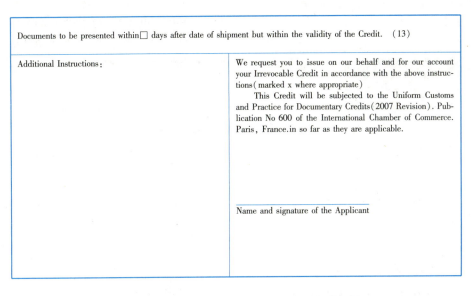

Figure 8. 5   **Irrevocable Documentary Application Form**

Section 7   The Contents of Documentary Credit

Documentary credit is issued based on the application form. When issuing a letter of credit, the issuing bank must make the credit consistent with the application. The International Chamber of Commerce (ICC) has drafted "Guidance Notes and Standard Forms for Banks, Noted Irrevocable Documentary Credit Form (Advice for the Beneficiary and for the Advising Bank)" for the issuance of irrevocable documentary credit by airmail(Figure 8. 6).

GUIDANCE NOTES AND STANDARD FORMS FOR BANKS

Noted Irrevocable Documentary Credit Form（Advice for the Beneficiary）

Name of Issuing Bank:	Irrevocable Documentary Credit（1）	Number（2）
Place and Date of Issue:（3）	Expiry Date and Place for Presentation of Documents Expiry Date: Place for Presentation:（4）	
Applicant: (5)		
	Beneficiary: (6)	
Advising Bank: Reference No (7)		
	Amount:（8）	
Partial shipments□allowed □not allowed（10）	Credit available with Nominated Bank: □by payment sight □by deferred payment at: □by acceptance of drafts at:（9） □by negotiation Against the documents detailed herein: □and Beneficiary's draft(s) drawn on:	
Transshipment□allowed □not allowed（11）		
□ Insurance covered by buyers （12）		
Shipment as defined in UCP600 Article 46 From: For transportation to:（13） Not later than:		

(14)~(20)

Documents to be presented within□ days after the date of shipment but within the validity of the Credit   （21）

We hereby issue the irrevocable Documentary Credit in your favor. It is subject to the Uniform Customs and Practice for Documentary Credits（2007 Revision）, International Chamber of Commerce, Paris, France. Publication No 600）and engages us in accordance with the terms thereof. The number and the date of the Credit and the name of our bank must be quoted on all drafts required. If the Credit is available by negotiation, each presentation must be noted on the reverse side of this advice by the bank where the Credit is available.

The document consists of □ signed page(s) （24）   (25)Name and signature of the issuing bank

GUIDANCE NOTES AND STANDARD FORMS FOR BANKS

Noted Irrevocable Documentary Form (Advice for the Advising Bank)

Applicant:	Irrevocable Documentary Credit	Number
Place and date of Issue: Applicant:	Expiry Date and Place for Presentation of Documents Expiry Date: Place for Presentation:	
Advising Banks:　Reference No:	Beneficiary:	
Partial shipments☐allowed　☐not allowed		
Transshipment☐allowed　☐not allowed	Amount:	
☐Insurance covered by buyers		
Shipment as defined in UCP600 Article 46 From: For transportation to: Not later than:	Credit available with Nominated Bank: ☐by payment sight ☐by deferred payment at: ☐by acceptance of drafts at: ☐by negotiation Against the documents detailed herein: ☐and Beneficiary's draft(s) drawn on:	

Documents to be presented within☐ days after date of shipment but within the validity of the Credit

We have issued the irrevocable Documentary Credit as detailed above. It is subject to the Uniform Customs and Practice for Documentary Credits (2007 Revision). International Chamber of Commerce, Paris, France. Publication No 600. We request you to advise the Beneficiary.
☐without adding your confirmation　☐adding your confirmation　☐adding your confirmation if requested by the Beneficiary (22)
Bank–to–Bank instructions (23)

The document consists of ☐ signed page(s)　　　　Name and signature of the issuing bank

Figure 8. 6　**Documentary Credit Issued by Airmail**

The major items of documentary credit are as follows:

(1) Type of the credit. The guidance notes and standard forms for banks have been drafted for the issuance of an irrevocable documentary credit. Other types of credit are stated or implied in applicable items throughout the credit.

(2) Credit number. The credit number is the running number for the credit opened by the issuing bank. This number is to be indicated in and tie up all the relevant documents.

(3) Place and date of issue. The place of issue is where the issuing bank is located. The date of issue is the date when the L/C is issued by the issuing bank.

(4) Date and place of expiry. All credits must stipulate a definite date not a period as an expiry date for presentation of documents for payment, acceptance or negotiation. The credit is expired after the expiry date. The period from the issuing date to the expiry date is called the validity period of the credit.

The place where the documents are to be presented on or before such expiry date is the place of expiry.

(5) Name and address of the applicant.

(6) Name and address of the beneficiary.

(7) Advising bank. Here is to indicate the name and address of the bank which is to advise the credit.

(8) Amount of the credit and its currency. The amount should be expressed both in figures and in words. The currency should be indicated in the ISO Currency Code, e.g. USD, GBP etc.

(9) Nominated bank and credit availability. A credit should nominate both the name of the bank and the way to effect payment.

Normally, a credit nominates two kinds of bank to effect payment:

①Credit available with the importer's bank (issuing bank). This means that the issuing bank nominates itself to be the paying or accepting bank to effect payment to the beneficiary upon receipt of documents or drafts "drawn on us". The credit is expired at the place of the issuing bank and documents are presented to the issuing bank within the validity of the credit. No other bank is to effect payment in the process but only to act as an intermediary bank to remit or forward the documents to the issuing bank on behalf of the beneficiary.

This type of credit is less favorable to the beneficiary because he will not receive the payment until the issuing bank pays and he will be responsible for the documents to reach the issuing bank within the validity of the credit. Any delay or loss in the transit of documents may hinder the exporter from his obtaining of the payments.

②Credit available with the exporter's bank. This means that the issuing bank nominates the exporter's bank to be the paying bank, accepting bank or the negotiating bank in the credit and to effect payment to the beneficiary upon receipt of documents or drafts. The credit is to be expired at the place exporter's bank and documents are to be presented to the exporter's bank within the validity of the credit.

This type of credit is more favorable to the exporter as there is no need for him to forward the documents to a foreign issuing bank.

Under L/C, the nominated bank is to effect payment to the beneficiary by one of the following four ways:

Firstly, Credit available by sight payment. Under this condition, the paying bank effects payment to the beneficiary against documents or sight drafts on the paying bank. Sometimes, no draft is required to present under sight payment to avoid the stamp duty and the paying bank simply effects sight payment to the beneficiary on documents.

Secondly, credit available by deferred payment. Under this condition, the paying bank effects payment to the beneficiary against documents on a specific future date but no draft is required to present.

Thirdly credit available by acceptance. Under this condition, the accepting bank effects payment to the beneficiary by acceptance and payment at maturity against documents and time drafts on the accepting bank.

Fourthly, credit available by negotiation. Under this condition, the negotiating bank effects payment to the beneficiary by negotiation of documents and drafts on the issuing bank.

(10) Partial shipment. Although partial shipment is allowed by the UCP, it is necessary to indicate clearly in a given credit whether partial shipment is allowed.

(11) Transshipment. Although transshipment is allowed by the UCP, it is necessary to indicate clearly in a given credit whether transshipment is allowed.

(12) Insurance covered by the buyer. The credit should indicate whether it requires insurance to be covered by the buyer. This should be made consistent with the chosen INCORTERM and the presentation requirement of insurance document.

(13) Port of shipment and port of discharge. The credit should indicate the port of shipment, the port of discharge and the latest date for shipment which should be within the validity of the credit.

(14) ~ (20) Description of goods and stipulated documents. Description of

goods in the credit should be made in a general term as a detailed description is to be provided in the commercial invoice. Documents here refer to the commercial documents and are normally listed in the following order：

①Commercial invoice.

②Transport documents.

③Insurance documents.

④Certificate of origin.

⑤Certificate of inspection.

⑥Packing list / Weight list.

The number of copies，either in original form or in duplicated form，the name of the maker，the order and other applicable stipulations should be indicated clearly.

（21）Presentation period. Every credit calls for documents to be presented at a stipulated time period after the date of shipment but within the validity of the credit.

In practice，this stipulated time period can be 14 to 21 days after the date of shipment. If the latest date for presentation period does not coincide with the expiry date of the credit，the latest date for presentation should fall on the earlier date.

（22）Instructions to the advising bank. The issuing bank instructs the advising bank of the credit in one of the following three ways：

①Without adding your confirmation.

②Adding your confirmation.

③Adding your confirmation if requested by the beneficiary.

（23）Bank to bank instructions. The issuing bank is to indicate to the nominated bank as the paying，accepting or negotiating bank the method of reimbursement as to where，how and when they will obtain funds.

（24）Number of pages. The issuing bank should always indicate in how many pages the credit is issued.

（25）The signature of the issuing bank. The signature of the issuing bank is required to validate both the advice of the credit for the beneficiary and the advising bank.

Section 8   Credit Draft

Drafts used in letter of credit must contain a drawn clause to indicate that the draft is established under a documentary credit. The drawn clause consists of the name of the issuing bank, the credit issuing date and the credit number.

In addition, drafts drawn under L/C should meet the following requirements as well:

(1) Drawer — the exporter.

(2) Drawee — a bank which can be.

① The issuing bank.

② The confirming bank.

③ The paying bank.

④ The accepting bank.

(3) Payee — the payee can be made as one of the following:

① The exporter. The exporter is required by the credit upon presentation to make endorsement, either in blank or in full, to the negotiating bank when the credit is a negotiable one.

② The negotiating bank. No endorsement is required.

(4) Tenor — either sight or time

Figure 8. 7 is a sample draft drawn under letter of credit.

E54621
Drawn under   First Union Bank, Dallas, Texas
Irrevocable L/C No.704481   Dated 20th Dec 2023
payable with interest@   %

No.T.0456   Exchange for USD 129 649.95   Shanghai 1st Feb 2024

At   ···   sight of this FIRST of Exchange (SECOND of Exchange)
being unpaid) Pay to the order of Bank of China, Shanghai
the sum of US DOLLARS ONE HUNDRED TWENTY NINE THOUSAND
SIX HUNDRED AND FORTY NINE AND 95/100 ONLY

To: First Union Trust Bank
       Dallas, Texas   China National Textiles Import & Export
                                              Corp., Shanghai Branch
                                                  signature

Figure 8. 7   **Credit Draft**

It should be noted that the particulars of the drafts drawn in different payment methods are varied. A comparison of them is made in Table 1. 1.

Table 1. 1　**Drafts in Payment Methods**

Items	Remittance（D/D）	Collection	Letter of Credit
Drawer	Remitting bank	Exporter	Exporter
Drawee	Paying bank	Importer	Issuing bank, or confirming bank, or paying bank, or accepting bank
Payee	Exporter	Exporter, or remitting bank, or collecting bank	Exporter, or negotiating bank
Tenor	Sight	Sight or time	Sight or time

Section 9　Normal Credit Types

Normal types of credit refer to those ones to meet the commercial purpose of the traders. Credit can be classified according to the following criteria：

1. According to the attachment of shipping documents

（1）Clean credit. A clean credit is one under which payment is to be effected only against a draft without any shipping documents attached thereto or sometimes, against a draft with a commercial invoice alone attached thereto.

（2）Documentary credit. A documentary credit is one which payment is to be made against shipping documents either with a draft attached or not. It is an important form of credit and against which other types of documentary credit will be made possible.

2. According to revocability

（1）Irrevocable credit. An irrevocable credit constitutes a definite undertaking of the issuing bank provided that the stipulated documents are presented to the nominated bank on or before the expiry date and that terms and conditions of the documentary credit are complied with, to pay or accept drafts or document（s） presented under the documentary credit.

An irrevocable documentary credit gives the beneficiary greater assurance of payment, though he remains dependent on an undertaking of a foreign issuing bank. The irrevocable documentary credit cannot be cancelled or modified without the express consent from the issuing bank, the confirming bank (if any) and the beneficiary.

An irrevocable credit normally should first be a documentary credit. The combination of a documentary and irrevocable credit makes the most popular form of credit and it is a requisite based on which other types of documentary credit are made possible.

Every credit should clearly indicate its revocability. In the absence of such indication, the credit will be deemed to be irrevocable. UCP 600, effective on 1st July, 2007, stipulates that banks can only issue irrevocable credits.

(2) Revocable credit. A revocable credit is one which can be modified or cancelled at any moment by the issuing bank without the beneficiary's consent or even without prior notice to the beneficiary.

The revocable documentary credit is less favorable to the exporter than the irrevocable documentary one. It involves risks to the beneficiary since the credit may be modified or cancelled while the goods are sent to shipment, or before the documents are presented, or, although documents may have been presented, before payment has been made. The exporter thus faces the problem of claiming payment directly from the importer without the issuing bank's payment undertaking.

Revocable credit is not a popular one. It is normally accepted as usage between affiliated parties or subsidiary companies.

3. According to the adding of confirmation

(1) Confirmed credit. A confirmation of an irrevocable documentary credit by a bank (the confirming bank) upon the authorization or request of the issuing bank constitutes a definite undertaking of the confirming bank, in addition to that of the issuing bank provided that the stipulated documents are presented to the confirming bank or any other nominated bank on or before the expiry date and the terms and conditions of the documentary credit are complied with, to pay, to accept draft(s) or to negotiate.

Confirmation usually adds to an irrevocable and documentary credit. A confirmed irrevocable documentary credit gives the beneficiary a double assurance of payment, since it represents both the payment undertaking of the issuing bank and that of the confirming bank. The sample credit shown in Figure 8. 2 is a confirmed one issued by airmail.

Normally, if an issuing bank is a smaller bank or if it is in a country of both politically and economically unstable, the beneficiary may desire that the credit be confirmed by a bank located in his own country so that to have an additional payment undertaking from a local bank.

(2) Unconfirmed credit. The issuing bank's credit is advised through an advising bank. When advising, the advising bank only acts as agent of the issuing bank and does not give its own payment undertaking to the beneficiary under the documentary credit except for taking reasonable care to check the apparent authenticity of the documentary credit which it advises, such a credit is an unconfirmed credit (Figure 8.8).

Normally, a beneficiary will consider the classification of the credit and the financial standing of the issuing bank before asking for confirmation. If the issuing bank is considered to be a first-class bank, there may not be any need to have its irrevocable documentary credit confirmed by another bank.

Name of issuing bank: The French Issuing Bank 38 rue FrancoisLer 75008 Paris, France	Irrevocable Documentary Credit	Number 12345
Place and Date of Issue: Paris, 1 January 2023	Expiry Date and Place for Presentation of Documents Expiry Date: May 29, 2023 Place for Presentation: The American Advising Bank, Tampa	
Applicant: The French Importer Co. 89 rue du Commerce Paris, France	Beneficiary: The American Exporter Co. Inc. 17 Main Street Tampa, Florida	
Advising Bank: Reference No The American Advising Bank 456 Commerce Avenue Tampa, Florida	Amount: US $ 100 000. - one hundred thousand U.S. Dollars	
Partial shipments ☒allowed ☐not allowed	Credit available with Nominated Bank: The American Advising Bank, Tampa ☒by payment at sight ☐by deferred payment at: ☐by acceptance of drafts at: ☐by negotiation	
Transshipment ☒allowed ☐not allowed		
☐ Insurance covered by buyers		
Shipment as defined in UCP 600 From: Tampa, Florida For transportation to: Paris, France Not later than: May 15, 2023	Against the documents detailed herein: ☒and Beneficiary's draft(s) drawn on: The American Advising Bank, Tampa	

● Commercial Invoice, one original and 3 copies
● Multimodal Transport Document issued to the order of the French Importer Co.
   marked freight prepaid and notify XYZ Custom House Broker Inc.
● Insurance Certificate covering the Institute Cargo Clauses and the Institute War
   and Strike Clauses for 110% of the invoice value endorsed to The French Importer Co.
● Certificate of Origin evidencing goods to be of U.S.A. Origin
● Packing List
Covering: Machinery and spare parts as per pro-forma invoice number 657
dated December 17, 2022-CIP   INCOTERMS   2010

Documents to be presented within [14] days after date of shipment but within the validity of the Credit

We hereby issue the Irrevocable Documentary Credit in your favor. It is subjected to the Uniform Customs and Practice for Documentary Credits and engages us in accordance with the terms thereof. The number and the date of the Credit and the name of our bank must be quoted on all drafts required. If the Credit is available by negotiation, each presentation must be noted on the reverse side of this advice by the bank where the Credit is available.

The document consists of [2] signed page(s)   The French Issuing Bank

Name of advising bank:
   The American Advising Bank
   456 Commerce Avenue
   Tampa, Florida
 	
Reference Number of Advising Bank: 2417
Place and Date of Notifications: January 14, 2023 Tampa
	Notification of Irrevocable
	Documentary Credit

Issuing Bank:
   The French Issuing Bank
   38 rue FrancoisLer
   Paris , France
	Beneficiary:
	   The American Exporter Co. Inc.
	   17 Main Street Tampa, Florida

Reference Number of the Issuing Bank: 12345	Amount: US $ 100 000. − one hundred thousand U.S. Dollars

We have been informed by the above-mentioned Issuing Bank that the above-mentioned Documentary Credit has been is-sued in your favor.
Please find enclosed the advice intended for you

Check the Credit terms and conditions carefully. In the event you do not agree with the terms and conditions, or if you feel unable to comply with any of those terms and conditions, kindly arrange an amendment of the Credit though your contrac-ting party(the Applicant).

Other information:

☒ This notification and the enclosed advice are sent to you without any engagement on our part.
☐ As requested by the Issuing Bank, we hereby add our confirmation to this Credit in accordance with the stipulations un-der UCP 600.

                                                      The American Advising Bank

Figure 8. 8   **Unconfirmed Credit by Airmail**

4. According to the way of credit availability

（1）Sight payment credit. Sight payment credit is one available by sight payment, under which a bank nominated therein is authorized to pay at sight on commercial documents with or without sight drafts presented in conformity with the terms of the credit. Figure 8.2 is a sample of sight payment credit.

Under sight payment credit, the exporter gets sight payment against commercial documents and sight drafts (if required) on the paying bank. The payment to the beneficiary made by the paying bank is final and without recourse against the beneficiary.

Sight payment credit also includes straight payment credit where the obligation of the issuing bank is extended only to the beneficiary in honoring drafts or documents and the credit usually expires at the counter of the issuing bank. This kind of credit is less favorable to the exporter since he will not obtain payment from his own bank, at the same time, he should be responsible for the documents to be presented to the counter of the issuing bank within the validity of the credit. Figure 8.9 is a sample of straight payment credit (advice for the beneficiary).

Name of issuing bank: The French Issuing Bank 38 rue FrancoisLer 75008 Paris, France	Irrevocable Documentary Credit	Number 12345
Place and Date of Issue: Paris, 1 January 2023	Expiry Date and Place for Presentation of Documents Expiry Date: May 29, 2023 Place for Presentation: The French Issuing Bank, Paris, France	
Applicant: The French Importer Co. 89 rue du Commerce Paris, France		
	Beneficiary: The American Exporter Co. Inc. 17 Main Street Tampa, Florida	
Advising Bank:　　　Reference No The American Advising Bank 456 Commerce Avenue Tampa, Florida		
	Amount: US $ 100 000. – one hundred thousand U.S. Dollars	
Partial shipments ☒allowed ☐not allowed	Credit available with Nominated Bank: The French Issuing Bank, Paris	
Transshipment ☒allowed ☐not allowed	☒by payment at sight ☐by deferred payment at: ☐by acceptance of drafts at: ☐by negotiation	
☐ Insurance covered by buyers		
Shipment as defined in UCP 600 From: Tampa, Florida For transportation to: Paris, France Not later than: May 15, 2023	Against the documents detailed herein: ☒and Beneficiary's draft(s) drawn on: The French Issuing Bank, Paris	

●Commercial Invoice, one original and 3 copies
●Multimodal Transport Document issued to the order of the French Importer Co.
　marked freight prepaid and notify XYZ Custom House Broker Inc.
●Insurance Certificate covering the Institute Cargo Clauses and the Institute War
　and Strike Clauses for 110% of the invoice value endorsed to The French Importer Co.
●Certificate of Origin evidencing goods to be of U.S.A. Origin
●Packing List
Covering:Machinery and spare parts as per pro-forma invoice number 657
dated December 17,2022-CIP　INCOTERMS　2010

Documents to be presented within ⎍14⎍ days after date of shipment but within the validity of the Credit

We hereby issue the Irrevocable Documentary Credit in your favor. It is subjected to the Uniform Customs and Practice for Documentary Credits and engages us in accordance with the terms thereof. The number and the date of the Credit and the name of our bank must be quoted on all drafts required. If the Credit is available by negotiation, each presentation must be noted on the reverse side of this advice by the bank where the Credit is available.

The document consists of ⎍2⎍ signed page(s)　　　　　　　　　The French Issuing Bank

Figure 8.9　**Straight Payment Credit** (**Advice for the Beneficiary**)

(2) Deferred payment credit. Deferred payment credit is one available by payment which is deferred to a specified future date, under which a bank nominated therein is authorized to pay on commercial documents complied with the terms and conditions of the credit. No draft is required for this credit.

Under deferred payment credit, the exporter gets time payment against commercial documents. The payment made to the beneficiary by the paying bank is final and without recourse against the beneficiary.

(3) Acceptance credit. Acceptance credit constitutes the nominated bank's undertaking to accept the time drafts upon presentation and to pay at maturity, provided that the commercial documents and time drafts are in compliance with the terms and conditions of the credit.

Under acceptance credit, the exporter gets time payment against commercial documents and time drafts on the accepting bank. The payment made to the beneficiary by the accepting bank is final and without recourse against the beneficiary.

(4) Negotiation credit. Negotiation credit is one under which the negotiating bank gives value for sight or time drafts and commercial documents presented to him. When negotiating, the bank will advance money to the beneficiary on presentation of the required documents and will charge interest on the advance from the date of the advance until such time as it receives reimbursement from the issuing bank.

Under a negotiation credit, the exporter gets sight payment against commercial documents and sight or time drafts on the issuing bank. The payment made by the negotiating bank to the beneficiary is not final, with right of recourse against the beneficiary if reimbursement to the negotiating bank is not ultimately forthcoming from the issuing bank. Figure 8. 10 is a sample of negotiation credit（advice for the beneficiary）.

Name of issuing bank： The French Issuing Bank 38 rue Francois 75008 Paris, France	Irrevocable Documentary Credit	Number 12345
Place and Date of Issue：Paris, 1 January 2023 Applicant： The French Importer Co. 89 rue du Commerce Paris, France	Expiry Date and Place for Presentation of Documents Expiry Date：May 29, 2023 Place for Presentation：The American Advising Bank, Tampa	

Advising Bank：   Reference No
The American Advising Bank
456 Commerce Avenue
Tampa, Florida
	Beneficiary：
	    The American Exporter Co. Inc.
	    17 Main Street
	    Tampa, Florida	

	Amount： US $ 100 000. – one hundred thousand U.S. Dollars	
Partial shipments ☒allowed ☐not allowed	Credit available with Nominated Bank： The American Advising Bank, Tampa ☐by payment at sight ☐by deferred payment at： ☐by acceptance of drafts at： ☒by negotiation	
Transshipment ☒allowed ☐not allowed		
☐ Insurance covered by buyers		
Shipment as defined in UCP 600 From：Tampa, Florida For transportation to：Paris, France Not later than：May 15, 2023	Against the documents detailed herein： ☒and Beneficiary's draft(s) drawn on： The French Issuing Bank, Paris, France	

●Commercial Invoice, one original and 3 copies
●Multimodal Transport Document issued to the order of the French Importer Co.
  marked freight prepaid and notify XYZ Custom House Broker Inc.
●Insurance Certificate covering the Institute Cargo Clauses and the Institute War
  and Strike Clauses for 110% of the invoice value endorsed to The French Importer Co.
●Certificate of Origin evidencing goods to be of U.S.A. Origin
●Packing List
Covering：Machinery and spare parts as per pro-forma invoice number 657
dated December 17, 2022–CIP INCOTERMS 2010

Documents to be presented within ⟦14⟧ days after date of shipment but within the validity of the Credit

We hereby issue the Irrevocable Documentary Credit in your favor. It is subjected to the Uniform Customs and Practice for Documentary Credits and engages us in accordance with the terms thereof. The number and the date of the Credit and the name of our bank must be quoted on all drafts required. If the Credit is available by negotiation, each presentation must be noted on the reverse side of this advice by the bank where the Credit is available.

The document consists of ⟦2⟧ signed page(s)   The French Issuing Bank

Figure 8. 10   **Negotiation Credit**（**Advice for the Beneficiary**）

5. According to the time of the credit availability

（1）Sight/Demand credit. Sight credit means that the credit amount is available to the beneficiary at sight. Sight credit includes sight payment credit and negotiation credit.

(2) Time/Usance credit. Time credit means that the credit amount is available to the beneficiary at a specific future time. Time credit includes deferred payment credit and acceptance credit.

In conclusion, the classification of credits is not a clear cut in the sense that one normal commercial credit is a combination of five types. Therefore, careful reading of the contents in a credit is essential to correctly interpret its types.

Section 10   Special Credit Types

In practice, the issuing bank can also add some special terms and conditions in the credit to serve the different purposes of the traders provided that they are not against the stipulations of the UCP 600. The addition of these special terms and conditions makes credits become special ones.

1. Buyer's usance credit

Buyer's usance credit is a special kind of acceptance credit which allows the exporter to get sight payment through discounting the time drafts, with the discounting interest and acceptance charges to be borne by the importer.

Buyer's usance credit is, in effect, an acceptance credit payable at sight to the exporter. It is issued to finance the importer and is used when the transaction is conducted on the sight basis. The importer is financed because it allows him to enter a sight contract with the exporter but to have a time credit (acceptance credit) issued. Similar wordings are to be found in the credit to indicate the nature of this type:

"Credit available with ourselves by acceptance against presentation of the documents and drafts at 180 days sight drawn on ourselves. Accepted draft will be paid by us on sight basis, discounting fee and interest charges being for the applicant's account."

2. Revolving credit

Revolving documentary credit is one by which, under the terms and conditions thereof, the amount is renewed or reinstated without specific amendments to the documentary credit being issued.

A revolving documentary credit is issued to facilitate the importer's continuously repeated purchases from the same supplier under which the issuing charges and the deposit margins for the repeated application of credits on the part of the applicant can be saved.

Revolving credit may revolve in relation to time or value. In the case of a documentary credit that revolves in relation to time, the credit is available for a fixed amount over a given period with regular shipments in between, irrespective of whether any sum was drawn during the previous interval. For example:

"This is a monthly revolving credit which is available up to the amount of USD 10 000 per month, and the full credit amount will be automatically renewed on the 1st day of each succeeding calendar month."

When there is no regular interval among shipments, the credit may revolve in relation to value with the amount being reinstated upon utilization after each shipment within a given overall period of validity. For example:

"This credit is revolving for six shipments only. The amount of each shipment is not exceeding USD 10 000. "

The amount of revolving credit can be cumulative or not-cumulative. Being cumulative means the amount of the credit available for a fixed calendar period or a shipment that is unused during that period or shipment may be used in the subsequent period or shipment. Non-cumulative means that the unused amount for a fixed calendar period or a shipment ceases to be available and is not carried over to the subsequent period or shipment.

Revolving credit involves an incalculable liability to the issuing bank because it is liable for the aggregate amount that might be drawn under the credit. Therefore, it is important for the issuing bank to specify the aggregate amount in the credit to maintain a certain degree of control. For example:

"This is a monthly revolving credit which is available up to the amount of USD 10 000 per month, and the full credit amount will be automatically renewed on the 1st day of each succeeding calendar month. Our maximum liability under this revolving credit dose not exceeding USD 60 000 being the aggregate value of six months. The unused balance of each month is non-cumulative to the succeeding month."

3. Transferable credit

Transferable documentary credit is normally issued when the transaction involves a middleman. The middleman is known as the first beneficiary and the actual supplier of the goods is known as the second beneficiary of the transferable credit.

Transferable documentary credit is one under which the beneficiary (the first beneficiary) may request the bank authorized to pay, incur a deferred payment undertaking, accept or negotiate, or in the event of a freely negotiable credit, the bank specially authorized in the credit as a transferring bank to make documentary credit available in whole or in part to one or more other beneficiaries (the second beneficiary). Figure 8. 12 shows the transferring of such a credit.

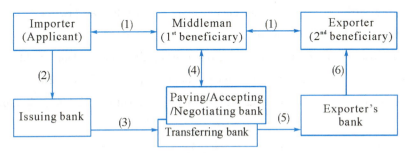

Figure 8. 11   **The Transferring of Transferable Credit**

(1) 1st sales contract is established between the importer and the middle man and 2nd sales contract between the middle man and the exporter with the amount less than the 1st contract.

(2) Importer applies for the issuance of the irrevocable documentary transferable credit based on the 1st contract in favor of the middleman (the 1st beneficiary).

(3) The issuing bank issues such a credit and forwards it to the middle man's bank which acts as the paying, or accepting or the negotiating bank of the credit.

(4) The middleman's bank advises the credit to the middleman who will give instruction to his bank to transfer the credit in favor of the exporter, with the amount less middleman's interest and with other applicable changes to the terms and conditions of the credit.

(5) The middleman's bank, acting as the transferring bank, forwards the transferred credit to the exporter's bank at the new amount and with other applicable changes to the terms and conditions of the credit.

(6) The exporter's bank advises the transferred credit to the exporter (the 2nd beneficiary).

The procedure of transferable credit is based on that of a normal commercial one, except for the part of transferring shown above. When the whole procedure is completed, the middleman's profit is realized.

4. Back-to-back credit

A back-to-back credit may be used when the credit issued in favor of the middle man is not transferable or, although transferable, cannot meet the middleman's requirements.

A back-to-back credit is formally defined as: "The benefit of an irrevocable documentary credit (the original credit) may be made available to a third party (the exporter) where the 1st beneficiary (the middle man) uses the documentary credit as security to obtain another documentary credit (the new credit) in favor of the actual supplier (the exporter)."

The back-to-back credit involves two legally independent credits: one opened in favor of the middle man and the other in favor of the exporter. The two credits are put back-to-back against each other. Figure 8.13 shows issuing of back-to-back credit.

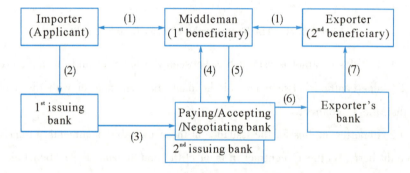

Figure 8.12   **The Issuing of Back-to-back Credit**

(1) 1st sales contract is established between the importer and the middle man and 2nd sales contract between the middle man and the exporter with the amount less than the 1st contract.

(2) Importer applies for the issuance of the irrevocable documentary credit based on the 1st contract in favor of the middleman (the 1st beneficiary).

(3) The issuing bank issues such a credit and forwards it to the middle man's bank, which acting as the paying, or accepting or the negotiating bank.

(4) The middleman's bank advises the credit to the middleman.

(5) Using it as a security, the middleman applies to his bank to issue a new credit in favor of the exporter, with the amount less the middleman's interest and with other applicable changes to the terms and conditions of the original credit.

(6) The middleman's bank, acting as the second issuing bank, forwards the new credit to the exporter's bank at the new amount and with other applicable

changes to the terms and conditions of the original credit.

(7) The exporter's bank advises the new credit to the exporter (the 2nd beneficiary).

Back-to-back credit resembles transferrable credit in many ways. However, it should be noted that there is only one credit in transferable credit but two credits in back-to-back credit. Another point is that the middle man's bank acts as the transferring bank in transferrable credit but as the 2nd issuing bank in back-to-back credit. While the transferring bank does not assume payment undertaking to the exporter, the 2nd issuing bank certainly does.

5. Counter/Reciprocal credit

The operation of counter/reciprocal credit involves two credits: the primary credit and the counter/reciprocal credit and it is in all respects similar to that of an ordinary commercial credit except that the applicant of the primary credit takes the position of the beneficiary of the counter/reciprocal credit, while the beneficiary of the primary credit becomes the applicant of the counter credit.

Counter/reciprocal credit is used mainly for the barter system with two underlying transactions, one being an import and the other an export with the amounts under the two credits being roughly equal with each other. Figure 8.13 shows the relationship of the two credits.

Figure 8.13   **The Relationship between Primary Credit and Counter Credit**

6. Anticipatory / Red clause credit

A red clause credit is a credit with a special condition/clause incorporated into it that authorizes the exporter's bank to make advances to the beneficiary before presentation of the documents. It is so called because this clause was originally written in red ink to draw attention to the unique nature of this credit.

Red clause credit is often used when the importer wants to extend finance to his reliable supplier (the exporter) by providing the funds prior to shipment. The special clause is incorporated in the credit at the specific request of the applicant, and the wording is upon his requirements.

The amount of the advance authorized specified in the clause may be for the partial or full amount of the credit. After advance payment, the exporter's bank will get repayment for the advances plus interest, from the proceeds to be paid to the beneficiary when the goods are shipped and documents are presented in compliance with the terms of the credit.

In the event that the beneficiary fails to ship the goods, the exporter's bank will have a right of recourse against the issuing bank, which will in turn have the similar right of recourse against the applicant/importer to demand repayment plus interest and other charges incurred. Therefore, this kind of advance arrangement is ultimately made at the risk of the applicant.

Section 11   Amendment of Credit

Although L/C is issued based on the application form which in turn on the sales contract, the three documents are legally independent from one another once issued. Any discrepancies between the credit and sales contract may lead to the amendment of the credit.

For the exporter/beneficiary, if he finds the terms and conditions in the credit are not in line with those mentioned in the sales contract, he may either accept the credit as it is or request the applicant to amend the credit through the issuing bank. On the other hand, if the amendment is initiated by the applicant, it must be issued by the issuing bank, and, in the case of an irrevocable credit, the amendment should also obtain the consent from the beneficiary and the confirming bank, if any. The issuing bank will charge a fee for such amendments to the account of the applicant.

When the issuing bank issues an amendment, the items amended should be attached to the original copy to replace the corresponding items in the original L/C and have a legal binding on all the parties concerned, such as the applicant, the beneficiary and the confirming bank, if any.

For the issuing bank, the amendment takes effect on the issuing date of the amendment; for the beneficiary, the effective date should be deemed either on the date of his formal certificate of acceptance or when he presents the documents in agreement with the amendment. To make sure whether the amendment is accepted or not by the beneficiary, the issuing bank may incorporate in the credit an additional document requirement to confirm the exporter's acceptance or rejection.

Section 12　Characteristics, Advantages and Disadvantages of Credit

1. Characteristics of L/C

(1) Letter of credit is a payment method based on the banker's credit in the sense that the issuing bank gives its payment undertaking to the exporter at the request of the importer. Therefore, compared with remittance and collection, L/C is a payment method where the bank's involvement is the greatest.

(2) Banks deal with documents in L/C operation. It should be noted that under L/C, banks deal with documents only rather than the physical goods, services or other performances to which the documents may relate.

(3) Banks effect payment only against the doctrine of strict compliance, that is, the documents presented must comply with the terms of the credit on the one hand and the documents themselves ought to be consistent with each other.

(4) Even dealing with documents, banks will enjoy the following escaping clauses:

①Banks assumes no liability or responsibility for the form, sufficiency, accuracy, genuineness, falsification or legal effect of any documents presented. Banks are only to examine that documents are on the face to be in compliance with the L/C.

②Banks assumes no responsibility for the acts of the third party taking part in one way or another in the credit operation or the acts of their correspondent banks to which they have instructed to carry out the documentary credit operation.

③Banks are not responsible for delays in the transmission of information over which they have no control.

On account of these characteristics, letter of credit carries with itself advantages as well as disadvantages.

2. Advantages of L/C

(1) Advantages to the exporter.

①The most outstanding benefit to the exporter is that he is free from the worry of non-payment on the part of the importer. He can rely on the bank's undertaking for payment provided the shipping documents are in line with the terms of the credit. In addition, L/C requires the importer to make application first. The exporter makes shipment after he has received the credit issued in his favor. In this sense, L/C is more favorable to the exporter rather than to the importer.

②Through various methods of financing available under the credit, he can obtain payment from his own bank immediately after the shipment provided that the documents presented are in line with the terms and condition of the credit, or even before the shipment is made. Thus his turnover is speeded up.

③The exporter can be freed from the worry of funds transfer to him or the prohibition of his goods from being imported, for the importer must have obtained the foreign exchange permit and import license before the credit is issued.

(2) Advantages to the importer.

①Once payment is made, the importer is protected from the risk of non-delivery from the exporter. Before he is required to make payment, title documents have been placed with the issuing bank and documents will be released to him against his payment.

②When applying for L/C, the applicant may be requested to place with the issuing bank a deposit margin of certain percentage of the credit amount and sometimes even no deposit margin. This brings benefits to the importer as the occupancy of his own flowing funds is reduced and he is thus financed.

③The importer can exercise certain control over the quality, quantity and the time of delivery of the goods, etc. through the terms and conditions under the credit. For example, the credit stipulates the latest shipment date to control the time of delivery of goods. The credit may call for the inspection certificates to control the quality and the quantity of the covered goods.

(3) Advantages to the issuing bank.

①The issuing bank can earn a commission by opening the credit. As letter of credit itself is a means of finance, an additional advantage for the bank is that from the time the credit is opened till the time the draft(s)/document(s) are presented for reimbursement, only its name and creditworthiness are lent out, no actual funds are granted.

②Before the importer makes payment, the title documents are in the hands of the issuing bank. With the ownership over the goods under the title documents, the bank can sell the goods to recover the loss in the event that the importer fails to fulfill his payment obligations.

(4) Advantages to other banks.

①The negotiation of the negotiating bank is done with the definite payment undertaking of the issuing bank and thus is normally risk－free. The negotiating bank is willing to negotiate the draft(s)/document(s) under the credit to gain profits though examining documents charges and discounting charges.

②Other banks will charge a fee and make a profit for every service they have provided in the credit operation.

3. Disadvantages of L/C

Because the operation of credit lays great emphasis on the documents to be on the face in consistence with the credit, the integrity of the contracting parties, namely the importer, the exporter as well as the credit standing of the issuing bank is of vital importance. Any deficiency in this respect may incur risks to the other parties concerned. Disadvantages imply risks to the relevant parties.

(1) Risks to the exporter. Although the exporter obtains a bank's payment undertaking by which he is protected from the risk of non－payment on the part of the importer, he still relies on the credit standing of the issuing bank. The exporter may suffer a loss if the L/C is a false L/C opened by a fictitious bank or a bank which goes bankruptcy after the shipment is made but before the payment is obtained. Another risk may occur to the exporter when the importer or the issuing bank or both incorporate soft clauses into the credit or intentionally and dishonestly find faults with the documents and refuse to make payment.

(2) Risks to the importer. Although the importer is freed from the risk of non－delivery from the exporter when banks deal with documents, he is exposed to the risk of getting "wrong" goods, goods that are inferior and quite different from those described in the sales contract. This may happen because under L/C, banks deal with documents rather than the physical goods, services or other performances to which the documents may relate. A dishonest exporter may fabricate "correct" documents to cover "wrong" goods.

(3) Risks to the issuing bank. The issuing bank can be cheated into issuing credit and making payment when the importer, or the exporter or both are dishonest. The exporter may make "correct" documents to cover the false transaction, and the importer may intentionally refuse to make payment to retire the documents after the issuing bank fulfils his payment undertaking to the exporter against the "correct" documents.

Exercises for Chapter 8

Ⅰ. Multiple-choice Questions (It is possible to make more than one choice)

1. A credit may be advised to a beneficiary through another bank (the advising bank) without engagement on the part of the advising bank, but that bank, if it chooses to advise the credit, shall _____.

   A. inform the issuing bank of the credit which it advises without delay

   B. endorse the amount negotiated on the reverse of the credit which it advises

   C. add his confirmation to the credit which it advises

   D. take reasonable care to check the apparent authenticity of the credit which it advises

2. Under _____ credit(s), the exporter gets sight payment.

   A. sight payment

   B. deferred payment

   C. acceptance

   D. negotiation

3. When a credit is available with the exporter's bank, _____ credit is most favorable to the exporter's bank.

   A. sight payment

   B. deferred payment

   C. acceptance

   D. negotiation

4. In a negotiable credit and in the event of dishonor, the negotiation bank has the right of recourse against _____.

   A. the issuing bank

   B. the drawer

   C. the exporter

   D. the beneficiary

5. Look at the four payment methods in international trade:

   (1) Payment under documentary credit.

   (2) Open account.

   (3) Collection in either documents against payment or acceptance of a bill of exchange.

   (4) Payment in advance.

   From an exporter's point of view, the order of preference is _____.

A. (4),(2),(3),(1)

B. (4),(3),(1),(2)

C. (4),(1),(3),(2)

D. (2),(4),(1),(3)

Ⅱ. Fill in the Blanks

1. The doctrine of strict compliance means that _____ on the one hand and _____ on the other hand.

2. Under L/C, payment to the exporter can be effected by payment, _____ or _____.

3. When a credit is confirmed, the exporter gets two payment undertakings from the _____ and _____.

4. Under acceptance credit, the exporter gets _____ payment against commercial documents and drafts drawn on the _____ bank.

5. If the tenor of the draft for a negotiable credit is made at two months sight, the export gets _____ payment against stipulated documents.

6. The drawn clause in a credit draft consists of _____, _____ and _____.

Ⅲ. Case Questions

Case One

Company A, Chengdu signs a contract with Company B, Bombay to export 1, 100 cartons of canned chicken at USD 20 000 with the shipment date no later than 15th, July 2023 under an irrevocable documentary confirmed negotiation credit. The credit is issued by Bank of India, Bombay on June 1, 2023 with the credit number as BOCCD2023060132. Bank of China, Chengdu is authorized to advise and confirm the credit and the bank is prepared to do so. After shipment, Company A, Chengdu submits sight drafts payable to his bank with commercial documents to his bank. After documents examination, the bank negotiates the documents and effects payments to the exporter. When the negotiating bank forwards the documents to the issuing bank to claim reimbursement, the issuing bank has already declared bankruptcy. Unable to get compensation from the issuing bank, Bank of China, Chengdu exercises its right of recourse against the exporter to call back its payment to the latter and at the same time suggests Company A, Chengdu to obtain sight payment from the importer directly.

Questions:

1. Specify the roles played by the two banks in this credit.

2. Can Bank of China, Chengdu call back the funds outlay to the exporter?

Why or why not?

3. Should Company A, Chengdu accept the suggestion by Bank of China, Chengdu? Why or why not?

Case Two

At the Canton Fair, a Chinese trading company established a sales contract with Company CD, Singapore for the export of a batch of white fungus. The terms of payment in the sales contract read as: "By irrevocable L/C available by Sellers' documentary draft at sight, to be valid by negotiation on China within 15 days after date shipment. L/C must reach the Sellers 30 days before the contracted month of shipment."

The Chinese trading company received the credit on 12 Nov, stipulating that "We hereby inform you that we have issued the irrevocable credit in your favor, available by negotiation of your draft at 120 days sight drawn on Bank ×××."

As the credit established was a time one and not in agreement with the sales contract, the Chinese trading company sent immediately an e-mail to Company CD, Singapore, requiring to have the credit amended to be a sight credit.

On 20 Nov., the Chinese trading company received the amendment notice of the credit as: "The credit with the No. ××× has been amended as follows: the usance draft can be negotiated on sight bases and discounted by Bank ×××."

Upon receiving the amendment notice, the Chinese trading company assumed that the amended credit was in agreement with the sales contract and made shipment and presentment accordingly.

But when checking its account after the completion of this transaction, the Chinese trading company found that the amount received was USD 5 000 less. After checking with the bank, the Chinese company was informed by the bank that the amount underpaid was the discount interest and other applicable charges deducted for negotiation and discounting. Although the Chinese trading company contacted the bank and the importer many times and insisted that he should be paid the full contract amount, his effort was futile and the Chinese trading company had to conclude the transaction at USD 5 000 short.

Questions:

1. Analyze the reasons for the loss suffered by the Chinese trading company.

2. What lessons should the Chinese company learn from this transaction?

Ⅳ. Practice Questions

Read the discussion between Mr. Dobson(the manager of a European export and import company) and Mr. Liang (the marketing manager of a Chinese export company) about the payment methods and then answer the questions below:

Mr. Dobson:　　　It's good that we've settled on the questions of price, quality, quantity and packing. Shall we discuss the payment methods now?

Mr. Liang:　　　Good idea. Let's get down to business. Since this is our first order in this field, we would like a lump sum payment. It saves time for both of us.

Mr. Dobson:　　　Lump sum advance payment? You mean we make all the payment before the goods are delivered? I don't think that's international practice. Besides, it's a bit demanding for such a trial order.

Mr. Liang:　　　That's our usual way when starting a new business relationship. What methods do you suggest?

Mr. Dobson:　　　I wonder if you can accept payment by installments? You know, our goods will also be delivered in partial shipments.

Mr. Liang:　　　What do you mean exactly?

Mr. Dobson:　　　I think the payment can be divided into two installments. 70% of the total can be paid at first delivery and the other 30% after the final acceptance.

Mr. Liang:　　　Well, I see your point. But normally we conduct our international sales with L/C. Actually, L/C provides us with guaranteed payment from the bank. How about L/C then?

Mr. Dobson:　　　That sounds reasonable. But an L/C is costly for us. Maybe we can make an advance payment to show you our sincerity.

Mr. Liang:　　　How much do you have in mind?

Mr. Dobson:　　　What about 25% of the total? In that case, we'd pay 25% in advance and pay 75% on final acceptance.

Mr. Liang:　　　OK. You drive a hard bargain! I'll accept your last proposal, but my company requires the final 75% payment to be paid within one month of the final delivery. Do you think that will be OK with you?

Mr. Dobson:　　　That's all right with us. And you can rest assured it will all go through OK. You know, we have an excellent reputation all over the world and we are the fourth largest European company in this line of business.

Mr. Liang:	Great. On our side, we'll ensure prompt shipment so as to be sure your products get to the market in your area quickly.
Mr. Dobson:	I appreciate your co-operation. I can envisage a sustainable and long-term relationship ahead. We can promise there'll be no problem with the payment. But I hope you can offer us more favorable conditions for later transactions.
Mr. Liang:	Of course. If these transactions prove successful and satisfactory, we can discuss many things later on. Right?
Mr. Dobson:	Yes. Then let's call it a deal.
Mr. Liang:	Yes, and now let's go and celebrate.

1. Determine the payment methods proposed by the buyer (Mr. Dobson) and the seller (Mr. Liang) respectively as they occur in the conversation and fill in the blanks:

The seller's suggestion

(1) _____

(3) _____

The buyer's suggestion

(2) _____

(4) _____,
which is finally accepted by the seller.

2. Give a definition to each payment method stated in question 1 and explain the most outstanding and obvious benefits as well as risks to the traders respectively.

V. Extended Discussions

On Oct 20, 2023, our company made an export at USD 52 500 under CFR 5% to ABC Trading, a middleman in Kuwait. The L/C amount issued was at USD 49 875 and was incorporated with the following clause: "When negotiating, 5% commission to be deducted from the amount negotiated and returned to the middleman, ABC Trading".

Unfortunately, however, the document clerk of our company failed to check the credit amount and when negotiating, submitted both commercial invoice and draft at USD 52 500, being the amount of the sales contract. Bank of China, Beijing, after deducted 5% commission from the amount, effected negotiation to our company at USD 49 875 and debited the same amount from the account of the issuing bank with Bank of China, Beijing. But the issuing bank refused to make reimbursement on the fact that the draft amount and that of the commercial invoice exceed the L/C amount. Our company contacted ABC Trading and the issuing bank and tried to make explanation but the effort was in vain in persuading either of them to accept the amount at USD 52 500.

As such, our company had no other choice but to issue new draft and commercial invoice complying the L/C amount at USD 49 875. In the end, after 5% commission being deducted from USD 49 875, our company got USD 2 493. 75 less for this export transaction.

Questions:

1. Explain the doctrine of strict compliance in L/C documentation and examination.

2. What lesson do we learn from the case?

Chapter 9 Factoring, Standby Credit and Letter of Guarantee

Objectives

◇Learn the definition and services offered by factoring.

◇Learn the definition and the use of standby credit.

◇Learn the definition of L/G.

◇Learn the differences between conditional guarantee and demand guarantee, between direct guarantee and indirect guarantee.

◇Learn the contents and classification of L/G.

◇Learn the selection and combination of various payment methods.

Section 1 Factoring

1. Definition of factoring

Factoring refers to the purchase of claim by a financial institution (the factor) from a business entity (the exporter) who has sold goods or provided services abroad to his trade debtors (the importer) whereby the factor purchases, normally without recourse, the exporter's account receivable, controls its credit extended to importers and administers its bookkeeping and collections.

In simple words, factoring refers to the purchase of claim arising from sales of goods or provision of services by a financial institution from the exporter to ensure payment from the importer.

Factoring is a new financial service provided for international trade and it is normally used together with open account and documents against acceptance.

Factoring originated in England and North America and there exist different worldwide organizations of factors with the development of international trade. Factors Chain International (FCI) established in 1968 is the largest one in the world with over a hundred factors from 40 different countries. China has become one of its member countries in 1993. FCI has completed *the Convention on International Factoring* (CIF), a set of rules and regulations governing the export factoring agreement between the exporter and the export factor and the correspondent contract between the export factor and import factor.

2. Parties to international factoring

There are four parties in the international factoring. They are:

(1) The exporter. The exporter is the factor's client who invoices on the importer for the supply of goods or the provision of services and whose accounts of receivable are factored by the factor. The invoice represents the exporter's account receivable or, in other words, his claim on the importer.

(2) The importer. The importer is liable for making payment for the account receivables arising from his purchase of goods or services.

(3) The export factor. The export factor is to factor the exporter's account receivables under an agreement to that effect. The export factor is normally the exporter's bank.

(4) The import factor. The import factor agrees to collect the account receivables invoiced by the exporter and consigned to him from the export factor. He is bound to pay such accounts receivable assigned to him and for which he has assumed the credit risk. The import factor is normally the importer's bank.

3. Services offered by the factors

The factor is to provide a package of financial services including the evaluation of the importer's credit, export trade finance, maintenance of sales ledger and collection of account receivable. The services in the service package offered by the factors are closely related. They are to minimize the risks on the part of the factors in the process.

(1) Evaluation of the importer's credit. The factors should evaluate the importer's credit standing and conclude a preliminary credit assessment. Based on it, the factors set a credit approval for a certain period of time for each order prior to its shipment. Any amount for each transaction within the approved credit is called approved account receivables by which the factors will assume the responsibility of payment. Any amount of transaction beyond the credit approval is unap-

proved receivables and the risk of bad debts is to be borne by the exporter himself. This method is to protect the factors themselves from the risk of the importer's non-payment.

(2) Export trade finance. It is up to the exporter whether to apply for trade finance from the export factor. If the exporter chooses to do so and if a transaction is within the credit approval, the export factor may grant financing to the exporter prior to the maturity of the invoice by negotiating without recourse the latter's accounts receivables. The payment is advanced and the exporter's turnover is speeded up. When the account receivables are assigned to the factor, the ownership to the goods will also be transferred to him.

(3) Maintenance of sales ledger. Once the invoice is sent to the factors, the factors will set up the corresponding sales ledger in his computer record system for the exporter. Professional services such as book keeping, calculation and making statements will be carried out by the factor.

(4) Collection of receivables. At maturity of the invoice, the factors will collect payment from the importer. The proceeds will be credited to the exporter if they have not been advanced to the exporter, normally less its commission of 1% to 2% of the invoice value. In the event that the importer fails to make payment on due date and if the payment is not advanced, the factors will make payments to the exporter, plus interest calculated from the due date to the date of the actual payment.

4. Procedure of international factoring

Figure 9.1 shows the procedure of international factoring.

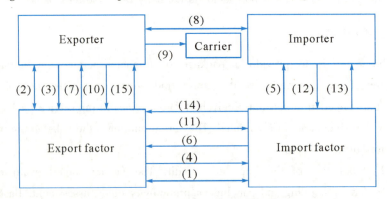

Figure 9.1 The Procedure of International Factoring

(1) A correspondent agreement is concluded between the export factor and the import factor.

(2) An export factoring agreement is established between the exporter and the

export factor.

(3) Exporter applies for a credit approval.

(4) Export factor transmits application for a credit approval.

(5) Import factor appraises importer's credit and set the approved receivables.

(6) Advise export factor of the approved receivables.

(7) Advise exporter of the approved receivables.

(8) Sales contract is established between the exporter and the importer within the approved receivables and with the payment terms as either O/A or D/A.

(9) Exporter delivers the goods for shipment.

(10) The exporter fills in and signs the "Notification and Transfer of Receivables" and submits it to the export factor with invoice and other documents. The exporter may also apply for finance at this stage.

(11) Invoices and other documents are transmitted by the export factor to the import factor.

(12) At maturity of the invoice, the import factor collects payment from the importer.

(13) The importer effects payment to the import factor, against which the import factor delivers documents to him.

(14) Proceeds are remitted by the import factor to the export factor.

(15) Proceeds are credited by the export factor to the exporter's account less the factoring commission. If the exporter has obtained finance by partial advance, discount charges should be deducted before the balance is credited to the exporter's account.

5. Advantages of international factoring

(1) Full payment is secured for the exporter within the approved receivables. Factoring is based on banker's credit whereby the factor undertakes to buy without recourse the exporter's claim within this limit.

(2) Proceeds will be obtained within maturity provided that the exporter makes shipment on time. The exporter may get financed at the time when he submits his invoices and other documents to the export factor.

(3) The exporter saves administrative and accounting costs because the factor will take full administrative control of the exporter's sales ledger. The exporter can get assistance from the factors through a service package offered by the latter, which ranges from an assessment of the creditworthiness of the overseas buyers to credit protection and collection services.

（4）Factoring enables the exporter to sell to his foreign trade partners on O/A and D/A terms, competitive against local suppliers while fully protected against bad debt losses by the factors.

（5）For the traders, the procedure under factoring is less complicated and less expensive than under L/C. Factoring can save the importer from the L/C issuing charges, deposit margin and possible L/C amendment fee. The doctrine of strict compliance of the credit does not apply to factoring, if the exporter makes shipment on time, he will get payment from the factors.

Section 2　Standby Credit

1. Definition of standby credit

According to UCP 600, a standby credit is defined as a letter of credit or a similar arrangement, however named or described, which represents an obligation to the beneficiary on the part of the issuing bank to:

（1）Repay money borrowed by, or advanced to or for the account of the applicant.

（2）Make payment on account of any indebtedness undertaken by the applicant.

（3）Make payment on account of any default by the applicant in the performance of an obligation, against stipulated documents which comply with the terms and conditions of the credit.

Under a standby credit, the payment will be called for only when the applicant fails to repay the loan or fails to fulfill its obligations. In other words, a standby credit will not be called for when the obligations are performed by the applicant. In a stand-by credit, the parties do not normally expect that the presentation of documents will occur. Figure 9. 2 is a sample of standby credit.

Name of issuing bank: The French Issuing Bank 38 rue FrancoisLer 75008 Paris , France	Irrevocable Documentary Credit	Number 12345
Place and Date of Issue: Paris, 1 January 2023		

| Name of issuing bank: The French Issuing Bank 38 rue FrancoisLer 75008 Paris , France | Irrevocable Documentary Credit | Number 12345 |

Name of issuing bank:
    The French Issuing Bank
    38 rue FrancoisLer
    75008 Paris , France

Irrevocable
Documentary Credit   Number 12345

Place and Date of Issue: Paris, 1 January 2023

Expiry Date and Place for Presentation of Documents
Expiry Date: May 29, 2023
Place for Presentation: The American Advising Bank,
Tampa

Applicant:
    The French ABC Co.
    89 rue du Commerce
    Paris, France

Beneficiary:
    The American XYZ Co. Inc.
    17 Main Street
    Tampa, Florida

Advising Bank: Reference No
    The American Advising Bank
    456 Commerce Avenue
    Tampa, Florida

Amount:
US $ 100 000. – one hundred thousand U.S. Dollars

Partial shipments ☒allowed ☐not allowed

Credit available with Nominated Bank:
The American Advising Bank, Tampa

Transshipment ☒allowed ☐not allowed

☐ Insurance covered by buyers

☒by payment
☐by acceptance of drafts at:
☐by negotiation

Shipment as defined in UCP 600
From: Tampa, Florida
For transportation to: Paris, France
Not later than: May 15, 2023

Against the documents detailed herein:
☒and Beneficiary's draft(s) at sight drawn on
The American Advising Bank, Tampa

Singed statement of The American XYZ Co. Inc. that The French ABC Co. failed to perform its contractual obligations under the agreement concluded on Dec.17, 2022 between The French ABC Co. and The American XYZ Co. Inc. in which The French ABC Co. was the successful bidder.

Special Conditions:
It is agreed that we may be released from our liability under this Letter of Credit Prior to the expiry date, only if we receive notification from The American Advising Bank, Tampa by tested telex to the effect that The American Advising Bank, Tampa has been duly advised by The American XYZ Co. Inc that the above agreement has been completely performed by The French ABC Co. The American Advising Bank, Tampa to advise the beneficiary adding its confirmation. We herebyauthorize The American Advising Bank, Tampa to drawn on us by means of telex for the value of all drafts drawn under this credit, provided the telex states that all terms and conditions of the credit have been complied with.

We hereby issue the Irrevocable Documentary Credit in your favor. It is subjected to The International Standby Practices (ISP98) issued by International Chamber of Commerce, publication No. 590 in 1998.

The document consists of ☐2 signed page(s)

The French Issuing Bank

Figure 9. 2   **Standby Credit** (**Advice for the Beneficiary**)

From a legal point of view, a stand-by credit is in effect a payment guarantee rather than a payment method. As a credit, some articles of UCP 600 are applicable to standby credit. In addition, it is also subject to The International Standby Practices (ISP 98) issued by International Chamber of Commerce, publication No. 590 in 1998.

2. Similarity between standby credit and commercial credit

Standby credit and commercial credit share the following similarities：

(1) Both types of credits are separate documents independent from the underlying contract.

(2) The payment undertakings under both credits are given by the issuing banks where payments are effected only against stipulated documents which comply with the terms and conditions of the credits.

3. Differences between standby credit and commercial credit

(1) Commercial credit is used for the purpose of payment settlement of international trade transactions while standby credit can be used for the purpose of guarantee for the fulfillment of both trade and non-trade contracts.

(2) The issuing bank's responsibilities under commercial credit end when payments are effected; the amount under standby credit may not be called for from the issuing bank when the applicant's obligations are fulfilled.

(3) Documents required under commercial credit are drafts plus those commercial documents evidencing the fulfillment on the part of the beneficiary; documents required under standby credit are drafts plus a statement attesting the non-performance on the part of an applicant. For this reason, standby credit is normally a clean credit and it is not typically used as a payment arrangement.

(4) Commercial credit is subject to all the articles stipulated in UCP 600. However, some articles under UCP 600 are not applicable to standby credit.

Section 3   Letter of Guarantee

1. Definition of letter of guarantee

A Letter of Guarantee (L/G) is a written promise by a bank at the request of its customer, undertaking to make payment to the beneficiary within the limits of time a stated sum of money against stipulated documents in the event of non-performance of the contractual obligations by the principal. It is also called a bank guarantee or a bond.

The underling contractual obligations might be payment, delivery, the repayment of a loan or the construction of a building, etc. In an international economic transaction, sometimes one party will insist the contract to be established under a bank guarantee in his favor.

It is obvious that the major difference of a bank's payment undertaking under L/C credit and that of L/G lies in the conditions to effect payments. Under L/C, the bank effects payment against the beneficiary's performance. While under L/G, the bank effects payment against the principal's non-performance. In this sense, letter of guarantee is similar to standby credit in effect.

2. Documents under letter of guarantee

Documents requirements vary according to the following two types of guarantee:

(1)Conditional guarantee."Uniform Rules for Contract Guarantee" issued by the International Chamber of Commerce in 1978 publication No.325 (URCG 325), stipulates the conditions under which a beneficiary can claim payment from the bank.

According to this rule, to attest the non-performance of the principal, the beneficiary should present such documentary evidence as a court decision, an arbitrary award or an approval to the claim from the principal in writing. The guarantee issued based on this rule is referred to as conditional guarantee.

Conditional guarantee requires documentary evidence giving maximum protection to the principal to be presented by the beneficiary when demanding payment. As a result, conditional guarantee is often deemed unacceptable to the beneficiary.

(2)(On) Demand guarantee. "Uniform Rules for Demand Guarantee" published by the International Chamber of Commerce in 1992 in its publication No.458 (URDG 458), is a new rule governing the letter of guarantee operation.

Under the new rule, the payment can be called "on demand" by simply a written demand from the beneficiary without a written proof from a neutral third party or from the principal himself, even in circumstances that the claim is wholly unjustified. The guarantee issued based on this new rule is referred to as "(on) demand" guarantee.

Compared with the conditional guarantee, this "on demand" guarantee is sometimes known as the "unconditional" guarantee. It is more favorable to the beneficiary and has gained general acceptance from prevailing banking and commercial practice.

3. Direct and indirect guarantee

According to the number of banks involved, L/G can be a direct guarantee or an indirect guarantee.

(1) Direct guarantee. A direct guarantee is issued directly from the foreign bank to the beneficiary. It normally involves the following three parties: the principal, the beneficiary and the guarantor.

①Principal/Applicant. The principal is the person at whose request the guarantee is issued. In the event that he fails to fulfill his contractual obligations, the principal will be claimed after the payment being effected by the guarantor. He is required to enter a counter indemnity with the guarantor at the time of application.

②The beneficiary. The beneficiary is the person in whose favor the guarantee is issued. In the event of default by the principal, he is entitled to obtain payment from the guarantor upon presentment of correct documents under the guarantee.

③The guarantor. The guarantor is the issuing bank of guarantee. It is a bank located in the applicant's country, who is responsible to issue the guarantee in agreement with the application form. Once a guarantee is established, the bank is under the obligation to make payments to the beneficiary under the terms stipulated in the guarantee. The bank has the right to claim compensation from the applicant to cover the funds outlay to the beneficiary.

Figure 9.3 shows the procedure of direct guarantee.

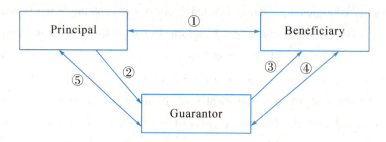

Figure 9.3 **The Procedure of Direct Guarantee**

①The contract is established between the two contracting parties.

②One contracting party is to apply to his bank for issuing a guarantee to the other contracting party in a foreign country. This party becomes the applicant and the other party becomes the beneficiary under the guarantee. The guarantee is issued against a counter indemnity contract or a reimbursement contract between the guarantor and the applicant.

③The guarantor forwards the guarantee to the beneficiary. In the event of performance by the principal, the guarantee is expired at the expired date or by an expired event. The expired guarantee is returned to the guarantor without any payment being made by him and the whole procedure ends here.

④In the event of non-performance by the principal, the beneficiary claims payment from the guarantor against the stipulated documents.

⑤After payment is effected to the beneficiary, the guarantor claims compensation from the principal against the counter indemnity contract or reimbursement contract.

（2）Indirect guarantee. In some countries, notably in the Middle East, local laws or customs prevent beneficiary from accepting guarantee issued directly by a foreign bank. Under this circumstance, the foreign bank instructs another bank domiciled in the beneficiary's locality to issue a guarantee against the foreign bank's own indemnity—the counter guarantee. As a result, the guarantee becomes an indirect guarantee which involves four parties and two guarantees where the beneficiary's bank becomes the guarantor and the applicant's bank becomes the instructing party.

Indirect guarantee involves the following four parties: the principal, the beneficiary, the instructing party and the guarantor.

①The principal/Applicant. The principal is the person at whose request the counter guarantee is issued. In the event that he fails to fulfill his contractual obligations, the principal will be claimed after the payment being effected by the instructing party. He is required to enter a counter indemnity with his bank at the time of application.

②The beneficiary. The beneficiary is the person in whose favor the guarantee is issued. In the event of default by the principal, he is entitled to obtain payment from the guarantor upon presentment of correct documents under the guarantee.

③The instructing party. The instructing party is the applicant's bank who issues a counter guarantee at the request of the applicant in favor of a foreign bank. A counter guarantee is so called because against which a guarantee is to be issued.

④The guarantor. The guarantor is the beneficiary's bank who issues a guarantee against a counter guarantee. The guarantor assumes double identities in this arrangement whereby it is the guarantor of the guarantee and the beneficiary of the counter guarantee.

Figure 9.4 shows the procedure of indirect guarantee.

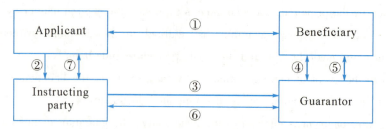

Figure 9.4 **The Procedure of Indirect Guarantee**

①The contract is established between the two contracting parties.

②One contracting party (the applicant) is to apply to his bank to issue a guarantee in favor of the other contracting party (the beneficiary) in a foreign country. This guarantee is issued against a counter indemnity contract or a reimbursement contract between the bank and the applicant.

③The applicant's bank issues such a guarantee in favor of another bank domiciled in the beneficiary's country and instructing the latter by this guarantee to issue a new guarantee on behalf of its client in favor of a specified party named therein. The original guarantee is the counter guarantee against which the new guarantee is issued. The applicant's bank becomes the instructing party because the new guarantee is established against his request and instruction.

④The bank domiciled in the beneficiary's locality issues the new guarantee at the request of the instructing party on behalf of the latter's principal to the beneficiary. The bank becomes the guarantor. In the event of performance by the principal, the guarantee and the counter guarantee are expired on their expiry dates or by expiry events. The expired guarantees are returned to their respective issuing banks without any payment being made by them and the whole procedure may end here.

⑤In the event of non-performance by the principal, the beneficiary claims payment from the guarantor against stipulated documents under the guarantee.

⑥The guarantor claims compensation from the instructing party against the counter guarantee.

⑦The instructing party claims compensation from the principal against the counter indemnity contract or reimbursement contract.

4. Major contents of letter of guarantee

A letter of guarantee should be made clear, specific and accurate and not to be too much in detail. It mainly includes:

(1)The name of beneficiary and the issuing date.

(2)The type and number of the guarantee.

(3) General information of the underlying transaction, such as the contract No., the two contracting parties, the date of the contract, the goods/services/projects and the relevant quantity, quality or performance requirements.

(4) The amount of the guarantee and its currency.

(5) The terms for effecting payment. A guarantee should specify the documentation to be produced in support of a claim. If the terms follow ICC publication No. 325, the guarantee is a conditional one which is less favorable the beneficiary. Or the guarantee can be a demand guarantee following ICC publication No. 458 which is more favorable to the beneficiary.

(6) The validity of the guarantee. According to ICC publication No. 458, a guarantee must specify a calendar date to be the expiry date or an expiry event. The guarantee shall be expired after the expiry date or a specified period after the occurrence of certain event, e.g. thirty days after shipment. If both the expiry date and the expiry event are specified, the guarantee shall be expired on whichever occurs first.

(7) Any other provisions such as the reduction of the amount, the governing law and jurisdiction.

(8) The name and signature of the guarantor. A guarantee is to be expired either after the expiry date/event or on settlement of claims under it. Under either case, the original copy of the expired guarantee must be returned to the guarantor.

5. Major types of letter of guarantee

According to *Uniform Rules for Contract Guarantees*, the major types of the bank guarantee are tender guarantee, performance guarantee, repayment guarantee, import guarantee, compensation guarantee, processing and assembly guarantee and loan guarantee, etc.

Types of guarantee can be numerous to serve the varied purposes of the contracting parties in their economic transactions. In fact, wherever there is a need for rights and interest protection, one contracting party can apply for a guarantee of a certain type by which he obtains the performance undertaking from a bank rather than his counterpart.

(1) Tender guarantee / Tender bond / Bid bond. A tender guarantee is an undertaking given by a bank at the request of a tenderer in favor of a party inviting tenders abroad, whereby the guarantor undertakes, in the event of non – performance by the principal in the obligations resulting from the submission of tender documents, to make payment to the beneficiary within the limits of time a

stated sum of money.

The three immediate parties to a tender guarantee are:

①The principal. The principal is the tenderer who submits his tender documents.

②The beneficiary. The beneficiary is the party inviting tenders.

③The guarantor. The guarantor is the bank to effect payment if the principal fails to meet his obligations resulting from his submission of tender documents.

When tenders are invited, the tender would make it as obligations for the tenderer that:

①The tender no to be modified and withdrawn before the award date.

②The tenderer undertakes to sign the contract with the party inviting tender if the tender is awarded to him.

③The tenderer is to procure the issuance of any performance or other required guarantee to replace the tender guarantee after the contract is established.

If the tender is not awarded, the expiry date of the tender guarantee is the award date or several days after the award date. On the other hand, if the tender is awarded, the expiry date is between 3 to 6 months till the signing of the awarded contract or the issuance of a performance guarantee or other required guarantee.

The amount of the tender guarantee is at a specific percentage, e.g., 1% ~ 5% of the project value. The purpose of the tender guarantee is to safeguard the beneficiary (the party inviting the tenders) against the principal's (the tenderer's) breach of their obligations to prevent the submission of frivolous tenders. Figure 9.5 is a sample tender guarantee.

(2) Performance guarantee / Performance bond. A performance guarantee is an undertaking given by the guarantor at the request of a supplier of goods or services or a contractor as the principal in favor of the buyer or an employer as the beneficiary, whereby the guarantor undertakes to make payment to the beneficiary within the limits of time a stated sum of money in the event of non-performance of the principal.

The three immediate parties are:

①The principal. The principal can be the exporter who supplies the goods and services under the sales contract or, he can be the contractor whom the project contract has been awarded. The principal is the tenderer under the tender guarantee.

TO: _____   Issuing Date: _____
                                           Bid security for Bid No. _____
                                           For supply of _____
This guarantee is hereby issued to serve as a Bid Security of _____

(name of Bidder) (hereinafter called the "Bidder") for invitation for Bid (Bid No. _____) for supply of _____ (description of goods) to _____ (Name of the Buyer).

_____ (Name of issuing bank) hereby unconditionally and irrevocably guarantee and binds itself, its successors and assigns to pay you immediately without recourse, the sum of _____ upon receipt of your written notification stating any of the following:

a) The Bidder has withdrawn his bid after the time and date of the bid opening and before the expiration of its validity period; or

b) The Bidder has failed to enter into Contract with you within thirty calendar days after the notification of Contract award; or

c) The Bidder has failed to establish acceptable Performance security within thirty calendar days after receipt of the Notification Award.

It is fully understood that this guarantee takes effect from the date of the bid opening and shall remain valid for a period of _____ calendar days, and during the period of any extension thereof that may be agreed upon between you and the Bidder with notice to us, unless terminated and or released by you.

                                           Issuing Bank _____
                                           Signed by _____
                                           (printed name and designation of
                                           official authorized to sign on behalf
                                           issuing bank)
                                           Official Seal _____

Figure 9.5   **The Tender Guarantee**

②The beneficiary. The beneficiary can be the importer who buys the goods or services under the sales contract or, he can be the employer who awards the project contract. The beneficiary is the party inviting tender under the tender guarantee.

③The guarantor. The guarantor is the bank to effect payment in the event of the principal's failure to fulfill the contract.

The purpose of the performance guarantee is to ensure the fulfillment of the contract on the part of the principal. Therefore, the performance guarantee is valid till the delivery of goods or services or the complete performance of the contract. The amount payable under this guarantee is often at $10\% \sim 15\%$ of the contract amount. Figure 9.6 is a sample performance guarantee.

```
To _____ ( Beneficiary )      Issuing Date _____
                                         Performance Bond No._____
                                         For the supply of _____
This Bond is hereby issued as the performance bond of _____ ( Applicant ) ( hereinafter
called the supplier ) for supply of _____ ( description of goods ) under the Contract No.
_____ to _____ ( the name of the beneficiary ) .
The _____ ( name of the guarantor ) hereby irrevocably guarantees itself, its successors
and assigns to pay you up to the amount of _____ ( the amount of the guaranteed
value ) representing _____ percent of the contract price and accordingly covenants and
agrees as follows :
a) On the supplier's failure of faithful performance of the contract ( hereinafter called the
   failure of performance ) , we shall immediately, on your demand in a written notification sta-
   ting the effect of the failure of performance by the supplier, pay you such amount or a-
   mounts as required by you not exceeding _____ ( the guaranteed amount ) in the man-
   ner specified in the said statement.
b) The covenants herein contained constitute irrevocable and direct obligations of the
   guarantor, no alternation in the terms of the contract to be performed thereunder and no al-
   lowance of time by you or any other act or omission by you, which but for this provision
   might exonerate or discharge the bank shall in any way release the guarantor from any lia-
   bility hereunder.
c) The performance bond shill become effective from issuing date and shall remain valid until
   _____ ( the date of expiry ) . Upon expiry, please return this bond for cancellation.
                                         Issuing Bank _____
                                         Signed by _____
                                         ( printed name and designation of
                                         official authorized to sign on behalf
                                         issuing bank )
                                         Official Seal _____
```

Figure 9.6 Performance Guarantee

（3）Import guarantee / Payment guarantee. An import guarantee or payment guarantee is an undertaking by the guarantor at the request of the importer to the exporter, whereby the guarantor undertakes to make payment to the beneficiary within the limits of time a stated sum of money in the event of non-payment by the principal for the goods he has received on open account terms.

The three immediate parties are :

①The principal. The principal is the importer who receives goods from the exporter on open account terms.

②The beneficiary. The beneficiary is the exporter who supplies goods to the importer on open account terms.

③The guarantor. The guarantor is to effect payment to the beneficiary in the event that the principal fails to make payment to the exporter.

The purpose of the import /payment guarantee is to secure the payment on an open account basis. The amount payable under this guarantee should be the unpaid value of the goods delivered plus any applicable interests.

（4）Repayment guarantee / Advance payment guarantee. A repayment guarantee or advance payment guarantee is an undertaking by the guarantor at the request of the exporter or contractor to the importer or employer, whereby the guarantor undertakes to make payment to the beneficiary within the limits of time a stated sum of money in the event of default by the principal to repay any sum or sums advanced by the beneficiary to the principal.

The three immediate parties are:

①The principal. The principal is the party who receives advance payment. He can be the exporter who is to supply the goods or services under payment in advance or the contractor who has been awarded the contract.

②The beneficiary. The beneficiary is the party who makes advance payment to the principal. He can be the importer who buys goods or services on the term of payment in advance or the employer who has made advance payment to the contractor.

③The guarantor. The guarantor is to effect payment in the event of default by the principal to repay any advance payments if the goods are not delivered or the services are not provided or if the contractual obligations are not performed.

The purpose of the repayment /advance payment guarantee is to secure that the delivery of goods or performance of the construction project. The amount payable is the amount of the advance payment and is automatically and proportionally reduced following each shipment or according to the progress in a construction project. In international trade, repayment guarantee can be used together with payment in advance to protect the importer. The period of validity of this guarantee is from the principal's actual receipt of advance payment to a specific date when the covered performance is fulfilled.

（5）Compensation guarantee. A compensation guarantee is an undertaking by the guarantor at the request of the importer of capital goods to the exporter, whereby the guarantor undertakes to make payment to the beneficiary within the limits of time a stated sum of money in the event of default by the principal to supply the future output of the factory in quantity, quality and time required.

The amount payable under compensation guarantee is normally made equal to the amount of the capital goods plus interest. The said guarantee is valid within half a month after the delivery of future output from the importing country.

（6）Processing and assembly guarantee. A processing and assembly guarantee is an undertaking by the guarantor at the request of the importer of raw material, components or machinery to the exporter, whereby the guarantor undertakes to make payment to the beneficiary within the limits of time a stated sum of money in the event of default by the principal to supply the finished products in quantity, quality and time required.

The amount payable under processing and assembly guarantee is normally made equal to the amount of the imported raw material, components or machinery plus interest. The said guarantee is valid within half a month after the delivery date or the finished goods from the importing country.

(7) Overdraft guarantee. When a contractor has established a complete production unit or infrastructure project in a foreign country, it will normally open an overdraft account with a local bank to obtain finance. And a bank guarantee is required before the overdraft account can be established.

An overdraft guarantee is an undertaking by the guarantor at the request of the contractor to an overseas bank, whereby the guarantor undertakes to make payment to the beneficiary within the limits of time a stated sum of money in the event of default by the principal to repay in due time the amount overdrawn in the account.

The amount payable is normally made equal to the stipulated overdraft facility in the overdraft account. The said guarantee is valid within half a month after the expiry date of the said account.

Section 4   Similarities Between L/G and L/C

L/G and L/C share the following similarities:

(1) Both L/G and L/C are based on banker's credit. This means that the issuing bank undertakes to effect payment to the beneficiary on behalf of the applicant/principal.

(2) Both L/G and L/C are legally independent from the underlying contract. Banks are bonded by the guarantee or the credit only.

(3) In both cases, banks deal with documents and bear no responsibilities for the form, sufficiency, accuracy, genuineness, or falsification of the documents presented. Banks are to take reasonable care for the apparent authenticity of the documents.

(4) Banks effect payment only against stipulated documents which comply with the terms and conditions of the guarantee or the credit.

Section 5　Differences Between L/G and L/C

The major differences between L/G and L/C are as follows:

(1) Applicable range. A letter of credit is applicable only to trade settlement where the payment undertaking by the issuing bank is extended to the exporter on behalf of the importer.

A letter of guarantee is applicable to both trade and non-trade transactions where the payment undertaking of the guarantor as a performance guarantee can be extended to either party of a contract.

(2) Payment undertaking. The purpose of a letter of credit is to effect payment against the beneficiary's fulfillment. In this sense, the issuing bank of L/C bears primary liability to the beneficiary. The documents required under a documentary credit should be documentary evidence of the beneficiary's performance, such as commercial invoice, bills of lading, insurance policy, etc.

The purpose of L/G is to effect payment against the principal's non-performance. In this sense, the issuing bank bears secondary liability to the beneficiary. That is to say, in the event of fulfillment, the amount under a guarantee will not be called for. The documents required should attest the non-performance of the principal. The stipulated documents can either be a written demand by the beneficiary or other documentary proof from a neutral third party.

(3) The number of banks effecting payment. Under L/C, more than one bank can effect payment to the beneficiary. They are the issuing bank, the confirming bank, the paying bank, the accepting bank or the negotiating bank. Therefore, the place of the presentation of documents can be made at the counter of any of these banks according to the stipulations in the credit.

Under L/G, only one bank can effect payment to the beneficiary of the guarantee. In the case of a counter guarantee, it is the instructing party and in the case of a guarantee, it is the guarantor. On either occasion, the presentation of documents should be made at the counter of the bank issuing the counter guarantee or the guarantee.

(4) The governing law. L/C should be subject to UCP 600. However, UCP 600 is only a set of rules and it does not stipulate the governing law and jurisdiction to be followed when there are any disputes.

L/G should be subject to either *the Uniform Rules for Contract Guarantee or the Uniform Rules for Demand Guarantee.* Although both of them are also rules, they indicate clearly the law and jurisdiction to be followed where there are any disputes, which are settled in the place of business of the guarantor if it is guarantee, or that of the instructing party if it is a counter guarantee.

(5)Transferability. L/C can be transferable whereas L/G cannot be transferable.

Section 6　Comparison of L/G and Standby Credit

1. Similarities

As one form of L/C, standby credit also shares those similarities with L/G stated above in Senction 4. In addition, the most unique similarity between standby credit and L/G is found in their effect, whereby the issuing bank of standby credit or the guarantor of L/G is to make payment to the beneficiary in the event of default on the part of the applicant/principal.

2. Differences

L/G and standby credit differ in the following aspects:

(1)Payment availability. Under standby credit, payment can be made available by sight payment, deferred payment, acceptance or negotiation with the issuing bank, the confirming bank, the paying bank, the accepting bank or the negotiating bank.

However, under L/G, amount will be payable only by payment available only with the guarantor of the guarantee or the instructing party of the counter guarantee.

(2)Place of presentation of documents. Under a standby credit, documents may be presented to the bank effecting payment. This means that the beneficiary may be required to present the documents to the counter of the issuing bank, confirming bank, paying bank, accepting bank or negotiating bank as stipulated in the credit, which, can be the exporter's own bank or a foreign bank in the importing country.

Under L/G, documents are to be presented to the counter of the guarantor under a guarantee or that of the instructing party under a counter guarantee.

Section 7   Summary of Payment Methods

In international trade, both the contracting parties will seek ways to protect himself from the breach of the other party while at the same time maintain their competitiveness in the world market.

Various payment methods provide different degrees of protection for either party against the risks of non-payment or non-delivery. For one transaction, traders may choose to use one payment method only, or they may choose to make a combination of different payment methods or the subtypes with a payment method to make a tradeoff between self-protection and competitive edge. The following are some popular selection and combination of payment methods in practice:

1. Payment in advance combined with O/A

In this combination, both parties agree that the importer makes partial payment in advance with the balance to be paid through O/A. The percentage for the amount under different payment methods is determined by putting into consideration of market condition, the intention of the transaction, the condition of the goods, as well as the credit standing of and the business relationship with the trade partner, etc. This overall consideration is also applicable to points 2, 3 and 4 below.

2. Remittance combined with collection

In this combination, both parties agree that the importer makes partial payment in advance with the balance to be paid through collection.

3. Letter of credit combined with remittance

In this combination, both parties agree to settle most proceeds through letter of credit, with the balance to be effected through remittance. This method is often used in the sales of bulk commodity, such as coal. The proceeds of the large part of the commodity are settled through L/C while the proceeds are T/T to the exporter after the delivery of the remainder.

4. Letter of credit combined with collection

It is also possible for the traders to arrange two invoices under letter of credit, one for the settlement through a clean credit for a percentage of the sales amount and the other for the settlement of the balance through D/P sight or D/P after sight.

5. Collection combined with standby credit or letter of guarantee

When the transaction is made on D/A, the exporter may require the importer to arrange a standby credit or letter of guarantee in his favor for the whole sales amount with the expiry date a period later than the due date of the drafts. In the event of default on the part of the importer, the exporter can claim compensation from the issuing bank of the stand-by credit or the guarantor of the bank guarantee.

6. Open account combined with import guarantee

When the transaction is made on open account term, the exporter may require the importer to arrange an import guarantee in favor of the exporter for the full amount of the contract. If the importer fails to make payment after exporter's delivery, the guarantor undertakes to make compensation to the exporter.

7. Payment in advance combined with repayment guarantee

When the transaction is made on payment in advance term, the importer may require the exporter to arrange a repayment guarantee in favor of the importer for the advance payment. If the exporter fails to make delivery after receiving payment, the guarantor undertakes to make repayment to the importer.

Exercises for Chapter 9

Ⅰ. Multiple-choice Questions (It is possible to make more than one choice)

1. The export factor _____.

A. purchases the exporter's account receivable, normally without recourse

B. controls the exporter's credit extended to the importer

C. administers the exporter's bookkeeping

D. collects payment for the exporter

2. _____ is concluded between the export factor and the import factor.

A. A sales contract

B. A correspondent agreement

C. An export factoring agreement

D. A preliminary credit assessment

3. _____ is the first service provided by the factors to the exporter.

A. Maintenance of sales ledger

B. Export trade finance

C. Collection of receivables

D. Evaluation of the importer's credit

4. _____ is/are applicable to standby credit.

A. INCOTERMS 2010

B. Some articles in UCP 600

C. ISP 98

D. URC 522

5. Standby credit is _____.

A. normally a clean credit

B. normally a documentary credit

C. in effect a payment guarantee

D. typically used as a payment arrangement

6. The obligations for the tenderer upon submitting tender are _____.

A. the tender is not to be modified and withdrawn before the award date

B. the tenderer undertakes to sign a contract for the successful bidding

C. the tenderer is to procure the issuance of repayment guarantee to replace the performance guarantee

D. the tenderer is to procure the issuance of performance guarantee to replace the tender guarantee

II. Fill in the Blanks

1. Factoring is a new financial service provided for international trade and it is normally used together with _____ and _____.

2. Under factoring, the amount of the sales contract should be made within _____.

3. The condition for the issuing bank of a normal documentary commercial credit to make payment is on _____, whereas the condition for the issuing bank of a standby credit to make payment is on _____.

4. _____ guarantee requires documentary evidence which gives maximum protection to the principal.

5. Under indirect guarantee, the beneficiary's bank is the _____ of the guarantee and the _____ of the counter guarantee.

6. The beneficiary of tender guarantee is _____, who can be the owner of a building or the party offering a project.

III. Case Question

Case One

Company A, a telecommunication equipment manufacturer, intends to sign an export sales contract with Company B, a telecommunication operator with the payment terms to be arranged as follows: 10% down payment to be made before delivery; 75% to be made against commercial documents; 15% to be made 6 months after the normal functioning of the equipment.

Questions:

1. What payment methods should be chosen to ensure delivery to Company B after 10% down payment is made by him in advance?

2. What payment methods should be chosen to ensure 75% payments to Company A after the equipment has been delivered?

3. What payment methods should be chosen to ensure 15% payments to Company A 6 months after the normal functioning of the equipment?

Case Two

Company A, a Chinese company, established a sales contract to export TV sets to Company B in country B. The Contract stipulated that the payment was to be settled through a documentary negotiation credit at full contract value and the credit would be effective upon the receipt of a performance guarantee at 10% of the contract value in favor of Company B issued by a bank in Country B.

Company A then went to his bank, Bank X, to apply for the establishment of the performance guarantee. After checking the credit standing of Company A, Bank X issued a guarantee in favor of Bank Y in country Y, instructing the latter to issue, based on the previous guarantee, a new guarantee in favor of Company B on behalf of Company A. Following the requirements of the applicant, Bank Y issued a performance guarantee, undertaking to make payment to Company B against his written demand that Company A had failed to perform his contractual obligations. The said guarantee was to be expired on May 10.

On April 30, Company A presented stipulated documents after shipment and obtained payment by negotiation. On May 2, Bank X received a message from Bank Y, requiring the guarantee to be extended for 3 months, which was not agreed by Company A. Bank X informed Bank Y of Company A's decision but received no response from Bank Y.

On May 15, Bank Y informed Bank X that he had made compensation to Company B against B's written demand of the non-performance on the part of the applicant, Company A, and required payment from Bank X.

Questions:

1. Specify the three immediate parties for the two guarantees.

2. Why are two guarantees issued for this transaction?

3. Is it reasonable and justifiable for Bank Y to claim compensation from Bank X?

Ⅳ. Practice Question

Fill in the blank repayment guarantee based on the following information:

ABC Exporting Company, New York (hereinafter referred to as the Exporter) signed an exporter sales contract, S/C No. 3505489, with China National Technical Import Corp., Beijing (hereinafter referred to as the importer) dated 11 Oct, 2023 at USD 2 400 000. 00 by which the importer is to make 10% down payment before delivery. At the request of the exporter, Bank of America, New York issued a repayment guarantee, No. 315/51040, on 29 Oct, 2023 in favor of the importer at USD 240 000. 00, being the amount of the advance payment of the abovesaid Contract.

Repayment Guarantee Form

To:_____   _____

_____
Our Guarantee No._____ as Repayment (Advance Payment) Guarantee

　　With reference to Contract No. _____ (hereinafter referred to as the Contract) signed between your Corporation and _____ (hereinafter referred to as the Seller) dated _____ amounting to _____ (say _____) in respect of the Seller's complete fulfillment of the obligations as specified in the Contract, we hereby undertake as follows:
　　Our liability under this Repayment (Advance Payment) Guarantee shall be limited to _____ of the total contract amount, namely _____ within 7 days after receipt of your written notice demanding refund from the Seller for reasons that the Seller fails to deliver all the goods to your corporation according to the stipulations of the Contract, we shall unconditionally refund to you the amount which has already been paid by you to the Seller as advance down payment, namely _____ and in addition to it together with the interest at the rate of 7% per annum from the date of your advance payment of the amount up to the actual date of refund.
　　This Guarantee shall become effective from today and shall remain valid until the date of the Bill of Lading when the Seller has delivered completely the goods.
　　This Guarantee is to be returned to us when our guarantee is no longer required or its validity has expired.

　　　　　　　　Guarantor:_____
　　　　　　　　　　Signature

V . Extended Discussions

Upon graduation as a Business English major, Miss Fang Yan has been employed by SINOCHEM GUANGDONG IMPORT& EXPORT, a trading company in Guangdong, China. Her company has recently got an order at USD 108 000 from METCH THAI ELECTRICAL APPLANCES COMPANY, BANGKOK, a new customer in Thailand. Now, Miss Fang is asked to make proposals on the payment terms for this transaction. What factors should Miss Fang take into consideration when selecting payment methods?

Part 4
Documents

Chapter 10   Commercial Invoice, Packing List and Insurance Policy

Objectives

◇Learn the classification and significance of documents.

◇Learn the definition and contents of commercial invoice.

◇Learn the definition and contents of packing list.

◇Learn the definition and contents of insurance policy.

◇Learn the classification of losses and coverages in insurance.

◇Learn the rules in coverage selection in insurance.

◇Learn the classification of insurance document.

Section 1   Documents in International Settlement

1. Classification of documents

Documents in international settlement include financial instruments and commercial documents which are made to facilitate both the payment and delivery of goods or provision of sevices. Financial instruments mainly include bills of exchange, promissory note and check, which are introduced in Chapter 3, Chapter 4, and Chapter 5. From Chapter 10 and onwards, the focus will move to commercial documents.

Popular types of commercial documents are commercial invoice, packing list, bills of lading, insurance policy, inspection certificate and certificate of origin, etc. These commercial documents can be grouped into basic documents and auxiliary documents.

Basic commercial documents are those that should be supplied by the exporter according to the requirement of the INCOTERMS like CIF, CIP or FOB etc. They are the commercial invoice, insurance policy and transport documents.

Auxiliary commercial documents refer to those ones which should be submitted according to the laws and regulations of the importing country or the special requirements of the importer concerning the conditions of the goods. They are mainly the certificate of origin, consular invoice and customs invoice, packing list and weight list, and inspection certificate, etc.

2. Payment methods, price terms and documents

Payment method can be remittance or reverse-remittance or can be based on trader's credit or banker's credit. In addition, price in sales contract is quoted in different price term. All these factors produce great effect on document as to its issuer, order or other applicable items. This means that the particulars of both financial instruments and commercial documents vary according to the payment methods chosen and price term selected in a transaction.

Under letter of credit, especially, as the issuing bank assumes maximum payment liabilities, it stipulates terms and conditions in the credit for the documents to be presented by the exporter, and the bank will fulfill its obligations only against the doctrine of strict compliance. Therefore, when a transaction is made under letter of credit, the maker or the issuer of a document must ensure that the documents made comply with the terms of the credit on the one hand and the documents presented ought to be consistent with one another on the other hand.

3. Significance of documents

Payment methods center around documents. The significance of documents in modern international settlements can be seen in the following points:

(1)Documents move through the settlement process. Modern international settlement has evolved from cash settlement to non-cash settlement where financial instruments have taken the place of cash as mediums of exchange. In the process of settlement, traders and the banks are dealing with financial instruments or commercial documents rather than cash and physical goods. Therefore, it is documents that are moving in the whole process of settlement.

(2) Documents are the evidence of performance of sales contract. As introduced in Chapter 1, financial instruments are made to settle payments. They are orders given to make or collect payments. When such orders are performed,

funds are transferred from one trader's bank account to another trader's bank account and thus payments are settled.

A sales contract describes and stipulates the conditions of the goods, shipment, insurance requirements and payment terms. All these obligations are reflected in the corresponding commercial documents. For this reason, commercial documents are varied and they signify whether the responsibilities in a transaction regarding the production, packing, shipment and insurance, etc of the goods have been fulfilled by the traders. When one type of commercial document is produced, it is considered that one obligation is taken up. Therefore, commercial documents are to provide documentary evidence that goods are produced, packed and insured properly and are delivered in correct quantity and quality and in timely fashion.

(3) Some commercial documents represent title to the goods. As introduced in Chapter 1, with the development in international settlement, two commercial documents, bills of lading and insurance policy, have evolved to become title documents.

In the case of bill of lading, the holder of bills of lading becomes the owner to the physical goods. For this reason, constructive delivery has come into being where the exporter is deemed to have made delivery once he surrenders title documents and the importer is expected to make payment when he is in possession title documents. In the case of insurance policy, the right to claim compensation can be transferred through endorsement. As a result, when goods have been documented, both delivery and payment are made against (title) documents rather than the physical goods.

Section 2　Commercial Invoice

1. Definition of commercial invoice

Commercial invoice or invoice is the accounting document prepared by the seller to claim payment from the buyer for the value of goods or service being supplied. It contains these major items as marks and numbers, description of goods, quantity, unit price and amount. In international settlement, it is a document to claim payment rather than an evidence of payment made.

Commercial invoice is issued based on the sales contract. The S/C No., the number of the sales contract, should be indicated in the commercial invoice. In the case of settlement by L/C, the name of the issuing bank, the L/C No. and the issuing date of the credit should also be indicated in the commercial invoice.

Commercial invoice is serves as a basic document against which other documents such as drafts, transport documents, insurance documents and packing list are established. It is usually made in the seller's letterhead with the wordings "commercial invoice" clearly indicated. Figure 10. 1 is a sample commercia invoice.

上海进出口贸易公司
SHANGHAI IMPORT & EXPORT TRADE CORPORATION
1123 ZHONGSHAN ROAD SHANGHAI, CHINA

COMMERCIAL INVOICE

TEL：021-65788866
FAX：021-65788867

INV. NO. : TX0053
DATE：FEB. 01, 2023
S/C NO. : TXT234
L/C NO. : TX0081

TO：
TKAMRA CORPORATION
302, KAWARA MACH OSAKA JAPAN
FROM SHANGHAI PORT　TO OSAKA PORT

MARKS & NO.	DESCRIPTIONS OF GOODS	QUANTITY	U/PRICE	AMOUNT
T.C TXT264 OSAKA C/NO.1-300	100%COTTON COLOUR WEAVE SHIRT TM 111 TM 222 TM 333 TM 444 PACKED IN ONE CARTON OF 20 PIECES EACH	2 000 PCS 2 000 PCS 1 000 PCS 1 000 PCS	CIFOSAKA USD 11. 00 USD 10. 00 USD 9. 50 USD 8. 50	USD 22 000. 00 USD 20 000. 00 USD 9 500. 00 USD 8 500. 00

TOTAL AMOUNT：SAY US DOLLARS SIX THOUSAND ONLY.

WE HEREBY CERTIFY THAT THE CONTENTS OF INVOICE HEREIN ARE CORRECT.

DRAWN UNDER JAPANESE ISSUING BANK, OSAKA, IRREVOCABLE DOCUMENTARY CREDIT NUMBER TX0081 DATED JAN 15, 2023

Authorized Signature

Figure 10. 1　Commercial Invoice

2. Major contents of commercial invoice

Commercial invoice usually includes the following items：

（1）Name and address of the seller. Both the name and address are pre-printed in the seller's letterhead. Under letter of credit, the name and address of the seller should be made consistent with those of the beneficiary.

(2) Name and address of the buyer. Under letter of credit, the invoice must be made out to the L/C applicant and with the name and address being in accordance with those appeared in the credit.

(3) The issuing date and invoice No. In practice, the issuing date of the commercial invoice can be the earliest one compared with other documents. Under letter of credit, the commercial invoice can be made on any day between the latest date for presentation and the expiry date of the credit. Invoice No. is the running number given by the seller.

(4) Shipping mark. Shipping mark is made for easy handling and recognition of commodities by the carrier and the consignee. It normally contains a mark, the name of the port/place of discharge, package No. etc.

When no shipping mark is used for a certain shipment, and the column "marks and numbers" will be entered with "N.M." or simply be left blank. However, when a shipping mark is used, it should be indicated thereon and the same shipping mark should also appear in other documents such as packing list or bills of lading.

(5) Description of goods. Commercial invoice shows a complete description of goods including their name, packing, and specification. Under letter of credit, it should conform to those in the credit, though the description of goods in L/C only appears in general terms.

(6) Quantity, unit price and amount. Price should be broken down into unit price and the seller should work out the total amount based on quantity which represents the invoice value payable by the importer. In international trade, price should be quoted in price terms. Under L/C, invoice value is normally the credit amount. Banks are not responsible for checking the mathematical calculation.

(7) Port/place of loading and port/place of discharge. The two ports/places should be made consistent with the chosen price term. Under L/C, they should also conform to the corresponding items in the credit.

(8) Payment method. Commercial invoice should indicate the chosen payment method in its subdivision when applicable, e.g. D/P sight or D/A 30 days sight. In the case of settlement by documentary credit, the name of the issuing bank, the L/C No. and the issuing date of the credit should also be indicated in the commercial invoice.

(9) Signature of the seller. According to UCP 600, commercial invoice may

not be signed unless otherwise stipulated in the credit.

Section 3   Packing List / Weight List

Packing list / weight list details the packing and assortment of goods item by item such as net and gross weight and measurement and serves as a supplementary document to the commercial invoice. It is made more convenient for the carrier, the buyer and the customs to count and check the goods.

Items such as the description of the goods and shipping marks on the packing list / weight list should be made in consistent with those on the commercial invoice. But those items pertaining to the unit price and amount in the commercial invoice should not be included in the packing list. The date of the packing / weight list can be made the same or a little later than but not earlier than that of the commercial invoice. Figure 10. 2 is a sample packing list.

上海进出口贸易公司
SHANGHAI IMPORT & EXPORT TRADE CORPARATION
1123 ZHONGSHAN ROAD SHANGHAI, CHINA

PACKING LIST

TEL: 021-65788866
FAX:021-65788867

INVOICE NO. TX0053
DATE: FEB. 01, 2023
S/C NO. : TXT233

MARKS & NOS
T.C

TO:
TKAMARA CORPOATION
302, KAWARA MACH OSAKA
JAPAN
FROM <u>SHANGHAI PORT</u>   TO   <u>OSAKA PORT</u>

TXT233
OSAKA
C/NO. 1-300

GOODS DESCRIPTIPN & PACKING	QUANTITY	CTNS	G.W. (KGS)	N.W. (KGS)	MEAS (M³)
100% COTTON COLOUR WEAVE SHIRT	2 000 PCS	100	11/1 100	10/1 000	0. 22/22
TM 111	2 000 PCS	100	11/1 100	10/1 000	0. 22/22
TM 222	1 000 PCS	50	11/550	10/500	0. 22/11
TM 333	1 000 PCS	50	11/550	10/500	0. 22/11
TM 444					
PACKED IN ONE CARTION OF 20 PIECES EACH					
TOTAL	6 000 PCS	300	3 300	3 000	66

SAY TATAL THREE HUNDRED CARTONS ONLY

DRAWN UNDER JAPANESE ISSUING BANK, OSAKA, IRREVOCABLE DOCUMENTARY CREDIT NUMBER TX0081 DATED JAN 15, 2023

Authorized Signature

Figure 10. 2 **Packing List**

Section 4　Insurance Documents

1. Definition of insurance document

Insurance document is a contract of indemnity between the insurer and the insured stipulating the premium, the amount insured, risks to be covered, procedures to establish a claim and other terms and conditions applicable, thereby indemnifying or making compensation to the latter by the former when a covered loss occurs. Concurrent with bills of lading, insurance documents have developed to become title documents.

The transportation of goods always involves risk and the cargo should be insured against the possible loss during transit. The obligations of cargo insurance have been stipulated in INCOTERM. The responsibility to insure the physical goods during the transit can fall either upon the exporter or the importer.

Price term should be chosen and indicated in the sales contract right at the beginning of the transaction. As price terms are the description of the responsibilities from the point of view of the exporter's rather than that of the importer. For example, in the case of CIF or CIP, it is agreed that the exporter will insure the goods and sign an insurance document with the insurance company. And in the case of FOB, FCA or CFR, the responsibility of entering into a contract of insurance with the insurance company falls on the part of the importer. Figure 10. 3 is sample insurance policy.

中国人民保险公司
大连分公司
The People's Insurance Company of China
DALIAN BRANCH
总公司设于北京一九四九年创立

HEAD OFFICE：BEIJING ESTABLISHED IN 1949

地址:中国大连中山路 141 号   CABLE：42001 DALIAN

ADDRESS：141 ZHONGSHAN ROAD DALIAN CHINA   FAX：336650 804558

TLX：86215 PICC CN

发票号次   保险单   保险单号次

INVOICE NO. 33563   **INSURANCE POLICY**

POLICY NO. PYIE2003210206000002

中 国 人 民 保 险 公 司 (以 下 简 称 " 公 司 ")

THIS POLICY OF INSURANCE WITNESSES THAT THE PEOPLE'S INSURANCE COMPANY OF CHINA

根 据

(HEREINAFTER CALLED"THE COMPANY")，AT THE REQUEST OF ___DALIAN I/E CO. LTD___

(以 下 简 称 被 保 险 人) 的 要 求,由 被 保 险 人 向 本 公 司 缴 付

(HEREIN CALLED THE " INSURED ") AND IN CONSIDERATION OF THE AGREED PREMIUM PAYING TO

约 定 的 保 险 费,按 照 本 保 险 单 承 保 险 别

THE COMPANY BY THE INSURED, UNDERTAKES TO INSURE THE GOODS IN TRNASPORTATION

和 背 面 所 载 条 款 与 下 列 特 款 承 保 下 列 货 物 运 输 保 险

SUBJECT TO THE CONDITIONS OF THE POLICY AS PER THE CLAUSES PRINTED OVERLEAF AND

特 立 保 险 单

SPECIAL CLAUSES ATTACHED HEREON.

标记 MARKS ANDNOS	包装及数量 PACKAGE & QUANTITY	货物描述 DESCRITION OF GOODS	保险金额 AMOUNT INSURED
N/M	4 CTNS	ART NO.42518	USD 1 700. 00

TOTAL AMOUNT INSURED 总保险金额：___US DOLLARS ONE THOUSAND SEVEN HUNDERD ONLY___

PREMIUM 保险费：___AS ARRANGED___   RATE 费率___AS ARRANGED PER CONVEYANCE 装载___ 运输工具:___S.S. EASTWIND V.009E___ SLG. ON OR ABT 开航日期.___JULY 4, 2023___ FROM 自 __ ___DALIAN CHINA___ TO 至 ___BUSHAN PORT, KOREA___

CONDITIONS 承保险别: Covering All Risks as per Institute Cargo Clauses (1.1.1963) and Risk of War as per Institute War Cargo Clause (11.3.80)

所 保 货 物,如 遇 出 险,本 公 司 凭 此 保 险 单 及 其 他 有 关 证 件 给 付 赔 款。

CLAIMS, IF ANY, PAYABLE ON SURRENDER OF THIS POLICY TOGETHER WITH OTHER RELE-VANT

所 保 货 物,如 发 生 本 保 险 单 项 下 负 责 赔 偿

DOCUMENTS. IN THE EVENT OF ACCIDENT WHEREBY LOSS OR DAMAGE MAY RESULT IN A CLAIM

的损失或事故,应立即通知本公司

UNDER THIS POLICY, IMMEDIATE NOTICE APPLYING FOR SURVEY MUST BE GIVEN TO THE

下述代理人查勘。

COMPANY'S AGENT AS MENTIONED HEREUNDER

NAME OF AGENTS:

CLAIM PAYABLE AT 赔付地点: __BUSHAN, KOREA__   中国人民保险公司

DATE 日期: __JULY 4 2023 DALIAN__   THE PEOPLE'S INSURANCE

               COMPANY OF CHINA

               大连分公司

               DALIAN BRANCH

Figure 10. 3 **Insurance Policy**

2. Contents of insurance document

The blank standard form of the insurance will be pre-printed by the insurer and be filled in and signed by the insured at the time when the latter decides to insure his goods with the former.

(1)The name and signature of the insurer. The insurer is the insurance company, the insurance underwriter or their agent. The insurer makes compensation to the insured against an insurance document. As the insurance document is normally preprinted on the insurer's letterhead, it is always pre-signed by the insurer.

(2)The name and signature of the insured. The insured is the party who pays premium and claims compensation from the insurer once a covered loss occurs to the insured goods. In international trade, an insurer can be made out to:

①The exporter: when the chosen shipping term, such as CIF, CIP etc. stipulates that it is the exporter's obligation to arrange insurance for the goods.

②The importer: when the chosen shipping term, such as FOB, CFR etc. implies that it is up to the importer to arrange insurance for the goods.

(3)Endorsement. Although the endorsement is made on the back of an insurance document, it is also an important item. By endorsement, the ownership of the insurance document is transferred to the endorsee who can file a claim to the insurer once a covered loss to the goods occurs during the transit. Claim often occurs in the country of the importer, so it is more convenient for the importer to file the claim. As the insured is made out differently, the requirements on endorsement also vary.

When the insured is the importer, no endorsement is required since the actual insured is the importer himself.

When the exporter is the insured, he will be required to endorse the document at the time when presentment is made. Under letter of credit, credit stipulations normally require the endorsee to be the issuing bank. The issuing bank will in turn endorse the document to the importer upon the latter's payment to retire the documents. Under other payment methods, however, the exporter may endorse the document to order or to the order of shipper, or directly to the importer who in turn will become the actual insured party. The exporter is not to endorse the documents to the bank without consent from the bank.

Endorsement of an insurance document can be made either in blank or in full. Under letter of credit, the insured should make proper endorsement as required by the stipulations in the credit.

(4) Description of goods. No detailed description is required on the insurance document and a general one will serve the purpose. However, other items such as the shipping mark, quantity and packing are to be made consistent with the invoice and other documents.

(5) The amount insured. The amount insured is the amount to be claimed by the insured. The amount will be expressed both in figures and in words. Normally the sum insured will be expressed in the same currency as that in the invoice and at 110% of the invoice value.

(6) The rate and the premium. Different rates will be decided by the insurer according to the types of goods, the types of risks, the types of vessels, the distance between the port of loading and the port of discharge and the target market. In practice, it usually appears as "as arranged" and need not to be filled in by the insured. Take All Risks for example, the rate can be 0.5%, 1.5% and 3.5% for the European and American market, the Asian market and the African market respectively.

The premium is the commission charged by the insurer on the insured, either the importer or the exporter. The premium is worked out against the formula below:

Premium = the insured amount × rate.

As the rate is not stated in the document, the premium will also appear as "as arranged".

(7) Conditions /coverage. Coverage specifies the risks chosen to cover the goods in transit and the insurer only makes compensation for the covered losses. Complete information of coverage consists of the type of the risk, its insurance clause and the effective date of that insurance clause.

（8）Shipping particulars. Shipping particulars include the information of the name of vessel, shipment date, the port of loading and the port of discharge. All the items concerning the shipping particulars should be made in consistent with the transport document such as bills of lading.

（9）Issuing date. The issuing date of the insurance document signifies the date on which the coverage takes effect. This date can be earlier than or the same as, but not later than the date of shipment (e.g. B/L date). A later issuing date of the insurance document indicates that the goods have been uninsured for some time and it is often found unacceptable on the part of the bank under letter of credit.

（10）Claim payable at. It should be clearly indicated in the insurance document as the place where the claim is payable as well as the name and address of the agent to whom the claim is to be directed.

The claim is normally made payable at the place of discharge, that is, in the country of the importer. The claim payable should be made in compliance with the stipulations in the credit when applicable.

（11）Full set. Normally, one original and one copy make a full set of insurance document.

3. Losses

Losses refer to the damage to the goods during the transit. According to the causes, losses can be divided into maritime losses and losses of external causes.

（1）Maritime losses. All natural disasters and accidents are referred to as maritime losses. Such disasters may happen when heavy weather, storm and lightning, earthquake, tsunami and flood cause accidents when the vessel or the cargo to be stranded, sunk or burned down. According to the degree of damage, the maritime losses can be further divided into total loss and partial loss.

The degree of damage is the most severe in a total loss where all the goods are lost or become worthless. It can take the following forms:

①Actual total loss. When the cargo has been completely destroyed or lost, it is referred to as actual total loss.

②Constructive total loss. A constructive total loss occurs when the damage may not reach the actual total loss but the repairing of the cargo will cost more than its original value.

Partial loss is also termed as "average" which indicates that some of the goods are lost or damaged but they still have some value or the necessary expenses to replace the goods will not exceed their original value. According to the causes of the average, partial loss can have the following subdivisions:

①General average (G.A.). It refers to a loss that one part of goods is intentionally sacrificed or the expenditure is voluntarily made by the captain in time of danger for the common benefit of the all parties concerned. General average will be inclusively sustained by all the parties involved.

②Particular average (P.A.). It refers to a loss that accidentally has occurred to part of the cargo and is not caused by the deliberate act of a party for the common benefit. Particular average will be sustained exclusively by the party upon whom the loss falls.

(2) Losses from external causes. Losses from external causes refer to losses brought about by causes other than maritime losses. They can be further divided into two types: general risks and special risks.

General risks to the goods are caused by mishandling in the process of transit. There are 11 subdivisions in general risks and a general understanding is necessary in connection with their names and nature.

①TPND: the initials for the risk of theft, pilferage and non-delivery. It refers to the risk that the cargo may be stolen in transit or may be lost or damaged due to improper unloading or some other types of mishandling, which leads to non-delivery.

②Risk of leakage: the risk of seepage and leakage of the liquid goods caused by the damaged container.

③Risk of clash and breakage: the risk of breakage of the fragile goods by vibration, clashing or pressing.

④Risk of hook damage: the risk of damage to the goods by the mishandling of a hook in the process of loading and unloading.

⑤Risk of fresh water or rain damage (FWRD): the risk of damage to the goods by being stained by fresh water or rain.

⑥Risk of shortage: the shortage of weight for the goods due to the broken external packing, not including, however, normal shortage of weight in transit.

⑦Risk of intermixture and contamination: the damage to the goods by being intermixed or contaminated with each other.

⑧Risk of taint of odor: damage to the goods by being tainted by odor of other goods.

⑨Risk of sweat and heating: the damage to the goods by sweat and heating caused by the sudden change of temperature or the malfunction of the ventilation on the vessel.

⑩Risk of rust: the damage to the goods by rust caused by contamination with sea water, not including goods getting rust by itself or due to its own flaw.

⑪Risk of breakage of packing: damage to the goods caused by rough handling in the process of loading and unloading.

Special risks refer to the damage or losses caused by political, military and administrative practices and procedures or any changes made in this regard. There are 9 types of special risks:

①War risk.

②Risk of strike riots and civil commotion (SRCC).

③Failure to deliver.

④Rejection.

⑤Aflatoxin.

⑥On deck.

⑦Import duty.

⑧Survey in customs clause.

⑨Survey at jetty clause.

4. Coverage

Various types of coverage are made to cover losses and they define the scope of liability of indemnity on the part of the insurer. In an insurance document, "conditions" and "risks" are sometimes two alternative terms to coverage. Coverage is divided into basic marine insurance coverage and additional risks.

(1) Basic marine insurance coverage. Three types of coverage will make the basic marine insurance coverage. "Basic" means that they can be insured on their own and is to be selected first before other additional types of coverage.

①Free from particular average (FPA). FPA means that the insurer is free from claiming for any particular average losses. It will provide coverage only for the total loss and general average of the partial loss. Compared with other types of risks, FPA provides the least coverage.

② With average (WA) or with particular average (WPA). WA, or with particular average (WPA), covers all the maritime losses, without being limited to particular average only. The scope of coverage of WA includes FPA plus particular average.

When WA does not cover small losses, it normally states the percentage over which the loss is to be covered. The minimum percentage of a loss to be covered is called a franchise. The percentage can be 3% or 5% of the insured amount. However, it is a tendency that a policy may not take the franchise into consideration. IOP, irrespective of percentage, means that the insurer provides complete coverage of the risk, no matter how small the loss is in monetary terms.

③All risks. All risks cover the maritime losses and the general risks, but not including special risks. All risks do not cover all the risks occurred in transit.

(2) Additional risks. Additional risks are made for the purpose to cover the 11 types of general risks and 9 types of special risks though each risk can be selected separately. Additional risks are so called because they cannot be chosen on their own. The insured can choose additional risks only after he has selected basic marine insurance coverage.

The insured should follow the rules below when selecting types of coverage:

①FPA, WA and all risks are not to be chosen at the same time in one insurance document since the coverage is overlapping with one another.

②When FPA or WA is chosen, the option is still open for selection from general risks and special risks.

③When all risks are chosen, the option is only open for selection from special risks since general risks are included in all risks.

Figure 10. 4 is an illustration of the rules.

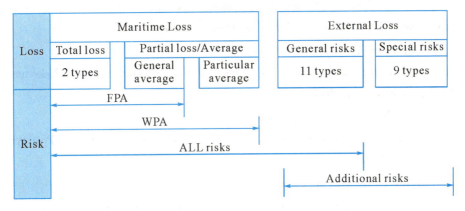

Figure 10. 4　**Rules for the Selection of Coverage**

5. Insurance clauses

In international insurance market, different marine associations have their own insurance clause concerning the risks and coverage.

(1) London Institute Cargo Clause. London Institute Cargo Clause (ICC) is constituted by the Institute of London Underwriters in 1912 and revised in 1982. ICC has found its wide application in the world insurance market as well as in Chi-

na. The institute has divided the coverage into two groups which are the basic Marine Risks and War/Strike Risks.

①Marine Risks.

Institute Cargo Clause A〔ICC（A）〕:this clause covers all risks.

Institute Cargo Clause B〔ICC（B）〕:this clause covers WA.

Institute Cargo Clause C〔ICC（C）〕:this clause covers FPA.

②War Strike Risks.

Institute War Clause － Cargo.

Institute Strikes Clauses － Cargo.

Malicious Damage Clauses.

（2）Ocean Marine Cargo Clause of the People's Insurance Company of China. Ocean Marine Cargo Clause of the People's Insurance Company of China（PICC）is constituted in 1972 and revised in 1976, 1981 and 1991. It can be divided as follows:

①Ocean Marine Cargo Insurance including FPA, WA and All Risks.

②Ocean Marine Insurance "Frozen Products".

③Ocean Marine Insurance "Wood oil in Bulk".

④Ocean Marin Cargo War Risks.

⑤Overland Transportation Cargo insurance "Train, Trucks" including Overland Transportation Risks and Overland Transportation All Risks.

⑥Overland Transportation Insurance "Frozen Products".

⑦Air Transportation Cargo Insurance including Air Transportation Risks and Air Transportation All Risks.

⑧Air Transportation Cargo War Risks.

⑨Parcel Post Insurance including Parcel Post Risks and Parcel Post All Risks.

⑩Parcel Post War Risks.

⑪Livestock & poultry insurance clause（by sea, land or air）.

Both the clauses in London Institute Cargo Clause（ICC）and Ocean Marine Cargo Clause of the People's Insurance Company of China（PICC）mostly are warehouse to warehouse clauses, whereby the goods are covered by insurance from the time they leave the consignor's warehouse to the time they reach the consignee's warehouse or the place of storage.

6. Classification of insurance documents

（1）Insurance policy. An insurance policy is a written contract between the insurance company (the insurer) and the trader (the insured), containing all the terms and conditions of the agreement with full details of the risks covered. The provisions concerning the rights and responsibilities of the two parties will normally be made on the reverse of the policy.

An insurance policy is a legal evidence of the agreement to insure and is the most popular insurance document in practice.

(2) Insurance certificate. An insurance certificate is a document similar to an insurance policy with the same details except that the provisions on the back of the policy are abbreviated. However, the provisions under an insurance policy are also applicable to an insurance certificate.

The insurance certificate takes the same effect as an insurance policy from the legal point of view. But, in some countries, the insured must have a policy before he can take a legal action against the insurer, where a certificate alone is insufficient to sue the insurer.

(3) Combined certificate. Combined certificate is an insurance certificate combined with a commercial invoice. The information about risks, insurance amount, and insurance No. etc. are indicated on the face of the commercial invoice.

(4) Open policy. When an exporter sells goods on a regular basis, he will normally arrange an open policy of insurance to cover all his exports during a specific time period at agreed terms and conditions. Each time a shipment is made, the insured (the exporter/importer) will declare the details of the shipment and pay a premium to the insurer. A certificate of insurance is then signed by the exporter who will in turn send one copy to the insurance company for his file and records.

The benefit of the open cover system is that it avoids the need to negotiate insurance terms each time a shipment is made and the necessity of issuing a separate policy for each individual shipment. In addition, if the exporter/importer does not give notice to the insurer due to careless omission, so long as the omission is not out of spite, the insurer shall renew and issue the insurance document. Even if the covered risks occur and goods are damaged or lost at the time of renewing and issuing, the insurance company shall make compensate.

However, if an exporter sells goods on a one-off basis, the exporter is to negotiate terms with the insurer and an insurance policy or insurance certificate will be issued. It should be noted that under UCP 600, open policy is not accepted by banks, unless stated otherwise therein.

Exercises for Chapter 10

Ⅰ. Multiple-choice Questions (It is possible to make more than one choice)

1. Under a documentary credit with no quantity specified and no partial shipment allowed, the bank will find the invoice amount less than USD 10 000 acceptable when the credit stipulates that the credit amount is _____.

A. for up to USD 10 000

B. for not exceeding USD 10 000

C. for maximum USD 10 000

D. to the extent of USD 10 000

2. Of the three basic risks, the coverage ranging from the least to the most should be like _____.

A. All Risks - W A - F P A

B. F P A - All Risks - W A

C. F P A - W A - All Risks

D. W A - F P A - All Risks

3. The correct combination(s) of risks is/are _____.

A. W A + Risk of hook damage + SRCC

B. TPND + War Risk

C. F P A + W A + SRCC

D. All Risks + Risk of taint of odor + War Risk

4. _____ is/are general risks.

A. Risk of leakage

B. On deck

C. Risk of shortage

D. Failure to deliver

5. According to the causes of the average, partial loss can be divided into _____.

A. general risks

B. special risks

C. particular average

D. general average

6. _____ details the packing and assortment of goods item by item and serves as the supplementary document to the commercial invoice.

A. Weight list

B. Combined certificate

C. Shipping mark

D. Packing list

II. Fill in the Blanks

1. Insurance documents include _____, _____, _____ and _____.

2. A commercial invoice is the accounting document by which the _____ claims payment from the _____ for the value of goods or services being supplied.

3. _____ indicates that the insurer provides complete coverage of the risk, no matter how small the loss is in monetary terms.

4. _____ is the amount to be claimed by the insured; whereas _____ is the commission charged by the insurer on the insured.

5. _____ refers to a loss that accidentally has occurred to part of the cargo and is not caused by the deliberate act of a party for the common benefit.

6. When the insured is _____, no endorsement is required to be made to the insurance document.

III. Case Questions

Case One

A Chinese textile trading company exported 1 500 silk shirts to a German company, CIF Hamburg. Shortly after the signing of the sales contract, the Chinese company arranged FPA with the insurer for the goods and an insurance policy was issued accordingly. On Feb. 20, the ship carrying the goods set sail. On Feb. 25, unfortunately, a heavy storm at sea damaged the ship seriously and on Feb. 26, the ship sank. On March 20, the Chinese textile trading company contacted the insurance company for compensation. But the claim was turned down and the insurer argued that they should not be held responsible because the loss to the goods was caused by partial loss, a risk not to be covered under FPA.

Questions:

1. What is FPA?

2. Should the insurance company honor the claim? Why or why not?

Case Two

A sales contract was established or the sale of leather gloves between Company ABC, Shanghai, the exporter, and Company XYZ, Stockholm, the importer, under CIF Stockholm covering P.I.C.C OCEAN MARINE CARGO CLAUSE ALL RISKS. The factory had dehumidified the gloves to the minimum before packed them with kraft paper and into double corrugated paper cartons and then into a 20-foot container. On arrival in Stockholm, the test results showed that all gloves were damaged by wet mildew stains and they were also discolored. The loss was estimated at USD 80 000. It was also found out that at the time of shipment, the weather was not extremely hot in the port of shipment, nor was it extremely cold in the port of destination. It was a normal journey and no abnormality occurred in transit.

Questions:

1. Should the insurance company make compensation for the goods? Why?

2. Should Company XYZ, Stockholm make payment for the goods? Why?

3. What should Company ABC, Chengdu do?

Ⅳ. Practice Questions

Practice One

A credit stipulates that China National Arts & Crafts Imp. & Exp. Corp., Chengdu, the insured, make special endorsement to transfer the insurance policy to The United Overseas Bank of Singapore, Singapore.

Practice Two

Fill in the black form of COMMERCIAL INVOICE based on the given information below:

1. L/C information to the ADVISING BANK.

FROM: NATIONAL COMMERCIAL BANK, NEW YORK, USA.

TO: BANK OF CHINA, GUANGDONG, CHINA.

DATE: 5 MARCH 2023.

L/C NO: GBD 6 688.

L/C AMOUNT: USD 28 820. 00.

APPLICANT: AMERICAN IMPORT & EXPORT COMPANY, NEW YORK.

BENEFICIARY: HONGSHUN TRADING COMPANY, GUANGZHOU.

DRAFTS TO BE DRAWN ON US AT SIGHT FOR 100 PCT OF INVOICE VALUE.

PARTIAL SHIPMENT: NOT ALLOWED.

MERCHADISE: 48 000 CANS OF MEILING BRAND CANNED ORANGE JAM, 250 GRM/CAN, 12 CANS IN A CARTON.

UNIT PRICE: USD 6. 55/CTN CIF NEW YORK.

COUNTRY OF ORIGIN: P.R. CHINA.

DOCUMENTS REQUIRED: COMMERCIAL INVOICE IN 3 COPIES DATED THE SAME DATE AS THAT OF L/C ISSUANCE DATE INDICATING COUNTRY

OF ORIGIN OF THE GOODS AND CERTIFIED TO BE TRUE AND CORRECT,
INDICATING CONTRACT NO. AND L/C NO.

ADDITIONAL CONDITIONS： ALL DOCUMENTS MUST INDICATE SHIP-
PING MARKS AS JAM IN DIMAOND NEW YORK.

2. Additional information.

INVOICE NO： HSH 123/2023.

CONTRACT NO： SC 888.

CONTRACT DATE： 10 JAN 2023.

THE AUTHORIAED SIGNATORY： LI MING.

GOODS SHOWN IN THE DELIVERY ORDER： 52 800 CANS OF MEILING
BRAND CANNED ORANGE JAM.

SHIPPING INFORMATION SHOWN IN B/L： FROM GUANGZHOU TO
NEW YORK.

VESSEL NAME： PUDONG V. 125.

SHIPPING MARK：

```
SC888
NEW YORK
C/NO. 1-4,400
```

HONGSHUN TRADING COMPANY
GUANGZHOU, CHINA
COMMERCIAL INVOICE

To:	Invoice No.: _____
	Invoice Date:_____
	S/C No.:_____
	S/C Date:_____
From:_____	To:_____
L/C No.:_____ L/C Date:_____	Issuing By:_____ _____

Marks & Numbers	Number & Package Description of Goods	Quantity	Unit Price	Amount
	TOTAL AMOUNT:			

....
SIGNATURE

AUTHOURISED

V. Extended Discussions

A Chinese exporter established a sales contract under an irrevocable sight credit CIF Rotterdam with an importer in Netherland. According the contract, the shipment was to be made in June. The importer's bank timely issued the credit and sent it to the exporter via his bank. After receiving the credit, the Chinese exporter made shipment accordingly. When making documentation, "the description of the goods" and "quantity" in the commercial documents were shown as below:

SAVING ENERGY 22W 2 000 PCS

SAVING ENERGY 15W 2 000 PCS

SAVING ENERGY 10W 2 000 PCS

The description of goods in the insurance policy was shown in general term as SAVING ENERGY.

After documentation, the Chinese exporter presented documents to the bank for payment, but the payment was refused by the issuing bank on that the documents presented were not complying with the credit stipulations and that the commercial invoice and insurance policy were not in agreement with each other.

Questions:

1. Is it justifiable for the issuing bank to refuse payment? Give your supporting reasons.

2. What inspiration can we get from this case?

Chapter 11　Transport Documents

Objectives

◇Learn the major types of transport documents.

◇Learn the definition, functions, contents and classification of marine bills of lading.

◇Learn the definition and functions of sea waybill.

◇Learn the definition, functions and contents of air waybill.

◇Learn the differences between B/L and waybill.

Transport documents include marine bills of lading, sea waybill, air waybill, road, rail or inland waterway transport documents, multimodal combined transport documents, and the courier receipt, post receipt or certificate of posting.

Section 1　Marine Bills of Lading

When the goods are transported by sea, a marine bill of lading is one of the most important shipping documents.

1. Definition of marine bill of lading

B/L, a marine bill of lading, is a transport document which is issued and signed by the carrier, the shipping company or his agent, and given to the shipper acknowledging that goods have been received for shipment to a particular destination and stating the terms on which the goods are to be carried. Figure 11. 1 is a sample of Marine B/L.

Shipper SHANGHAI IMPORT & EXPORT TRADE CORPARATION 1123 ZHONGSHAN ROAD SHANGHAI CHINA		B/L NO. HJSHBI 142939 *ORIGINAL* 中国对外贸易运输总公司 CHINA NATIONAL FOREIGN TRADE TRANSPORT CORPORATION 直运或转船提单 BILL OF LADING DIRECT OR WITH TRANSSHIPMENT
Consignee or order TO THE ORDER OF SHIPPER		SHIPPED on board in apparent good order and condition (unless otherwise indicated) the goods or packages specified herein and to be discharged or the mentioned port of discharge of as near there as the vessel may safely get and be always afloat.
Notify party TKAMRA CORPORATION 302 KAWARA MACH OSAKA JAPAN		THE WEIGHT, measure, marks and numbers, quality, contents and value, being particulars furnished by the Shipper, are not checked by the Carrier on loading. THE SHIPPER, Consignee and the Holder of this Bill of Lading hereby expressly accept and agree to all printed , written or stamped
Pre-carriage by	Port of loading SHANGHAI	provisions, exceptions and conditions ofthis Bill of Loading, including those on the back hereof.
Vessel PUDONG V.503	Port of trans-shipment	IN WITNESS where of the number of original Bill of Lading stated below have been signed, one of which being accomplished, the other (s) to be void.
Port of discharge OSAKA	Final destination	

Container Seal No. or marks and Nos.	Number and kind of packages Designation of goods	Gross weight (kgs)	Measurement (m^3)
GATU0506118 T.C TXT233 OSAKA C/NO.1-300	100% COTTON COLOUR WEAVE-SHIRT SAY THREE HUNDRED(300) CARTONS ONLY TOTAL ONE 40'CONTAINER CY TO CY FREIGHT PREPAID	3 300 KGS ON BOARD	66 CBM

DRAWN UNDER JAPANESE ISSUING BANK, OSAKA, IRREVOCABLE DOCUMENTARY CREDIT NUMBER TX0081 DATED JAN 15, 2023			
REGARDING TRANSSHIPMENT INFORMATION PLEASE CONTACT		Freight and charge FREIGHT PREPAID	
Ex. rate	Prepaid at	Freight payable at SHANGHAI	Place and date of issue SHANGHAI FEB. 18, 2023
	Total prepaid	Number of original Bs/L THREE	Signed for or on behalf of the Master as Agent

Figure 11.1 **Marine B/L**

2. Functions of marine bill of lading

Bill of lading performs all the four functions as follows:

(1)A receipt of goods. A bill of lading serves as a receipt for goods shipped, acknowledging that the goods have been received in said quality, quantity and in apparent good order for shipment on board a vessel. It is the responsibility of the carrier to deliver the goods accordingly to the consignee named in the bill of lading.

(2)A contract of carriage. A bill of lading is a contract of carriage made between the carrier and the shipper. The detailed provisions are made on the reverse of the document which stipulate the rights and responsibilities of the two parties. On the one hand, it is the responsibility of the carrier to transport the goods by sea and make the delivery to the consignee. On the other hand, the obligation for the shipper is to consign the goods in apparent good order and in conformity with packing requirements of the shipment.

(3)A title document. A bill of lading is a title document. The legal owner of the bill of lading is the legal owner of the goods. The carrier releases the goods against the production of the original bill of lading. Original bills of lading are issued in a set and the number of originals should be indicated on the bill of lading.

As any one original B/L will enable the possessor to obtain the goods, possession of a full set is required to secure the ownership of the goods. The exporter is deemed to make delivery once he has submitted B/L. As a result, on the basis that B/L has become the title document, constructive delivery has come into being.

(4) A negotiable document. As a title document, B/L is a negotiable document for ownership transfer. When B/L is transferred, the ownership over the goods has also been transferred. Any transferee who takes possession of an endorsed B/L for value obtains a good title to it.

3. Contents of B/L

(1)The name of the carrier. The carrier is a shipping company who can either be the owner of the ship or the hirer of the vessel. In the case when the contract of carriage is made through an agent of the shipping company, the carrier should be the shipping company instead of the agent. It is the shipping company who enters into the contract of carriage with the shipper.

(2)The name of the shipper. The shipper is also called the consignor who dispatches the goods to the carrier. He can either be the exporter or the exporter's agent. Under letter of credit, the shipper is the beneficiary of the credit.

(3)The name of the consignee. The consignee is the party who has the right to take delivery of the goods at the stated destination. The consignee can be made out differently by which B/L takes different orders:

①Demonstrative order. A bill of lading so made can be transferred by endorsement and delivery.

Firstly, "to order" and "to the order of shipper". "To order" indicates that the ownership of goods belong to the exporter/shipper. In effect, it is the same as "to the order of shipper". The B/L so made is usually required by L/C or used in collection.

Under L/C, when presenting the documents, the exporter is required by the terms and conditions of the credit to endorse the B/L to the bank who in turn endorses the B/L to the importer against the latter's payment. In this way, the ownership of the B/L is eventually transferred to the importer to get the goods. In practice, bills of lading under letter of credit may be required to be made out to order and blank endorsement.

Under collection, when presenting the documents, the exporter endorses the B/L specially to the importer and the bank will release the B/L to the importer against his payment (D/P) or his acceptance (D/A).

Secondly, "to the order of the issuing bank". Under a letter of credit, the credit may stipulate that the B/L is made out to the order of the issuing bank. When B/L is so made, the bank has absolute ownership over the goods. Once the importer makes payment, the bank is to endorse the B/L specially to transfer the ownership to the importer to get the goods.

This kind of B/L is normally used under letter of credit only. Under collection, however, B/L is not to be made out to the order of a bank before getting the express consent from the bank.

Thirdly, "to the order of the importer". When a bill of lading is made out to the order of the importer, no endorsement is required and the importer can take delivery from the carrier against an original B/L.

A B/L so made is normally used under O/A or payment in advance. Such a bill of lading is not to be used under L/C. As banks do not have the ownership over the B/L, they will be reluctant to accept the B/L so made.

As the exporter does not maintain the ownership of goods when a B/L is so made, it is recommended that such a B/L is not to be used in collection, either.

②Restrictive order. When a B/L is made out to a named consignee, the importer, it is a restrictive order. In this case, the importer can obtain the goods by presenting the original bill of lading upon his identification is proved.

This type of B/L is used under O/A or payment in advance with the purpose to enable the importer to obtain goods through least formalities. It is not to be used under L/C and it is not recommended to be used in collection.

(4) The notify party. The notify party is the person whom the shipping company will notify upon arrival of the goods, usually he is the importer or his agent. When the importer is not shown to be the consignee in a B/L, information of importer is to be given in the notify party.

When a B/L is made out "to order" "to the order of the shipper" "to the order of the issuing bank", the name and address of the importer or those of his agent is indicated in the notify party. However, when a B/L is made out "to the order of the importer" or "to the name consignee (importer)", the notify party is to be left blank.

(5) The name of the carrying vessel and the voyage No.. The name of the vessel is to be given in a B/L and the voyage is abbreviated as "V".

(6) The port of shipment and the port of destination. The port of shipment is also called the port of loading. The port of destination is also referred to as the port of discharge or the port of unloading.

When a B/L is made for marine transport only, the name of the two ports only will serve the purpose. On other occasions, however, the B/L may be made for combined transport shipment where door to door service is provided. In this case, the place of receipt and the final place of delivery are given in addition to those of the two ports.

(7) Marks and numbers. The marks and numbers should be made consistent with those on other documents such as the invoice or the packing list, etc. The same marks will appear on the boxes, cartons or cases where the goods are contained to indicate that they are covered by the same bill of lading.

(8) Description of goods. A general or a brief description of the goods is sufficient to be given in a B/L. If the transaction is under L/C, the credit number, the name of the issuing bank and the credit issuing dated should be indicated in the B/L as well.

(9) Total packages. This shows how many boxes/cartons/cases into which the goods are packed.

(10) Freight charges. Freight charges can be made as prepaid or collect. Freight prepaid indicates that the freight costs have already been paid by the exporter, which is usually the case under INCOTERMS like C & F or CIF. Freight collect means that the payment of the sea-freight is due at the destination and is to be collected from the importer on arrival, which is, for example, the case under INCOTERMS like FAS or FOB.

(11) Number of original B/L and the carrier's signature. This item indicates how many original bills of lading makes a full set. In practice, full set may contain 2, 3 or 4 originals.

An original bill of lading is one which is signed by the by the shipping company or his agent. For an original B/L, the very word "original" should be clearly indicated thereon to distinguish itself from a copy. The carrier often issues unsigned copies for record purpose, these unsigned copies are not title documents.

(12) The B/L issuing date. The B/L issuing date is the date on which the carrier received the goods for shipment or loaded the goods on board the ship.

If the transaction is under letter of credit, the B/L date should comply with the stipulations of the credit and is usually to be made between the invoice date and the latest date of shipment.

4. Major types of marine bill of lading

(1) According to whether the goods are on board the ship.

①On board B/L or shipped B/L. An on board B/L bears the wordings "Shipped in apparent good order and condition ..." which confirms that the exporter has delivered the goods on board the vessel at the port of shipment.

Date of issuance of a shipped B/L will be deemed to be the date of shipment. An onboard B/L is a satisfactory type to the shipper for an early bank settlement.

②A received for shipment B/L. A received B/L bears the wordings "Received in apparent good order and condition ..." which merely expresses that the goods have been handed over to the carrier and are in his custody.

The absence of the word "shipped" will make the bill of lading unacceptable by the bank for settlement unless provisions have been made in the credit otherwise. For this reason, A received for shipment B/L needs to be converted to an on board B/L by adding an on board notation with the name of the vessel on which the goods have been loaded as well as the on board dated clearly indicated. For a received for shipment B/L, the date of the on board notation, rather than the date of issuance, is the date of shipment.

(2) According to the conditions of the shipped goods.

①Clean B/L. When the statement "Shipped/Received in apparent good order and condition ..." is not modified by the carrier, such a bill of lading is regarded a "clean" B/L.

When a carrier finds no defective conditions concerning the goods or their packaging, he will issue a clean B/L. A clean and on board bill of lading is most favored by banks for settlement under letter of credit.

②Unclean B/L. If the carrier dose not agree with the statement "Shipped/Received in apparent good order and condition ...", he will add a clause on the B/L indicating the defective condition of the goods or their packaging. Such a clause will make the bill of lading an "unclean" B/L. Under L/C, an unclean bill of lading is not acceptable to the bank.

（3）According to the order of the B/L

①Negotiable B/L. Negotiable B/L refers to the demonstrative order B/L. This type of bill can be made to order, to the order of shipper, to the order of the issuing bank and to the order of the importer.

An order B/L can be transferred by endorsement and delivery. Negotiable B/L has found wide application in payment methods.

②Non-negotiable B/L. Non-negotiable B/L refers to the one made out to a named consignee, usually the importer. It is also called straight B/L.

Non-negotiable B/L is often used in open account or payment in advance, and on other occasions, in non-commercial basis transactions.

（4）According to whether the goods are transshipped.

①Direct B/L. Direct B/L is issued when the goods are shipped by one vessel direct from the port of loading to the port of discharge without transshipment being made on the route.

When the transaction is under L/C and if the credit bears such indications as "transshipment not allowed", a direct B/L is required to be presented.

②Transshipment B/L. Transshipment B/L is issued when there is no direct service between the port of loading and the port of discharge where at least two vessels will be involved. The goods will be transshipped from one vessel to another at the port of transshipment.

When the transaction is under L/C and if the credit bears such indications as "transshipment allowed", transshipment B/L is to be issued by the carrier and will be acceptable to the bank.

（5）According to whether the details of the contract of carriage are stated

①Long form B/L. The long form B/L is a complete form of bill of lading with full details of the contract of carriage printed on the reverse of the B/L.

②Short form B/L. The short form B/L is a regular bill of lading except that the detailed information of the contract of the carriage is omitted and is subject to that contained in the carrier's long form bill of lading. Banks will normally accept this type of B/L unless stated otherwise the in the credit.

（6）Liner B/L. The liner B/L is issued by the carrier when the goods are shipped on regular line vessels with scheduled route and reserved berth at destination.

The most obvious advantage of the liner B/L is that the carrier can inform the shipper, before or shortly after the sea voyage, the estimated date of departure

(ETD) and the estimated time of arrival (ETA). The importer will, in turn, be informed that the goods are dispatched and will arrive on a set date. Liner B/L is a popular type in practice.

(7) Container B/L. With the container shipping service, a container can be hauled, by a forwarder, to the premises of the exporter's and those of the importer's, thus the goods can be loaded by the exporter and unloaded by the importer.

A container B/L is issued when the goods are packed in either less than a container load (LCL) or full container load (FCL), by which the carrier provides the shipping service from a container yard in the exporting country to a container yard in the importing country.

Container bills of lading can be issued to cover goods being transported on a traditional port to port basis, or they can be issued for combined transportation to provide door to door service. However, not all the seaport can offer container shipping services.

(8) Multimodal transport documents (MTD). According to UCP 600, multimodal transport documents (MTD) are newly developed shipping documents to cover at least two different modes of transport from the place of departure to the place of final destination by sea, inland waterway, air, rail or road.

In the single mode of transportation under a marine bill of lading, the carrier only provides port to port service; whereas in multi-modes transportation under MTD, the carrier can provide door to door service. Since the 1980s, marine bills of lading have been made applicable to either marine transportation of port to port shipment or to combined transport shipment of door to door service.

Parties to MTD are:

①Multimodal transport operator (MTO). The multimodal transport operator (MTO) issues the MTD and will be responsible for the whole journey, no matter whether he arranges the whole journey or just a part of the transportation. MTO corresponds to the carrier of marine bill of lading.

②Consignor. The consignor consigns the goods for transportation to the multimodal transport operator and with whom the MTD is established. The consignor corresponds to the shipper of marine bill of lading.

③Consignee. The consignee is the party entitled to take delivery of the transported goods at destination. Similar to consignee of marine bill of lading, the consignee of MTD can also be made out to demonstrative order or restrictive order. Table 11.1 shows the way MTD consignee is made and the negotiability of the MTD.

Table 11. 1   **The Consignee and Negotiability of MTD**

Items	Consignee	Negotiability	The way to negotiate
Demonstrative order	To order	Negotiable	Endorsement is required
	To the order of shipper		
	To the order of ××× Bank		
	To the order of ××× Co.		
Restrictive order	To ××× Co.	Not negotiable	NA

It is found from Table 11. 1 that when the consignee is made out to demonstrative order, the MTD is negotiable whereas when the consignee is made out to restrictive order, the MTD is non-negotiable. In addition, when the transaction is under L/C, the endorsement should be made according to the stipulations in the credit.

The differences between MTD and marine bill of lading are shown in Table 11. 2.

Table 11. 2   **Differences between MTD and Marine B/L**

Marine Bills of Lading (B/L)	Multimodal Transport Documents (MTD)
The issuer must be a carrier, namely a shipping company	The issuer is the Multimodal transport operator (MTO) who can either be the carrier or a manager of the whole journey
The carrier provides a port to port shipment for a journey of a single mode of marine transportation	The MTO provides a door to door service for a journey which involves at least two modes of transportation
The responsibility of the carrier is from the time when the goods are received or loaded onboard the ship at the port of loading to the time when they are discharged from the ship at the port of destination	The MTO assumes the liability from the place where the goods are taken into his charge in the place of receipt to the place of the final destination
The carrier is neither liable for the loss or damages to the goods before they are received or put onboard the ship at the port of shipment, nor after they are discharged from the vessel at the port of destination	The MTO is responsible for the loss or damages to the goods whenever and wherever occurred in the course of the whole journey

(9) Through B/L. Through B/L resembles an MTD except that it is issued by the first carrier who is only responsible for his part of the journey.

It should be remembered that the classification of the B/L is based on their various functions and there is no clear-cut among them. It is allowed that one B/L can simultaneously take several types in combination.

Section 2　Sea Waybill

A sea waybill is a transport document issued by the shipping company as an alternative to marine B/L.

A sea waybill only performs two functions of B/L, namely as a receipt of goods and a contract of carriage. However, unlike B/L, a sea waybill is not a document of title and it is not negotiable. As a result, a sea waybill can only be made out to a named consignee — the importer.

When an exporter agrees to sell the goods on open account terms, payment in advance or on a non-commercial basis, it follows that the exporter may ask the shipping company for a sea waybill rather than B/L with the purpose for the importer to obtain the goods with minimum formalities and in the possible shortest time. Waybills can meet this requirement because the goods will be released by the carrier to the named consignee (the importer) against identification proven and a facsimile copy of the sea waybill, without requiring the presentment of the original sea waybill.

Compared with straight B/L, sea waybill is also made out to the named consignee, the importer. However, straight B/L is a document of title and the goods are to be released at the presentment of an original straight B/L. But a sea waybill is not a title document and the original sea waybill may not be required by the carrier for the release of the goods.

Section 3　Air Waybill

1. Definition and functions of air waybill

Air waybill (AWB) is issued by an airline when goods are dispatched by air. It is a contract between the carrier (the airline) and the shipper.

Similar to a sea waybill, air waybill also performs two functions only, namely as a receipt of goods and as a contract of carriage. Unlike marine B/L, AWB is not a document of title and is not negotiable. Upon arrivals at the airport of destination, goods are to be released to the consignee against identification proven and a facsimile copy of the air waybill, without requiring the presentment of an original air waybill. Figure 11. 2 is a sample of air waybill.

Shipper's Name and Address	shipper's Account Number	Not Negotiable Air Waybill
SPEIRS AND WILLIAMS LTD., SHANGHAI BRANCH 320 ZHONGSHAN ROAD, SHANGHAI,CHINA		中国民航　　CAAC ISSUED BY THE CIVIL AVIATION ADMINISTRATION OF CHINA Beijing, China Copies 1, 2 and 3 of this Air Waybill are originals and have the same validity
Consignee's Name and Address	Consignee's Account Number	It is agreed that the goods described herein are accepted in apparent good order and condition (except as noted) for carriage SUBJECT TO THE CONTIDITIONS OF CONTRCT ON THE REVERSE HEREOF. ALL GOODS MAY BE CARRIED BY ANY OTHER MEANS INCLUDING ROAD OR ANY OTHER CARRIER UNLESS SPECIFIC CONTRARY INSTRUCTIONS ARE GIVEN HEREON BY THE SHIPPER. THE SHIPPER'S ATTENTION IS DRAWN TO THE NOTICE CONCERNING CARRIER'S LIMITATION OF LIABILITY. Shipper may increase such limitation of liability by declaring a higher value for carriage and paying a supplemental charge if required.
BANK OF CHINA, HONG KONG WAICHAI BRANCH L/C NO. 01-192545		

Issuing Carrier's Agent Name and City	Accounting Information
RTW SHIPPING, SHANGHAI	02100 8843 2

Agent's IATA Code 93-5-3386	Account No. CS 123678	

Airport of Departure (Addr. Of First Carrier) and Requested Routing SHANGHAI

To	By First Carrier	Routing and Destination/	to	by	to	by	Currency	WT/VAL PRD	COLL	Other PRD	COLL	Declared value for carriage	Declared Value for Customs
HK	CA						CNY	X		X		NVD	

Airport Destination	Flight/Date	For Carrier Use Only Flight/Date	Amount of insurance	Insurance: —If carrier offers insurance and such insurance is reque sted in accordance with the conditions thereof, indicate amount to be insured in figures in box marked "amount of insurance"
HONGKONG	CA509/	16 OCT	NIL	

Handling Information

13 CTNS. NOTIFYING: PHILMEN INT. CO. E2, 3/F HANG FUNG IND. BLDG., PHASE-22G HOK YUEN ST. KLN

No. of Pieces RCP	Gross Weight	Kg lb	Rate Class Commodity Item No.	Chargeable weight	Rate Charge	Total	Name and quantity of Goods (incl. Dimensions or Volume)
13	390	K	4401	398.5	2.89	1 151.67	13 WOODEN CASES CONTAINING 26 CEMENT SPARY GUNS MODEL 435 SWG HONGKONG NO.435 C/NO. 1-13

Prepaid	Weight Charges	Collect	Other Charges
1 151.67			
	Valuation Charge		
	Tax		
	Total Other Charges Due Agent		Shipper certifies that the particulars on the face hereof are correct and that insofar as any part of the consignment contains dangerous goods, such part is properly described by nam3e and is in proper condit ion for carriage by air according to the applicable Dangerous Goods Regulations.
	Total Other Charges Due Carrier		
49.85			SPEIRS AND WILLIAMS LTD., SHANGHAI BRANCH
			Signature of Shipper or his agent
Total Prepaid	Total Collect		
1 201.52			
Currency Conversion Rate	CC Charges in Dest. Currency		2023-10-16 SHANGHAI SHANGHAI RTW SHIPPING, Executed on (date) of (place) Signature of Issuing Carrier or his Agent
For Carrier's Use Only at destination	Charges at Destination	Total Collect Charges	

999-1950 3022

Figure 11. 2　Air Waybill

2. Contents of AWB

（1）Name of the carrier. The carrier is the airline and the issuer of the AWB who enters the air transport document with the shipper.

The word non-negotiable on the AWB indicates clearly that it is not a title document.

（2）The name and address of the shipper. The shipper is normally the exporter.

（3）The name and address of the consignee. The consignee can be made out to one the following ways：

①The importer, it is normally used in O/A and payment in advance.

②The issuing bank, it is normally used in letter of credit. Under collection, the AWB can be made out to a bank only after getting the latter's consent and permission.

③An agent of the exporter, it is normally used under collection.

When the consignee is made out in the last two cases, the issuing bank or the exporter's agent can press the importer into payment. After payment is made, the bank or the exporter's agent will instruct the airline to place the goods at the disposal of the importer.

（4）Carrier's agent. To facilitate the business in different cities or countries, the carrier has its agent in various places. The information concerning the agent's name, its code and account No are indicated in the AWB.

（5）The names of the airports. The name of the airport of departure and the name of the airport of the destination together with the flight no. should be furnished accordingly.

（6）The declared value for customs purposes. If there are no goods to be declared for customs purposes, NVD is to be indicated, meaning no value declared.

（7）Handling information. Handling information corresponds to the notify party on a bill of lading. It should be entered with the name and address of the importer when he is not shown as the consignee. Otherwise, this box should be left blank.

（8）Marks. The marks perform the same function as the shipping marks on a bill of lading. The same marks will appear on all the boxes/cartons/cases and on all the other relevant documents.

（9）Brief description of the goods. Normally the nature and quantity of goods with the weight and dimensions or volume are normally indicated.

（10）Air freight charges. Similar to the freight charges in bills of lading, air freight charges are indicated as prepaid or collect. Prepaid indicates that the freight costs have already been paid by the exporter while collect means they are to be due at the destination and to be paid by the importer. The amount of the air freight charges is normally shown on the AWB. To indicate prepaid or collect should be made consistent with the chosen INCOTERM.

(11) Signature of shippers or his agent. The shipper should certify that the particulars on the face of the AWB are correct and if any part of the consignment contains dangerous parts, such part is properly described by name and is in proper condition for carriage by air according to the applicable *Dangerous Goods Regulations*.

(12) The issuing date. The issuing date is the date on which the goods are received by the airline and in his custody. Normally, this is also the flight date.

(13) The signature of the carrier or his agent. AWB is to be signed by the carrier or by his agent on his behalf. Any signature by an agent must indicate that the agent has signed for or on behalf of the carrier.

(14) The full set. Normally, 3 originals, 6 copies and 3 extra copies make a full set of AWB. The 1st original is for the carrier, the 2nd one is for the consignee and the 3rd one is for the shipper.

If the transaction is under L/C and according to UCP600, the 3rd original for the shipper is to be presented to the bank, even if a credit may require full set of AWB to be presented.

Section 4   Other Transport Documents

Other transport documents include road, rail, inland waterway transport documents, and courier receipt, post receipt, and certificate of posting. These types of transport documents perform two functions only. They are a receipt of the goods by the carrier and a contract of carriage. But they are not documents of title and they are not negotiable.

1. Road, rail, inland waterway transport documents

When the goods are sent by truck, a road waybill is to be issued. *The Convention on Contract for the International Carriage for Goods by Road* (CMR) was established in 1956 in Geneva by 17 European Countries. China is not a signatory country of CMR. For this reason, it should be noted that although CMR consignment note is also a land transport document, if a transaction is shipped by a Chinese carrier and under a L/C stipulating the presentment of CMR, the Chinese exporter should require the credit to be amended because a CMR cannot be issued by a Chinese carrier.

When the goods are shipped by inland waterway transport, an inland waterway waybill is to be issued.

When the goods are sent by railway, a railway bill will be issued. It is subject to *the International Convention for the Transport of Goods by Rail* (CIM) established in some form in 1893 with additional protocol made in 1970 after various revisions to meet the needs of the international trade of the modern time.

These transportation documents, however named, contain the following major items:

(1) Date of issuing. According to UCP 600, the issuing date of the transport document is deemed to be the shipment date, unless the waybill contains a different dated reception, stamp, an indication of the date of receipt or a date of shipment.

(2) Name and address of the shipper and consignee. Waybills must be made out to a named consignee and not to be made out to order, to the order of the shipper, to the order of xxx bank or to the order of xxx Co., unless the credit stipulates otherwise.

(3) Place of receiving the goods and the place of delivery. According to UCP 600, the transport document should indicate the place of receiving goods and the place of destination stated in the credit.

(4) Description of goods. General description of goods will be sufficient, together with their quantity expressed in weight or measurement, indicating credit number, credit issuing bank and the issuing date.

(5) Marks and numbers. The marks and numbers should be made consistent with those on other documents and the same marks and numbers shall appear on the boxes, cartons or cases where the goods are contained.

(6) Carriage charges. The transport document should indicate the charges to be borne by the shipper or the consignee.

(7) Instructions for customs and other formalities. The shipper should provide his information for customs clearance and other formalities.

(8) Originals. According to UCP 600, the transport document must appear to be the original for consignor or shipper or bear no mark indicating for whom the document has been prepared. A rail waybill marked "duplicate" will be accepted

as an original. A rail or inland waterway waybill will be accepted as an original whether marked as original or not. In the absence of an indication on the transport document as to the number of originals issued, the number presented will be deemed to constitute a full set.

(9)Signing of the transport document. According to UCP 600, the transport document must appear to indicate the name of the carrier, and be signed by the carrier or named agent for or on behalf of the carrier, or indicate receipt of goods by signature, stamp or notation by the carrier or a named agent for or on behalf of the carrier.

Any signature, stamp or notation of receipt of the goods by the carrier or agent must be identified as that of the carrier or agent.

Any signature, stamp or notation of receipt of the goods by the agent must indicate that the agent has signed or acted for or on behalf of the carrier.

If a rail transport document does not identify the carrier, any signature or stamp of the railway company will be accepted as evidence of the document being signed by the carrier.

2. Courier receipt, post receipt, or certificate of posting

When the goods are sent through the post office, by a courier or an expedited delivery service, a post receipt,a courier receipt or a certificate of posting will be issued. In recent years, with the fast development of e-commerce, small on-line transactions are getting increasingly popular in international trade.

The worldwide famous expedite services are EMS, DHL, UPS and FedEx. This mode of postal transportation will be chosen when the goods are of a great value, or of a small quantity such as samples and when the speed of delivery is of the greatest concern. Courier service and the expedited services can provide desk-to-desk service.

According to UCP 600, a postal transport receipt, however named, evidencing receipt of goods for transport, must appear to:

(1)Indicate the name of the courier service and be stamped or signed by the named courier service at the place from which the credit states the goods are to be shipped; and indicate a date of pick-up or receipt or wording to this effect. This date will be deemed to be the date of shipment.

(2)A requirement that courier charges are to be paid or prepaid may be satisfied by a transport document issued by a courier service evidencing that courier charges are for the account of a party other than the consignee.

A post receipt or certificate of posting, however named, evidencing receipt of goods for transport, must appear to be stamped or signed and dated at the place from which the credit states the goods are to be shipped. The date will be deemed to be the date of shipment.

Exercises for Chapter 11

Ⅰ. Multiple-choice Questions (It is possible to make more than one choice)

1. A bill of lading serves as _____.

A. contract of carriage

B. title to the goods

C. unconditional payment order

D. a receipt of goods

2. A bill of lading made out _____ is/are non-negotiable.

A. to ABC Co., Chengdu

B. to the order of XYZ Co., Shanghai

C. to the order of Bank of China, Beijing

D. to order

3. Under which trade terms should the column of freight and charge marked as "freight collect"?

A. CIF

B. CFR

C. FAS

D. FOB

4. Which of the following types of B/L are unacceptable to banks? _____

A. Long form B/L

B. Received for shipment B/L

C. Unclean B/L

D. Container B/L

5. Sea waybill may be used when _____.

A. the importer wants to transfer the document to another buyer

B. the transaction is for non-commercial purpose

C. the payment is made in advance

D. the payment term is open account

6. _____ is/are not title documents.

A. Air waybill

B. MTD made out to order

C. Rail waybill

D. Courier receipt

Ⅱ. Fill in the Blanks

1. A bill of lading has two basic parties, namely the _____ and _____ .

2. According to the indication about the goods on the bill of lading, there are _____ B/L and _____ B/L.

3. A sea waybill must be consigned to a _____ consignee, to whom goods are delivered upon proof of his identification without surrendering _____ sea waybill. It is convenient to goods which will arrive at _____ before the sea waybill reaches the consignee.

4. _____ issues the MTD and will be responsible for the whole journey, no matter whether he arranges the whole journey or just a part of the transportation.

5. By an air waybill, goods are delivered to a named _____ whereas in a demonstrative order MTD, goods are delivered to a person against an original document duly _____ .

6. A rail or inland waterway transport document will be accepted as an original whether _____ as an original or not.

Ⅲ. Case Questions

Case One

A credit states: "Full sets of clean shipped on board marine bills of lading made out to the order of ABC Bank, Shanghai."

Questions:

1. Indicate the type of the required B/L.

2. How to indicate the consignee in the B/L?

3. Is endorsement needed at the time of taking delivery? If no, state your reasons. If yes, who should make the endorsement?

Case Two

A documentary negotiable credit issued for a transaction under CIF New York between Company A, Beijing, the exporter, and Company B, New York, the importer, indicates the following terms:

1. COMMERCIAL INVOICE IN 6 ORIGINALS

2. FULL SET CLEAN ON BOARD MARINE BILLS OF LADING MADE OUT TO ORDER AND BLANK ENDORSED, MARKED "FREIGHT PREPAID"

3. INSURANCE POLICY COVERING P. I. C. C. OECAN CARGO CLAUSES ALL RISKS AND WAR RISKS DATED 1ˢᵀ JANUARY, 1981.

The credit also states that it is subject to the Uniform Customs and Practice for Documentary Credits [2007 Revision. International Chamber of Commerce. Paris, France. Publication No. 600 ("UCP")].

After receiving the credit, Company A, Beijing makes shipment accordingly, obtains marine bills of lading in 3 originals and presents the stipulated documents to the negotiating bank who makes negotiation and then forwards the documents to the issuing bank for reimbursement. But the issuing bank refuses to make reimbursement on account of the following discrepancies:

1. The Commercial Invoices are not signed.

2. Only one original B/L, not a full set is presented, which does not comply with the terms and conditions of the credit.

3. The insured amount is made the same as that of the Commercial Invoice.

Questions: Analyze whether the discrepancies pointed out by the Issuing Bank are all proper and reasonable? State your supporting reasons.

IV. Practice Questions

A credit issued by Barclays Bank Ltd., London at the request of Allen Co., London in favor of China National Arts & Crafts Imp. & Exp. Corp., Chengdu stipulates that the B/L must be made out to order and endorsed to the order of the issuing bank.

Questions:

1. Please make the shipper's endorsement as per credit stipulation.

2. Please make the issuing bank's special endorsement to the importer.

V. Extended Discussions

In 2023, a Chinese company AAA made a deal with an American buyer for a batch of toys at USD 31 500 under a negotiable credit. BBB Company wanted to have 1/3 original named consignee bills of lading to be sent directly to them. BBB Company also said that this was a very popular and accepted practice in America and if their request was not met, the deal would be cancelled. Considering that the Christmas season was drawing near, the contract value was relatively big and the L/C was a safe payment method to the exporter, AAA Company finally agreed to their request.

After shipment was made, AAA Company sent one copy of original named consignee bills of lading to BBB Company as agreed and submitted documents immediately at the same time to the bank for negotiation. More than ten days later,

AAA asked BBB about the payment and BBB explained that the payment was under processing. More than 20 days later, not having received any payment, AAA pushed for payment again but BBB asked for the payment to be delayed for a few more days because their money was tight at the time being. But what was actually going on was that BBB had already taken delivery of goods against that original B/L. More than 30 days later, AAA pushed again, but BBB again found some excuses to put off the payment till finally, AAA could not reach BBB any longer.

Questions:

1. Explain the meaning of "soft clauses" in a credit.

2. Make a comment on the statement "Ethics is more important than knowledge". You may give concrete examples to support your opinion.

Chapter 12　Certificate of Origin, Inspection Certificate and Documents Examination

Objectives

◇Learn the definition and major forms of certificate of origin.

◇Learn the major contents of GSP form.

◇Learn the definition, types and contents of inspection certificate.

◇Learn the definitions and functions of consular invoice, customs invoice and proforma invoice.

◇Learn the principles of documents examination under L/C.

Section 1　Certificate of Origin

1. Definition and functions of certificate of origin

A certificate of origin is a document certifying that the goods originated from a particular country. It is served as the basis for exercising discriminatory tariffs, implementing quotas and import control, ensuring that the quality of the imports meet the standards of the country of origin and conforms to the sanitation requirements of the importing country.

Some countries may insist that a certificate of origin should be produced before goods will be allowed into the country. Certificate of origin can be issued by an independent party such as inspection bureau or a chamber of commerce, with the relevant details of the certificate will be supplied by the exporter. In China, the independent party can be the General Administration of customs of the People's Republic of China or the China Council for the Promotion of International Trade

（CCPIT）. Figure 12. 1 is a certificate of origin issued by CCPIT.

1. Exporter (full name and address) TIANJIN ANIMAL BY–PRODUCT IMP & EXP CORP 80 YANTAI STR., TIANJIN CHINA	CERTIFICATION NO: A2–489C
2. Consignee (full name, address, country) CRISTAL WILLIAMS LTD., 1445 BROADWAY, #0803 NEW YORK,N.Y. 10018 USA	CERTIFICATE OF ORIGIN OF THE PEOPLE'S REPUBLIC OF CHINA
3. Means of transport and route FROM TIANJIN TO NEW YORK BY SEA	5. For Certifying authority use only
4. County / region of destination U.S.A.	

6. Marks and numbers	7. Number and kind of packages; description of goods	8. H.S. Code	9. Quantity	10. Number and date of invoices
CR 612 WILLIAMS C/NO. 1–9	NINE BALES WHITE DEHAIRED COATWOOL	51. 05	953 NET	CR013073061 NOV. 10th 2023

11. Declaration by the exporter The undersigned hereby declares that the above details and documents are correct; that all the goods were produced in China and that they comply with the Rules of Origin of the People's Republic of China TIANJIN ANIMAL BY–PRODUCT IMP & EXP CORP 80 YANTAI STR., TIANJIN CHINA	12. Certification It is hereby certified that the declaration by the exporter is correct CHINA COUNCIL FOR THE PROMOTION OF INTERNATIONAL TRADE, SHANGHAI, NOV. 10th 2023
Place and date, signature and stamp of authorized signatory	Place and date, signature and stamp of certifying authority

Figure 12. 1   **Certificated of Origin Issued by CCPIT**

If a credit does not indicate an issuing party, the certificate of origin can be issued by the exporter or manufacturer of the merchandize themselves, or to be combined with commercial invoice incorporated the exporter's declaration that, for example, "we (a Chinese exporter) hereby certify that the goods shipped are of

Chinese Origin" or wordings of the same effect. Figure 12.2 is a certificate of origin issued by the exporter.

CERTIFICATE OF ORIGIN

DATE _____

1. THE NAME OF EXPORTER _____

ADDRESS _____

2. NAME OF IMPORTER OR CONSIGNEE _____

ADDRESS _____

3. THIS IS TO CERTIFY THAT THE MERCHANDISE DESCRIBED IS GROWN/PRO-CESSED/MANUFACTURED IN _____ (COUNTRY, PALCE)

MARKS & NOS	DESCRITION OF GOODS	QUANTITY	REMARKS

THE ABOVE DESCRIBED MERCHANDISE HAS BEEN LOAD _____ (NAME OF CARRIER) ON/ABOUT _____ (DATE) DESTINED FOR _____ PORT.

4. THIS CERTIFICATE SHALL INVALID IN CASE OF ANY UNAUTHORIZED ALTERAT-TION.

ISSUED BY _____

Figure 12.2   Certificate of Origin Issued by the Exporter

As is often the case, letter of credit will usually stipulate an independent third party as the issuer of the certificate of origin. In this case, the certificate should be made on the issuer's company letterhead and should be made into a separate document which is not to be combined with any other document.

2. Generalized system of preferences form（GSP）

（1）Definition and functions of GSP. General System of Preference（GSP）form is another widely used form of certificate of origin. GSP is a treatment of customs duties preference imposed by the developed countries on the goods from the developing countries, with the purpose of increasing in the developing countries the revenue of export and speeding up their industrialization and their economic growth. It signifies:

①General. This favorable treatment is granted to every developing country.

②Non-discriminatory. The preference is conducted on a non-discriminatory basis.

③Non-reciprocal. The preferences are granted by the developed country to the developing country without any requirements of a counter preference from the developing countries. Any exporter in a developing country will obtain this favorable treatment after he has made out the certificate on a GSP form.

A GSP certificate of origin takes standard forms worldwide and should be issued by an authorized entity in the exporting country. Figure 12. 3 is a sample of GSP certificate of origin.

<table>
<tr><td colspan="3">1. Goods consigned from (Exporter business name, address, country)
SHANGHAI XIAGUANG IMPORT AND EXPORT CORPORATION
1123 ZHONGSHANROAD, SHANGHA, CHINA</td><td colspan="3">Reference NO.

GENERALIZED SYSTEM OF PREFERENCES
CERTIFICATE OF ORIGIN
(Combined declaration andcertificate)
FORM A</td></tr>
<tr><td colspan="3">2. Goods consigned to (Consignee's name, address, country)
YABAHARA TRADE CORPORTAION
302 KAWARA MACH, OSAKA, JAPAN</td><td colspan="3">Issued in: THE PEOPLE'S REPUBLIC OF CHINA
- -
(country)
See Notes overleaf</td></tr>
<tr><td colspan="3">3. Means of transport and route (as far as known)

FROM SHANGHAI TO OSAKA
BY S.S</td><td colspan="3">4. Forcertifying authority use only</td></tr>
<tr><td>5. Item number</td><td>6. Marks and Numbers of packages</td><td>7. Number and Kind of packages; description of goods</td><td>8. Origin criterion (see Notes overleaf)</td><td>9. Gross weight or other quantity</td><td>10. Number and date of invoices</td></tr>
<tr><td>1</td><td>YTC
50053
OSAKA
C/NO. 1-300
(in triangle)</td><td>LADIES SILK SHIRT SAY TOTAL TRHEE HUNDRED CARTONS ONLY
* * * * * * *
* * * * * * * *
* *</td><td>"P"</td><td>G.W.
3 300 KGS</td><td>YTC50053
FEB.01,2023</td></tr>
<tr><td colspan="3">11. Certification
  It is hereby certified, on the basis of control carried out, that the declaration by the exporter is correct.
ENTRY-EXIT INSPECTION AND QUARANTINE OF THE PEOPLE'S REPUBLIC OF CHINA, SHANGHAI
(company stamp)

SHANGHAI JUNE 05,2023(signature)
- - - - - - - - - - - - - - - - - - - -
Place and date, signature and stamp of certifying authority</td><td colspan="3">12. Declaration by the exporter
  The undersigned hereby declares that the above details and statements are correct; that all the goods were produced in

CHINA
- - - - - - - - - - - - - - - - - - - -
(county)
and that they comply with the origin requirementsspecified for those goods in the Generalized System of Preferences for goods exported to

JAPAN
- - - - - - - - - - - - - - - - - - - -
(importing country)
SHANGHAI XIAGUANG IMPORT AND EXPORT CORPOARATION, SHANHAI (company stamp)
SHANGHAI JUNE 04, 2023 (signature)
- - - - - - - - - - - - - - - - - - - -
Place and date, signature of authorized signatory</td></tr>
</table>

NOTES

Ⅰ. Countries which accept Form A for the purposes of the generalized system of preferences (GSP):

		European Economic Community	
Australia	New Zealand		
Austria	Norway	Belgium	Ireland
Bulgaria	Poland	Denmark	Italy
Canada	Sweden	France	Luxembourg
Czechoslovakia	Switzerland	Germany	Netherlands
Finland	Soviet Union	Greece	United kingdom
Hungary	United states	Spain	Portugal
Japan			

Full details of the conditions covering admission to the GSP in these countries and obtainable from the designated authorities in the exporting preference-receiving countries or from the customs authorities of the preference-giving countries listed above. An information note is also obtainable from the UNCTAD secretariat.

Ⅱ. General conditions:

To qualify for preference, products must:

(a) fall within a description of products eligible for preference in the country of destination. The description entered on the form must be sufficiently detailed to enable the products to be identified by the customs officers examining them.

(b) Comply with the rules of origin of the country of destination. Each article in a consignment must qualify separately in its own right; and

(c) Comply with the consignment conditions specified by the country of destination. In general, products must be consigned direct from the country of exportation to the country of destination but most preference-giving countries accept passage through intermediate countries subject to certain conditions. (for Australia, direct consignment is not necessary.)

Ⅲ. Entries to be made in Box 8

Preference products must either by wholly obtained in accordance with the rules of the country of destination or sufficiently worked or processed to fulfill the requirements of that country's origin rules.

(a) Products sufficiently obtained: for single country shipments, enter the letter-P—in Box 8 (for Australia or New Zealand Box 8 may be left blank).

(b) Products sufficient worked or processed: for export to the countries specified below, the entry in Box 8 should be as follows:

(1) United States of America: for single country shipments, enter the letter -Y—in Box 8, for shipments from recognized associations of countries, enter the letter -Z— followed by the sum of the cost or value of the domestic materials and the direct cost of processing, expressed as a percentage of the ex-factory price of the exported products; (example -Y—35% or -Z—35%)

(2) Canada: for products which meet origin criteria from working or processing in more than one eligible least developed country, enter letter -G—in Box 8; otherwise -F—

(3) Austria, Finland, Japan, Norway, Sweden, Switzerland and the European Economic Community:

enter the letter-W—in Box 8 followed by the Customs Co-operation Council Nomenclature tariff heading of the exported product. (example -W—98. 02).

(4) Bulgaria, Czechoslovakia, Hungary, Poland and the USSR: for products which include value added in the exporting preference-receiving country, enter the letter-Y—in Box 8 followed by the value of imported materials and components expressed as a percentage of the f.o.b. price of the exported products (example -Y—45%); for products obtained in a preference-receiving country and worked or processed in one or more than such countries, enter -PK—

(5) Austria and New Zealand: completion of Box 8 is not required. It is sufficient that a declaration be properly made in Box 12.

* For Australia, the main requirement is the exporter's declaration on the normal commercial invoice Form A, accompanied by the normal commercial invoice, is an acceptable alternative, but official certification is required.

Figure 12. 3　**GSP Certificate of Origin**

(2) Contents of the GSP. For most exports, the Generalized System of Preferences Form A is to be used. However, for some distinctive products such as textile products or textile handicrafts, the credit may indicate that the Certificate of Origin for Textile Products or the Certificate in Regard to Textile Handicrafts and Traditional Textile Products of the Cottage Industry to be presented respectively instead of the GSP Form A.

Items 4 and 11 of GSP Form A are to be filled in by the issuing authority and the other items are to be filled in by the exporter：

In the first box of the right-hand column，"Certificate No." is to enter the running number provided by the issuing authority. "Issued in" is to enter the name of the country where the GSP Form A is issued. It should be noted that the country name should be made in full，for example，THE PEOPLE'S REPUBLIC OF CHINA.

①Goods consigned from (exporter's business name, address, country). A GSP form requires the complete name of the country of origin to be supplied. For a Chinese exporter，the address should be spelt in Hanyu Pinyin，the Chinese phonetic alphabet.

If goods are routed through other traders in intermediary country (region)，indicate "VIA" behind the exporter，then fill in the name, address and country (region) of the transit trader.

②Goods consigned to (Consignee's name, address, country). A GSP form requires the complete name of the country of the importer to be supplied. The bank generally accepts the consignee to be made to be the L/C applicant, the notify party in the B/L, the addressee of the commercial invoice. If the credit stipulates the consignee in a transport document is not to be clearly indicated, the bank generally also allow the consignee to be made as "to whom it may concern" or "to order".

It should be noted that the name of the middlemen is not to be indicated here because the consignee should be in the preference-giving countries.

③Means of transport and route (as far as known). Details of the shipment to which the certificate relates，including the issuing date of B/L or other transport documents，mode of transportation by sea，land or air，and the place of shipment, the place of transit and the place of the final destination.

Transit transportation via a third country is to be indicated when the goods are exported to such countries as Switzerland or Austria who do not have a coastline. For example，"On Oct 6, 2023 by sea from SHA to Hamburg transit to Switzerland."

④For certifying authority use only. This is to be filled in by the issuing authority.

⑤Item number. For Individual commodity，enter the number "1" or to be left blank. For different types of commodities，enter the number "1""2""3"，and so on for each commodity.

⑥Marks and numbers of packages. Shipping marks should be shown in complete form，including the text，pattern and package number and should not be simply indicated as "AS PER INVOICE NO..." or "AS PER B/L NO...". For a Chinese export, the shipping marks should not indicate that the goods shipped are produced in places outside P. R. of China.

⑦Number and kind of packages; description of goods. Number of packages should be indicated both in Arabic numbers and in English. For example, "ONE HUNDERED AND TWENTY (120) CARTONS OF WORKING GLOVES". If goods are packed, the type of package should be indicated. If the goods are not packed, "NUDE CARGO" "IN BULK" or "HANGING GARMENTS" should be properly indicated.

The description of goods should indicate the specific name of the commodity, the detail of which should be accurately found in commodity code HS 8 digits. Brand name or article number need not to be supplied, as these have nothing to do with the commodity code and the customs tariff.

⑧Origin criterion (see notes overleaf). This is a key item to be checked by the importing customs. Different letters indicate whether the goods are purely domestic products or not. For example, the letter "P" means a 100% local production, while "W" indicates that the products contain foreign ingredients or components, the value of which is below 50% of that of the FOB price. "F" indicates that the value of foreign contents is below 40% of that of the ex-factory price.

For goods to be exported to Australia and New Zealand, the item can be left blank.

⑨Gross weight or other quantity. Goods should be indicated by normal measurement unit, such as pieces/pcs, dozen/doz, or set, etc. When the goods are measured by weight, G.W., gross weight, is to be indicated. N.W. is to be indicated for goods being measured by net weight only.

⑩Number and date of invoices. The month in the date should be indicated in English, either in complete or abbreviated form. The date indicated in this item should be the same as that in the commercial invoice and is not to be later than the shipment date. This item cannot be left blank.

⑪Certification. The issuing authority is to certify in this item that the declaration by the exporter is correct. The issuer is to indicate the place and date of issue, and sign and stamp the GSP form after checking the items filled in by the exporter. The signature and the stamp shall not overlap each other.

The issuing date is not to be earlier than that of the commercial invoice indicated in item 10, nor is it made earlier than the declaration date in item 12. In addition, it is to be made no later than the shipment date.

⑫ Declaration by the exporter. For a Chinese export, the manufacturing country should be indicated as "CHINA". The name of the importing country should be consistent with the information supplied in item 3. The date can be the same date as, but not earlier than the invoice date indicated in item 10.

In a GSP form, a separate declaration by the exporter independent from the certification of the issuer is required. The exporter certifies that the merchandize is grown / processed / manufactured in that country.

Section 2　Inspection Certificate

1. Definition of inspection certificate

An inspection certificate is a document to be issued by an independent party inspecting the commodity to ensure the quality, quantity, packing and other conditions of the export. An inspection certificate may be issued either under the legal requirement of regulations of the authorities of the exporting/importing country or be issued at the request of the exporter, the importer, the carrier or the insurer for notarial survey.

In international goods transaction, for the fulfillment of sales contract, the inspection can be carried out by the exporter, the importer, a third-party surveyor, or a government inspection bureau. The inspection entity may take various names as authentic surveyor, swore measurer or laboratory, etc. and they can be official, semi-official or non-official organizations. Food and Drug Administration (FDA), in the USA, Societe General De Surveillance (SGS) in Geneva, Switzerland and Lloyd's Surveyor in the United Kingdom are recognized international authorized inspection entities. In China, the official issuer of the certificate is the General Administration of Quality Supervision Inspection and Quarantine (AQSIQ), the former China Exit and Entry Inspection & Quarantine Bureau (CIQ).

Compulsory legal inspection is to be carried out when goods inspection is by the law and regulations and under the requirement of the authorities of the exporting/importing country. In this case, goods inspection should be carried out by an official inspection entity or a third independent authorized inspection organization designated by the authorities of the exporting/importing country.

2. Functions and types of inspection certificate

Inspection and quarantine of import and export commodities constitutes an important part in international trade transactions. Inspection certificate performs the following functions. Firstly, the certificate is the documentary evidence to customs examination, taxation, clearance and duty preferences. Secondly, handling customs declaration and inspection procedures in a timely manner is to guarantee that the goods will be shipped in conformity with the quality, quantity weight or packing and within the agreed time period as stated in the sales contract. Thirdly, the certificate is part of the documents stipulated under L/C to be presented to banks for settlement and payment. Furthermore, the certificate is a document against which the importer can return the goods or lodge a claim against the liable parties, the exporter, the carrier or the insurer, etc.

Different types of inspection certificate are made to inspect the different aspects of the exports as required. The major types are as follows:

(1) Inspection certificate of quality.

(2) Inspection certificate of quantity.

(3) Inspection certificate of weight.

(4) Inspection certificate of health.

(5) Inspection certificate of veterinary.

(6) Inspection certificate of value.

(7) Inspection certificate of plant quarantine.

(8) Inspection certificate of disinfection.

(9) Inspection certificate of sanitation.

(10) Inspection certificate of fumigation.

(11) Inspection certificate of conditioned weight.

3. Contents of inspection certificate

A certificate of inspection should be made on the issuer's company letterhead. Figure 12. 4 is a sample of inspection certificate of quality.

中华人民共和国出入境检验检疫
ENTRY-EXIT INSPECTION AND QUARANTINE
OF THE PEOPLE'S REPUBLIC OF CHINA

共一页 第 1 页 Page 1 of 1
编号 No. : 210100223013678

CERTIFICATE OF QUALITY 品质证书

发货人
Consignor HONG YUN GROUP COMPANY LIMITED
收货人
Consignee ＊＊＊
品名 CHINESE LIGHT SPECKLED KIDNEY BEANS
Description of Goods 2009 CROP.(INNER MONGOLIA ORIGIN)

报检数量/重量
Quantity/Weight Declared -108. 575 - M/T
包装种类及数量
Number and Type of Packages -2 150- GUNNY BAGS
运输工具
Means of Conveyance VICTORY V. 146E

标记及号码
Mark & No.
N/M

This is to certify that we, did, at the request of consignor, attend at the warehouse of commodity on 17 Nov, 2023. The representative sample was drawn at random for inspection according to the stipulations of the L/C, the results were as follows:
　　　　　　　　　Moisture 14. 0 PCT
　　　　　　　　　Admixture 0. 1 PCT
　　　　　　　　　Imperfectgrains, other color beans and water stain beans 4. 8 PCT
Conclusion:The quality of the above commodity conform with the stipulations of the L/C No. 1201N10028
＊ ＊
印章　　签证地点 Place of Issue　DALIAN, CHINA　　签证日期 Date of Issue
18 Nov, 2023
Official Stamp
授权签字人 Authorized Officer Wang Xiaoyan　签名　Signature

我们已尽最大能力实施上述检验,不能因为我们签发本证书而免除卖方或其他方面根据合同和法律所承担的产品质量和其他责任。All inspections are carried out conscientiously to the best of our knowledge and ability. This certificate does not in any respect absolve the seller and other related parties from his contractual and legal obligations especially when product quality is concerned.

Figure 12. 4　**Inspection Certificate of Quality**

（1）Name of certificate and No.. The name of inspection should be specified as required by L/C, e.g. Certificate of Quality. The 15-digit code is to be provided by the issuer. The first 6 digits are the number for the Inspection and Quarantine

Bureau, the 7th digit is for the inspection type, such as, code "2" is for the exports, and the 8th and 9th digits are for the issuing year and the digits 10th to 15th are the running number.

(2) Consignor. Consignor should be made out to be the "shipper" of the B/L. As the exporter/beneficiary is generally the shipper, so the consignor will normally show the exporter's name.

(3) Consignee. The consignee is generally made out "to whom it may concern" or "to order". It is also acceptable that this item is left blank or entering " ＊ ＊ ＊ ", without showing the importer's name as the consignee. One reason is that the inspection certificate is a notarial certification legally valid for any holder. The other reason is to make the certificate consistent with the B/L especially when the B/L is made out to order.

Under letter of credit, this item can show the importer's name as the consignee, unless the credit stipulates otherwise.

(4) Description of goods. Description of goods is to be made consistent with the credit stipulations and the commercial invoice. It is acceptable to describe the goods in general term.

(5) Marks & No.. Marks and No. is to be made consistent with the stipulations of the credit and those in the other commercial documents. N/M is entered when no shipping mark is made for the shipment.

(6) Quantity/weight declared. This item is to be made consistent with commercial invoice and transport document. When the goods are priced by net weight, this is to enter the net weight; when by gross weight, enter the gross weight of the goods.

(7) Number & type of package. This item is to be made consistent with those in the commercial invoice and transport document. When the goods are bulk cargo, enter "in bulk" and then add the weight.

(8) Means of conveyance. This item is to enter the name of means of conveyance.

(9) Results of inspection. This is the core part in the certificate. The results stated in the results are made according to the requirement of the inspection as weight, quality and quantity etc. of the goods. The results are given by the issuer after checking and inspection and should conform to the inspection requirements stipulated in the credit. The issuer must comply and indicate the manufacturing month of the goods if it is required and stipulated by the credit.

The beneficiary shall inform the inspection entity of the credit stipulations and requirements so that the required type of certificate in compliance with the credit can be issued. Do not enter the certificate any extra and needless information not required by the credit and, if any stipulation cannot be complied with by the issuing party, the beneficiary should have credit amended.

Enter " ＊ ＊ ＊ ＊ ＊ ＊ " at the end of the message.

(10) Place of issue. Enter the business address of the issuing entity of the inspection and quarantine certificate.

(11) Date of issue. The issuing date is provided by the issuer based on the date of inspection. On one hand, the inspection certificate should not be made later than the B/L date. On the other hand, it should not be made too early as the certificate may be expired before documents are presented.

A credit may require, for example, "This Certificate should indicate that inspection had been carried out just before loading." In practice, the issuing date can be made the same or a little earlier than the shipment date.

(12) Stamp and signature, The certificate is to be signed by the chief inspector and stamped by the issuer. If a specific insurance organization is specified in the credit, the certificated must be made by that organization only. If a credit does not make that indication, the certificate can be issued, signed and stamped by any authorized and eligible inspection entity.

Section 3   Other Commercial Documents

1. Consular invoice

A consular invoice is a special type of invoice issued by the embassy or consulate of the importing country located in the exporting country. A consular invoice may be required by some countries as a basic shipping document to present. A consular invoice can both increase the revenue for the consulate, as well as perform the functions of the certificate of origin to serve as a basis for levying discriminatory duties on different countries and to prevent dumping of the foreign goods. It can also take the place of the import permit. A high tariff or even an embargo will be imposed for the shipment without a consular invoice.

Consular invoice is parallel to commercial invoice. It is an official document with fixed format to be available from the consulate. The common practice is, if required by the credit, that the consular is to make statements of certification, for a fee to be borne by the exporter, on the commercial invoice to verify the origin of the goods. If this is the case, the exporter should take this charge into consideration when calculating the export price.

As to the exporter, it is both time-consuming and costly to apply for a consular invoice, especially when there is no consulate located in the city of the exporter's premises. For this reason, the exporter, e.g. in China may ask to have the consular invoice to be issued by the China Councils for the promotion of International Trade.

2. Customs invoice

A customs invoice is a special invoice made and specified by the customs of the importing country and to be issued by the exporter by filling in a given form specified by the customs of the importing country. It usually takes three different forms:

Firstly, customs invoice.

Secondly, combined certificate of value and origin.

Thirdly, certified Invoice in accordance with ×××customs regulations.

The customs invoice format varies from country to country but the content provided by the customs invoice must be exactly consistent with that in the commercial invoice. Except the frequently used Canada Customs Invoice, other types of customs invoice are rare.

Similar to the consular invoice, a customs invoice can perform the following functions:

(1) To certify the origin of goods against which differential tariffs will be levied by the customs of the importing country.

(2) To ensure that the value of the imports is not lower than their domestic value so that dumping will be prevented.

To serve these purposes, though varied in forms according to the different customs regulations of the importing countries, a customs invoice will feature the origin of the goods with detailed information on the price formation. For example, if the price term is FOB, then the net export price stated should be worked out by the FOB price less the packing charges and inland transportation charges or other applicable charges incurred during the process of the exportation. Under CIF, the net export price would further less out the freight and insurance premium. It should be noted that the domestic price must be lower than the net export price.

The difference between a customs invoice and a consular invoice is not in effects but in procedures. A customs invoice can be printed in the exporting country conforming to the original form of the importing country while consular invoice will be made and printed by the embassy or the consulate of the importing country. This means that it is not necessary for the exporter to pay a fee to obtain a customs invoice while he is asked for a fee in the case of a consular invoice.

3. Pro-forma invoice

Proforma invoice, also known as preliminary invoice, is often issued before the establishing a sales contract between the exporter the importer. It normally takes the same form and with the same items as those in a commercial invoice except the word "pro-forma" clearly indicated therein. Figure 12. 5 is a sample of pro forma invoice

ABC IMPORT & EXPORT CORPORATION, CHENGDU
12 SHAWAN STREET, JINGNIU DISTRICT, CHENGDU, CHINA
TEL: 028-87873456   FAX: 028-87873457

PRO-FORMA INVOICE

TO:
CUDA TEXTILES TRADING
BLK43,05-06,
MARSILING RISE
733180 SINGPORE

PRO FORMA INVOICE NO.: P2023AE0930-8
PURCHASE ORDER NO.:
DATE: 9 MAY 2023

FROM:
SHANGHAI PORT

TO:
SINGAPORE PORT

ART NO.	COMMODITY & DESCRIPTION	QUANTITY	UNIT PRICE & TERMS	AMOUNT
			FOB SHANGHAI	
1652	WOMENS SILK SHIRT	2 311 PCS	USD 2. 850/PC	USD 6 586. 35
1750	WOMENS SILK SHIRT	2 517 PCS	USD 3. 100/PC	USD 7 802. 70
		4 828 PCS		USD 14 389. 05 ===========

TOTAL VALUE: SAY US DOLLARS: FOURTEEN THOUSAND THREE HUNDERED AND EIGHTY NINE AND CENTS FIVE ONLY

TERMS AND CONDITONS:
● TERMS OF PAYMENT: L/C AT SIGHT
● PACKING: TO BE PACKED IN CARTTON 23CM × 30CM × 45CM
● DATE OF SHIPMENT: ON OR BEFORE 30 AUG. 2023
● TOLERANCE: 5% MORE OR LESS ALLOWED

CONFIRMED AND ACCPTED BY (BUYER)

SELLER:

SIGNATUE   DATE

SIGNATURE

Figure 12. 5   Pro-forma Invoice

Functions of pro-forma invoice are as follows:

(1) The pro-forma invoice can be supplied by the exporter as a quotation to the importer. The price and sales terms will be negotiated between the two parties and once the terms are accepted by the importer, there will be a firm contract to be made in accordance of the contents in the pro-forma invoice, against which commercial invoice will also be made accordingly. In practice, the exporter will be required to certify on the commercial invoice such wordings: "the goods are in accordance with the pro-forma invoice No..."

(2) As L/C is normally established before a commercial invoice, a pro-forma invoice is required by the importer when applying for the import license or foreign exchange permit. Also, letter of credit is generally established with reference to the pro-forma invoice rather than the commercial invoice. In practice, the credit will bear a statement such as "as per pro-forma invoice No ... dated ...". In this case, the commercial invoice should also quote the same indication.

(3) Under advance payment where payment is required before the shipment, the exporter will normally forward a pro-forma invoice instead of a commercial invoice for the advancement.

(4) Under consignment where goods are in the hands of a middleman, a pro-forma invoice will serve as a reference to him in his offer to a potential buyer. And a commercial invoice will be established only after a potential buyer is available.

(5) In international bidding, a pro-forma invoice is required by the party inviting tender from the tenderer. The party inviting tender will make comparisons against pro-form invoices submitted from different tenderer before deciding and establishing the contract with the most competitive candidate.

Though closely related to commercial invoice, pro-forma invoice is not a formal invoice to be used in payment settlement. It is only a price offer, has no legal binding upon the seller or the buyer and is to be replaced by commercial invoice after the establishment of sales contract.

4. Manufacturer invoice

Manufacturer invoice is issued by the manufacturer to the exporter for the sale of goods. It is priced in local currency and represents the products' price in the domestic market of the exporting country.

The purpose of requiring the submission of manufacturer invoice in the credit stipulation is to check whether there is dumping behavior in the sale and determine whether to impose "anti-dumping duties" on the export commodity. Manufacturer invoice has the following basic items:

(1) The words "Manufacturer Invoice" in bold font should be clearly indicated on the top of the document.

(2) It should be made out to the exporter.

(3) The issuing date of the manufacturer invoice should be earlier than that of the commercial invoice.

(4) Commodity name, specification, quantity, number of packages must be consistent with those in the commercial invoice.

(5) Price shall be made in the local currency of the exporting country, to be less than the quoted price in the corresponding commercial invoice, e.g. 8.5% or 9% discount of the FOB basis.

(6) When goods leave the factory, there is no need to bear shipping marks on the ex-factory products or in the manufacturer Invoice, unless the credit states otherwise.

(7) Manufacturer Invoice is to be signed by the authorized official in the factory and stamped and issued by the manufacturer.

5. Shipping advice

After loading the goods on board on the ship or onto the carrying vehicle, the exporter should timely send shipping advice to the buyer, so that the latter can make necessary preparation and get ready to make payment, retire documents, go through formalities for import customs clearance and take delivery of the goods.

Especially under CFR/CPT, the seller is responsible for signing the contract of carriage and paying the cost of carriage, whereas the insurance of the cargo is to be arranged by the buyer himself. As soon as the goods are loaded on board the vessel/delivered to the carrier, the risks are transferred from the seller to the buyer. Therefore, the seller must send shipping advice sufficient in details and in time to enable the buyer to insure the goods on time. Otherwise, the seller is held responsible for any loss to the goods thus incurred.

The content of the shipping advice generally includes the order number or contract number, L/C number, the bill of lading number, commodity name, quantity, total amount and shipping mark, port/place of loading, name of vessel/vehicle, ETD and ETA, etc. Figure 12.7 is a sample of shipping advice.

```
ABC IMPORT & EXPORT CORPORATION, CHENGDU
12 SHAWAN STREET, JINGNIU DISTRICT, CHENGDU, CHINA
         TEL: 028-87873456        FAX: 028-87873457

                        SHIPPING ADVICE


To:                              No.:
                                 Date:
                                 L/C No. :
                                 Insurance Cover Note No.:
                                 Port of Shipment:
                                 Port of Destination:
                                 Date of Shipment:
                                 Vessel Name:

SHIPPING MARK      DESCRIPTION OF GOODS      QUANTITY/WEIGHT




SPECIAL CONDITIONS IN SHIPPING ADVICE


                                        SIGNATURE AND STAMP
```

Figure 12. 6　**Shipping Advice**

6. Beneficiary's certificate

Beneficiary's certificate is a statement made out on the exporter/beneficiary's company letterhead to certify that he has performed certain tasks according to the stipulation in the credit. For example, the tasks may generally include the mailing of a duplicated copy of shipping documents to the importer, cabling the issuing bank that the shipment has been made, or certifying that the shipment is in conformity with the contract, etc.

Always, the beneficiary's certificate will be accompanied by a post registered receipt or a courier receipt from EMS, DHL, FedEx, UPS, etc., as an evidence. It is to be issued and stamped by the exporter, with the issuing date not to be later than the stipulated date in the credit but not to be earlier than the shipping date. It is acceptable to have a same date as that of the shipping date. Figure 12. 7 is a sample of beneficiary's certificate.

ABC IMPORT & EXPORT CORPORATION, CHENGDU
12 SHAWAN STREET, JINGNIU DISTRICT, CHENGDU, CHINA
TEL: 028-87873456   FAX: 028-87873457

BENEFICIARY'S CERTIFICATE

INVOICE NO.:   NO.:
                                                     DATE:

BUYER:
L/C NO.:

THIS IS TO CERTIFY THAT THE GOODS ARE SHIPPED FROM SHANGHAI AND THECOLOR AND PATTERN ARE IN COMFORMITY WITH THE SELLER'S CATALOGUE NO. 3-B-948 STATED IN THE SALES CONTRACT NO. SC-OH0223-10.

....
Authorized Signature

Figure 12. 7   **Beneficiary's Certificate**

Beneficiary's certificate has no fixed format, but it should include both the L/C number and the invoice number. For the certifying part, it is recommended to be made the same as the original wordings shown in the credit, except for the necessary changes made to person and tense.

Section 4   Documents Examination under Letter of Credit

In international settlement, documents are to be presented by the exporter. However, different payment method decides how an individual document is to be made and whether the documents are to be sent to the importer, or to be presented to the importer's bank or to the exporter's bank. Documents examination is to be carried out by the relevant party afterwards. For payment methods other than letter of credit, it is necessary to refer to the previous chapters for the understanding of the documentation requirements, presentation requirements as well as the reasons behind these requirements. In this chapter, the focus is on the documentation and examination of documents under letter of credit.

1. General principle in documents examination

(1) The principle of independence. The principle of independence signifies

that the credit is a separate document independent from the sales contract or the credit application form on which it is based. This means only the wordings in the credit have the binding on banks.

(2) The principle of strict compliance. Under letter of credit, documents must be made according to the terms and conditions stipulated in the credit. The International Chamber of Commerce has drafted the principle of strict compliance to guide and govern the documentation and examination of documents. The principle consists of the following two aspects:

①Documents must comply with terms and conditions of the credit.

②Documents themselves must be consistent with each other.

Any failure of these two requirements will result in "discrepancies" of documents, causing problems for the exporter to obtain payments from the bank.

When the documents are found to be in strict compliance, the issuing bank is to take up the documents and make reimbursements to the nominated bank after payments have been effected by payment, acceptance or negotiation to the beneficiary.

When discrepancies are found in the documents, banks may reject the documents and give notice by telecommunication stating all the discrepancies within 7 banking days after the receipt of the documents.

(3) Banks deal exclusively with documents. In international settlement, banks will deal with documents rather than with the physical goods. Banks will never be involved in contractual disputes between the traders about the actual conditions of the goods while they should ensure that the documents presented meet the terms and conditions of the credit.

Payment must be made by the issuing bank on stipulated documents, regardless of whether the actual goods are in conformity with the contractual description. Any disputes concerning the quality or quantity of the goods, the importer should lodge the claim directly on the exporter.

However, non-stipulated documents will not be examined by banks. When banks receive such documents, they shall return them to the presenter or pass them on without responsibility.

(4) Banks' escaping clauses.

①Banks are required to examine documents with reasonable care but assume no responsibilities for the authenticity, form or validity of the documents. "Reasonable care" means that banks should make use of their background and special knowledge to make sure that the documents presented are in face consistent with the credit and with each other. In addition，banks are not responsible for the presentment of false or forged documents.

②Banks are not liable for the act of a third party involved in the operation. The third party may be another bank when the original bank，acting as the issuing bank，instructs the latter，as his correspondent bank，to advise，confirm，or negotiate the credit but whose act is beyond the control of the original issuing bank.

(5)Reasonable time. The issuing bank，the confirming bank or the nominated bank shall each be allowed a reasonable time to examine the documents. According to UCP 600，the notice of payment refusal must be given by telecommunication or，if that is not possible，by other expeditious means no later than the close of the fifth banking day following the day of presentation.

2. Documents examination

All documents should be issued no later than the expiry date of the credit. The following are the guiding points to be considered in the bank's examination of each individual document.

(1)Examining commercial invoice.

①Ensure that the commercial invoice is not named as "proforma invoice" or "provisional invoice".

②Ensure that the invoice is issued by the beneficiary of the credit to the applicant of the credit. Ensure that it is not made out to the name of a third party other than the applicant，unless otherwise stipulated in the credit.

③Ensure that the description of goods is in agreement with that shown in the credit. As only a general description of goods is made in the credit，the additional and detailed information of the description of goods in the invoice are not considered to be inconsistent with the requirements of the credit.

④Ensure that the details of the goods，the price terms and the breakdowns of prices as mentioned in the credit are included in the invoice.

⑤Ensure that there are no extra，additional or unfavorable descriptions，such as the indications of "used"，"junk"，or "assembly"，etc. on the packages，to arouse suspicion to the conditions and value of the commodity.

⑥Ensure that any other pieces of information supplied in the invoice，such as marks，numbers，transportation information etc. are in agreement with that of the other documents.

⑦Ensure that the value of the invoice corresponds with that of the draft and it does not exceed the available balance of the credit.

⑧Ensure that the currency of the invoice is the same as that of the credit.

⑨Ensure that the invoice value covers the complete shipment if partial shipments are allowed in the credit.

⑩Ensure that the invoice is signed when required by the credit.

⑪Ensure that the correct number of original(s) and copy(s) are presented.

（2）Examining draft.

①Ensure that a drawn clause is included to indicate that the draft is established on a credit. Ensure that the credit number, the name of the issuing bank and the issuing date will be included in the drawn clause.

②Ensure that the name of the drawer corresponds with the name of the beneficiary.

③Ensure that the drawee should always be a bank, may it be the issuing bank, the confirming bank or other nominated bank as the paying bank or the accepting bank. The draft should not be drawn on the applicant.

④Ensure that the draft is issued within 14 to 21 days after the B/L date but within the validity date of the credit. Ensure that the draft is presented before or on the latest date of presentation which will fall on the earlier date of the above mentioned two dates.

⑤Ensure that the tenor is as required by the credit.

⑥Ensure that the draft amount dose not exceed the balance available in the credit. The amount of the draft expressed in figures and words should be made identical. Ensure that the value of the draft and that of the invoice corresponds.

⑦Ensure that the draft is properly endorsed and there are no restrictive endorsements.

⑧Ensure the draft drawn is not "without recourse", unless the credit states otherwise.

（3）Examining marine bills of lading.

①Ensure that the B/L is a "clean" and "on board" one. Banks do not accept a B/L which contains a clause to render it "unclean".

②Ensure that an "on board" notation is dated and made on a "received for shipment" B/L.

③Ensure that the B/L is not a "chartered contract" of the transport, unless the credit states otherwise.

④Ensure that the B/L bears the name of the shipper or his agent.

⑤Ensure that the B/L is made out to the consignee as required in the credit. If the importer's name is not shown as the consignee, it will be shown as the notify party as required in the credit.

⑥Ensure that the B/L is correctly endorsed as required in the credit.

⑦Ensure that the general description of goods is identical with that shown in the credit and that the shipping marks and numbers as well as other specifications, if any, are in agreement with those appeared on other documents.

⑧Ensure that the "freight prepaid" or "freight collect" is indicated correctly on the B/L as required by the terms of the credit.

⑨Ensure that the full set of originals issued is presented, unless the credit states otherwise.

⑩Ensure that the B/L is presented no later than the 14 to 21 days after shipment but within the validity of the credit.

(4) Examining insurance document

①Ensure that the insurance document is the right type of policy, certificate or declaration required by the credit.

② Ensure that it is issued and signed by an insurance company, an underwriter or their agent.

③Ensure that if it is issued to the order of the beneficiary of the credit, the insurance document is correctly endorsed so that the title can be transferred to the applicant of the credit.

④Ensure that the document does not bear a date later than the B/L date, the date of shipment or the date of taking in charge of the carrier.

⑤Ensure that the insured amount is as required in the credit and is expressed in the same currency as that of the credit, unless otherwise stated in the credit. Banks will not accept an under-insured document.

⑥Ensure that the general description of goods corresponds to that in the credit and other details such as the shipping marks and numbers, etc. are consistent with other documents.

⑦Ensure that it covers the goods from the designated port of loading or place of taking in charge to the port of destination or the place of delivery.

⑧Ensure that the claim under the insurance document is made payable at the destination.

⑨Ensure that the risk(s) is correctly chosen and covered as required in the credit.

⑩Ensure that the full set is issued and presented as required by the credit.

(5) Examining certificate of origin.

①Ensure that the country of origin specified meets the requirement of the credit.

②Ensure that if a certificate of origin is required under the credit, it is a separate document and not combined with any other document(s).

③Ensure that the certificate of origin is issued, signed and legalized as required by the credit.

④Ensure that the right form of certificate of origin is issued and presented.

⑤Ensure that the description of goods is consistent with that of the other documents.

⑥Ensure that correct number of original(s) and copy(s) are issued and presented.

(6) Examining inspection certificate.

①Ensure that the inspection certificate is issued and signed by the party required in the credit.

②Ensure that the certificate is the right type complying with the inspection requirements of the credit.

③Ensure that the description and mark of goods are in agreement as to those mentioned in the commercial invoice and other documents. Ensure that the goods inspected in the documents are exactly those exported.

④Ensure that the certificate is issued on a date earlier than the shipment date on the B/L. Ensure that the inspection date is to be made on a date required by the credit.

⑤Ensure that the document contains no detrimental clause as to the goods, specifications, quality, packaging, etc., unless authorized by the credit.

(7) Examining packing/weight list.

①Ensure that it is a separate document and not combined with any other document(s).

②Ensure that it contains a detailed list as to show its packing, weight or measurement of the goods in accordance with the requirements of the credit.

③Ensure that the data on it is consistent with that of the invoice and other documents.

④Ensure that it is signed if it is required in the credit.

(8) Examining other miscellaneous documents. According to UCP 600, when miscellaneous documents other than commercial invoice, transport documents and insurance documents are called for, the credit should stipulate by whom such documents are to be issued, their wordings and their data content. If the credit dose not so stipulate, banks will accept such documents as presented, provided that their

data content is not inconsistent with any other stipulated documents presented.

(9)Examining covering letter. When the exporter presents the documents to the bank for payment, acceptance or negotiation, he will usually fill in a standard form made by and addressed to the bank, covering L/C stipulated documents and indicating their numbers of original(s) and copy(s). This standard form will serve as a covering letter and will be placed on the top of the other documents which will be orderly arranged according to the sequence of their appearance in the covering letter. Figure 12.8 is a sample of cover letter.

To Malayan Banking Berhad　　　　　　　　　　　　　　　　　Bank's Copy

　　　　　　　　　　　　　　　　　　　　　　　　　　　　　　Date

Dear Sirs

We enclose draft/s and documents as listed, please follow the instructions marked ☒

☐PURCHASE/DISCOUNT/NEGOTIATE subject to that payment

☐PURCHASE/DISCOUNT/NEGOTIATE subject to final payment (without advance) and to credit our account only upon receipt of funds from the reimbursing/paying bank.

OR

☐Present to the issuing bank for payment

Our Ref. No.	Drawee & Address	Tenor	Bill Amount

Documents attached	Draft	B/L	Comm. Inv.	Ins. Cert.	Cert. Orgn.	Pkg List	Wt. List	Bene. Cert.	Shpg Co. Cert.	AWB	DO	
Number of copies												

Enclosed also: 1 copy of Invoice and 1 photocopy of the original transport document for your file.

Covering:

Drawn under L/C No. ---------------------------- Issued by ------------
　　　　　　　　　　　　　　　　　Dated
---　---------------

Please follow instruction marked ☒

☐Advise acceptance and maturity date by cable/telex

☐In case of dishonor advise us by cable/telex giving reasons

Please utilize against Forward Contract No.

Date　　　　　　　　　　　　　　　For

Please credit our Current Account No.　　　　　　　　　with you.

It is expressly agreed and we hereby undertake to repay or hold you harmless and fully indemnify you on demand the a-mount which you have paid us or will pay to us together with all costs and charges which you may have incurred. If payment is not made to you by the drawee of the draft and or the issuing bank of the letter of credit which has been discounted/purchased/negotiated or presented for payment by you for any reasons whatsoever including but not limited to any discrepancies in the documents.

We further agree that your bank assumes no responsibility for the authenticity or genuineness of documents delivered to your bank, nor for the quantity, quality, condition, genuineness, identity, title or delivery of the goods to which the documents relate.

For Bank's Use		
Bank's Ref. No.	Date E.P.	Initial

Yous faithfully

....
Authorized Signatures & Stamp

Figure 12. 8   **Cover Letter**

When a bank examines a covering letter, it should:

①Ensured that the letter is addressed to this bank.

②Ensure that it has a current date.

③Ensure it is correctly related to the Credit number reference.

④Ensure that the documents enumerated are attached in correct numbers of original(s) and copy(ies) with the same amount and currency.

⑤Ensure that the bank remitting the documents is acting as a paying, accepting, negotiating bank.

⑥Ensure that the payment instructions are clear and understandable. It should clearly indicate whether any discrepancy(ies) have been noted and whether payment, acceptance, or negotiation has been effected against an indemnity or under reserve.

3. Banks' common practices in documents discrepancies

(1) The practices of the nominated bank. In the event that the documents presented are inconsistent with the terms and conditions of the credit or with each other, the nominated bank will adopt the following practices:

①Return all the documents or just the discrepant documents to the beneficiary/exporter to have them corrected or amended for resubmission within the validity of the credit and before the latest date for presentation of documents.

②Upon requested by the exporter, cable or write to the issuing bank/confirming bank, if any, for authority to pay, accept, or negotiate against such discrepant documents.

For example:"Documents presented under your L/C No._____ Bill's a-mount _____ Our reference No._____, all terms are complied with except _____. Please cable us whether we may negotiate the documents."

③Call for an indemnity from the beneficiary to pay, accept or negotiate with the understanding that any payment, acceptance or negotiation made will be refunded by the party issuing the indemnity, together with the interest and all charges if the issuing bank refuses to make reimbursement against these discrepant documents. In this case, the nominated bank should indicate clearly in the covering letter that "due to discrepancy(ies) we have paid/accepted/negotiated documents against Letter of Indemnity".

④Based on practical experience and with the agreement of the beneficiary, pay, accept or negotiate "under reserve", i. e. the bank retains the right of recourse against the beneficiary if the issuing bank refuses to make reimbursement against the discrepant documents. In this case, the nominated bank will indicate clearly in the covering letter that "due to discrepancy(ies), we have effected payments under reserve".

⑤Return all the documents to the beneficiary/exporter for his direct action to forward them to the issuing bank.

(2)The practices of the issuing bank. When the documents presented by the beneficiary or sent by the nominated bank abroad are found to be on their face to be in consistence with the terms of the credit and with each other after checking, the issuing bank is bound to:

①Take up the documents.

②Effect payments to the beneficiary or make reimbursement to the nominated bank who has paid, accepted or negotiated under the credit.

However, when the documents are found to be inconsistent, the issuing bank may seek advice from the applicant and if the applicant accepts the discrepancy(ies), the issuing bank will deliver documents against applicant's payment of the invoiced amount and effect payments to the beneficiary or to the nominated bank. If the applicant does not accept the discrepancy(ies), the issuing bank may exercise the right of refusal and no payments will be effected. The issuing bank will not be entitled to exercise the right of refusal until it has acted in accordance with the following requirements stipulated in the *Uniform Customs and Practice for Documentary Practice*:

①Payments are refused on the basis of documents discrepancies but not of goods discrepancies. This is because that document examination is made on documents but not on the underlying goods.

②Issuing bank gives the notice of refusal at the time no later than the close of the fifth banking day following the day of receipt of the documents. The issuing bank may make the decision to dishonor on its own or it is the result that the issuing bank fails to approach the applicant for the latter's approval of the discrepancies.

③Issuing bank gives the notice of refusal by SWIFT, Cable or Telex but not by airmail. It should be clearly stated in the message that the dishonor comes from the issuing bank and not from the applicant. For example, any message contains

"Buyers refuse …" or "Our customer rejects …" or similar wording is wrong because letter of credit is a payment method based on banker's credit.

④The notice of refusal must state all discrepancies. Issuing bank is not allowed to raise discrepancies in several notices. According to UCP, the issuing bank will not be entitled to raise subsequently any further discrepancies if the first discrepancy mentioned in the notice of refusal turned out to be inadequate grounds for rejection of documents.

⑤Notice of refusal must also state that issuing bank is holding the documents at the disposal of, or is returning them, to the presenter (the exporter or the nominated bank). The issuing bank is not permitted to give notice of refusal on one hand and deliver the documents to the applicant on the other hand.

4. Beneficiary's common practices in documents discrepancies

(1) Determine whether the issuing bank's payment refusal is proper. Under letter of credit, the issuing bank fulfills its payment undertaking to the beneficiary against stipulated documents which comply with the terms and conditions of the credit. In reality, however, it is possible that an issuing bank without a reputable credit standing may collude with a dishonest applicant to refuse payment on alleged discrepancies. Therefore, when receiving a bank's notice of payment refusal, the beneficiary is recommended to determine whether the notice is reasonable on the following check points:

①Whether there are points listed in the notice not complying with the terms and conditions of the UCP.

②Whether the bank requires the submission of documents not stipulated in the credit.

If the discrepancies raised by the issuing bank are not reasonable, the beneficiary and the nominated bank shall write or cable the issuing bank immediately to press for prompt payment with incurred interest for delayed payment, if any. In this case, the beneficiary and the paying bank, the accepting bank or the negotiating bank must be cautious and work closely with each other to make effort to receive payment as soon as possible.

(2) Measures taken when the issuing bank's payment refusal is proper. If actual discrepancies do exist, the beneficiary is to take the following measures as the case may be:

①Correct the documents immediately and present the corrected documents within the time limit of the credit.

②Contact the applicant directly, asking him to accept the discrepant documents and effect payments. It is necessary to contact the applicant because even if reimbursement is effected to the paying, accepting or negotiating bank, it might be made under reserve in chance of being called back by the issuing bank when the importer chooses not the accept the discrepancies.

③Send the discrepant documents on collection. Although it is a possible solution, the payment method has thus been changed from L/C to collection, and the issuing bank is in no way to effect payment if the applicant refuses to pay.

As any discrepancy may hinder payment settlement to the beneficiary， it is important for the traders and other relevant parties in import and export business to know the way banks exam documents to make correct documentation and present stipulated documents accordingly.

In conclusion， documents play very important roles in international settlement. No payment method can exist on its own without the participation of documents. Documents are used to facilitate settlement to the exporter and delivery to the importer. It is documents that move in various payment methods. In a word， documents are essential for the smooth operation of settlement， based on which international trade can be made successful.

Exercises for Chapter 12

I . Multiple-choice Questions (It is possible to make more than one choice)

1. Consular invoice can _____ .

A. perform the functions of certificate of origin

B. take the place of an import permit

C. prevent the dumping of foreign goods

D. increase the revenue for the consulate

2. Of the following documents under a documentary credit, _____ bears the earliest issuing date.

A. inspection certificate

B. certificate of origin

C. commercial invoice

D. packing list

3. When the beneficiary presents documents not required by the credit, the bank will _____ .

A. return the documents to the presenter

B. forward the documents as received

C. be liable for the documents

D. not be liable for the documents

4. Generalized System of Preferences (GSP) is made with the purpose of _____

A. increasing the revenue of export in the developing countries

B. increasing the revenue of import in the developing countries

C. speeding up the industrialization of the developing countries

D. speeding up the economic growth of the developing countries

5. When the credit is not transferable, the commercial invoice must _____ .

A. be signed

B. appear to have been issued by the beneficiary

C. must be made out to the name of the applicant

D. must be made out in the same currency as that in the credit

6. Banks are required to examine the _____ of the documents.

A. form

B. genuineness

C. sufficiency

D. apparent authenticity

7. The drawee of the draft established on a letter of credit could be any of the following EXCEPT _____.

A. issuing bank

B. negotiating bank

C. paying bank

D. confirming bank

Ⅱ. Fill in the Blanks

1. In L/C settlement, all documents should be issued no later than the _____ date of the credit.

2. Generalized System of Preferences is a treatment of _____ preference imposed by the developed countries to the developing countries. In a GSP form, a separate declaration by the _____ independent from the certification of the issuer is required.

3. When a B/L issued without any modification made to the pre-printed phrase "in apparent good order and condition" thereon, it is a/an _____ one.

4. The insurance document presented shall bear a date not _____ than the B/L or shipment date and show that the claim is made payable at the _____.

5. When presenting the inspection certificate, the presenter shall ensure that the document is issued on a date a little _____ than the shipment date on the B/L.

6. _____ can be supplied by the exporter as a quotation to the importer.

7. Date of _____ notation as evidenced on a "Received for Shipment B/L" is deemed to be the date of shipment.

Ⅲ. Case Question

Case One

A Chinese foreign trading company established an export sales contract with a Republic of Korean company under a CIF letter of credit. The Chinese company delivered the goods within the credit validity period and in correct quality and quantity ordered. After shipment, the Chinese company presented through a Chinese bank such documents as draft, commercial invoice, B/L, insurance policy and inspection certificates of quality and quantity to the Republic of Korean issuing bank to claim payment. The documents reached the issuing bank, unfortunately, at a time when the market was shrinking and the price was decreasing. Against such a market situation, the issuing bank decided to refuse making payment, pointing it as a discrepancy that the commodity names in the B/L were made in shortened form.

Question: Should the Chinese company press the issuing bank for payment? On what grounds?

Case Two

Yiran Company, Chengdu, a trading company specializes in Chinese tea export, established a sales contract under CFR to export certain amount of Chinese Green Tea to Company A, Dubai. The credit read: "Insurance covered by the Buyer and Shipping Advice to be sent by DHL immediately after shipment to Commerce Insurance Co., Address: Post Box No. 3345, Dubai. under open policy No. B/OPEN3567 and a copy of this advice to accompany the documents for negotiation." (Figure 12.9)

After shipment, Yiran Company, Chengdu sent the shipping advice shown below by DHL to Commerce Insurance Co., Dubai according to the credit stipulation.

SHIPPING ADVICE

TO: Commerce Insurance Co.,
Post Box No. 3345, Dubai

L/C No.: 22/39875
Open Policy No.: B/OPEN3567
Under captioned credit and open policy, please insure the goods as particulars given below:
Commodity: Chinese Green Tea
Quantity: 200 cases
Carrying Vessel: HONGQI V051
Shipping date: 20 April 2023
Port of loading: Shanghai
Port of Discharge: Dubai

Authorized Signature & Company Stamp

Figure 12.9   **Shipping Advice**

Then, Yiran Company, Chengdu presented the copy of the shipping advice together with other documents to the bank for negotiation. But when the documents were forwarded to the issuing bank, the bank sent to the exporter a notice of payment refusal on the following grounds: the information about the invoice value of goods was not given in the shipping advice, on account of which the open policy could not become effective and thus the goods were not covered by insurance.

Question: How can Yiran Company, Chengdu respond to the bank's notice to obtain payment?

Ⅳ. Calculation

Please calculate the amount insured and insurance premium for an export transaction for 110% invoice value at CIF USD 20 000 against all risk at the rate of 0.5% and war risk at the rate of 0.03%.

V. Extended Discussions

A Chinese Company made an export contract at USD 78 000 for a batch of bulk goods of 1 000 M/T with an American buyer under an irrevocable negotiation credit CIF New York. The American buyer timely opened the credit through its bank. The credit stated that it was subject to UCP 600, with the amount not exceeding USD 78 000 and the expiry date on Nov 30. The Chinese company made shipment of 950 M/T on Nov 4 and obtained the B/L issued on the same date.

On Nov 29, the Chinese company presented documents to the bank but the bank refused to negotiate the documents.

Questions:

1. Analyze the reasons for not getting negotiation from the bank.

2. What lesson should be drawn from this case?

第一部分　引入篇

第一章　国际结算概述

学习目标

◇了解国际贸易销售合同的主要内容。

◇了解国际结算的概念及分类。

◇了解国际结算所涉单据。

◇思考国际贸易、国际结算以及跨境电子商务之间的联系。

第一节　国际贸易与销售合同

国际贸易是一种跨越国家边界交换货物与服务的商业活动。一方面，它包括进口与出口两方面的交易活动；另一方面，它包括有形的货物贸易与无形的服务贸易。个人、公司乃至国家向国外售出货物或服务为出口贸易，而它们从国外购进货物或服务为进口贸易。

经过询盘、发盘与还盘的磋商过程后，国际贸易的下一个环节便是与国外贸易伙伴签订贸易协议。贸易协议可以称为贸易合同或贸易确认书，并可以由进口商、出口商任意一方拟定。如由出口商拟定，贸易协议被称为销售合同或销售确认书；如由进口商拟定，贸易协议被称为购货合同或购货确认书。无论如何称呼，贸易协议都是一份法律文书，对契约双方具有法律约束力。

如图 1.1 所示，销售合同的主要内容有货物描述、数量、单价和金额、价格术语、包装、运输、支付和投保等。其主要条款有质量或数量不符、索赔条款、不可抗力条款以及仲裁条款。

售 货 合 同
SALES CONTRACRT

卖方：SINOCHEM GUANGDONG IMPORT& EXPORT

Sellers：CORPORATION, CHINA

Contract No.：98SGQ468001

Date：APR. 28, 2023

Signed at：GUANGZHOU

地址：

Address：97,ZHANQIAN ROAD, GUANGZHOU, CHINA

Telex： 0925

Fax： 83556600

Buyers：METCH THAI ELECTRICAL APPLANCES COMPANY

Address：124 MAITRICHITR RD., BANGKOK,THAILAND

Telex：

Fax：

This Sales Contract is made by and between the Sellers and the Buyers，whereby the Sellers agree to sell and the Buyers agree to buy the under-mentioned goods according to the terms and conditions stipulated below：

（1）货号、品名及规格 Name of Commodity and Specification	（2）数量 Quantity	（3）单位 Unit	（4）单价 Unit Price	（5）金额 Amount
TRIANGLE BRANDREFERIGERATOR ACD-150W ACD-150G ACD-150Y 5% more or less both in amount and quantity allowed	200 200 200	SET SET SET	CIF BANGKOK USD 180.00 USD 180.00 USD 180.00	USD 36 000.00 USD 36 000.00 USD 36 000.00
	Total Amount			USD108 000.00

（6）Packing： CARTON   （7）Delivery Form GUANGZHOU to BANGKOK

（8）Shipping Marks： N/M

（9）Time of Shipment：within   30   days after receipt of L/C. transshipment allowed.

（10）Terms of Payment：By 100% Confirmed Irrevocable Letter of Credit in favor of the Seller to be available by sight draft to be opened and to reach China before MAY 20, 2023 and to remain valid for negotiation in China until the 15th days after the foresaid Time of Shipment. L/C must mention this contract number. L/C advised by BANK OF CHINA GUANGZHOU BRANCH. TLX：444U4K GZBC. CN. ALL banking Charges outside China（the mainland of China）are for the account of the Buyer.

（11）Insurance：To be effected by Seller for 110% of full invoice value covering WA up to BANGKOK

~~To be effected by the buyer.~~

（12）Quality/Quantity Discrepancy and Claim：

Incase the quality or quantity/weight are found by buyer to be not in conformity with the

Contract after arrival of the goods at the port of destination, the Buyers may lodge claim with the Seller supported by survey report issued by an inspection organization agreed upon by both parties, with the exception, however, of those claims for which the insurance company and the shipping company are to be held responsible, claim for quality discrepancy should be filed by the Buyer within 30 days after arrival of the goods at the port of destination, while for quantity/weight discrepancy claim should be filed by the buyer within 15 days after arrival of the goods at the port of destination. The Seller shall, within 30 days after receipt of the notification of the claim, send reply to the Buyer.

(13) Force Majeure: In case of Force Majeure, the Seller shall not be held responsible for late delivery or non-delivery of the goods but shall notify the Buyer by cable. The Seller shall deliver to the Buyer by registered mail, if so requested by the Buyer, a certificate issued by the China Council for the Promotion of International Trade or competent authorities.

(14) All disputes arising from the execution of or in connection with this contract shall be settled amicably by negotiation. In case of settlement can be reached through negotiation the case shall then be submit to China International Economic & Trade Arbitration Commission. In Shenzhen(or in Beijing) for arbitration in act with its sure of procedures. The arbitral award is final and binding upon both parties for setting the Dispute. The fee for arbitration shall be borne by the losing party unless otherwise awarded.

The Seller _____   The Buyer _____

图 1.1　销售合同

　　合同中的价格术语也称为 INCOTERMS。INCOTERMS 是《国际贸易术语解释通则》的英语首字母缩合词,该解释通则由位于法国巴黎的国际商会出台。销售合同中的报价必须包含价格术语。

　　每笔贸易业务,无论是出口业务还是进口业务,其目的都是履行合同,实现商品的交换和货款的支付。销售合同中的"付款条件"是指支付方式。此销售合同样例中所选择的支付方式是信用证。

第二节　国际结算

　　国际结算是指为结清不同国家之间的债务、欠账以及债权而通过银行所进行的跨国资金转移。

　　国际结算起因于国与国之间的有形贸易与无形贸易,还起因于国与国之间的非贸易活动,如国家间的借贷与投资、国际援助以及跨境个人汇款业务等。据此,国际结算分为两类:服务国际贸易而形成的贸易结算和服务非贸易业务而形成的非贸易结算。在国际商务领域,虽然非贸易结算同样重要,但本书的重点是介绍国际贸易结算。

国际结算以支付方式为中心。在销售合同中,支付方式也可以表述为"支付条件"或"付款"。支付方式分为五大类:汇款、托收、保理、信用证以及保函。每一种支付方式都包括不同的亚类。在这五大类中,汇款、托收和信用证是国际贸易中最常用的支付方式。

第三节　单据

支付方式有两大组成要素:金融票据和商业单据。没有单据,支付方式便无从运作。

1. 金融单据

金融单据中的"金融"二字表明金融单据的目的是支付货款。金融单据也称为"金融票据"或"票据",主要包括汇票、本票和支票,其目的是便利货款的结算。

由于国际贸易的贸易双方地处两国,货物跨境流动,现金结算会给贸易商带来极大的不便与风险。因此,在现代国际结算中,金融票据取代现金,用作货款结算的交换媒介。

简言之,金融票据是为货款的收付而发出的"指令"。一旦执行了"指令",货款就结清了。因此,由于金融票据的介入,国际结算步入了非现金结算时代。金融票据(而非现金)在国际贸易的整个结算过程中运行。

2. 商业单据

商业单据是货物正确生产、包装、保险以及货物保质、保量、按时交付的单据证明。商业单据的目的是便利货物的交付。

商业单据种类各异,各种商业单据表示在货物运输过程中贸易商是否承担了对货物相应的生产、包装、发货以及保险等责任。常见的商业单据有商业发票、装箱单、提单、保单、检验单以及原产地证书等。贸易商一旦提交一种商业单据,就意味着贸易商履行了其所代表的相应责任。

总而言之,支付方式的实现需要金融单据和商业单据的参与。支付方式、金融单据、商业单据三者紧密相连,三者共同构成国际结算的核心内容。

3. 物权单据

"物权"一词代表着所有权。随着货运业和保险业的发展,商业单据中提单和保单这两种单据成为物权单据。

就提单而言,提单持有人便是货主。因此,当卖方提交物权,即交货;当买方收到提单，即收到货物。这种基于物权单据的交货称为象征性交货，与早期国际结算中的实际交货相对。在实际交货中，货物只有在实际交给买方时才为交货。

货物的单据化使国际结算发生了巨大的变化。首先，交货和支付可以不凭实际货物而凭单交货和凭单付款。其次，单据业务成为国际结算业务的中心业务。

第四节　国际贸易、国际结算与跨境电子商务的联系

1. 国际贸易与国际结算的联系

国际结算业务关乎销售合同的成功履行。国际贸易与国际结算的相互关系阐释如下：

（1）国际贸易产生的欠账、债务以及债权需通过国际结算进行结清偿付。

（2）国际结算中的支付方式的正确选择与运作是贸易合同的签订和履行的基础。

（3）在国际结算的支付方式中，商业单据履行向进口商交货的任务，金融票据履行向出口商付款的任务，从而实现货款与单据（货物）的对流，完成一笔进出口贸易交易。

（4）支付方式不同，其贸易步骤也随之不同。

（5）支付方式不同，其贸易中开立的金融票据和商业单据细节也随之不同。

2. 跨境电子商务与国际贸易的联系

随着互联网、国际物流和在线支付的发展，消费者可以通过互联网购物平台在全球进行买卖，出现了跨境电子商务（CBEC）。近年来，跨境电子商务的迅猛发展加速了全球消费，成为国际贸易的一股强大的驱动力量。

根据交易的主体不同，跨境电子商务可以分为企业对企业模式（B2B）、企业对消费者模式（B2C）、消费者对消费者模式（C2C）等不同模式。目前，在中国跨境电子商务市场交易规模中，B2B 跨境电子商务市场交易规模占总交易规模的近 90%。在跨境电子商务市场中，企业及市场仍处于主导地位。

主要的跨境电子商务平台有亚马逊、易趣网、阿里巴巴、敦煌网、速卖通、Wish 以及虾皮网等。在这些平台中，亚马逊是美国最大的电子商务平台，也是开展电子商务业务最早的平台之一。阿里巴巴是中国的一个大型电子商务平台。易趣网主要为全球的消费者对消费者和企业对消费者的线上交易提供

便利。

作为一种新型的运作模式,表 1.1 展示了传统国际贸易与跨境电子商务的区别。

表 1.1　传统国际贸易与跨境电子商务的区别

项目	传统国际贸易	跨境电子商务
交易模式	以 B2B 为主的大批量、少批次、大额贸易	多以 B2B、B2C、C2C 的小批量、多批次、小额贸易
交易环节	生产商→出口商→进口商→批发商→零售商→消费者	生产商→零售商→消费者或生产商→消费者
支付方式	传统支付方式,如汇款、托收、信用证	第三方网络支付(如贝宝、国际支付宝)、国际信用卡、汇款、信用证
运输方式	70%以海运为主,多采用集装箱运输,运输成本占交易额的比例较低	以航空小包、国际快递为主(如 EMS、DHL、FedEx、UPS、TNT),运输成本占 30%~40%或更多
报关方式	需经过申报、查验货物、缴纳税费和海关放行四个阶段缴纳进口税费,出口时符合条件可享受出口退税优惠	委托运输公司集中申报和查验。从 2019 年 1 月 1 日起,跨境电商零售进口产品的单次贸易量不超过人民币 5 000 元,年度交易额不超过人民币 26 000 元的,免征关税,但也无法享受出口退税

与传统外贸相比,基于网络平台的跨境电子商务的优势是参与方可以是厂商,也可以是贸易商;可以是大企业,也可以是小公司,还可以是个人。跨境电子商务卖家可以真切地向成千上万的国外潜在买家展示其产品和服务。由于跨境电子商务的交易过程比传统外贸更短、更扁平,消费者可以通过跨境电子商务模式购买在国内市场买不到的或在国内市场价格昂贵很多的国外产品和服务。

跨境电子商务的支付与结算是指参与国际买卖的债务人通过使用一定的支付工具和支付方式,向国外债权人清偿其债务和欠账。其支付结算方式包括传统支付方式和跨境电商支付方式。传统支付方式主要用于企业对企业的 B2B 模式,包括汇款、托收和信用证方式。跨境电商支付方式包括银行卡、银行转账以及通过贝宝、国际支付宝、西联汇款等第三方线上支付平台支付等方式。

传统外贸支付方式历史悠久。信用证在跨境电子商务中使用广泛,特别是在交易量和金额都很大的时候。近年来,随着互联网的普及以及人们对跨境网购的持续认可,跨境电子商务的支付结算方式也发展迅速。从市场来看,由于传统外贸与跨境电子商务相互补充,传统外贸结算方式和跨境电子商务结算方式也会继续相互补充、相互共存。

第二章　常用价格术语

学习目标

◇学习价格术语的定义及分类。
◇具体学习6种常用价格术语。
◇了解其他价格术语。
◇学习影响交易中价格术语选择的因素。

第一节　价格术语概述

在国际贸易中,每笔交易的价格须包含价格术语。价格术语为三个英语首字母的缩合词,规定买卖双方的责任。总体来说,价格术语明确界定卖方的责任,通过排除卖方责任暗示出买方责任。因此,在某一价格术语中未出现的责任,便可以由买方来承担。

国际商会制定出了一套称为"INCOTRMS"的规则——《国际贸易术语解释通则》,又称为"贸易术语"或"价格术语",最早于1936年出版。随着时间的推移,国际商会对价格术语进行了几次修订,价格术语的最新版本为《2000通则》,于2000年1月1日生效。

受商业习惯和个人偏好等影响,《2010通则》在短时间内不会完全取代《2000通则》。这两个规则会共存一段时间,但会逐渐被《2010通则》取代。在实务中,贸易商在销售合同中应指明其报价遵循的是《2000通则》还是《2010通则》。

价格术语以极为简洁的方式界定了在货物运输过程中进出口商的风险和费用(责任)起止地点。合同签订时,进口商/买方和出口商/卖方在交易之初就会具体参照《通则》来界定双方各自的责任,以避免在运作过程中产生误会和后续争端的可能性。

货物从卖方所在地运往买方所在地的责任主要包括货物生产和包装的成本、进出口国国内内陆运输的费用、进出口海关通关的费用、装卸费用、从装运港/装运地至目的港/目的地的主运输费用以及货物投保的费用。国际贸易货物运输主要责任如图 2.1 所示。

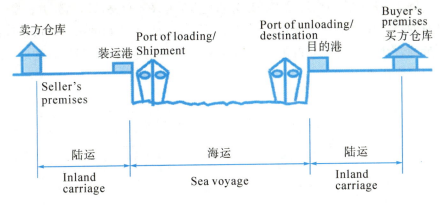

图 2.1　国际贸易货物运输主要责任

1.《2000 通则》

《2000 通则》共有 13 个价格术语,分为 E、F、C 和 D 四组(见表 2.1)。

表 2.1　《2000 通则》

E 组	EXW(指定地点)工厂交货价	出发地
F 组	FCA(指定地点)货交承运人价	主运费未付
	FAS(指定装运港)船边交货价	
	FOB(指定装运港)船上交货价离岸价	
C 组	CFR(指定目的港)成本加运费价	主运费付讫
	CIF(指定目的港)成本、保险加运费价	
	CPT(指定目的地)运费付讫价	
	CIP(指定目的地)运费、保险费付讫价	
D 组	DAF(指定地点)边境交货价	抵达地
	DES (指定目的港)船上交货价	
	DEQ (指定目的港)码头交货关税付讫价	
	DDU (指定目的地)关税未付价	
	DDP (指定目的地)关税付讫价	

　　E 组只有“工厂交货价”,即卖方在己方所在地让买方获得货物。从这一地点起,其后的所有费用皆由买方承担;F 组包括 FCA、FAS、FOB,要求卖方将货物运至买方指定的承运人处;C 组的 CFR、CIF、CPT 和 CIP 要求卖方签订运输合同将货物运至目的港目的地,但卖方不承担货物出险、损失的风险;D 组

DAF、DES、DEQ、DDU 和 DDP 要求卖方承担风险将货物运至抵达地。从 EXW 到 DDP，卖方责任从最小增至最大，而买方的责任变化刚好相反。

图 2.2 从进出口商运输责任划分起止点简单图示价格术语的分类。需要注意的是，价格术语中的装运港/装运地不总是指生产货物的出口商所在地；同样地，价格术语中的目的港/目的地也不总是指这笔交易的最终目的地，即进口商所在地。

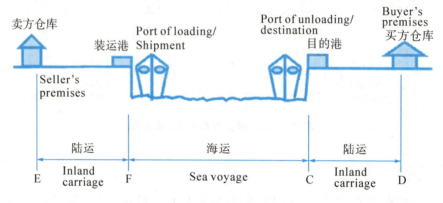

图 2.2　运输责任划分起止点

2.《2010 通则》

《2010 通则》中的价格术语从 13 个降至 11 个，这种减少主要涉及 D 组中的术语。除 DDP 保持不变外，《2010 通则》用 DAP 和 DAT 融合和取代 DAF、DES、DEQ 和 DDU。

《2010 通则》中的 EXW、FCA、CPT、CIP、DAP、DAT、DDP 这 7 个价格术语适用于任何运输方式，而 FAS、FOB、CFR、CIF 这 4 个价格术语只适用于海运和内陆水道运输（见表 2.2）。

表 2.2　《2010 通则》

适用于任何运输方式	
EXW	工厂交货（指定交货地）
FCA	货交承运人（指定交货地）
CPT	运费付至（指定目的地）
CIP	运费保险费付至（指定目的地）
DAT	运输终端交货（指定终端港或目的地）
DAP	目的地交货（指定目的地）
DDP	完税后交货（指定目的地）

表 2.2（续）

只适用于海运和内陆水道运输	
FAS	船边交货（指定装运港）
FOB	船上交货（指定装运港）
CFR	成本加运费（指定目的港）
CIF	成本加保险加运费（指定目的港）

在这 11 个价格术语中，经常使用的有 6 个，即用于海运的 FOB、CRF 和 CIF 以及用于陆上运输和多式联运的 FCA、CPT 和 CIP。多式联运至少包括陆上运输、海上运输、空运、铁路运输、公路运输以及内陆水道运输中的两种类别。

第二节　FOB、CFR 和 CIF

1. FOB：船上交货（指定装运港）

根据《2010 通则》的规定，FOB 是指当货物送到指定装运港买方指定的船上时，卖方即完成交货，货物灭失或损坏的一切风险转移，买方承担从自那一点起的一切费用和风险。

（1）FOB 卖方主要责任如下：

①在商定的日期或期限内将货物交至指定装运港买方指定的船上。

②承担交货前货物的风险、损失以及相关费用。

③自担费用，获取出口许可证或其他官方许可，并为货物出口办理相应的海关手续。

④向买方发出有关交货的详尽通知。

⑤自担费用，向买方提供交货的常规证明。

（2）FOB 买方主要责任如下：

①签订从装运港启运的运输合同，费用自担并支付海运费。

②在商定期限内向卖方发出有关船只、船名、装货地点以及订立的发货时间的详尽通知。

③在货物交至装运港船上时收货。

④承担交货后货物损坏或灭失的一切风险以及货物相关费用。

⑤自担费用，取得任何进口许可证或其他官方许可，并为货物进口办理相应的进口手续。

同时，买方可以安排货物的海运保险并支付从装运港开始的保险费。

图 2.3 显示了 FOB 买卖双方的责任。

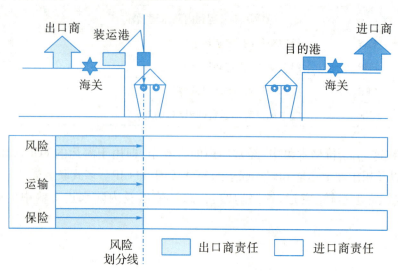

图 2.3　FOB 买卖双方的责任

为了进一步明确装船费的责任，避免日后纷争，FOB 产生以下术语变形：

（1）FOB 班轮条件：装船费由承运人承担，卖方不承担装船费。

（2）FOB 吊钩下交货：卖方负责将货物交到船只停泊码头吊钩所及之处，以后发生的装船费用将由买方承担。

（3）FOB 理舱费在内：卖方将货物装入船舱并承担包括理舱费在内的装船费用。理舱费是指货物入舱后进行安置和整理的费用。在实务中，该术语用 FOBS 表示。

（4）FOB 平舱费在内：卖方负责包括平舱费在内的装船费用。平舱费是指对入舱的散装货进行包括理舱在内的平整的费用。在实务中，该术语用 FOBT 表示。

FOB 变形术语出现在《2010 通则》出版之前。尽管《2010 通则》并未包括这些变形术语，但如签约方在销售合同中载明这些变形术语，《2010 通则》并不反对其使用。

2.　CFR：成本加运费（指定目的港）

根据《2010 通则》的规定，CFR 是指卖方在货物交至船上即完成交货，货物灭失或损坏的一切风险转移，卖方签订运输合同，承担将货物运至目的港的费用和海运费。

（1）CFR 卖方的主要责任如下：

①签订运输合同，支付海运费。

②在商定的日期和期限内将货物交至指定装运港船上。

③承担交货前货物的风险、损失以及货物相关费用。

④自担费用，获取出口许可证或其他官方许可，并为货物出口办理相应的海关手续。

⑤向买方发出有关交货的详尽通知。

⑥自担费用，向买方提供交货的常规证明。

（2）CFR 买方的主要责任如下：

①在货物交至装运港船上时收货。

②承担交货后货物损坏或灭失的一切风险以及货物相关费用。

③自担费用，取得任何进口许可证或其他官方许可，并为货物进口办理相应的进口手续。

同时，买方可以安排货物的海运保险并支付从装运港开始的保险费。需要注意的是，卖方应及时并详尽地向买方发送装船通知，以便买方及时为货物购买保险。否则，卖方应为未及时购买保险而产生的货物损失承担责任。图2.4 显示了 CFR 买卖双方的责任。

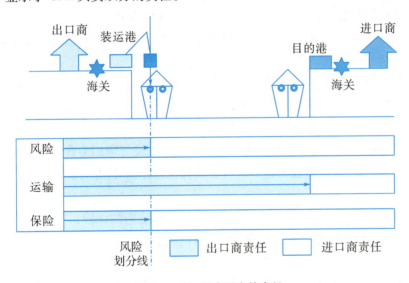

图 2.4　CFR 买卖双方的责任

为了进一步明确卸货费的责任，避免日后纷争，CFR 产生以下术语变形：

（1）CFR 班轮条件：船方负责卸货，卸货费已包括在卖方已支付的海运费中。

（2）CFR 卸至码头：货物需卸至码头，卖方负责卸货并承担包括驳船费、码头费在内的卸货费。

（3）CFR 吊钩下交货：卖方负责将货物从船舱吊起一直卸到码头或驳船吊钩能及之处的费用。船舶不能靠岸时，驳船费用由买方负责承担。

（4）CFR 舱底交货：卖方一旦将货物交至买方可以卸货时即完成交货责

任。买方承担将货物从舱底卸货的费用

CFR 变形术语出现在《2010 通则》出版之前。尽管《2010 通则》并未包括这些变形术语，但如签约方在销售合同中载明这些变形术语，《2010 通则》并不反对其使用。

3. CIF：成本加保险加运费（指定目的港）

根据《2010 通则》的规定，CIF 是指卖方在货物交至船上即完成交货，货物灭失或损坏的一切风险转移，卖方签订运输合同，承担将货物运至目的港的费用和海运费。卖方签订保险合同，为买方货物在运输途中的货物损坏或灭失的风险投保。

（1）CIF 卖方的主要责任如下：

①签订运输合同，支付海运费。

②签订货物保险合同，支付保费。

③在商定的日期和期限内将货物交至指定装运港船上。

④承担交货前货物的风险、损失以及货物相关费用。

⑤自担费用，获取出口许可证或其他官方许可，并为货物出口办理相应的海关手续。

⑥自担费用，向买方提供交货的常规证明。

（2）CIF 买方的主要责任如下：

①在货物交至装运港船上时收货。

②承担交货后货物损坏或灭失的一切风险以及货物相关费用。

③自担费用，取得任何进口许可证或其他官方许可，并为货物进口办理相应的进口手续。

买方应注意，CIF 术语只要求卖方购买最低险别的保险。如买方希望投保更高险别，则需要与卖方明确达成这样的协议或自行安排额外保险。图 2.5 显示了 CIF 买卖双方的责任。

为了进一步明确卸货费的责任，避免日后纷争，CIF 产生以下术语变形：

（1）CIF 班轮条件：船方负责卸货，卸货费已包括在卖方已支付的海运费中。

（2）CIF 卸至码头：货物需卸至码头，卖方负责卸货并承担包括驳船费、码头费在内的卸货费。

（3）CIF 吊钩下交货：卖方负责将货物从船舱吊起一直卸到码头或驳船吊钩能及之处的费用。船舶不能靠岸时，驳船费用由买方负责承担。

（4）CIF 舱底交货：卖方一旦将货物交至买方可以卸货时即完成交货责任。买方承担将货物从舱底卸货的费用。

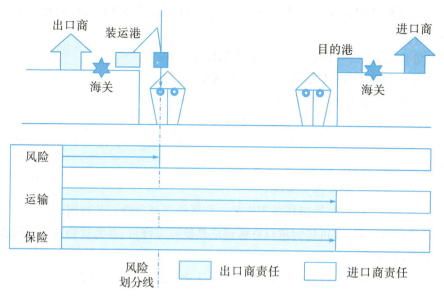

图 2.5　CIF 买卖双方的责任

　　FOB、CFR 和 CIF 的价格构成不同。FOB 代表一笔出口业务的基本成本构成，CFR 是成本价格加上海运费，CIF 是成本价格加上海运费再加保费。但是以上术语的风险划分点相同，货物在装运港交至船上时，货物损毁的风险转移至买方。在以上术语下，卖方在装运港交货并将合同规定的物权单据交与买方即完成交货责任，卖方并不承担实物货物交与买方的责任。这种交货称为象征性交货，即凭单交货，而非凭实物交货。

第三节　FCA、CPT 和 CIP

　　FCA、CPT 和 CIP 这三个术语适用于任何运输方式以及多式联运。多式联运是指货物的运输涉及铁路运输、公路运输、空运、海运以及内陆河道运输的至少两种运输方式。

1. FCA：货交承运人（指定交货地）

　　根据《2010 通则》的规定，FCA 是指当货物送到买方指定的承运人或另一方时，卖方即完成交货，各方需明确指出交货地的具体地点，自那一点起的风险转移至买方。

　　（1）FCA 卖方的主要责任如下：

　　①在商定的期限和地点将货物交至买方指定的承运人或另一方。

　　②承担交货前货物的风险、损失以及相关费用。

③自担费用，获取出口许可证或其他官方许可，并为货物出口办理相应的海关手续。

④向买方发出有关交货和承运人的详尽通知。

⑤自担费用，向买方提供交货的常规证明。

（2）FCA 买方的主要责任如下：

①签订运输合同，费用自担并支付运费。

②在充足的时间内向卖方发出有关承运人、运输方式以及交货地内的交货地点的详尽通知，以便卖方交货。

③在货物交至承运人时收货。

④承担交货后货物损坏或灭失的一切风险以及货物相关费用。

⑤自担费用，取得任何进口许可证或其他官方许可，并为货物进口办理相应的进口手续。

同时，买方可以安排货物保险并支付从交货地点开始的保险费。

2. CPT：运费付至（指定目的地）

根据《2010 通则》的规定，CPT 是指在商定地点把货物交至卖方指定的承运人或另一方时即完成交货，卖方负责签订运输合同，承担将货物运至指定目的地的相关运费。

（1）CPT 卖方的主要责任如下：

①签订运输合同，承担相关运费。

②在商定的日期和地点内将货物交至卖方指定的承运人或另一方。

③承担交货前货物的风险、损失以及货物相关费用。

④自担费用，获取出口许可证或其他官方许可，并为货物出口办理相应的海关手续。

⑤向买方发出以便其收货的详尽通知。

⑥自担费用，向买方提供交货的常规证明。

（2）CPT 买方的主要责任如下：

①在货物于商定时间和地点交至卖方指定的承运人或另一方时收货。

②承担交货后货物损坏或灭失的一切风险以及货物相关费用。

③自担费用，取得任何进口许可证或其他官方许可，并为货物进口办理相应的进口手续。

同时，买方可以安排货物保险并支付从交货地点开始的保险费。

3. CIP：运费保险费付至（指定目的地）

根据《2010 通则》的规定，CIP 是指在商定地点把货物交至卖方指定的承运人或另一方时即完成交货，卖方负责签订运输合同，承担将货物运至指定目的地的相关运费。卖方签订保险合同，为买方货物在运输途中的货物损坏或灭失的风险投保。

（1）CIP 卖方的主要责任如下：

①签订运输合同，支付运费。

②签订货物保险合同，支付保费。

③在商定的日期和地点内将货物交至卖方指定的承运人或另一方。

④承担交货前货物的风险、损失以及货物相关费用。

⑤自担费用，获取出口许可证或其他官方许可，并为货物出口办理相应的海关手续。

⑥向买方发出以便其收货的详尽通知。

⑦自担费用，向买方提供交货的常规证明。

（2）CIP 买方的主要责任如下：

①在货物在商定时间和地点交至卖方指定的承运人或另一方时收货。

②承担交货后货物损坏或灭失的一切风险以及货物相关费用。

③自担费用，取得任何进口许可证或其他官方许可，并为货物进口办理相应的进口手续。

买方应注意，CIP 术语只要求卖方购买最低险别的保险。如买方希望投保更高险别，则需要与卖方明确达成这样的协议或自行安排额外保险。

4. FOB、CFR、CIF 与 FCA、CPT、CIP 的比较

由于 FOB、CFR 和 CIF 术语只适用于海运和内陆水道运输，便相应出现了适用于海运、陆运和铁路运输以及多式联运的 FCA、CPT 和 CIP 术语，多式联运至少包括两种不同的运输方式。FCA、CPT 和 CIP 术语的出现满足了以集装箱运输和多式运输为特点的现代物流业迅猛发展的需要。

买卖双方在 FCA、CPT 和 CIP 术语下的责任与在 FOB、CFR 和 CIF 术语下的责任相对应。在 FCA、CPT 和 CIP 术语下，货物损毁的风险在指定地点货交指定承运人时转移至买方。买方承担从承运人处受领货物后至最终目的地的所有费用与风险。它们在成本、运费以及保险方面的责任可以清楚地从图 2.6 中通过与 FOB、CFR 和 CIF 的比较得以体现。

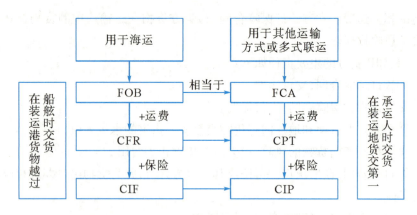

图 2.6　FOB、CFR、CIF 与 FCA、CPT、CIP 的比较

第四节　其他价格术语

其他价格术语为《2010 通则》中的 EXW、FAS、DAT、DAP 和 DDP，与 FOB、CFR、CIF、FCA、CPT 和 CIP 相比，这五个术语不常用。

1. EXW：工厂交货（指定交货地）

根据《2010 通则》的规定，EXW 是指卖方在己方所在地或另一指定地点（如工厂、车间或库房等）将货物交由买方处置时完成交货。卖方无需将货物装车，也无需办理相应出口清关手续。

（1）EXW 卖方的主要责任如下：

①卖方在指定地点将货物交由买方处置，无需装车。

②承担交货前货物的风险、损失以及货物相关费用。

③向买方发出有关交货的详尽通知。

（2）EXW 买方的主要责任如下：

①在商定的时间地点收货。

②承担交货后货物损坏或灭失的一切风险以及货物相关费用。

③自担费用，取得任何出口和进口许可证或其他官方许可，并为货物出口和进口办理相应的进口手续。

EXW 术语下卖方责任最小而买方责任最大。如果买方不能直接或间接办理出口货物清关，建议不要选用 EXW。

2. FAS：船边交货（指定装运港）

根据《2010 通则》的规定，FAS 是指当货物送到指定装运港买方指定的船边(如码头或驳船上)时,卖方即完成交货,货物灭失或损坏的一切风险自船边转移,买方承担从自那一点起的一切费用和风险。

(1)FAS 卖方的主要责任如下:

①在商定的日期将货物交至指定装运港买方指定的船边。

②承担交货前货物的风险、损失以及相关费用。

③自担费用,获取出口许可证或其他官方许可,并为货物出口办理相应的海关手续。

④向买方发出有关交货及运载船只的详尽通知。

⑤自担费用,向买方提供交货的常规证明。

(2)FAS 买方的主要责任如下:

①签订运输合同,费用自担并支付海运费。

②在商定期限内向卖方发出有关船名、装货地点以及订立的发货时间的详尽通知。

③在货物交至装运地点买方指定货船船边时收货。

④承担交货后货物损坏或灭失的一切风险以及货物相关费用。

⑤自担费用,取得任何进口许可证或其他官方许可,并为货物进口办理相应的进口手续。

FAS 只适用于海运和内陆水道运输。同时,买方可以安排货物的海运保险并支付从装运港开始的保险费。

3. DAT:运输终端交货(指定终端港或目的地)

根据《2010 通则》的规定,DAT 是指货物一旦在目的港或目的地终端从抵达的运输工具上卸下并交至买方处置即完成交货。"终端"包括任何地方,无论是否覆盖,如码头、仓库、集装箱堆场或公路、铁路、航空货运码头。卖方承担将货物运至指定目的地的终端并卸货的所有风险。

(1)DAT 卖方的主要责任如下:

①签订运输合同,支付运费,将货物运至目的港或目的地终端。

②在商定的期限于指定目的港或目的地将货物从抵达的运输工具上卸下并交至买方处置。

③承担交货前货物的风险、损失以及货物相关费用。

④自担费用,获取出口许可证或其他官方许可,并为货物出口办理相应的海关手续。

⑤自担费用,向买方提供交货的常规证明。

(2)DAT 买方的主要责任如下:

①在货物交至目的港或目的地终端时收货。

②承担交货后货物损坏或灭失的一切风险以及货物相关费用。

③自担费用,取得任何进口许可证或其他官方许可,并为货物进口办理相应的进口手续。

4. DAP：目的地交货（指定目的地）

根据《2010通则》的规定,DAP是指货物在抵达指定目的地运输工具上做好卸货准备时交至买方处置即完成交货。卖方承担将货物运至指定目的地的所有风险。

（1）DAP卖方的主要责任如下：

①签订运输合同,支付运费,将货物运至目的港或目的指定地点。

②在商定的期限将货物在抵达指定目的地运输工具上做好卸货准备时交至买方处置。

③承担交货前货物的风险、损失以及货物相关费用。

④自担费用,获取出口许可证或其他官方许可,并为货物出口办理相应的海关手续。

⑤自担费用,向买方提供交货的常规证明。

（2）DAP买方的主要责任如下：

①在目的地货物交付时或从承运人处受领货物时收货。

②承担交货后货物损坏或灭失的一切风险以及货物相关费用。

③自担费用,取得任何进口许可证或其他官方许可,并为货物进口办理相应的进口手续。

DAP与DAT非常相似,除了DAT的交货地点是在目的国的运输终端,而DAP是在买方所在地或其附近的最终目的地。DAP经常用于地处同一经济区的进口国、出口国之间的贸易。由于经济区内的国家间不设海关,因此货物无需清关。如果是这样的贸易,买方希望货物在其所在地交货。

5. DDP：完税后交货（指定目的地）

根据《2010通则》的规定,DDP是指货物在抵达指定目的地运输工具上做好卸货准备时交至买方处置即完成交货。卖方承担将货物运至指定目的地的所有风险,为货物的出口和进口办理清关,支付出口关税和进口关税,完成所有海关手续。

（1）DDP卖方的主要责任如下：

①签订运输合同,支付运费,将货物运至目的港或目的指定地点。

②自担费用,获取出口和进口许可证或其他官方许可,并为货物出口和进口办理相应的海关手续。

③在商定的期限将货物在抵达指定目的地运输工具上做好卸货准备时交至买方处置。

④承担交货前货物的风险、损失以及货物相关费用。

⑤自担费用,向买方提供交货的常规证明。

(2)DDP买方的主要责任如下:

①在目的地货物交付时或从承运人处受领货物时收货。

②承担交货后货物损坏或灭失的一切风险以及货物相关费用。

在DDP术语下,卖方责任最大而买方责任最小。如果卖方不能直接或间接办理进口货物清关,建议不要选用DDP。

第五节　总结

基于上述价格术语的介绍,我们可以得出这样的结论:当价格术语从EXW向DDP移动时,出口商的责任从最小逐渐增至最大,进口商的责任大小则刚好相反。此外,我们还需注意下面几点:

1. 报价必须包含价格术语

《通则》指出了价格的构成条件。这些条件代表着贸易商的责任。因此,国际贸易中完整正确的报价包括三个项目:单价及币种+某价格术语+装运港/地或目的港/地。

例如,国际贸易中报出的单价"USD 100/bag FOB Shanghai or USD 120/bag CIF Shanghai"。在第一个报价中,上海是装运港,而在第二个报价中,上海是目的港。其原因是上海用在了不同的价格术语中。

除此之外,一些如"佣金"等词语也可能用于某价格术语中。佣金是给中间商做成的每笔交易的酬金。当某价格术语指明含佣金时,中间商向买方抽取佣金。例如,"CFR New York C3 USD 10.00/CTN"表示该价格术语为3%的含佣金价,佣金由买方支付。给中间商的佣金也可以不在某价格术语中指出。在这种情形下,如果含佣金,则由卖方支付

2. 价格术语不同,报价不同

当某种价格术语下出口商承担的责任较大时,其报价就会较高;相反,如进口商承担的责任较大,出口商的报价就会较低。

对于一份销售合同而言,价格术语不同,报价也不同。图2.7显示了这种报价的变化趋势。

EXW	FOB	CFR	CIF	DES	DDP
$ 98	$ 100	$ 110	$ 115	$ 120	$ 140

图 2.7　价格术语与报价高低

（注：图中金额数字只是对价格变化趋势的演示，非实际价格）

3. 货物在任何价格术语下都可投保

使用价格术语需牢记《通则》是从卖方而非买方的角度描述责任的。因此，当投保没有在某价格术语中显示时，该价格术语只是载明投保不是卖方的责任，但是投保可由买方承担。

例如，货物在 FOB 术语下与在 CIF 术语下都一样可以投保。简言之，货物在任何价格术语下都可投保，唯一的区别是哪一个贸易商与保险公司签订合同，哪一个贸易商支付保费。

4. 装运合同和到达合同

当销售合同在 FOB、FAS、FCA、CFR、CIF、CPT 或 CIP 价格术语下签订时，该合同为装运合同，交货为象征性交货。卖方在指定装运港交货并向买方提交合同规定的包括物权单据在内的商业单据后即完成交货责任，不承担将货物运至目的地的责任。买方应根据物权单据凭单付款。在装运合同中，货物损毁的风险在装运港将货物装船或将货物越过船舷，或者在装运地货交承运人时转移至买方。

当销售合同在 EXW 价格术语下签订时，该合同也是装运合同，但交货为实际交货。当货物在卖方所在地交至买方后即完成交货责任。货物损毁的风险在卖方所在地货物交由买方处置时转移至买方。

当销售合同是在 DAT、DAP 或 DDP 价格术语下签订时，合同称为到达合同，交货为实际交货。当货物在目的地终端或指定地点交至买方时完成交货。货物损毁风险在目的地终端或指定地点货物交由买方处置时转移至买方。

5. 价格术语的选择

价格术语决定了销售合同的性质以及货物交付的条件，合理选择价格术语能反映出贸易商的履约能力，提高交易的效率。价格术语的选择通常应考虑以下几个方面：

（1）运输方式。由于 FOB、FAS、CFR 和 CIF 只适用于海运和内陆水道运输，因此如果运输方式为空运、公路运输、铁路运输或多式运输，贸易商应从 EXW、FCA、CPT、CIP、DAT、DAP 和 DDP 中进行选择。

（2）履约能力。根据《2000 通则》的规定，价格术语分为 E、F、C 和 D 四组，E 组进口商承担责任最多，D 组出口商承担责任最多。鉴于此，如果贸易商不能直接或间接从对方国家获得进口或出口许可证或其他官方许可证，或者不能为货物办理相关的进口或出口清关手续，买方不应选择 EXW 价格术语，卖方不应选择 D 组价格术语。

在 F 组和 C 组价格术语下，贸易商分摊责任。因此，如果贸易商能获得优惠的运费和保费，买方应选择 FOB、FCA 或 FAS 价格术语，卖方应选择 CFR、CIF、CPT 或 CIP 价格术语。

（3）运费变化。如果运费价格上行，卖方应选择 FOB、FCA 或 FAS 价格术语，买方应选择 CFR、CIF、CPT 或 CIP 价格术语。如果运费价格下行，双方做相反的选择。如果运费价格不好预测，卖方最好选择 F 组价格术语而买方最好选择 C 组价格术语。

（4）支付方式。在汇款、托收和信用证这三种常用支付方式中。如果选择的支付方式是托收或信用证，卖方应选择合同为装运合同和象征性交货的 F 组和 C 组价格术语。这样卖方或卖方的银行可以通过物权单据控制货物。进口商只有在对出口商或银行进行支付后，才能得到物权单据。

一般而言，如果选择汇款，贸易商无需做上述考虑。

第二部分　票据篇

第三章　汇票（Ⅰ）

学习目标

◇了解金融票据的定义及主要分类。

◇了解分析汇票的定义。

◇学习汇票的要件。

◇学习对价、议付和承兑等概念。

◇学习汇票的主要当事人，其票据责任与票据权利。

◇思考汇票持票来人与持票人的关系。

第一节　金融票据

金融票据（financial instrument），又称为"credit instrument"，简称"票据（instrument）"，是指一人开出的，在一定时间内，由其本人或由其指定的第三方，对另一人无条件支付一定金额的书面单据。

金融票据在国际结算中扮演着重要的角色。金融票据的目的是进行款项的收取或支付。金融票据已取代现金，用作贸易交易中的支付工具，避免在进出口结算过程中的现金使用。

国际结算中常用的金融票据有汇票、本票和支票。在这三种票据中，汇票是结算过程中最常用的，票据法对汇票的大部分规定也适用于本票和支票。本票和支票将在第五章进行介绍。

第二节　汇票概述

1882 年的英国《票据法》对汇票的界定如下：汇票是一人向另一人开出的，由出票人签字，要求汇票开给的那一人对某一特定人或其指定人或持票来人，即期或在固定的未来某一日期或在可以确定的未来某一日期，支付一定货币金额的无条件支付命令。

汇票(bill of exchange)又称为"draft"或"bill"。汇票样例如图 3.1 所示。

```
         (8)
Exchange for USD100 000. -                              New York, June 3, 2023
                    (6)
    (7)                (1)              (9)
    At 60 days sight pay XYZ company, Hong Kong or order
                         (8)
    the sum ofUnited States Dollars One Hundred Thousand only value received.


         (3)(5)
To:BBB Bank,
    2 Hill Road
    Hong Kong                                    (2)(4)
                                        For: AAA Co., Ltd, New York
                                            (authorized signature)
```

图 3.1　汇票样例

为便于更好理解,上例汇票可以细分如下:

(1)无条件的书面命令。

(2)由一人开出(出票人)。

(3)向另一人开出(受票人)。

(4)由开出的人签字。

(5)要求汇票开给的那一人。

(6)支付。

(7)即期或在固定的未来某一日期或在可以确定的未来某一日期。

(8)一定金额的货币。

(9)付给某一特定人或其指定人或持票来人(收款人)。

图 3.2 是实务中的汇票样例。

如图 3.2 所示,实务中使用的汇票一般是一式两联,但只代表一项责任。当其中的一联被支付后,另一联即告失效。因此,第一联汇票会载有字句"付一不付二",而第二联会载有字句"付二不付一",以避免出现一套汇票被重复付款的情况。

"对价付讫"表明收款人基于其已向出票人支付过对价而获得付款。对价是能以货物、服务以及货币形式给出的任何事物,是合同成立的基础。

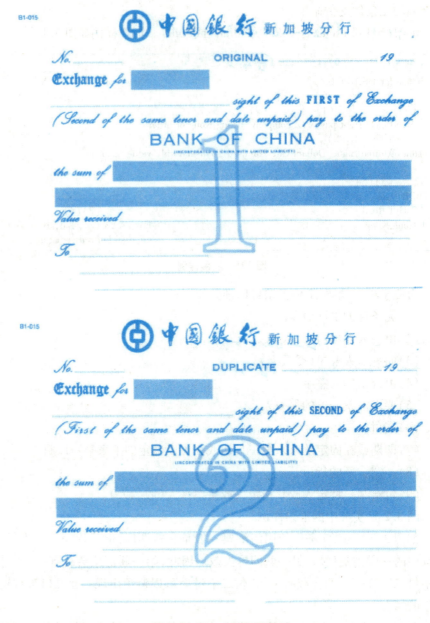

图 3.2　实务中的汇票样例

第三节　汇票的要件

汇票的要件是指使汇票完整有效的先决条件。汇票定义中的 9 个细分部分都是汇票的要件。以下详细介绍其中 2 个要件，即期限和抬头。

1. 汇票的期限

期限在汇票的定义中以"即期或在固定的未来某一日期或在可以确定的未来某一日期"加以表述。期限既表示汇票的付款时间，又表示汇票的到期日。根据期限，汇票可以即期或在某一固定的或可以确定的未来日期进行支付。

（1）即期汇票。即期汇票（demand bill）又称为"sight bill"，表述为要求受票人一经要求时、受票人见票时或汇票向他提示付款时进行支付。汇票如果载有这样的表述，或者汇票没有载明付款时间，都是即期汇票。对于即期汇票而言，汇票的提示日就是汇票进行付款的到期日。

即期汇票的表述方式总结如下：

①即期支付："On demand pay …"

②提示即付："On presentation pay …"

③见票即付："At sight pay …"

④支付："Pay …"

（2）远期汇票。远期汇票（usance bill）又称为"time bill"或"term bill"，是指汇票在未来某一固定日或未来某一确定日支付。远期汇票有如下表述方式：

①在未来某一固定日支付。未来日期指的是汇票期限迟于汇票的开立日期。

②在出票日后某一固定日支付。例如，"pay 60 days after date …"，其到期日为出票日后 60 天。此处的"日期（date）"指的是汇票的出票日。

③在见票日后某一固定日支付。"见票"是指将汇票向受票人进行提示要求其进行承兑。当这种汇票的受票人见票后，其必须承兑汇票。

承兑是受票人做出的一种承诺，保证在汇票到期时进行支付。对于这种汇票而言，承兑是必须的，因为需确定承兑日后继而据此确定到期日。

例如，"pay one month after sight …"表示承兑日后 1 个月为付款到期日。假设汇票于 2023 年 1 月 9 日提示并于同日承兑，那么到期日就是 2023 年 2 月 9 日。

④在某一确定会发生的具体事件发生后的某一固定日。在实务中，这类汇票往往是在提单日后某一固定日支付。由于发货是一件确定会发生的具体事件。因此，提单日后某一日期是一可以确定的未来日期。

例如，"pay 3 months after the B/L date …"。

2. 汇票的抬头

汇票定义中对汇票的抬头的表述为"付给某一特定人或其指定人或持票

来人（收款人）"。

根据对收款人的不同表述,汇票有三种抬头:限制性抬头、指示性抬头和持票来人抬头。汇票的不同抬头决定汇票的可流通性及其流通方式。流通指汇票所有权转移的过程,表明汇票的收款人/持票人具有将汇票转让给他人的权利。

(1)限制性抬头。限制性抬头的汇票只能支付给某一特定人。举例如下:

只支付给上海 A 公司(Pay to A Co., Shanghai only)。

支付给上海 A 公司不可议付/不可转让/不可指定(Pay to A Co., Shanghai not negotiable / not transferable / not to order)。

限制性抬头的汇票不可流通,即上述汇票的收款人"上海 A 公司"不能将此汇票转让给他人。

(2)指示性抬头。指示性抬头的汇票可以支付给某一特定人或由其指定的其他人,没有限制其转让或流通的字句。举例如下:

支付给上海 A 公司(Pay to A Co., Shanghai)。

支付给上海 A 公司的指定人(Pay to the order of A Co., Shanghai)。

支付给上海 A 公司或其指定人(Pay to A Co., Shanghai or order)。

支付给指定人(Pay to order)。

指示性抬头的汇票可以流通,表示汇票收款人上海 A 公司通过背书和交付将汇票流通或转让给他人。背书使汇票的流通变得安全。因此,国际贸易中广泛使用指示性抬头的汇票。

(3)持票来人抬头。持票来人抬头的汇票支付给持票来人,即没有特定的汇票收款人。任何一个持有持票来人抬头的汇票的人即汇票的所有人。举例如下:

支付给持票来人(Pay to bearer)。

支付给上海 A 公司或持票来人(Pay to A Co., Shanghai or bearer)。

注意:"bearer"一词使汇票成为持票来人抬头,不管是否有一特定人与这一词在汇票中同时载明。

持票来人抬头的汇票可以流通。这类汇票无需背书,仅通过交付就能由持票来人将其转让他人。这类汇票具有全流通性,但由于缺少背书而使其流通不安全。

第四节　汇票的主要当事人

汇票的主要当事人有出票人、受票人、收款人、背书人、被背书人和持票人。他们各自具有不同的权利和义务，充当汇票的债权人或债务人。其中，出票人、受票人和收款人是汇票在转让给他人之前的基本当事人。流通后，汇票产生背书人、被背书人和持票人等其他当事人。

1. 出票人

出票人是向受票人开立并签署汇票并将汇票交付给收款人的当事人。

出票人是汇票的债务人。在一张即期汇票得到付款和一张远期汇票被受票人承兑之前，出票人对收款人或汇票的持票人承担第一责任。当受票人以不付款或不承兑的方式退票时，出票人必须赎回汇票并进行支付。但当一张远期汇票被承兑后，出票人的责任成为第二责任。

2. 受票人

受票人是汇票向其开出的当事人，依照出票人的指令对汇票进行兑付，即承兑与付款的当事人。

受票人是汇票的另一债务人。但是，当一张汇票向其提示时，受票人有权做出兑付（同意进行承兑和付款）或退票（拒绝做出承兑和付款）的选择。这是因为受票人不能阻止任何一个其并不欠账的当事人开立以其为受票人的汇票。这意味着在受票人同意兑付汇票之前，其还不是汇票的债务人；一旦同意，其便认可对汇票的负债，在远期汇票的情形下，成为承兑人。

承兑人是特殊受票人。当远期汇票的受票人在汇票正面签名，表示其承诺在到期日付款，便成为承兑人。这种承兑使承兑人对汇票承担第一责任。此时，如上所述，出票人便对汇票承担第二责任。

3. 收款人

收款人是收取汇票金额，汇票向其进行支付的当事人。收款人是汇票的第一债权人，也是汇票的第一合法所有人。收款人可以凭汇票索取支付也可以将汇票转让（流通）给他人。如果汇票被转让，收款人成为汇票的原持票人/转让人，汇票从他处转走。而受让人，即获取汇票的当事人，成为汇票的新持票人。

汇票由出票人向受票人开立，支付给收款人。汇票三个直接当事人表示，出票人向受票人发出指令，要求其向收款人进行承兑或付款。需要注意的是，一方面,汇票的出票人和受票人可以为同一人;另一方面,汇票的出票人和收款人也可以是同一人。

当汇票为指示性抬头或持票来人抬头时,汇票可以从一个持票人转让给另一个持票人。这样,汇票的所有权便从前手持票人转让给后手持票人。这一转让过程称为流通。在汇票的流通过程中,汇票将产生其他当事人。

4. 背书人

背书人原本是汇票的收款人或持票人,为流通汇票的目的在汇票背面签名的当事人。背书人是汇票的债务人,收款人是汇票的第一背书人。当收款人成为背书人后,他自己也由债权人变为债务人,承诺对被背书人及其后手持票人承担责任。

例如,背书人对其被背书人可做如下承诺:"如果你方,现票据持票人,在进行恰当提示承兑和提示付款但被退票,一经接到你方通知,我会按汇票票面价值对你进行付款。"票据在流通过程中可以产生第一背书人、第二背书人、第三背书人等,背书人可以一直记录下去。

5. 被背书人

被背书人是汇票向其转让的当事人。被背书人是汇票的债权人,是汇票的新持票人。被背书人可以在汇票背面签名,继续向其人转让汇票。一旦转让,其便又成为背书人,并使自己成为债务人。

汇票流通过程能产生一系列背书人。图3.3显示了汇票的流通过程。汇票从A转让给B,B再转让给C。此时,从C的角度看,A和B为其前手。如果C继续转让汇票给D,D再转让给E,D和E成为C的后手。

图3.3　汇票的流通过程

6. 持票人

持票人是汇票持有人,为汇票的债权人。持票人可以是收款人/持票来人或被背书人,收款人是第一持票人。但是,一个持有伪造汇票的人或一个盗取支付给他人的汇票的人是非法持有人,不是持票人,只有合法持有人才能成为持票人。图3.4显示了汇票持有人和持票人的相互关系。

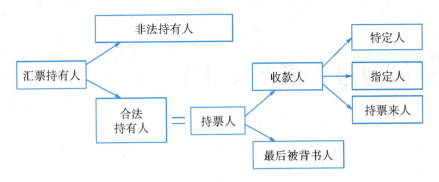

图 3.4　汇票持有人和持票人

作为债权人,持票人对汇票拥有如下完全票据权利:

(1)有到期对票据进行提示要求承兑与付款的权利。

(2)有向他人转让汇票的权利。

(3)有对汇票背书的权利。

(4)有向前手发出拒付通知的权利。

(5)有向前手行使追索权的权利。

(6)有以自己之名起诉的权利。

(7)有要求复制已丢失汇票的权利。

(8)有对支票或银行即期汇票划线的权利,有将票据交付银行请求托收的权利。

总体来说,汇票的债权人有收款人/持票来人、被背书人和持票人。汇票的债务人有对汇票承担付款责任的出票人、受票人、承兑人和背书人。他们的债务顺序如下:

承兑前:第一,出票人;第二,第一背书人;第三,第二背书人……

承兑后:第一,承兑人;第二,出票人;第三,第一背书人;第四,第二背书人……

第四章　汇票（Ⅱ）

学习目标

◇学习主要的票据行为。

◇学习如何背书与承兑。

◇学习汇票的运行过程。

◇学习汇票的分类。

◇学习商业汇票与银行汇票、光票与跟单汇票的区别。

◇学习计算贴现净款与贴现息。

第一节　主要的票据行为

票据行为是指以承担票据的债务为目的所做出的法律行为。主要的票据行为有出票、背书、提示、承兑、付款、退票、发拒付通知、发拒绝证书以及行使追索权。每种票据行为由不同的当事人向不同的当事人做出以实现不同的目的。

1. 出票

出票由出票人做出，包括两个动作：一个动作是出票并签字，另一个动作是将汇票递交收款人。债务责任因此确立，汇票被开立。

出票人出票时须开立完整汇票，包含规定的所有要件。出票人还须对汇票签字。没有出票人签字的汇票或伪造签字的汇票不是有效汇票。汇票的责任仅凭签字确立。如未签字，当事人不对汇票承担债务责任。汇票可以由个人、公司或经个人授权的另一人开出。汇票一经开立，出票人即对汇票承担第一责任。

递交汇票是指由出票人把汇票交至收款人。收款人据此有权收款，成为汇票的第一持票人和汇票的债权人。

2. 背书

背书在汇票的背面做出，包含两个动作：一是在汇票背面签字，另一个是将汇票递交给被背书人/受让人。

背书是一个流通行为。当汇票从一人转至另一人，受让人成为汇票持票人时汇票被流通。只有持票人，即收款人/持票来人和被背书人能背书汇票。

背书仅对指示性抬头的汇票做出。指示性抬头的汇票通过背书和递交完成转让。

背书有以下几种方式：

（1）特别背书（记名背书）。特别背书包含背书人的名字与签字且同时清楚指出受让人姓名。特别背书也被称为记名背书。

例如：

Pay to the order of B Co., Shanghai ………… 被背书人

For A Co., Shanghai　　　　　　………… 背书人

<u>Signature</u>（背书人做出）

上例表示汇票从上海 A 公司转让给上海 B 公司。

这样背书后的汇票仍然为指示性抬头的汇票。该汇票可以继续通过背书和递交行为转让。一组连续的背书可以清晰地显示一系列背书人和被背书人。

（2）空白背书（不记名背书）。空白背书只包含背书人/转让人的姓名和签字而不显示被背书人/受让人的姓名。空白背书又称为不记名背书。

例如：

For A Co., Shanghai　………… 背书人

<u>Signature</u>（背书人做出）

当汇票的背书为空白背书时，汇票从原来的指示性抬头变为持票来人抬头，汇票仅凭递交就可继续转让。当一个空白背书后又跟一个空白背书时，后一个背书的背书人就被认为是前一个背书的被背书人。因此，一系列空白背书也可以是连续的。

但是，在空白背书的背书人姓名上面加上"pay to"或"pay to the order"并在其后载明受让人姓名后，空白背书就转化为特别背书。

（3）限制性背书。限制性背书载有"only（只转给）""not negotiable（不可流通）""not transferable（不可转让）""not to order（不转指定人）"等表述，以限制汇票的进一步流通。

例如：

Pay to ABC Bank, Shanghai only ………… 被背书人

For A Co., London　　　　　………… 背书人

Signature（背书人做出）

或

Pay to ABC Bank，Shanghai not negotiable ⋯⋯⋯⋯ 被背书人

For A Co.，London　　　　　　　　⋯⋯⋯⋯ 背书人

Signature（背书人做出）

限制性背书使汇票从指示性抬头变为限制性抬头。被背书人只能凭汇票索取付款而不能再次转让汇票。

（4）托收背书。"请托收"是背书人向被背书人发出的要求托收汇票金额的指示。托收背书要求被背书人按要求处置汇票，但汇票的所有权并没有转让给被背书人。

例如：

Forcollection pay to Bank A，New York　⋯⋯⋯⋯被背书人

ABC Co.，Shanghai　　　　　　　⋯⋯⋯⋯ 背书人

Signature（背书人做出）

或

Pay to Bank A，New York for collection　⋯⋯⋯⋯ 被背书人

ABC Co.，Shanghai　　　　　　　⋯⋯⋯⋯ 背书人

Signature（背书人做出）

由于受让人并非汇票所有人，因此托收背书使汇票不能再进行转让。

3. 提示

提示（presentment）也表述为"presentation"，是由汇票持票人向汇票受票人做出的，在即期汇票下要求付款，在远期汇票下要求承兑和付款的票据行为。

持票人应在汇票指定的地点以及合理时间内提示汇票。如未指定地点，汇票应在受票人或承兑人的办公场所提示。如未指明办公场所，汇票在受票人或承兑人的居所提示。

如果受票人为银行，其有以下三种途径提示汇票：

（1）在受票行柜台提示。

（2）通过票据交换所向受票行提示。

（3）联行和代理行通过航空邮寄或快递方式向受票行提示。

如果汇票按期提示但被受票人退票，持票人即获追索权，可向所有前手直至出票人进行追索。

4. 承兑

承兑是远期汇票受票人表示同意执行出票人命令的票据行为。但受票人

在对汇票签字表示接受承担支付汇票所载金额责任之前，受票人对汇票不承担责任。

有效承兑包括两个动作：一个动作是受票人在汇票正面载明"承兑"字样并签字。如只有受票人的签字而无其他表述，也为有效承兑。另一个动作是将已承兑汇票交还收款人，以便收款人在到期日再次提示汇票。如果远期汇票为在见票后某一固定日支付，承兑日被视作见票日，据此计算汇票到期日。

为方便起见，承兑时可载明承兑日和到期日。图 4.1 显示了全式承兑所包括的条目。

```
ACCEPTED（已承兑）
On（accepting date 承兑日）
to mature（到期）
On（due date 到期日）
受票人姓名
签字
```

图 4.1　全式承兑

一旦受票人做出承兑，受票人便成为承兑人，对汇票承担第一付款责任。这样，出票人便承担第二责任。在实务中，由于已承兑汇票载有承兑人给出的到期付款的明确承诺，已承兑汇票比未承兑汇票更易于流通转让。

限制性承兑是指受票人在承兑时加上了条件，以清楚明白的表述改变了汇票的出票效果。限制性承兑可以改变汇票金额、付款时间或付款地点等。如图 4.2 所示，一张面额为 USD 10 000 的汇票在受票人做出如下限制性承兑时被改为 USD 9 700。

```
ACCEPTED（已承兑）
1 FEB., 2023（2023 年 2 月 1 日）
Payable for amount of USD 9 700 only（支付 USD 9 700 整）
For ABC Bank, London（伦敦 ABC 银行）
签字
```

图 4.2　限制性承兑

允许受票人做出限制性承兑的原因是受票人对是否同意执行出票人命令具有选择权。其可以选择同意或不同意执行出票人命令，或者在承兑前坚持先满足某种条件。只要汇票在开出时是有效的，限制性承兑并不会使这张汇票无效。但是，持票人也有权选择拒绝接受限制性承兑的汇票，如果拒绝，持票人可以以拒绝承兑将该汇票认定为退票。

5. 付款

付款这一票据行为可以由汇票任一债务人向汇票任一债权人做出。但单凭付款并不能注销汇票。注销是指汇票的任一债务人，即受票人、承兑人或可能出现的背书人，对其所承担的汇票债务责任终结的票据行为。

只有当付款满足如下条件时，才是正当付款，汇票才能被注销：

（1）付款须由受票人或承兑人，或者代表受票人或承兑人做出，而非由出票人或任一背书人做出。因为由出票人或任一背书人做出的付款不具有终结性，其会再向受票人或承兑人索取付款。

（2）付款须在到期日或到期日后支付，而非提前支付。

（3）付款须付给持票人。汇票如经转让，且受票人是银行，银行在付款前须检查背书或至少检查背书的连续性。

（4）付款须为善意付款，即对持票人票据权利的缺陷并不知情。

简言之，正当付款须由受票人或承兑人在到期日或到期日后向持票人做出善意付款，且对持票人票据权利的缺陷并不知情。当付款成为正当付款后，付款才为终结性付款，汇票才能被注销。注销使票据责任得以终结，票据运行过程结束。

6. 退票

退票是当汇票向受票人提示时，受票人对汇票拒绝做出承兑或拒绝做出付款的票据行为。

汇票的退票方式可以是拒绝承兑或拒绝付款。另外，当汇票只做限制性承兑时，持票人也可以将汇票视为退票。退票的其他方式还包括受票人的故意躲避、破产甚至死亡等，致使汇票无法获得承兑或付款。

当汇票被退票后，持票人即获追索权，可向其前手背书人直至出票人行使追索权，索取付款。

7. 发拒付通知

当汇票被退票后，持票人须向出票人或所有背书人发出拒付通知，以期他们承担责任。发此通知的目的是通知出票人以及前手背书人，汇票未获得承兑或付款，他们须做好支付准备。

拒付通知可以通过两种方式送达前手背书人和出票人。第一种方式是持票人在退票的下一个工作日向他的直接前手背书人发出通知，此直接前手背书人立即再通知他的直接前手背书人直至通知送达出票人。如果在此过程中，任何当事人未能如此发送通知，其在失去对前手背书人以及出票人追索权的同时，仍须对持票人承担责任。第二种方式是持票人单独通知汇票每个背书人和出票人,以便使他们承担责任。

第一种方式对持票人来说更方便可行,因为其可能不是对每一位背书人都了解,但能肯定每一位背书人都会传递退票通知。

如果出票人或背书人在其汇票签字的旁边载明"免除拒付通知",意思是如果汇票被退票,持票人可以在不对他发出拒付通知的情况下向他索取付款。

8. 作拒绝证书

拒绝证书是由公证人或其他授权方开出,证明汇票被退票的票据行为。拒绝证书须在汇票被退票当天或不迟于下一个工作日做出。

当汇票被退票并发出拒付通知后,持票人将汇票交由公证人向受票人再次提示,以获取退票的法律证明。如果汇票再次被退票,公证人会开立拒绝证书并连同被退票汇票交还持票人,持票人据以向前手背书人直至出票人行使追索权。

公证费由出票人承担,在索赔时收取。但是,出票人如在其汇票签字旁载明"免做拒绝证书"或"退票时请勿做拒绝证书",出票人便不会承担拒绝证书公证费。在这种情形下,持票人可不做拒绝证书而向他索取付款,而如果持票人仍寻求公证人开立拒绝证书,拒绝证书费则由持票人自己承担。

9. 行使追索权

追索权表示在汇票被退票的情况下,持票人有向出票人和背书人索取赔付的权利。行使此权利便成为一种票据行为。赔付金额应该是汇票应付金额加上利息、发出拒付通知和做拒绝证书以及产生的其他相关费用。

持票人在完成下列票据行为后可行使追索权:

(1)向受票人提示汇票要求承兑或付款但被退票。

(2)在退票日后一个工作日内向其前手背书人和出票人发拒付通知。

(3)在退票日后一个工作日内为拒绝承兑或拒绝付款做拒绝证书。

当出票人或任一背书人在汇票上载明"无追索权"时,其对汇票的责任即被免除,但这样的表述会影响汇票流通。

第二节　汇票的运行

汇票通过票据行为从出票向注销运行。但是,受以下两个因素的影响,汇票运行有着不同的轨迹:

第一,汇票是否被流通转让。

第二,汇票是否被退票。

图 4.3 显示了运行中的汇票既没有被流通转让也没有被退票。该运行过程简单，只涉及汇票的三个基本当事人和四个或五个票据行为。

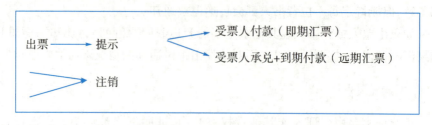

图 4.3　汇票基本运行过程

图 4.4 显示了运行中的汇票既被流通转让也被退票。该运行过程比上面的过程复杂，在被注销前，将涉及更多的当事人和更多的票据行为。

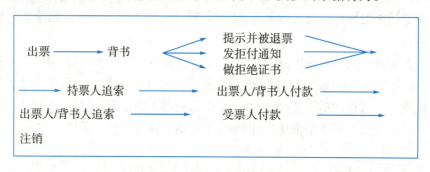

图 4.4　汇票复杂运行过程

汇票还可以有其他运行过程，也可能会涉及更多当事人与票据行为。但无论运行过程如何，汇票的运行都是从出票人出票开始到受票人或承兑人付款，汇票注销而结束。

第三节　汇票的分类

汇票按下列标准进行分类：

1. 按三个直接当事人的所在地分类

（1）国内汇票。当汇票的三个直接当事人，即出票人、受票人和收款人都在同一个国家，汇票为国内汇票。通常，国内汇票在同一国出票和支付。

（2）国际汇票。当三个直接当事人中的两个在不同的国家，汇票为国际汇票。通常，国际汇票在一个国家出票，在另一个国家支付。

2. 按期限分类

（1）即期汇票。即期汇票在受票人见票时立即支付。它可以被表述为见票即付、一经要求即付或一经提示即付。

（2）远期汇票。远期汇票在固定的未来时间或可以确定的未来时间支付。远期汇票可以再细分为在未来某一固定日、在出票日后某一固定日、在见票日后某一固定日或在某一确定会发生的具体事件发生后的某一固定日支付。

3. 按汇票抬头分类

（1）限制性抬头。汇票只支付给某一特定人，不可流通。

（2）指示性抬头。汇票支付给某一特定人或其指定人，通过背书和递交可流通。

（3）（持票）来人抬头。汇票支付给（持票）来人，通过递交便可流通，无需背书。

4. 按出票人和受票人分类

（1）银行汇票。银行汇票由一家银行向另一家银行或其总行/分行开出。当银行汇票由受票行承兑，便成为银行承兑汇票。银行承兑汇票代表银行承诺，因此在国际结算业务中最受欢迎。

（2）商业汇票。商业汇票由一家贸易商向另一家贸易商或一家银行开出。当商业汇票向另一家贸易商开出并由此贸易商承兑，便成为商业承兑汇票。当商业汇票向一家银行开出并由该银行承兑，便成为银行承兑汇票。

5. 按是否附带货运单据分类

（1）光票。光票是没有附带货运单据的汇票，通常在结算过程中单独使用。货运单据属于商业单据，结算中最常用的货运单据是海运提单。

开出光票的原因各异，主要有对服务款项的收取、个人汇款业务以及国际贸易中无货运单据的服务贸易的款项收取。当然，光票也可用于国际货物贸易的款项收取。

（2）跟单汇票。在结算过程中必须附带相关货运单据才能完成一笔出口交易的汇票是跟单汇票。跟单汇票在国际货物贸易中普遍使用。

光票和跟单汇票外观形式上无异。两者的区分点是看该汇票在结算过程中是单独运行还是附带货运单据运行。

总体来说，汇票的分类并不是非此即彼的。事实上，国际结算中的任一汇票都是五个类别的组合。例如，一张汇票可以是国际远期银行承兑只支付某一特定人的汇票,此汇票是光票还是跟单汇票则取决于其在某一具体结算过程中的运行方式。

第四节　贴现

持票人可以通过贴现汇票获得融资,在汇票到期日之前得到支付。

1. 贴现的定义

贴现汇票是指承兑汇票的持票人在汇票到期前以低于其面额的价格将汇票出售给一家金融机构的行为。

开办贴现业务的金融机构称为贴现行,持票人获得的贴现金额称为净款,汇票面额与净款之间的差额称为贴现息。

持票人贴现汇票的目的是在到期日之前提前获取款项,加速其资金周转,获得融资。贴现汇票的金融机构的目的是赚取利润。贴现息代表金融机构的利润,贴现息也是持票人为获得融资所支付的成本。

2. 贴现的程序

贴现的程序如图4.5所示。贴现的程序一结束,持票人便获得融资,金融机构便赚取了利润。

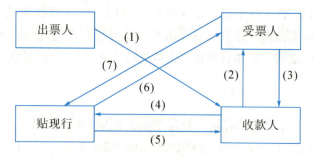

图4.5　贴现的程序

(1)出票人向受票人开出一张远期汇票并递交收款人/持票人。

(2)收款人向受票人提示承兑。

(3)受票人承兑汇票并将汇票交还收款人。

(4)到期日前,收款人作为汇票第一持票人向贴现行贴现(出售)汇票。

(5)贴现行贴现(购买)汇票,向收款人支付净款。贴现行成为新持票人。

(6)到期日时,贴现行向受票人提示付款。

(7)受票人向贴现行支付票面金额。

3. 贴现中的计算

贴现息和净款的计算如下：

贴现息＝（面额×贴现天数×贴现率）÷360（365）天

净款＝面额－贴现息

净款＝面额×［1－贴现天数÷360（365）天×贴现率］

公式中的贴现天数是指从贴现日至到期日之间的天数。贴现率是金融机构为贴现而设置的比率。

例如：

一张金额为 USD 10 000、见票后 90 天的汇票在 2023 年 6 月 20 日承兑并在 2023 年 6 月 30 日贴现。如果贴现率为 10%，一年按 360 天计，计算其贴现息与净款。

计算如下：

当持票人在 6 月 30 日贴现汇票时，距到期日剩余的天数为 90－10＝80 天。因此，贴现天数为 80 天。

贴现息＝（10 000×80×10%）÷360＝USD 222. 22

净款＝10 000－222. 22＝USD 9 777. 78

上例表明，持票人在 2023 年 6 月 30 日贴现汇票时获得 USD 9 777.78。贴现行在到期日向受票人提示付款时获得 USD 10 000。因此，贴现行赚取的利润为 USD 222.22。

4. 贴现行的角色

从汇票流通的角度看，贴现行是被背书人，从背书人（收款人/第一持票人）处获取汇票。但是，该流通是以向背书人提供融资为其特殊目的的贴现。在通常情况下，如汇票不再继续流通，贴现行成为汇票的新持票人。

作为持票人，贴现行将承担在到期日汇票被拒付的风险。因此，承兑行非常看重承兑人的资信。总体来说，银行资信高于贸易商资信，一流银行的资信高于小银行的资信。因此，在贴现市场，一张一流银行承兑汇票比一张商业承兑汇票更易被贴现。

同时，与任何持票人一样，如受票人拒绝付款，贴现行将获得向其前手背书人和出票人追索的权利。如发生这种情况，原收款人获得的融资金额将被追回。

第五章　本票和支票

学习目标

◇学习本票的概念。

◇学习支票的定义和分类。

◇学习支票结清程序。

◇思考不同金融票据的关联性。

第一节　本票

本票是由一人（出票人）向另一人（收款人）开出的，由出票人签字，保证对某一特定人或其指定人、持票来人即期或在某一固定未来日期或在某一可以确定的未来日期支付一定金额的书面无条件付款承诺。

本票（promissory note）又称为"note"，如图5.1所示。

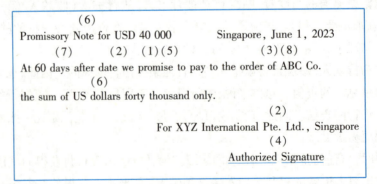

图 5.1　本票

1. 本票的要件

与汇票相似，本票的定义规定出本票的要件。要件是使本票成为有效票据的先决条件，具体如下：

（1）书面无条件承诺。

（2）由一人（出票人）开出。

（3）开给另一人（收款人）。

（4）由出票人签字。

（5）保证支付。

（6）一定金额。

（7）在即期或在某一固定未来日期或在某一可以确定的未来日期支付。

（8）支付给某一特定人或其指定人、持票来人。

2. 本票与汇票

作为一种主要的金融票据，与汇票一样，在中国，本票也遵循《中华人民共和国票据法》的相关条款，但有下列与汇票不同之处：

（1）本票是一种无条件承诺，而汇票是一种无条件命令。

（2）直接当事人。本票只有两个直接当事人，即出票人和收款人；汇票有三个基本当事人，即出票人、受票人和收款人。本票的出票人相当于汇票的出票人和受票人。

（3）承兑要求。由于本票的出票人承担第一付款责任，承兑不适用于本票。因此，本票鲜有在见票后某一固定日支付的远期本票。远期汇票常要求承兑，特别是在见票后某一固定日支付的远期汇票。

（4）对做拒绝证书的要求。做拒绝证书的要求不适用于被退票的国际本票；退票后的国际汇票须做拒绝证书，才能使持票人获取追索权。

（5）出票人和收款人。本票的出票人和收款人不能为同一人，汇票的出票人和收款人可以为同一人。

（6）全套份数。本票单张签发，汇票成套签发。当一张汇票获得付款后，另一张失效。

3. 本票的主要类别

（1）银行本票。银行本票在银行业务中用途广泛。

由银行开出支付给特定人的本票可视为现金。即期支付给持票来人的银行本票是"法定货币"，属于一个国家的货币范畴。银行即期持票来人抬头本票的发行受特别法律监管，只能由央行或授权银行发行。

如果对商业银行发行持票来人抬头即期本票失控，势必会扰乱一个国家的金融体系。因此，商业银行只能签发支付给特定人的本票。

（2）商业本票。商业本票（trader's note）又称为"commercial papers"，是由公司或贸易商开出的远期持票来人抬头的本票。任何人一经向出票人支付了本票面额后，即成为商业本票的收款人。

商业本票不用作支付工具。出票人签发商业本票的目的是向公众筹资，因此发行时带有支付给商业本票购买者的利息。地方政府或大企业也可以发行一年期远期本票向公众筹资，这种远期本票便称为债券。

（3）国库券。国库券虽然称为"treasury bill"，但它不是汇票（bill）而是远期持票来人抬头本票（note），由财政部授权央行发行。国库券按一定年利率以贴现方式向投资者销售，其期限一般是出票日后 90 天支付，国库券的主要购买者为各个商业银行。

国库券的售价为净款。投资者购买时支付净款，到期时获得国库券票面金额，贴现息为其赚取的利润。

与商业本票一样，国库券不用作支付工具，中央政府可用其进行筹款，收款人可用其赚取利润。更为重要的是，中央政府还可利用国库券来调节市场的资金余缺。

第二节　支票

支票是由银行客户向银行开出，由银行客户签字，授权银行对某一特定人或其指定人或持票来人即期支付一定金额的书面无条件支付命令。

简言之，支票可以理解为向银行开出的即期汇票。支票（check）也可以写为"cheque"，如图 5.2 所示。

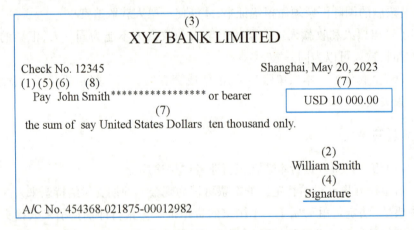

图 5.2　支票

支票由银行为其客户预先印制并将空白支票簿交由客户，客户在需要时填写（出票）支票，递交收款人。

1. 支票的要件

与汇票、本票相似,支票的定义规定出支票的要件。要件是使支票成为有效票据的先决条件,具体如下:

(1)无条件的支付命令。

(2)由客户(出票人)开出。

(3)向银行(受票人)开出。

(4)由此客户签字。

(5)授权银行支付。

(6)即期支付。

(7)一定金额。

(8)支付给某一特定人或其指定人或(持票)来人(收款人)。

2. 支票的直接当事人

支票有三个直接当事人:

(1)出票人。"出票"是指从银行账户里填写出一定金额的支票。换言之,出票人就是填写支票的人。

首先,出票人应是在银行开立了账户的客户。其次,当出票人出票时,其责任是确保其账户里的余额足以支付支票金额。否则,支票会被跳票。

(2)受票人。受票人是支票开给的银行。该银行是出票人开立账户的银行。

银行的责任是对客户支票金额在其账户余额内或在其透支额度内的支票付款。如果受票行对客户支票做出了不当退票,银行须承担全责并做出赔偿。

(3)收款人。收款人是支票向其支付的当事人。

3. 支票的划线与结清

(1)非划线支票。非划线支票是指只是对银行"空白"支票进行了填入,其正面没有两条划出的平行线的支票。当持票人在受票行提示付款时,非划线支票可以在银行柜台提现(见图5.3)。

(2)划线支票。划线支票是指在支票正面,通常是在支票的左上角划有两条平行线的支票。划线支票的持票人不能在柜台提现,支票金额必须通过银行账户划转。对支票划线的目的是确保款项付给正确的持票人。划线支票分为以下两种:

①普通划线支票。普通划线支票是指支票正面划有两道平行线,其间可以带有也可以不带有"和公司""& Co.""不可流通""账户收款人"等字样(见图5.4)。

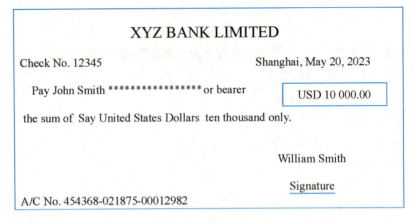

图 5.3　非划线支票

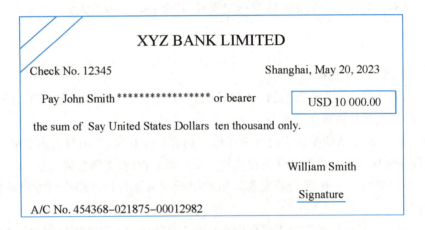

图 5.4　普通划线支票

普通划线的目的是使支票仅通过银行账户划转。普通划线并不指定托收行。只要支票是完整有效的，受票行须对通过任何银行提示的支票进行付款。

②特别划线支票。当支票正面的两道平行线之间添加了一家银行的名字，无论是否再带有"和公司""& Co.""不可流通""账户收款"等字样，增添的银行名称使划线成为特别划线（见图 5.5）。

特别划线的目的是使支票只能通过指定的那家银行的账户收取，此时该银行为托收行。其他银行不对支票进行提示付款。

出票人和收款人可以做出以下行为：

第一，对未划线支票进行划线。

第二，将支票的普通划线改为特别划线。

（3）划线支票的结清。收款人/持票人要兑现划线支票金额，必须首先将支票存入一家其开立了账户的银行，要求银行为其收款。这家银行称为托收行，它可以是也可以不是支票受票行。

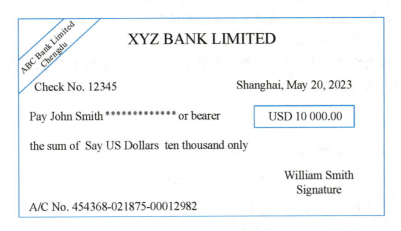

图 5.5　特别划线支票

图 5.6 显示了划线支票结清程序,其收款人/持票人将支票存入非受票行的银行(托收行)。

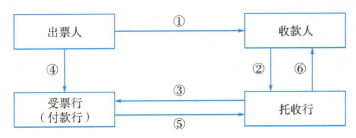

图 5.6　划线支票结清程序

①出票人开出支票并将其递交收款人。

②收款人将支票存入托收行,要求此银行为其收款。

③核查后,托收行代表收款人将支票递交受票行。

④核查后,受票行借记出票人在该行的账户。

⑤付款行将金额转至托收行。

⑥托收行将金额贷记收款人账户。

4. 支票与汇票

作为主要的金融票据之一,与汇票一样,支票也遵循《中华人民共和国票据法》的相关条款,但有下列与汇票不同之处:

(1)汇票可由任何一人向另一人开出,支票只能由在银行开立了账户并有足够余额的银行客户向其银行开出。

(2)汇票的期限可以是即期或远期,支票只能是即期。

(3)汇票承兑后,承兑人对汇票付款承担第一责任;承兑不适用于支票,支票的出票人须对支票承担第一责任。

（4）汇票承兑人对支票做出的承兑不可撤销，支票受票行对支票付款的职责和权利可以被出票人的止付命令加以终止。

（5）划线规则只适用于支票。支票开立的目的不是用于流通，因此流通规则对支票意义不大。

5. 汇票、本票和支票

这三种金融票据的主要区别如表 5.1 所示。

表 5.1　汇票、本票和支票

项目	汇票	本票	支票
特点	命令	承诺	命令
出票人	A/A/A	A	A/A （客户）
受票人	B/A/B	A	B/B （银行）
收款人	C/C/A	C	C/A
期限	即期/ 远期	即期/ 远期	即期
承兑	适用	不适用	不适用

第三部分　结算篇

第六章　汇款

学习目标

◇学习支付方式的分类。

◇学习汇款的定义及分类。

◇学习信汇、电汇和票汇的程序。

◇学习票汇汇票的开立要求。

◇学习汇款在国际贸易中的应用。

◇学习汇款的特点。

第一节　支付方式概述

资金需进行跨国转移有以下目的：

第一，对国际贸易所产生的债务进行结算。

第二，向国外亲朋进行个人汇款。

第三，对政府的对外援助调拨款项。

当资金的跨国转移是对国际贸易所产生的债务进行结算，这便是国际贸易结算，也是本书的重点。当资金的跨国转移是为实现后两个目的，则是国际非贸易结算。

资金的转移须通过银行，银行应其客户的要求跨国转移资金。或者说，贸易商要求银行向其应支付的国外贸易伙伴转移资金。在这一结算过程中，客户（贸易商）是"委托人"，指示银行向贸易另一方，即"受益人"转移资金。银行成为其客户，即"委托人"的"中间人"或"代理"。这种委托-代理关系在国际结算中很重要。国际结算中的任何支付方式都反映了这种关系，都涉及两个贸易商及其各自的银行。

此外，在国际结算中区分支付方式和支付工具这两个概念也很重要。支付工具是指现金或金融票据。在非现金结算时代，虽然需要使用现金来计算付款金额，出口商在结算过程完结之后也会获得现金支付，但在整个结算过程中运行的是金融票据,即汇票。支付方式包括两个部分:金融票据和商业单据。因此,尽管支付方式涉及支付工具,但单凭支付工具并不能称其为支付方式。

第二节　支付方式的分类

1. 按实际应用分类

(1)汇款。

(2)托收。

(3)信用证。

(4)保理。

(5)保函。

2. 按支付工具分类

(1)现金结算。现金结算是指当国际结算还未得到充分发展时,用现金充当交换媒介,运行于结算过程之中。

(2)非现金结算。非现金结算是指金融票据(多以汇票为主),充当交换的媒介,运行于结算过程之中。非现金结算标志着国际结算进入现代期,上述按实际应用分类的五种支付方式都属于非现金结算方式。

3. 按资信分类

(1)商业信用。在商业信用中,出口商获得的付款承诺来自进口商。汇款和托收这两种支付方式是建立在商业信用基础上的支付方式。

(2)银行信用。在银行信用中,出口商获得的付款承诺来自银行而非进口商。信用证、保理和保函都是建立在银行信用基础上的支付方式

银行信用一般被视为高于商业信用。因此,如果选用的支付方式是建立在银行信用基础上,出口商获得的付款保证更为安全。当然,出口商要获得付款,仍然需要依赖银行的资信。

4. 按票据的运行方向与资金的流动方向分类

(1)顺汇。在顺汇中,债务人(进口商)将款项(付款资金)交给银行,要求银行通过某种金融票据或付款指令向债权人(出口商)转移资金。金融单据的出票人或付款指令的签发人为进口商银行,金融单据的受票人或付款指令的收件人为出口商银行。

顺汇表示资金的流动方向与金融票据或付款指令的运行方向一致,其资金流动方向与运行方向如图6.1所示(图中直线代表资金流动方向,虚线则表示票据或付款指令的运行方向)。

图6.1 顺汇

在按实际应用分类的五种支付方式中,只有汇款属于顺汇。

(2)逆汇。在逆汇中,债权人(出口商)向债务人(进口商)或债务人的银行开立汇票,要求银行凭汇票为他人收取款项。

逆汇表示资金流动方向与金融票据运行方向相反。托收、信用证、保理和保函都属于逆汇。其资金流动方向和运行方向如图6.2所示(图中直线代表资金流动方向,虚线则表示票据的运行方向)。

图6.2 逆汇

第三节 汇款概述

如图6.3所示,汇款是指某一银行(汇出行),在其客户(汇款人)的要求下,将一定金额转移至其国外分行或其代理行(付款行),指示其向居住在该国的某一指定人(收款人/受益人)付款。

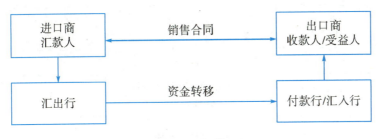

图 6.3　汇款

汇款的四个直接当事人如下：

1. 汇款人

汇款人是进行汇款的当事人,向其银行提出向国外受益人汇出款项的要求。在国际贸易中,汇款人为买方或进口商。

2. 汇出行

汇出行是按汇款人的要求,向付款行汇出款项并指示付款行向受益人支付一定金额的银行。在国际贸易中,汇出行是进口商银行。

3. 付款行/汇入行

付款行/汇入行是从汇出行收入款项,并按汇出行指示向受益人支付一定金额的银行。在国际贸易中,付款行/汇入行是出口商银行。

4. 收款人/受益人

收款人/受益人是接受汇款款项的当事人。在国际贸易中,收款人/受益人为卖方或出口商。

第四节　汇款的分类

按付款命令的不同发出方式,汇款分为通过航空邮寄的信汇(M/T)、电子转账的电汇(T/T)和使用银行即期汇票的票汇(D/D)

1. 信汇

(1)信汇的定义。汇出行在汇款人的要求下,通过向付款行发送/邮寄付款指令,要求付款行向受益人支付一定金额。信汇的定义如图6.4所示。

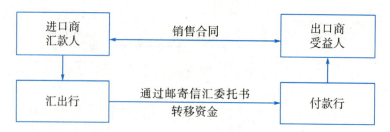

图 6.4　信汇的定义

信汇利用邮政服务邮寄付款指令。付款指令是由汇出行向付款行发出的经过证实的书面命令。在信汇中，付款指令以信汇委托书形式发出。

信汇委托书基于信汇申请书开立。信汇申请书在汇款人要求银行为其转移资金之前填写。当银行在客户填写完毕并签字的信汇申请书上签章后，信汇申请书成为银行（汇出行）与客户（汇款人）之间的契约，银行据此转移资金。

空白申请书由银行预先成套印制，其中第一联为信汇申请书，第二联为信汇委托书，第三联为客户存根。汇出行在信汇委托书上签字后邮寄给付款行。

图 6.5 为信汇申请书，图 6.6 为信汇委托书。

图 6.5　信汇申请书

图 6.6 信汇委托书

（2）信汇的程序。信汇的详细步骤如图 6.7 所示。

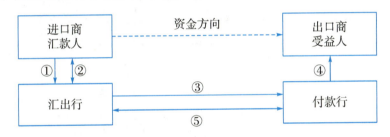

图 6.7 信汇的详细步骤

①汇款人向其银行提交已签字的书面申请书，要求银行通过信汇方式转移资金。

②汇出行核查汇款人账户。如账户余额足够，汇出行在申请书上签章并将客户存根交还汇款人存档。汇出行按汇出金额加上其佣金和航空邮寄费用借记汇款人账户（如客户无账户，客户则将现金与申请书一并提交银行）。

③汇出行开立信汇委托书并邮寄给付款行。

④付款行对照汇出行有权签名样本验证信汇委托书，核实受益人身份后付款。

⑤付款行向汇出行索取偿付。

2. 电汇

（1）电汇的定义。汇出行在汇款人的要求下，通过电报、电传、SWIFT 方式向付款行转移资金，要求付款行向受益人支付一定金额。电汇的定义如图 6.8 所示。

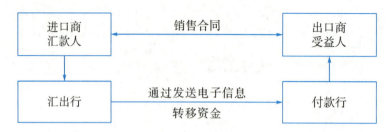

图 6.8　电汇的定义

银行为客户预先印制空白电汇申请书，如图 6.9 所示。

APPLICATION FOR TELEGRAPHIC/ELECTRONIC TRANSFER

图 6.9　电汇申请书

　　电子信息由电报、电传或 SWIFT 发送。SWIFT 是环球间电讯金融协会的英语首字母缩略词，协会成员行之间发送的 SWIFT 信息为电子信息。信汇中的信函信息须由汇出行有权签名加以验证，而电汇中的电子信息须由密押或

SAK 密押(SWIFT 密押)加以验证。

密押或 SAK 密押是两家银行为验证电子信息而提前协商的密码编码。密押的密码由一系列的列表数字构成,每一个数字代表某月、某日、金额、币种以及其他相关项目。这些数字相加的总和构成密押或 SAK 密押,与电子信息一并发送以达验证目的。

(2)电汇的程序。电汇的详细步骤如图 6.10 所示。

图 6.10　电汇的详细步骤

① 汇款人向其银行提交已签字的书面申请书,要求银行通过电汇方式转移资金。

② 汇出行核查汇款人账户。如果账户余额足够,汇出行在申请书上签章并将客户存根交还汇款人存档。汇出行按汇出金额加上其佣金和电汇费用借记汇款人账户(如果客户无账户,客户将现金与申请书一并提交银行)。

③ 汇出行以电报、电传、SWIFT 方式发出付款指令。

④ 付款行对照密押或 SWIFT 密押验证电子信息,核实受益人身份后付款。

⑤ 付款行向汇出行索取偿付。

3. 票汇

(1)票汇的定义。汇出行在汇款人的要求下,向付款行开出汇票,要求付款行向汇票收款人/受益人即期支付一定金额。票汇的定义如图 6.11 所示。

图 6.11　票汇的定义

银行可预先印制票汇或电汇申请书,客户在要求银行票汇或电汇时对相应方框进行勾选。汇票/电汇申请书如图 6.12 所示。

OVERSEAS UNION BANK LIMITED

APPLICATION FOR DEMAND DRAFT/TELEGRAPHIC TRANSFER

DD/TT No.

Name of Applicant
Address

Agent/Correspondent

Contact Tel. No.

I/We wish to apply for a
☐ Demand Draft Drawn on ________ (Location)
☐ Telegraphic Transfer to ________ (Location)

FOR BANK USE

FX Contract No.
(if applicable)

For Demand Draft only
Beneficiary's Name

Currency/Amount

Exchange Rate | SGD Equivalent

Commission

Cable Charges

For Telegraphic Transfer only
Beneficiary's Bank

Total

Beneficiary's
Account No
Name

This application and the issue of the above item is subject to the Bank's Terms and Conditions (printed overleaf) receipt of which I/we hereby acknowledge, and which I/we have read and agree to abide by.

Details of Payment

In Settlement:
☐ Debit my/our Account No.
☐ Bank ________ Cheque No.
☐ Cash

Charges Imposed by Agent/Correspondent
☐ To be borne by me/us ☐ To be borne by beneficiary

Signature(s) of Applicant(s) Date

Instruction for Beneficiary's Bank (if any)

TELLER OFFICER

OUB 1924 (1) Bank Copy

图 6.12　票汇/电汇申请书

票汇中付款指令是通过银行即期汇票的方式发出的，该汇票由汇出行向付款行开出，收款人为出口商。

银行即期汇票如图 6.13 所示。该汇票也可视为支票，其三个直接当事人如下：

出票人：The Royal Bank of Canada，Mongkok Branch，Hong Kong.

受票人：The Royal Bank of Canada，Toronto，Canada.

收款人：ABC Co.，Toronto，Canada.

The Royal Bank, Limited
Hong Kong

REF. No.
No. R 12345

Date: June 8, 2023

Pay to the order of : ABC Co., Toronto *************** CAD 10 000.00

the sum of Canadian dollars ten thousand only ***

TO:
The Royal Bank of Canada
International Centre
22 XY ST. Toronto, Canada

The Royal Bank of Canada
Mongkok Br. HK

authorized signature

图 6.13　票汇汇票

（2）票汇的程序。票汇的详细步骤如图 6.14 所示。

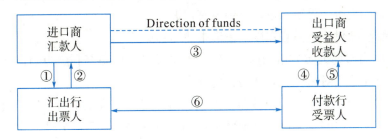

图 6.14　票汇的详细步骤

① 汇款人向其银行提交已签字的书面申请书，要求银行通过票汇方式转移资金。

② 汇出行核查汇款人账户。如果账户余额足够，汇出行在申请书上签章并将客户存根交还汇款人存档。汇出行按汇款金额加上其佣金借记汇款人账户，向付款行开立支付给出口商的汇票。汇票开出后交由汇款人（如果客户无账户，客户将现金与申请书一并提交银行）。

③ 汇款人将汇票寄送出口商。

④ 收到汇票后，出口商/收款人向付款行提示汇票。

⑤ 在凭有权签字验证汇票后，付款行向出口商支付款项。

⑥ 付款行向汇出行索取偿付。

与信汇和票汇相比，电汇付款速度最快、最安全，但银行费用也最高。鉴于其快捷及安全性，贸易商一般选择电汇，特别是当汇款金额大，付款又有时限要求时，更是如此。

第五节　汇款的应用

当贸易商在进出口交易中选用汇款时，除对信汇、电汇或票汇进行选择外，还须再对预付货款和赊销进行选择。

1. 预付货款

预付货款是指付款的时间先于提交货物或服务的时间。进口商先通过信汇、电汇或票汇付款，出口商收到款项后再安排发货。显然，预付货款对出口商有利，但对进口商风险极大。

预付货款对进口商不利的原因如下：

（1）进口商提前付款，在收到货物或服务前其资金被冻结。

（2）进口商承担出口商不交货的风险。

（3）进口商对合同下的货物是否会交付、是否会收到、是否会在约定的时间内收到、是否会保质保量地收到没有把握。

因此，预付货款一般在以下情形中使用：

（1）当市场为卖方市场时，此时市场情形对出口商有利。为确保获得货物，进口商选用对出口商有利的支付方式。

（2）当货物的生产过程或服务的提供过程专业化程度很高且属于资金密集型时，进口商同意通过部分预付货款和部分按进程付款的方式对出口商进行融资。

（3）出口商在对进口商资信不确定时，或者当进口商国家的政治经济状况不稳定，可能致使付款延误且出口商不可控时，出口商可能坚持以预付货款的支付方式进行结算。

总体来说，为保护自己，进口商在选用预付货款前应确定出口商资信优良，否则进口商应只同意将预付货款用于结算部分款项，余额通过其他支付方式进行结算。

2. 赊销

赊销与预付货款刚好相反。赊销是指出口商在进口商通过信汇、电汇或票汇付款前先行发货。尽管双方已预先约定付款时间，但事实上出口商是在以赊账的方式销售，对进口商是否履约付款并无把握。赊销对进口商有利，但对出口商风险极大。

赊销对出口商不利的原因如下：

（1）出口商承担进口商不付款的风险。

（2）出口商在付款没有把握的情况下放弃了对货物的所有权。

（3）在收到货款前，出口商的资金已冻结。

（4）有可能因政治风险而实施的规则延缓或阻碍资金流动，影响出口商收款。

赊销一般在以下情形中使用：

（1）当市场为买方市场时，此时市场对进口商有利。为保持竞争力，出口商选用对进口商有利的支付方式。当然，赊销不是使出口商具有竞争力的唯一方式。

（2）进口商、出口商之间有着长期的、经常的贸易关系。

（3）当跨国公司向其海外分公司或附属公司发货时使用。

总之，为了保护自己，出口商在选用赊销前应确定进口商资信优良。否则出口商应要求赊销在银行保函情形下使用或只将其用于交易的部分款项的结算。

第六节　汇款的特点

　　汇款是基于商业信用的支付方式。银行只按汇款人/进口商的要求向出口商转移资金,并不给与出口商付款承诺。在汇款的过程中,银行不运作单据。商业单据和金融单据,如有的话,也是直接由贸易商自己寄送。换言之,银行在汇款中承担的责任少、介入的程度低。因此,汇款具有如下利弊:与托收和信用证相比,一方面,由于银行介入程度低,汇款是最简单、最便宜的支付方式。另一方面,由于同样的原因,汇款对贸易商的风险最大。在预付货款情况下,进口商承担出口商不交货的极大风险,当不交货的情况发生时,进口商钱货两失。在赊销情况下,出口商承担进口商不付款的极大风险,当不付款的情况发生时,出口商也是钱货两失。汇款并不能降低这些风险。

第七章　托收

学习目标

◇学习托收的定义及当事人。

◇学习托收的分类。

◇学习即期付款交单、远期付款交单和承兑交单的程序。

◇学习托收汇票的开立要求。

◇学习托收的特点。

第一节　托收的定义

1. 定义一

托收是指银行按其收到的以下指示运作单据：

（1）获得付款或承兑。

（2）付款交单或承兑交单。

"单据"是指金融单据和商业单据。

2. 定义二

托收是指这样的安排，出口商发货并向进口商开立相关汇票，汇票随附或不随附单据提交给出口商银行，明确指示该银行通过其在进口商处的代理行（总行/分行）进行款项托收。托收的定义二如图7.1所示。

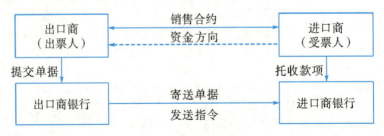

图7.1　托收的定义二

第二节　托收的当事人及 URC

1. 委托人

委托人是将托收项(单据)提交给其银行的当事人，是委托-代理关系的委托方，也是出口商和汇票的出票人，还是将货物发运的发货人。

2. 受票人

受票人是汇票开出的当事人，应该对汇票进行付款或承兑，是进口商。

3. 汇出行/托收行

汇出行/托收行是出口商银行，从委托人/出口商处接受托收项(汇票或其他单据)，向其海外代理行或海外总行/分行寄送托收项，要求后者从进口商处收取款项(在下文中，"remitting bank"将统一采用第一种译法，即译为"汇出行")。

4. 托收行/代收行

托收行/代收行从汇出行处接受托收项并向受票人提示汇票，是进口商银行，也是汇出行的海外代理行或其海外总行/分行(在下文中，"collecting bank"将统一采用第一种译法，即译为"托收行")。

当委托人指定了托收行时，汇出行便向这家银行发送单据。如果委托人未指定托收行，汇出行将为委托人选择托收行。在实务中，最好由汇出行选择托收行。因为并非所有海外银行都值得信赖，所以由汇出行选择一家其了解的银行来执行指令的做法更为稳妥。

《托收统一规则》(URC)由国际商会出台，是国际上认可的有关跟单托收的执业守则，对相关各方和所有银行具有法律约束力。托收指示须明确载明此托收业务受 URC 规则制约。托收业务一般总是遵循 URC 规则，除非托收指示另有规定，或者某些国际法律与 URC 规则相左。URC 522 是 URC 的最新版本，于 1996 年 1 月 1 日生效。前一个版本是 URC 322，于 1978 年 1 月 1 日生效。

第三节　托收的分类

根据金融票据是否附带物权单据（货运单据）向汇出行提交，托收可分为光票托收和跟单托收。

1. 光票托收

光票托收是只针对不附带货运单据的金融票据的托收。如有货运单据，出口商直接寄送至进口商。当提交的金融票据还附带有如商业发票的非货运单据时，这种托收也视为光票托收。

光票托收主要用于对贸易产生的诸如运费、保费、佣金或其他从属费用等杂费的收取。光票托收使用于定金的收取或没有货运单据的服务贸易款项的收取。

2. 跟单托收

跟单托收是对附带货运单据的金融票据的托收或对没有金融票据的货运单据的托收。当不使用金融票据时，对金融票据出票人所征收的印花税可避免，托收金额则在商业发票中指明。

与光票托收相比，银行在跟单托收中须运作货运单据，因而承担的责任更大，跟单托收也更为广泛地运用于国际货物贸易的托收业务中。

基于向进口商交单的不同条件，跟单托收又可分为付款交单和承兑交单。总体来说，付款交单对出口商更有利，而承兑交单对进口商更有利。

（1）即期付款交单。即期付款交单是指托收行凭进口商对即期汇票的付款或只凭进口商的即期付款便进行交单，出口商获得即期支付。即期付款交单中使用的汇票，如有，须为即期汇票。当进口商/受票人即期付款后，托收行立即向其交单。

即期付款交单并不一定要求使用汇票，托收行可以凭对商业发票的付款而交单。商业发票是一种商业单据，会清楚载明应支付的金额。即期付款交单的程序如图 7.2 所示。

①出口商发货获得货运单据后，以货物价值向进口商开立即期汇票，填写托收申请书。托收申请书中清楚指明单据交付条件为即期付款交单。之后出口商将此申请书与汇票和商业单据提交其银行要求托收（如果不用汇票，将不开立、不提交汇票）。

②基于申请书，汇出行开立银行托收指示并将该指示与其收到的托收项寄送托收行。

图 7.2　即期付款交单的程序

③作为汇出行的代理,托收行在收到托收指示和托收项后,向进口商提示汇票要求其付款(如无汇票,托收行则直接通知进口商即期付款)。

④进口商向托收行进行即期付款。

⑤托收行凭进口商的即期付款向其交单。

⑥托收行按托收指示的指令将款项汇至汇出行。

⑦汇出行将款项贷记出口商在他处开立的账户。

(2)远期付款交单。远期付款交单是指托收行凭进口商对远期汇票的付款而进行交单,出口商获得远期支付。远期付款交单中使用的汇票是远期汇票。当进口商在远期汇票到期日付款后,托收行才向其交单。远期付款交单的程序如图 7.3 所示。

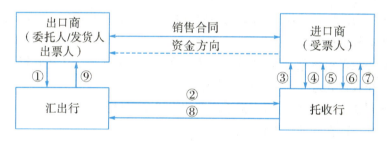

图 7.3　远期付款交单的程序

①出口商发货获得货运单据后,以货物价值向进口商开立远期汇票,填写托收申请书。托收申请书中清楚指明单据交付条件为远期付款交单。之后出口商将此申请书与汇票和商业单据提交其银行要求托收。

②基于申请书,汇出行开立银行托收指示并将该指示与其收到的托收项寄送托收行。

③作为汇出行的代理,托收行在收到托收指示和托收项后,向进口商提示汇票要求其承兑。

④一经提示承兑,进口商承兑汇票并将此已承兑汇票交还托收行。

⑤到期日时,托收行再次提示汇票要求进口商付款。

⑥进口商在到期日付款(远期付款)。

⑦托收行凭进口商的远期付款向其交单。

⑧托收行按托收指示的指令将款项汇至汇出行。

⑨汇出行将款项贷记出口商在他处开立的账户。

（3）承兑交单。承兑交单是指托收行凭进口商对汇票的承兑而进行交单,出口商获得远期支付。承兑交单下的汇票为远期汇票。承兑交单的程序如图7.4所示。

图7.4　承兑交单的程序

①出口商发货获得货运单据后,以货物价值向进口商开立远期汇票,填写托收申请书。托收申请书中清楚指明单据交付条件为承兑交单。之后出口商将此申请书与汇票和商业单据提交其银行要求托收。

②基于申请书,汇出行开立银行托收指示并将该指示与其收到的托收项寄送托收行。

③作为汇出行的代理,托收行在收到托收指示和托收项后,向进口商提示汇票要求其承兑。

④一经提示承兑,进口商承兑汇票并将此已承兑汇票交还托收行。

⑤托收行凭进口商的承兑向其交单。

⑥到期日时,托收行再次提示汇票要求进口商付款。

⑦进口商在到期日进行付款。

⑧托收行按托收指示的指令将款项汇至汇出行。

⑨汇出行将款项贷记出口商在他处开立的账户。

第四节　托收指示

托收指示是一种标准授权书,出口商在此授权书中就跟单托收向其银行写入具体指令。托收业务按托收指示中的具体指令运作。国际商会制作的托收指示标准格式如图7.5所示。

PLEASE COLLECT THE UNDERMENITIONED FOREIGN BILL OR DOCUMENTS

Full Name and Address of Drawer/Exporter		For Bank Use Only	Date	I.S.B. Collection No.	
		Drawers reference (to be quoted in all correspondence)			
		For Bank Use Only	Due Date	Correspondence Reference	
Consignee-Full Name and Address		Drawee (if not Consignee)-full Name and Address			
		For Bank Use Only	Fate Dates		
TO Barclays Bank PLC S.W.I.F.T. ADDRESS BARC GB22		Drawers Bankers Barclays Bank	Sorting Code No. 20-	Ref. No.	
		Account No.			

PLEASE FORWARD DOCUMENTS ENUMERATED BELOW BY AIRMAIL FOLLOW SPECIAL INSTRUCTIONS AND THOSE MARKED X

Bill of Exchange	Comm'l Invoice	Cert'd /Cons Inv.	Cert.of Origin	Ins'ce Pol/ Cert.	Bill of Lading	Parcel PostRec'pt	AirWaybill

Combined Transport Doc.	Other Documents and whereabouts of any missing original Bill of Lading				

Release Documents on	Acceptance	Payment	If unaccepted and advise reason by	Protest	Do Not Protest
If documents are not taken up on arrival of goods	Warehouse Goods	Do Not Warehouse		Cable	Airmail
	Insure Against File	Do Not Insure		Protest	Do Not Protest
Collect All Charges	Yes	No	If unpaid and advise reason by	Cable	Airmail
Collect Correspondent's Charges ONLY	Yes	No	Acceptance /Payment may be deferred until arrival of goods	Yes	No
Goods and carrying vessel			After final payment Remit proceeds by	Cable	Airmail

For Bank Use Only				
In case of need refer to			For Guidance	Accept their Instructions

SPECIAL INSTRUCTIONS 1. Represent on arrival of goods if not honored on first presentation

Date of Bill of Exchange	Tenor		Amount of Collection
Bill of Exchangeclaused	Please apply Proceeds of this collection as indicated with an "X"	Credit us in Sterling	
		Credit our Foreign Currency Account No.	
		Apply to Forward Contract No.	
	I/We agree that you shall not be liable for any loss, damage, or delay however caused which is not directly due to the negligence of your own officers and servants. Any charges and expenses not recovered from the drawees, including any costs of protecting the merchandise, may be charged to us		
For Bank use Only	Dates & Signature		

Subject to uniform rules for collections (1978 Revision) International Chamber of Commerce Publication No. 322

图 7.5 托收指示标准格式

当出口商填写签字并向汇出行提交后,此授权书为托收申请书。基于此申请书,银行缮制托收指示并寄交托收行。当出口商在托收程序开始提交时,此授权书也可用作涵盖托收项的面函。跟单托收申请书样例如图 7.6 所示。

TO：BANK OF CHINA   DATE：
     SINGAPORE

Dear Sirs

I/we enclose herewith the following draft(s) and document(s) for collection subject to the terms and conditions set out overleaf：

Bill No.	Amount	Due Date/Tenor	Drawee

Documents	Drafts	B/L	Invoice	P/W List	Ins Cert	Cert Origin	Cert of Qly /Qty	AWB	D.O.	

kindly act in accordance with my/our instructions marked "X" as indicated hereinbelow：

( ) Deliver document(s) against payment   ( ) Deliver Document(s) against acceptance

( ) All banking charges are for the account of the drawee.

( ) All collecting bank's charges are for the account of drawee and your charges are for my/our account.

( ) Protest for non-payment   ( ) Protest for non-acceptance

( ) Overdue interest to be collected from the drawee at % per annum from due date to the approximate date of return remittance in Singapore.

( ) Interest to be collected from the drawee at % per annum from first presentation to the approximate date of return remittance in Singapore.

In case of need or difficulties, please communicate with (seller's representative)：

Address：

Tel：

Who will endeavor to obtain the honoring of the aforesaid draft(s), without any alteration of my/our instructions.

In case of dishonor, the goods may, in the option of your correspondent or agent, be landed, cleared through the customs, warehoused and insured at my/our costs and expenses.

It is understood and agreed that, having exercised due care in the selection of any correspondent to whom the abovementioned items any be sent for collection, you shall not be responsible for any act, omission, default, suspension, insolvency or bankruptcy of any such correspondent or sub-agent thereof, or for any delay in remittance, loss in exchange or loss of items or their proceeds during transmission or in the course of collection, but your responsibility shall be only for your own acts.

PAYMENT INSTRUCTIONS：

( )   Please advance/discount the bill.

( )   Please pay us only upon receipt of funds

( )   Please credit proceeds to our account no.：

( )   Please offset Import Bill(s) ref.：

( )   Please utilize Forward Contract no.：

( )   Hold proceeds and contact：   at Tel. No.

SPECIAL INSTRUCTIONS：

Please deliver the documents through：   Yours faithfully

(Drawee's Banker)

(X) Whichever is applicable.

(Subject to Uniform Rules for Collections ICC Publication No. 322)

图 7.6　跟单托收申请书样例

　　托收指示与托收申请书的内容基本一致，下面以跟单托收申请书为例阐释其主要内容。

　　(1)出票人/出口商名称及地址。

　　(2)汇出行(出票人银行)名称及地址。

　　(3)汇票细节。此栏填入受票人/进口商的信息。

（4）涉及提交单据。出口商应清楚指明其提交的单据名称及单据份数。

（5）交单条件。此栏指明交单是按付款交单还是按承兑交单运作。如果未给出指令，交单条件将按付款交单运作。

（6）仓储和保险条款。如果在货物抵达时单据未被受领，指令须指明是否对货物进行仓储和保险。在进口商对汇票不付款或不承兑的情形下，该条款将指示托收行对货物进行仓储和保险，其支出将由出口商承担。

（7）拒绝证书条款。明确指示对拒绝付款或拒绝承兑产生的退票是否做拒绝证书。拒绝证书费用在由托收行先行支付后由出口商银行进行偿付，并最终借记其客户。

（8）需要时的代理。需要时的代理是出口商在进口商国家的代理。在违约发生时，托收行向其咨询结算事宜。

（9）出票人/出口商签字。

（10）特别指示。托收行信息在此显示。托收行可以由出口商指定，出口商也可以交由汇出行指定。

（11）遵循 URC。托收指示一般须清楚载明：此托收指示遵循《托收统一规则》（1978 年修正版）、国际商会第 322 号出版物或其后续版本 URC 522（于 1996 年 1 月 1 日生效）。

第五节　托收汇票

托收中使用的汇票需满足下列要求：

（1）出票人：出口商。

（2）受票人：进口商。

（3）收款人：受益人、汇出行、托收行三个当事人之一。

①受益人。受益人，即出口商为收款人。出口商在向汇出行提交汇票与单据时，须对汇票进行托收背书，背书给托收行。

②汇出行。收款人也可作为汇出行。托收汇票的出票条款表明汇出行作为收款人是为托收款项。汇出行在向托收行寄送汇票与单据前，须对汇票进行托收背书，背书给托收行。

③托收行。收款人也可作为托收行。同样，托收汇票的出票条款表明托收行作为收款人是为托收款项。此类汇票无需背书。

（4）期限：即期或远期。托收汇票如图 7.7 所示。

```
                Documents are to be delivered only against payment of this bill
                representing      100% value of our Invoice No.

No.TA.60153   Exchange for USD 19 800.00                  Shanghai Dec,25 2023


At 60 days after sight sight of this FIRST of Exchange(Second of Exchange being unpaid)
Pay to the order of Bank of China,Shanghai
The sum of U.S.DOLLARS NINETEEN THOUSAND EIGHT HUNDRED ONLY


To:Ewing General Trading
   Post Box No.1489                    China National Import & Export Corporation
   Dubai                               Shanghai Branch,Shanghai,China
                                             Authorized Signature
```

图 7.7　托收汇票

第六节　托收的特点

托收是建立在商业信用之上的支付方式,银行在托收业务中不给与出口商付款承诺,但银行在托收过程中须运作单据。根据《托收统一规则》的规定,开办托收业务的银行须秉持善意,合理谨慎,须核实其收到单据与托收指示中的指令达到表面的一致,即使银行没有责任继续进一步深入检查单据。与汇款相比,银行在托收中承担的责任更大,介入的程度更高。

1. 托收的优点

托收,尤其是跟单托收,是对预付货款和赊销的一种折中,在一定程度上降低了进口商、出口商的风险。

(1)对出口商的优点。在赊销中单据直接寄交进口商,而在托收中单据提交银行,银行因此就可凭借物权单据(货运单据)对货物拥有物权。通常,只有在买方对汇票进行了付款(付款交单)或承兑(承兑交单)后,银行才将货物的物权交至买方。因此,在赊销情形下出口商面临的进口商不付款所产生的钱货两失的极大风险被降低。在跟单托收情形下,如果进口商想要获得物权单据提货,须先向托收行进行付款或承兑。

(2)对进口商的优点。进口商在进行付款(在付款交单情形下)或进行承兑(在承兑交单情形下)时,可以确定出口商已发货并已将单据提交银行。因此,在预付货款情形下进口商面临的出口商不交货所产生的钱货两失的极大风险被降低。在跟单托收情形下,如果出口商想要获得付款或承兑,须先发货并向汇出行交单。

2. 托收的风险

总体来讲,托收对进口商更有利一些,因为无论是在付款交单还是在承兑交单情形下,出口商总须先发货并将单据提交银行。

(1)对出口商的风险。

①在付款交单情形下。在付款交单情形下,出口商面临进口商不付款的风险。例如,在进口货物的市场萎缩、价格下降时,买方就可能故意不提货、不付款。尽管进口商不付款就不能得到货物,出口商没有失去货物,但是此时货物已抵达国外港口,有可能出现货物受损被盗的风险,或者产生滞期费。滞期费是指港务局对不及时提货的货物征收的费用。

一旦出现上述情况,出口商会处于非常不利的境地,要么能找到一名替代的买方, 要么支付费用将货物运回,要么降价与进口商进行货款结算。因此,当支付方式是建立在商业信用上时,贸易伙伴的资信非常重要。

②在承兑交单情形下。在承兑交单情形下,出口商除面临进口商不付款的风险之外,还可能失去货物。单据,即货物,是凭承兑交付的,并不担保进口商会在汇票到期日付款。一旦汇票被承兑,出口商面临的风险与其在赊销情形下的风险一样大,区别只是出口商手中有一张已承兑汇票,如果汇票在到期日被退票,可以凭此对进口商提起诉讼。因此,汇票被承兑后,出口商同样面临钱货两失的风险。

为了保护自己,出口商应只将承兑交单用于部分货款的结算,余额则通过其他支付方式进行结算。

(2)对进口商的风险。尽管托收总体来说对进口商有利,但其也面临如下风险:

①在付款交单情形下。尽管进口商没有出口商不交货的风险,但进口商收到的货物可能有问题,可能是次品或与合同描述不符的。在付款交单情形下,进口商是先付款后提货,因此没有机会检查货物。发出的货物是否符合合同规定完全依赖于出口商的资信。

②在承兑交单情形下。在承兑交单情形下,进口商凭承兑获取货物,因此有机会在付款前检查货物。但是,如果进口商因发现进口货物与合同规定不符而对已承兑汇票拒绝付款,根据《中华人民共和国票据法》的规定,进口商本身的资信将受损。因此,虽然进口商没有收不到货物的风险,但是面临收到有问题的货物的风险。同样,当支付方式是建立在商业信用上时, 贸易伙伴的资信非常重要。

第八章　信用证

学习目标

◇学习信用证的定义及当事人。

◇学习跟单信用证的程序。

◇学习信用证汇票开立要求。

◇学习信用证的分类。

◇学习信用证的修改。

◇学习信用证审单及信用证的特点。

第一节　信用证的定义

1. 定义一

国际商会第 415 号出版物对信用证做出如下界定：

信用证是银行（开证行）在买方（申请人）的要求下并按照其指示向卖方（受益人）开出的，凭符合信用证条款的合规单据即期或在可以确定的未来某一时间进行付款的书面承诺。

信用证强调银行有条件的付款承诺。"条件"是指受益人须在规定的时间内按信用证条款提交合规单据。"进行付款"是指信用证下的付款方式可以是付款、承兑或议付。

2. 定义二

无论如何命名或描述，跟单信用证是指一种安排，据此安排银行（开证行）在客户（申请人）的要求和指示下，或者代表银行自己，凭合规单据以及符合信用证条款的情形下，进行如下运作：

（1）向第三方（受益人）或其指定人进行付款，或者对此受益人开出的汇票进行承兑和付款。

（2）授权另一家银行进行这样的付款,或者对汇票进行这样的承兑或付款。

（3）授权另一家银行进行议付。

信用证的定义二如图8.1所示。

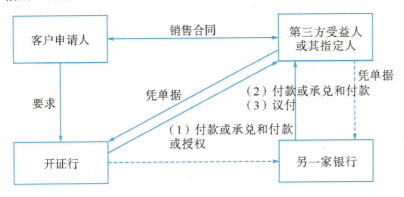

图8.1　信用证的定义二

在实务中,更普遍的做法是受益人将单据寄交他的银行(另一家银行),如图8.1中虚线所示,而不是直接向开证行提交,如图8.1中实线所示。

信用证有信开本(见图8.2)和由电报、电传、SWIFT开出的电开本(见图8.3)。如信开,信用证须由签字加以验证;如电开,须由密押和SAK密押加以验证。

Name of issuing bank: The French Issuing Bank 38 rue FrancoisLer 75008 Paris , France	Irrevocable Documentary Credit	Number 12345
Place and Date of Issue: Paris, 1 January 2023	Expiry Date and Place for Presentation of Documents Expiry Date: May 29, 2023 Place for Presentation: The American Advising Bank, Tampa	
Applicant: The French Importer Co. 89 rue du Commerce Paris , France		
	Beneficiary: The American Exporter Co. Inc. 17 Main Street Tampa,Florida	
Advising Bank:　　　　　　Reference No The American Advising Bank 456 Commerce Avenue Tampa,Florida	Amount: US $ 100 000. – one hundred thousand U.S. Dollars	
Partial shipments ☒allowed　☐not allowed	Credit available with Nominated Bank: The American Advising Bank, Tampa	
Transshipment　☒allowed　☐not allowed	☒by payment at sight ☐by deferred payment at: ☐by acceptance of drafts at: ☐by negotiation	
☐ Insurance covered by buyers		
Shipment as defined in UCP 600 From: Tampa,Florida For transportation to: Paris, France Not later than: May 15, 2023	Against the documents detailed herein: ☒and Beneficiary's draft(s) drawn on: The American Advising Bank, Tampa	

- Commercial Invoice, one original and 3 copies
- Multimodal Transport Document issued to the order of the French Importer Co. marked freight prepaid and notify XYZ Custom House Broker Inc.
- Insurance Certificate covering the Institute Cargo Clauses and the Institute War and Strike Clauses for 110% of the invoice value endorsed to The French Importer Co.
- Certificate of Origin evidencing goods to be of U.S.A. Origin
- Packing List

Covering: Machinery and spare parts as per pro-forma invoice number 657 dated December 17, 2022-CIP INCOTERMS 2010

Documents to be presented within 14 days after date of shipment but within the validity of the Credit

We hereby issue the Irrevocable Documentary Credit in your favor. It is subjected to the Uniform Customs and Practice for Documentary Credits and engages us in accordance with the terms thereof. The number and the date of the Credit and the name of our bank must be quoted on all drafts required. If the Credit is available by negotiation, each presentation must be noted on the reverse side of this advice by the bank where the Credit is available.

The document consists of 2 signed page(s)   The French Issuing Bank

Name of advising bank: The American Advising Bank 456 Commerce Avenue Tampa, Florida Reference Number of Advising Bank: 2417 Place and Date of Notifications: January 14, 2023, Tampa	Notification of Irrevocable Documentary Credit
Issuing Bank: The French Issuing Bank 38 rue FrancoisLer Paris, France	Beneficiary: The American Exporter Co. Inc. 17 Main Street Tampa, Florida
Reference Number of the Issuing Bank: 12345	Amount: US $ 100 000. – one hundred thousand U.S. Dollars

We have been informed by the above-mentioned Issuing Bank that the above-mentioned Documentary Credit has been issued in your favor
Please find enclosed the advice intended for you

Check the Credit terms and conditions carefully. In the event you do not agree with the terms and conditions, or if you feel unable to comply with any of those terms and conditions, kindly arrange an amendment of the Credit though your contracting party(the Applicant).

Other information:

☐ This notification and the enclosed advice are sent to you without any engagement on our part.
☒ As requested by the Issuing Bank, we hereby add our confirmation to this Credit in accordance with the stipulations under UCP 600.

The American Advising Bank

图 8.2　信用证信开本

OF SGD35.00 / S$0.00

RECEIVED = issue of a documentary credit FM700 ================== S-COPY 0002 =

* DESTINATION   FCBKSGSGAXXX   SW19961108FS000000009400
* SESS   2097   DATE RCVD 08-NOV-96 17:10
* SEQU 154575

* ORIGINATOR   FCBKTWTPAXXX   FROM SWIFT
* SESS   2307   FIRST COMMERCIAL BANK   DATE SENT 08-NOV-96 17:10
* SEQU 374328   TAIPEI

------------------------- NORMAL -------------------------

FIRST COMMERCIAL BANK
SINGAPORE BRANCH
No. 6696-3116

* :27 /sequence of total	:1 / 1
* :40A/form of documentary credit	:IRREVOCABLE
* :20 /documentary credit number	: 6NF2/00508/1163
* :31C/date of issue	:08/11/96
* :31D/date and place of expiry	:15/12/96 SINGAPORE
* :50 /applicant	:FUBC INDUSTRIAL CORP
	P.O. BOX 84-2
	TAIPEI TAIWAN
* :59 /beneficiary	:O INTERNATIONAL PTE LTD.
	14 WOODLANDS INDUSTRIAL PARK
	SINGAPORE
* :32B/currency code amount	:USD 17660,00
1D/available with/by-name,addr	:AVAILABLE WITH ANY BANK
	BY NEGOTIATION
* :42C/drafts at	:DRAFTS AT SIGHT
	FOR FULL INVOICE VALUE
* :42D/drawee - name and addr	:DRAWN ON US
* :43P/partial shipments	:PROHIBITED
* :43T/transshipment	:PROHIBITED
* :44A/on board/disp/taking charge	:SINGAPORE
* :44B/for transportation to	:KAOHSIUNG
* :44C/latest date of shipment	:30/11/96
* :45A/descr goods and/or services	:FOB SINGAPORE

RECEIVED 16 NOV 1996

      BUILDING MATERIALS
      MORTAC SEALER, CEMENTITIOUS STUCCO AND STUCCO SPRAY GUN
* :46A/documents required   :
      . SIGNED COMMERCIAL INVOICE IN 6 COPIES INDICATING THIS
       CREDIT NUMBER.
      . FULL SET LESS ONE OF CLEAN ON BOARD MARINE BILLS OF LADING
       MADE OUT TO THE ORDER OF FIRST COMMERCIAL BANK
       NOTIFY APPLICANT, MARKED ''FREIGHT COLLECT'' AND INDICATING
       THIS CREDIT NUMBER.
      . PACKING LIST IN 3 COPIES SIGNED BY BENEFICIARY.
      . BENEFICIARY'S CERTIFICATE STATING THAT ONE SET OF SHIPPING
       DOCUMENTS, INCLUDING: 1/3 CLEAN ORIGINAL ON BOARD OCEAN
       BILL OF LADING HAS BEEN SENT TO THE APPLICANT.
      . CERTIFICATE OF ORIGIN OF SINGAPORE.
* :47A/additional conditions   :
      . THE NUMBER AND THE DATE OF THE CREDIT AND THE NAME OF OUR BANK
       MUST BE QUOTED ON ALL DRAFTS.
* :71B/charges   :ALL BANKING CHARGES INCLUDING

** = = = = = = = = = = = = = = = CMT7/00024791/12-NOV-96/09:01:13 = P 1/2 =

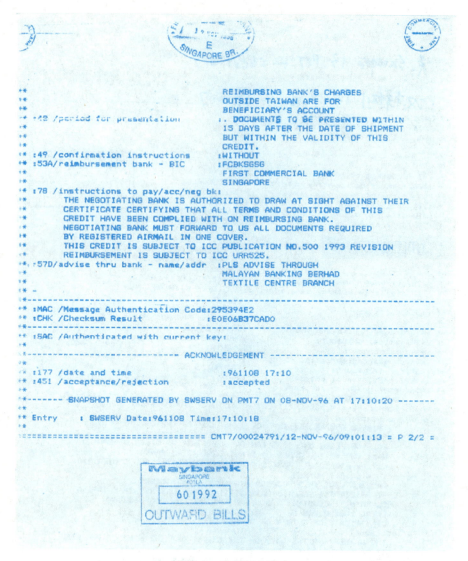

图 8.3　信用证电开本

第二节　跟单信用证直接当事人

1. 申请人

信用证申请人是进口商。

当销售合同规定用信用证结算时，进口商填写信用证申请书并签字，要求其银行开立以出口商为受益人的信用证。进口商须确保开出的信用证与销售合同严格一致。因为虽然信用证是基于销售合同开立的，但是一旦开出，信用证将成为独立于销售合同的文件。

2. 受益人

受益人是出口商,信用证为其开立。

收到信用证后,出口商须对照销售合同核查信用证条款。一旦出口商接受信用证条款,出口商须按要求安排生产和发货,并且确保提交的单据与信用证的规定完全相符。受益人也是安排发货的发货人和开立汇票的出票人。

3. 开证行

开证行是进口商银行,按申请人的要求开立信用证。

一旦开证,开证行承担向出口商履行付款承诺的全部责任,也使信用证成为建立在银行信用上的支付方式。开证行应是一家资信一流的银行。

4. 通知行

通知行是出口商银行,向受益人通知信用证。

通知行不给予出口商付款承诺。但是,在通知信用证前,通知行应谨慎合理地核查信用证的表面真实性。

出口商在按照一份"跟单信用证"运作前,须让信用证由一家当地银行进行通知,这一点很重要。因为在实务中,有可能信用证是由国外一家并不存在的"银行"开立的欺诈性信用证。因此,出口商有必要由当地的通知行对开证行和信用证本身的真伪进行核实。

第三节　信用证的其他当事人

为便利信用证的运作,开证行会指定其他银行参与运行过程。这些银行主要有保兑行、付款行、承兑行、议付行和偿付行。这些银行被称为信用证的其他当事人。

1. 保兑行

当通知行在开证行授权和要求下并愿意在信用证上加上其保兑,通知行会在给受益人的通知中加以注明并由此成为保兑行。

保兑构成保兑行对受益人无追索的付款或承兑,条件是出口商须完整提交跟单信用证中规定的所有单据并且提交的单据与信用证的规定完全相符。

当信用证被保兑后,受益人凭一份信用证得到两个银行的独立的付款承诺,一个承诺来自开证行,另一个承诺来自保兑行。保兑行进行的付款对出口商无追索权。

2. 付款行

当信用证为付款信用证时，开证行可以指定自己或另一家银行，通常是出口商银行，作为付款行。

付款行对出口商进行无追索权的付款，条件是出口商须完整提交跟单信用证中规定的所有单据并且提交的单据与信用证的规定完全相符。

3. 承兑行

当信用证为承兑信用证时，开证行可以指定自己或另一家银行，通常是出口商银行，作为承兑行。

承兑行进行承兑并对出口商进行无追索权的付款，条件是出口商须完整提交跟单信用证中规定的所有单据并且提交的单据与信用证的规定完全相符。

4. 议付行

当信用证为议付信用证时，开证行可以指定另一家银行，通常是出口商银行，成为议付行。一家银行可以因信用证的指定而成为议付行，但当信用证为自由议付信用证时，任何一家银行都可以成为议付行。应注意，开证行自己不可以充当议付行。

议付行议付（购买）出口商提交的汇票或单据，条件是出口商须完整提交跟单信用证中规定的所有单据并且提交的单据与信用证的规定完全相符。议付后，议付行成为汇票的新持票人，有权向受票人索取付款。当汇票以拒绝付款被退票后，开证行获得向出口商进行追索的权利。因此，议付行对出口商的付款具有追索权。

5. 偿付行

偿付行由开证行指定，代表开证行对付款行、承兑行或议付行的索偿进行偿付。为便利资金转移，偿付行一般都是开证行在出口商国家的分行/总行。

当对出口商进行了付款后，索偿行，即付款行、承兑行或议付行，将单据寄送开证行，同时向偿付行索偿。由偿付行做出的偿付不是终结性付款。也就是说，开证行一旦发现单据与信用证之间存在不符点，开证行将从索偿行处追回已偿付款项。

当开证行在信用证中并未指定偿付行时，偿付则由开证行自己做出。开证行在进行偿付前将审核单据是否相符，一旦开证行做出偿付，其偿付没有追索权。

需要注意的是，不同的银行名称表示银行在信用证运作中所扮演的不同角色,并非参与银行的实际个数。不同的银行名称并非绝对排他,因为在一个信用证程序中,一个银行可以同时扮演不同的角色。

第四节　UCP 600

UCP 是《跟单信用证统一惯例》的英文首字母缩略词,由位于法国巴黎的国际商会出台。

UCP 是有关跟单信用证的一系列规则,相关银行的责任须受其条款的制约并与其条款的规定严格相符。任何开立的信用证须清楚载明所涉及信用证"受《跟单信用证统一规则》制约"。

UCP 600 是国际商会第 600 号出版物,是 UCP 的最新版本,于 2007 年7 月1 日生效。前一个版本是 UCP 500,于 1994 年 1 月 1 日生效。

第五节　跟单信用证程序

跟单信用证程序如图8.4 所示。

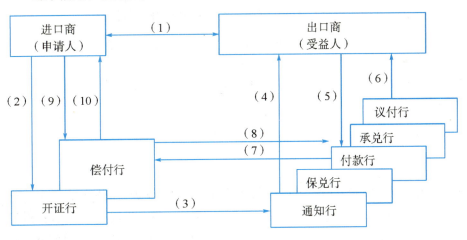

图 8.4　跟单信用证程序

(1)进出口商双方签订销售合同,确定用信用证结算款项。

(2)进口商(申请人)填写申请书并签字,要求其银行(开证行)签发信用证,以出口商为受益人。进口商须确保申请书内容与销售合同内容一致。

(3)进口商银行在开立信用证前核查买方资信。如果申请人是银行的新客户,可能需要支付信用证金额的 20% 作为开证押金。开立后,信用证寄交在受益人的国家代表受益人的出口商银行。

（4）出口商银行应在核实真伪后将跟单信用证交予受益人并充当：

①通知行——当出口商银行自己不给与付款承诺时。

②保兑行——在开证行的授权或要求下，在通知信用证时对信用证加上自己的保兑。

（5）出口商须对照销售合同核查信用证的条款。如有不符点且不符点并不重要，受益人可以原样接受信用证；如有重大不符点，受益人须要求申请人通过开证行修改信用证，以便信用证与合同保持一致。

出口商发货，获得货运单据，并按信用证要求备好其他单据后，通常向出口商银行交单。出口商银行充当：

①付款行——如果信用证为付款信用证，对受益人进行即期付款或远期付款。

②承兑行——如果信用证是承兑信用证，对受益人须先承兑汇票，在到汇票期日进行付款。

③议付行——如果信用证是议付信用证，对受益人提交的汇票和单据进行议付。

（6）付款行、承兑行或议付行对照信用证条款审核单据。如果单据合规，上述银行将以付款、承兑或议付的形式进行付款。

（7）付款行、承兑行或议付行向偿付行寄送单据索取偿付。如果信用证没有指定偿付行或偿付行未能进行偿付，偿付则由开证行做出。

（8）偿付行或开证行做出偿付。

（9）进口商付款。

（10）开证行凭进口商的付款向其交单。

第六节　跟单信用证申请书

银行预先印制空白跟单信用证申请书，由申请人/进口商填写并签字。一旦签字，申请书成为申请人与开证行之间的契约文件。当填写申请书时，进口商须确保申请书的内容与销售合同的内容一致。申请书的主要内容如下：

（1）受益人名称全称和地址。

（2）跟单信用证金额和币种。

（3）跟单信用证类别，常见类别为不可撤销和跟单信用证。

（4）信用证金额的兑用方式。

（5）汇票的受票人及期限。

（6）货物的笼统描述，指明其价格术语，如 CIF、CFR、FOB 或其他《通则》中的术语。

（7）单据的详细要求。

（8）申请书应指明装运港/地和目的港/地。

（9）运费预付或到付,须与所选《通则》术语保持一致。

（10）是否允许转船装运。

（11）是否允许分船装运。

（12）最后的船期。

（13）交单期限。

（14）信用证的到期日和到期地点。

（15）跟单信用证是否为可转让信用证。

（16）跟单信用证通知方式,如函送还是电送。在实务中,如通知行与受益人在同一城市,受益人也可前往通知行领取信用证。

国际商会制作的跟单信用证申请书标准格式如图 8.5 所示,不同的银行可以基于此标准格式设计自己的申请书。

（3）Irrevocable Documentary Credit Application

Applicant：	Issuing Banks：
Date of Application： □issue by（air）email □with brief advice by teletransmission （see UCP 600 Article 11）（16） □issue by teletransmission（see UCP 600 Article 11） □Transferable Credit−as per UCP 600 Article 48（15）	Expiry Date and Place for Presentation of Documents Expiry Date： Place for Presentation： （14）
Confirmation of the Credit： 　　　　（3） □not requested □requested □authorized if requested by Beneficiary	Beneficiary： 　　（1）
	Amount in figures and words（please use ISO Currency Codes）： 　　（2）
Partial shipments□allowed □not allowed（11）	
Transshipments □allowed □not allowed（10） Please refer to UCP 600 transport Articles for exceptions to this condition	Credit available with Nominated Bank：C□by payment sight □by deferred payment at： （4） □by acceptance of drafts at：
□ Insurance will be covered by us	□by negotiation Against the documents detailed herein： □and Beneficiary's draft（s）drawn on：（5）
Shipment as defined in UCP 600 Article 46 From： For transportation to： （8） Not later than： （12）	
Goods（Brief description without excessive details−See UCP 600 Article 5）： 　　（6）	Terms □ FAS □ CIF □ FOB □ Other terms （6） □ CFR □as per INCOTERMS

Commercial invoice☐ signed original and ☐copies

Transport Document：
☐ Multimodal Transport Document Covering at least two different modes of transport（7）
☐ Marine/Ocean Bill of Lading covering a port-port shipment
☐ Non-negotiable Sea Waybill covering a port-port shipment
☐ Air Waybill original for the consignor
☐ Other transport document
☐ to the order of
☐ endorsed on blank
☐ marked freight　☐ prepaid　☐ payable at destination（9）
☐ notify

Insurance Document：
☐ Policy　☐ Certificate　Declaration under an open cover covering the following risks

Certificates：
☐ Origin
☐ Analysis
☐ Health
☐ Other

Other Documents：
☐ Packing　List
☐ Weight　List

Documents to be presented within☐ days after date of shipment but within the validity of the Credit.（13）

Additional Instructions：	We request you to issue on our behalf and for our account your Irrevocable Credit in accordance with the above instructions(marked x where appropriate)　　This Credit will be subjected to the Uniform Customs and Practice for Documentary Credits(2007 Revision). Publication No 600 of the International Chamber of Commerce. Paris, France.in so far as they are applicable.
	Name and signature of the Applicant

图 8.5　不可撤销跟单信用证申请书

第七节　跟单信用证的内容

跟单信用证基于申请书开出。开立信用证时,开证行须确保信用证内容与申请书内容一致。国际商会为不可撤销跟单信用证信开本的开立制作了"(致受益人和通知行的)不可撤销跟单信用证标准通知书",如图 8.6 所示。

GUIDANCE NOTES AND STANDARD FORMS FOR BANKS

Noted Irrevocable Documentary Credit Form（Advice for the Beneficiary）

Name of Issuing Bank：	Irrevocable　Documentary Credit（1）	Number（2）
Place and Date of Issue：（3）	Expiry Date and Place for Presentation of Documents Expiry Date： Place for Presentation：（4）	
Applicant： 　　　　　　　（5）	Beneficiary： （6）	
Advising Bank：　　Reference No 　　（7）		
	Amount：（8）	

Partial shipments□allowed　□not allowed（10）	Credit available with Nominated Bank： □by payment sight □by deferred payment at： □by acceptance of drafts at：（9） □by negotiation Against the documents detailed herein： □and Beneficiary's draft（s）drawn on：
Transshipment□allowed　□not allowed（11）	
□ Insurance covered by buyers　（12）	
Shipment as defined in UCP600 Article 46 From： For transportation to：（13） Not later than：	

（14）~（20）

Documents to be presented within□ days after the date of shipment but within the validity of the Credit　（21）

We hereby issue the irrevocable Documentary Credit in your favor. It is subject to the Uniform Customs and Practice for Documentary Credits（2007 Revision）, International Chamber of Commerce, Paris, France. Publication No 600）and engages us in accordance with the terms thereof. The number and the date of the Credit and the name of our bank must be quoted on all drafts required. If the Credit is available by negotiation, each presentation must be noted on the reverse side of this advice by the bank where the Credit is available.

The document consists of □ signed page（s）（24）　　　　（25）Name and signature of the issuing bank

Noted Irrevocable Documentary Form（Advice for the Advising Bank）

Applicant：	Irrevocable Documentary Credit	Number
Place and date of Issue： Applicant：	Expiry Date and Place for Presentation of Documents Expiry Date： Place for Presentation：	
Advising Banks： Reference No： Partial shipments□allowed □not allowed	Beneficiary：	
Transshipment□allowed □not allowed □Insurance covered by buyers	Amount：	
Shipment as defined in UCP600 Article 46 From： For transportation to： Not later than：	Credit available with Nominated Bank： □by payment sight □by deferred payment at： □by acceptance of drafts at： □by negotiation Against the documents detailed herein： □and Beneficiary's draft(s) drawn on：	

Documents to be presented within□ days after date of shipment but within the validity of the Credit

We have issued the irrevocable Documentary Credit as detailed above. It is subject to the Uniform Customs and Practice for Documentary Credits（2007 Revision）. International Chamber of Commerce，Paris，France. Publication No 600. We request you to advise the Beneficiary.
□without adding your confirmation □adding your confirmation □adding your confirmation if requested by the Beneficiary（22）
Bank-to-Bank instructions（23）

The document consists of □ signed page(s)

Name and signature of the issuing bank

图 8.6 信用证信开本

信用证的主要内容如下：

（1）信用证类别。标准通知书格式是为开立不可撤销跟单信用证而制定。信用证其他类别在信用证其他项目中指出。

（2）信用证号码。信用证号码是开证行所开信用证的流水号。该号码须在所有相关单据中载明，以便绑定这些单据。

（3）开证地点和开证日期。开证地点是开证行所在地。开证日期是开证行开立信用证的日期。

（4）到期日和到期地点。信用证须规定一个确切日期而非一个时间段作为提交单据要求付款、承兑或议付的最后到期日。信用证在到期日之后过期失效。从开证日至到期日的这段时间称为信用证有效期。

到期地点是在到期日当天或之前单据提交的交单地点。

（5）申请人名称及地址。

（6）受益人名称及地址。

（7）通知行。此处指明通知信用证的银行的名称和地址。

（8）信用证金额和币种。币种须以国际标准化组织货币代码表示，如美元用 USD、英镑用 GBP 表示。

（9）指定银行和信用证兑用方式。信用证须指定进行付款的银行名称以及银行进行付款的方式。

通常，以下两类银行可以进行付款：

①由进口商银行（开证行）对信用证进行付款。这意味着开证行指定自己为付款行或承兑行，在收到单据或"以我行为受票人"的汇票时对受益人进行付款。此类信用证在开证行所在地到期，单据须在信用证有效期内交单至开证行。其他银行在此过程中不进行付款，只充当中介银行，为受益人向开证行转递单据。

此类信用证对受益人不太有利，因为受益人在开证行付款前不能得到支付而且还须为单据在信用证有效期内送达开证行担责。单据传递过程中的任何延误或遗失都将妨碍出口商获得支付。

②由出口商银行对信用证进行付款。这意味着开证行指定出口商银行为信用证的付款行、承兑行或议付行，在收到单据或汇票时对受益人进行付款。此类信用证在出口商银行所在地到期，单据须在信用证有效期内交单至出口商银行。

此类信用证对出口商较有利，因为出口商无需将单据寄送海外开证行。

信用证指定银行可以有四种方式对受益人进行付款：

第一，信用证以即期付款方式兑用。在此情形下，付款行凭单据或即期汇票对受益人进行即期支付。有时，为避免印花税，即期付款不要求提交汇票，此时付款行只凭单据对受益人进行即期付款。

第二，信用证以延期付款方式兑用。在此情形下，付款行对受益人在一确定的未来日期凭单据对受益人进行支付，不要求提交汇票。

第三，信用证以承兑方式兑用。在此情形下，承兑行凭单据和远期汇票进行承兑，于到期日对受益人进行支付。

第四，信用证以议付方式兑用。在此情形下，议付行议付单据和汇票，对受益人进行支付。

（10）分船装运。虽然 UCP 允许分船装运，但在具体信用证中须指明是否允许分船装运。

（11）转船装运。虽然 UCP 允许转船装运，但在具体信用证中须指明是否允许转船装运。

（12）买方负责保险。信用证须指明是否需要买方购买保险。这一条款须与所选《通则》术语以及保险单的提交要求一致。

（13）装运港和卸货港。信用证须指明装运港、卸货港以及须在信用证有效期内的最后装船日期。

（14）～（20）货物描述及单据要求。信用证中的货物描述为笼统描述，因为详细描述将在商业发票中提供。此处的单据仅指商业单据，通常按如下顺序排列：

①商业发票。

②运输单据。

③保险单据。

④原产地证书。

⑤检验证书。

⑥装箱单/重量单。

单据须清楚指明提交单据的份数、正本或副本、单据签发人、单据抬头以及其他相关规定。

（21）交单期限。信用证将要求单据须在装运日后一规定期限内，且不超过信用证有效期交单。

在实务中，交单期限可以是装运日期后 14～21 天。如果交单期限的最后一天与信用证的到期日不在同一天，那么最后交单日为较早的那个日期。

（22）给通知行的指示。开证行可按下列三种方式之一指示通知行：

①无需贵行保兑。

②请加上贵行保兑。

③如受益人要求请加上贵行保兑。

（23）银行对银行指令。开证行向指定付款、承兑或议付的银行指明他们获取偿付的地点、方式以及时间。

（24）页数。开证行须指明开立信用证的页数。

（25）开证行签字。信用证致受益人的通知和致通知行的通知须经开证行签字方能生效。

第八节 信用证汇票开立要求

信用证中使用的汇票须包含出票条款,表明该汇票是在一跟单信用证下开立。出票条款包括开证行名称、信用证开证日期以及信用证号码。

除此之外,信用证下开立的汇票还须满足以下要求:

（1）出票人:出口商。

（2）受票人:银行。其可以是:

①开证行。

②保兑行。

③付款行。

④承兑行。

（3）收款人：收款人可以是下面两种情形之一。

①出口商。信用证将要求出口商在交单时对汇票做空白背书或记名背书,背书给议付信用证的议付行。

②议付行。议付行无需对汇票背书。

（4）期限:即期或远期。

信用证汇票如图 8.7 所示。

E54621
Drawn under First Union Bank, Dallas, Texas
Irrevocable L/C No.704481   Dated 20th Dec 2023
payable with interest@_____%

No.T.0456   Exchange for USD 129 649.95   Shanghai 1st Feb 2024

At _____sight of this FIRST of Exchange (SECOND of Exchange)
being unpaid)Pay to the order of Bank of China, Shanghai
the sum of US DOLLARS ONE HUNDRED TWENTY NINE THOUSAND
SIX HUNDRED AND FORTY NINE AND 95/100 ONLY

To:First Union Trust Bank
    Dallas,Texas   China National Textiles Import & Export
                                    Corp.,Shanghai Branch
                                        Signature

图 8.7 信用证汇票

需要注意的是,在不同支付方式下开立的汇票细节是不一样的,对其不同点的比较总结如下,如表8.1所示。

表8.1 支付方式中的汇票

项目	汇款（票汇）	托收	信用证
出票人	汇出行	出口商	出口商
受票人	付款行	进口商	开证行, 或者保兑行, 或者付款行, 或者承兑行
收款人	出口商	出口商, 或者汇出行, 或者托收行	出口商, 或者议付行
期限	即期	即期或者远期	即期或者远期

第九节 信用证普通分类

信用证普通分类可以满足贸易商的常规贸易目的,按以下标准分类:

1. 按是否附带货运单据分类

(1)光票信用证。光票信用证是指仅对不附带货运单据的汇票进行付款,或者仅对附带有商业发票的汇票进行付款的信用证。

(2)跟单信用证。跟单信用证是指对附带或不附带汇票的货运单据进行付款的信用证。跟单信用证为信用证的一个重要类别,是开立其他类别信用证的基础。

2. 按可撤销性分类

(1)不可撤销信用证。不可撤销信用证构成开证行对在信用证情形下提交的汇票或单据付款或承兑的明确承诺,条件是出口商在跟单信用证到期日当天或之前向指定银行提交合规单据,完全符合信用证条款。

虽然受益人也须依赖国外开证行的资信,但是不可撤销跟单信用证向受益人提供了更为可靠的付款保证。在没有得到开证行、保兑行(如果有)和受益人明确表示同意的情况下,不可撤销信用证不得被撤销和修改。

不可撤销信用证须首先为跟单信用证。跟单与不可撤销的组合构成最常用的信用证类别组合,这种组合是其他类别信用证得以开立的先决条件。

信用证须清楚指明其撤销性。如无此明示,信用证将被视为不可撤销。根据2007年7月1日生效的UCP 600,银行只能开立不可撤销信用证。

（2）可撤销信用证。可撤销信用证可在任何时候，在受益人不同意甚至在其不知情的情况下，被开证行撤销或修改。

与不可撤销信用证相比，可撤销信用证对出口商不太有利，使其面临风险。因为在货物发运过程中，或者在单据提交前，或者虽然已交单但在支付前，信用证都可能被修改或撤销，导致出口商在无开证行的付款承诺的情况下，只能直接向进口商索取付款。

可撤销信用证不常用，通常只用于附属公司和子公司之间的贸易。

3. 按加保兑分类

（1）保兑信用证。在开证行的授权和要求下，一家银行（保兑行）对不可撤销跟单信用证的保兑构成了在开证行承诺之外保兑行的明确的付款、承兑汇票或议付的承诺，条件是受益人在跟单信用证到期日或在到期日前将规定的单据向保兑行或其他指定银行提交且提交的单据完全符合信用证条款。

保兑通常基于不可撤销跟单信用证做出。经保兑的不可撤销跟单信用证向受益人提供了来自开证行和保兑行的双重付款承诺。本章第一节中的图8.2信用证信开本是不可撤销跟单保兑信用证。

在通常情况下，如果开证行较小或其所在国政治经济形势不稳定，受益人会希望信用证得到本国一家银行的保兑，以获得这家本地银行的付款承诺。

（2）未保兑信用证。未保兑信用证是指通知行通知开证行开出的信用证。作为开证行的代理，在通知时，通知行对跟单信用证受益人不给予任何付款承诺，只是对其通知的信用证的表面真实性进行谨慎合理的核查，这样的信用证为不可撤销跟单未保兑信用证（见图8.8）。

在通常情形下，受益人在要求保兑前会考虑信用证和开证行的资信情况。如果开证行被认为是一流银行，一般不需要要求另一家银行对其开出的不可撤销跟单信用证进行保兑。

Name of issuing bank： The French Issuing Bank 38 rue FrancoisLer 75008 Paris，France	Irrevocable Documentary Credit	Number 12345
Place and Date of Issue：Paris，1 January 2023	Expiry Date and Place for Presentation of Documents Expiry Date：May 29, 2023 Place for Presentation：The American Advising Bank, Tampa	
Applicant： The French Importer Co. 89 rue du Commerce Paris，France		
	Beneficiary： The American Exporter Co. Inc. 17 Main Street Tampa，Florida	
Advising Bank： Reference No The American Advising Bank 456 Commerce Avenue Tampa，Florida		
	Amount： US $ 100 000. – one hundred thousand U.S. Dollars	

Partial shipments ☒allowed ☐not allowed

Transshipment ☒allowed ☐not allowed

☐ Insurance covered by buyers

Shipment as defined in UCP 600
From：Tampa，Florida
For transportation to：Paris，France

Not later than：May 15，2023

Credit available with Nominated Bank：
The American Advising Bank，Tampa
☒by payment at sight
☐by deferred payment at：
☐by acceptance of drafts at：
☐by negotiation

Against the documents detailed herein：
☒and Beneficiary's draft（s）drawn on：
The American Advising Bank，Tampa

● Commercial Invoice，one original and 3 copies
● Multimodal Transport Document issued to the order of the French Importer Co.
  marked freight prepaid and notify XYZ Custom House Broker Inc.
● Insurance Certificate covering the Institute Cargo Clauses and the Institute War
  and Strike Clauses for 110% of the invoice value endorsed to The French Importer Co.
● Certificate of Origin evidencing goods to be of U.S.A. Origin
● Packing List
Covering：Machinery and spare parts as per pro-forma invoice number 657
dated December 17，2022-CIP INCOTERMS 2010

Documents to be presented within 14 days after date of shipment but within the validity of the Credit

We hereby issue the Irrevocable Documentary Credit in your favor. It is subjected to the Uniform Customs and Practice for Documentary Credits and engages us in accordance with the terms thereof. The number and the date of the Credit and the name of our bank must be quoted on all drafts required. If the Credit is available by negotiation，each presentation must be noted on the reverse side of this advice by the bank where the Credit is available.

The document consists of 2 signed page（s）

The French Issuing Bank

Name of advising bank：
    The American Advising Bank
    456 Commerce Avenue
    Tampa，Florida

Reference Number of Advising Bank：2417
Place and Date of Notifications：January 14，2023 Tampa

Notification of Irrevocable
Documentary Credit

Issuing Bank：
    The French Issuing Bank
    38 rue FrancoisLer
    Paris ，France

Beneficiary：
    The American Exporter Co. Inc.
    17 Main Street Tampa，Florida

Reference Number of the Issuing Bank：
                                12345

Amount：
US $ 100 000. - one hundred thousand U.S. Dollars

We have been informed by the above-mentioned Issuing Bank that the above-mentioned Documentary Credit has been issued in your favor.
Please find enclosed the advice intended for you

Check the Credit terms and conditions carefully. In the event you do not agree with the terms and conditions, or if you feel unable to comply with any of those terms and conditions, kindly arrange an amendment of the Credit though your contracting party(the Applicant).

Other information:

☒This notification and the enclosed advice are sent to you without any engagement on our part.
☐As requested by the Issuing Bank, we hereby add our confirmation to this Credit in accordance with the stipulations under UCP 600.

The American Advising Bank

图 8.8　未保兑信用证信开本

4. 按信用证的兑用方式分类

（1）即期付款信用证。即期付款信用证是指兑用方式为即期付款的信用证。信用证中被授权的银行对提交的符合信用证条款的附带或不附带即期汇票的商业单据进行即期付款,如本章第一节中的图 8.2 所示。

在即期付款信用证下,出口商凭商业单据和以付款行为受票人的即期汇票(当要求提交汇票时)获得即期支付。付款行对受益人的付款为终结性付款,对受益人无追索权。

即期付款信用证也包括直交付款信用证。在这种信用证下,开证行对汇票和单据的兑付责任只针对出口商,信用证到期地点在开证行柜台。此类信用证对出口商不太有利,出口商不能从出口商银行获得款项,同时还须为单据在信用证有效期内在开证行柜台进行提示担责。图 8.9 为信开本直交付款信用证(致受益人的通知)。

Name of issuing bank: The French Issuing Bank 38 rue FrancoisLer 75008 Paris, France	Irrevocable Documentary Credit	Number 12345
Place and Date of Issue: Paris, 1 January 2023	Expiry Date and Place for Presentation of Documents Expiry Date: May 29, 2023 Place for Presentation: The French Issuing Bank, Paris, France	
Applicant: The French Importer Co. 89 rue du Commerce Paris, France	Beneficiary: The American Exporter Co. Inc. 17 Main Street Tampa, Florida	
Advising Bank:　　　Reference No The American Advising Bank 456 Commerce Avenue Tampa, Florida	Amount: US $ 100 000. – one hundred thousand U.S. Dollars	

Partial shipments ☒allowed ☐not allowed	Credit available with Nominated Bank: The French Issuing Bank, Paris
Transshipment ☒allowed ☐not allowed	☒by payment at sight ☐by deferred payment at: ☐by acceptance of drafts at: ☐by negotiation
☐ Insurance covered by buyers	
Shipment as defined in UCP 600 From: Tampa, Florida For transportation to:Paris, France Not later than:May 15, 2023	Against the documents detailed herein: ☒and Beneficiary's draft(s) drawn on: The French Issuing Bank, Paris

●Commercial Invoice, one original and 3 copies
●Multimodal Transport Document issued to the order of the French Importer Co.
　marked freight prepaid and notify XYZ Custom House Broker Inc.
●Insurance Certificate covering the Institute Cargo Clauses and the Institute War
　and Strike Clauses for 110% of the invoice value endorsed to The French Importer Co.
●Certificate of Origin evidencing goods to be of U.S.A. Origin
●Packing List
Covering:Machinery and spare parts as per pro-forma invoice number 657
dated December 17,2022-CIP　INCOTERMS　2010

Documents to be presented within ⏍14⏍ days after date of shipment but within the validity of the Credit

We hereby issue the Irrevocable Documentary Credit in your favor. It is subjected to the Uniform Customs and Practice for Documentary Credits and engages us in accordance with the terms thereof. The number and the date of the Credit and the name of our bank must be quoted on all drafts required. If the Credit is available by negotiation, each presentation must be noted on the reverse side of this advice by the bank where the Credit is available.

The document consists of ⏍2⏍ signed page(s)　　　　　　　　　The French Issuing Bank

图 8.9　信开本直交付款信用证（致受益人的通知）

（2）延期付款信用证。延期付款信用证是指付款时间延至未来一个确定时间进行支付的信用证。信用证中被授权的银行对符合信用证条款的商业单据进行付款。这种信用证不要求提交汇票。

在延期付款信用证下，出口商凭商业单据获得远期支付。付款行对受益人的付款为终结性的，对受益人无追索权。

（3）承兑信用证。承兑信用证构成指定银行给予远期汇票提示承兑以及到期付款的承诺。条件是受益人提交的商业单据和远期汇票符合信用证条款。

在承兑信用证下，出口商凭商业单据和以承兑行为受票人的远期汇票获得远期支付。承兑行对受益人的付款是终结性的，对受益人无追索权。

（4）议付信用证。议付信用证是指议付行对向其提交的即期或远期汇票和商业单据进行议付。当议付时，议付行在受益人提交了合规单据后对受益人提前预付款项，并收取从预付款项日起至收到开证行偿付款项时止的利息。

在议付信用证下，出口商凭商业单据和以开证行为受票人的即期或远期汇票获得即期支付。议付行对受益人的付款不是终结性的，如果开证行最终没有对议付行进行偿付，议付行对受益人具有追索权。图 8.10 为信开本议付信用证（致受益人的通知）。

Name of issuing bank： The French Issuing Bank 38 rue Francois 75008 Paris，France	Irrevocable Documentary Credit	Number 12345

Place and Date of Issue：Paris，1 January 2023	Expiry Date and Place for Presentation of Documents Expiry Date：May 29，2023 Place for Presentation：The American Advising Bank，Tampa
Applicant： 　The French Importer Co. 　89 rue du Commerce 　Paris，France	Beneficiary： 　The American Exporter Co. Inc. 　17 Main Street 　Tampa，Florida
Advising Bank：　　　　　Reference No 　The American Advising Bank 　456 Commerce Avenue 　Tampa，Florida	Amount： US $ 100 000. – one hundred thousand U.S. Dollars
Partial shipments ☒allowed　☐not allowed	Credit available with Nominated Bank： The American Advising Bank，Tampa ☐by payment at sight ☐by deferred payment at： ☐by acceptance of drafts at： ☒by negotiation
Transshipment　☒allowed　☐not allowed	
☐ Insurance covered by buyers	
Shipment as defined in UCP 600 From：Tampa，Florida For transportation to：Paris，France Not later than：May 15，2023	Against the documents detailed herein： ☒and Beneficiary's draft(s) drawn on： The French Issuing Bank，Paris，France

● Commercial Invoice，one original and 3 copies
● Multimodal Transport Document issued to the order of the French Importer Co.
　marked freight prepaid and notify XYZ Custom House Broker Inc.
● Insurance Certificate covering the Institute Cargo Clauses and the Institute War
　and Strike Clauses for 110% of the invoice value endorsed to The French Importer Co.
● Certificate of Origin evidencing goods to be of U.S.A. Origin
● Packing List
Covering：Machinery and spare parts as per pro-forma invoice number 657
dated December 17，2022–CIP INCOTERMS 2010

Documents to be presented within ⎡14⎤ days after date of shipment but within the validity of the Credit

We hereby issue the Irrevocable Documentary Credit in your favor. It is subjected to the Uniform Customs and Practice for Documentary Credits and engages us in accordance with the terms thereof. The number and the date of the Credit and the name of our bank must be quoted on all drafts required. If the Credit is available by negotiation，each presentation must be noted on the reverse side of this advice by the bank where the Credit is available.

The document consists of ⎡2⎤ signed page(s)　　　　　　　　The French Issuing Bank

图 8.10　信开本议付信用证（致受益人的通知）

5. 按信用证兑用时间分类

（1）即期信用证。即期信用证是指受益人即期获得信用证金额。即期信用证包括即期付款信用证和议付信用证。

（2）远期信用证。远期信用证是指受益人在未来某一特定时间获得信用证金额。远期信用证包括延期付款信用证和承兑信用证。

总体来说,信用证的分类并不是非此即彼的,一份普通贸易信用证总是五个类别的组合。因此,仔细阅读信用证的内容对正确解读信用证类别至关重要。

第十节　信用证特殊类别

在实务中,开证行可以在信用证中加入特殊条款以满足贸易商的不同目的,只要这样的条款与 UCP 600 的规定不相违背。这些特殊条款一旦写入,信用证成为特殊类别信用证。

1. 买方远期信用证(假远期信用证)

买方远期信用证(假远期信用证)是一种特殊的承兑信用证,通过贴现远期汇票,进口商承担贴现息和承兑费用而使出口商获得即期支付。

实际上,买方远期信用证(假远期信用证)是使出口商获得即期支付的承兑信用证,在所签订的交易合同为即期时开立,目的是为进口商提供资金便利。签订的合同为即期合同,但开立的信用证为远期信用证(承兑信用证),进口商因此获得融资。此类信用证有下列类似字句说明其性质:

"我行凭提交的单据和开立以我方为受票人的 180 天远期汇票,以承兑方式对信用证进行支付。我方可对已承兑汇票进行即期支付,贴现费和利息将记入申请人账户。"

2. 循环信用证

循环信用证是指按照此信用证的条款,信用证金额可以更新或恢复至原金额且无需对所开立信用证进行具体修改的信用证。

开立循环信用证是为便利进口商连续且反复从同一供货商购货,使申请人避免重复申请开证所支出的开证费用和开证押金。

循环信用证可以按时间或按金额进行循环。当跟单信用证按时间循环时,信用证金额在其规律发货的商定期限内按固定金额循环,不管在前一期限内信用证金额是否被提取。

例如:"此循环信用证按月循环,每月可用金额不超过 USD 10 000,且信用证金额从下一个日历月的 1 号起自动更新,全额可用。"

当发货不规律时,信用证可按金额循环,信用证金额在商定的总的有效期内,每次发货被提取后自动恢复至原金额。

例如:"此信用证按发货限循环 6 次,每次发货的金额不超过 USD 10 000。"

循环信用证的金额分可累加或不可累加。可累加是指在某固定日历周期内或某次固定发货的未用金额可以在下一日历周期和下一次发货中使用。不可累加是指在某固定日历周期内或某次固定发货的未用金额不再可用,不能转入下一个日历周期和下一次发货。

循环信用证可能使开证行的责任不好预估,因为开证行须对循环信用证下可能被提取的总金额承担责任。因此,明确循环信用证的累计总金额,使风险责任可控,对于开证行来说至关重要。

例如:"此信用证按月循环,每月可用金额为 USD 10 000。信用证金额从下一个日历月的 1 号起自动更新,全额可用。我行在此循环信用证下的责任不超过 USD 60 000,为 6 个月的累计金额。每月未用余额不可累加至下一个月。"

3. 可转让信用证

可转让跟单信用证通常在交易涉及中间商时使用。中间商为可转让信用证的第一受益人而货物实际供货方为第二受益人。

可转让跟单信用证是指信用证的受益人(第一受益人)可要求被授权付款、延期付款、承兑或议付的银行,或者在自由议付信用证的情况下,信用证特别授权的银行作为转递行,将跟单信用证可用的全部或部分金额转让给一个或多个其他受益人(第二受益人)。可转让信用证的转让程序如图 8.11 所示。

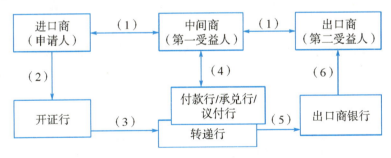

图 8.11　可转让信用证的转让程序

(1)进口商与中间商之间签订第一销售合同,中间商与出口商之间签订合同金额小于第一合同的第二销售合同。

(2)进口商基于第一合同申请开立不可撤销跟单可转让信用证,以中间商为受益人(第一受益人)。

(3)开证行开立可转让信用证并将此信用证寄送至在信用证中作为付款行、承兑行或议付行的中间商银行。

(4)中间商银行向中间商通知信用证,中间商向此银行发出指令,要求以出口商为受益人转让信用证,转让金额须扣除中间商的利润并对信用证条款做出相应修改。

(5)中间商银行作为转让行,把按照新金额以及对信用证条款已做相应修改的已转让信用证寄送至出口商银行。

(6)出口商银行将已转让信用证通知出口商(第二受益人)。

可转让信用证的程序,除上面所示的转让部分外,都按普通贸易信用证的程序运作。当整个程序结束后,中间商的利润得以实现。

4. 背对背信用证

当以中间商为受益人的信用证不能转让时,或者虽然可以转让,但并不能满足中间商的要求时,各方可以使用背对背信用证。

背对背信用证的正式定义如下:"不可撤销跟单信用证(原证)的金额可以使第三方(出口商)获得,其第一受益人(中间商)将此跟单信用证作为质押,开出以实际供货方(出口商)为受益人的另一信用证(新证)。"

背对背信用证涉及两个在法律上相互独立的信用证:一个信用证以中间商为受益人,另一个信用证以出口商为受益人。这两个信用证一个凭另一个开出。图8.12显示了背对背信用证的开立程序。

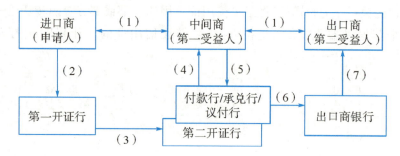

图8.12 背对背信用证的开立程序

(1)进口商与中间商签订第一销售合同,中间商与出口商签订合同金额小于第一合同的第二销售合同。

(2)进口商基于第一销售合同开立以中间商为受益人(第一受益人)的不可撤销跟单信用证。

(3)开证行开出信用证并将信用证寄送至在信用证中作为付款行、承兑行或议付行的中间商银行。

(4)中间商银行将信用证通知中间商。

(5)以此信用证为质押,中间商向其银行申请开立新证,新证以出口商为受益人,金额须扣除中间商利润并对原证条款做出相应修改。

(6)中间商银行作为第二开证行,把已按新金额开立并对原证条款已做相应修改的新证寄送至出口商银行。

（7）出口商银行将新证通知出口商（第二受益人）。

背对背信用证与可转让信用证在许多方面相似。但是，可转让信用证只涉及一个信用证而背对背信用证却涉及两个信用证。再有，中间商银行在可转让信用证中为转让行而在背对背信用证中为第二开证行。转让行对出口商不给予付款承诺，而第二开证行需给予出口商付款承诺。

5. 对开/互惠信用证

对开/互惠信用证的运作涉及两个信用证：原证和对开/互惠信用证。其运作与普通贸易信用证的运作无异，只是原证的申请人成为对开/互惠信用证的受益人，而原证的受益人成为对开信用证的申请人。

对开/互惠信用证主要用于易货贸易，涉及相互关联的两笔交易：一笔为进口，另一笔为出口。两证的金额也大致相当。对开/互惠信用证的相互关系如图 8.13 所示。

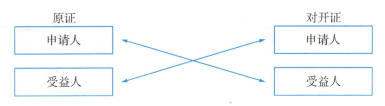

图 8.13　对开/互惠信用证的相互关系

6. 预支 / 红条款信用证

红条款信用证是指在信用证中写入特别条件/条款，授权出口商银行在受益人交单前预支其货款。之所以称为红条款信用证是因为该条款最初是用红笔写出，以引起对这种信用证的这一特点的注意。

当进口商希望对其信赖的供货方（出口商）授信，使其在发货前获得付款时，会使用红条款信用证。该特别条款是应申请人的要求，因此其表述将遵照申请人的具体要求写入。

红条款指明的授权预付金额可以是信用证的部分或全部金额。预付之后，出口商银行将在受益人发货并提交符合信用证条款的单据后，从付给受益人的款项中扣除其预付款项并加上利息获得偿还。

如果受益人最终未能发货，出口商银行对开证行具有追索权，开证行依次对申请人/进口商也具有追索权，要求进口商进行偿还并支付利息以及其他产生的费用。因此，这种预付安排的风险最终是由申请人承担的。

第十一节　改证

虽然信用证基于申请书开出，而申请书又基于销售合同开出，但信用证一经开出，这三个文件在法律上相互独立。信用证出现任何与销售合同的不符点都可能导致改证。

对于出口商来说，如果其发现信用证条款与销售合同中的条款不一致，其可以选择原样接受信用证也可以要求申请人通过开证行对信用证进行修改。另外，如果改证由申请人提出，修改也必须通过开证行进行修改，并且当信用证为不可撤销信用证时，修改还须得到受益人的同意（如有保兑行的话，还须得到保兑行的同意）。开证行对改证将收取改证费并计入申请人账户。

开证行签发改证后，被修改的各项须随附原证以替换原证的相关项目，并对申请人、受益人、保兑行（如有的话）各方具有法律约束力。

对于开证行来说，改证在修改日生效；对于受益人来说，改证可以在其发出正式接受改证的确认函时或在其按改证条款提交单据时生效。为确定受益人是否接受改证，开证行可以在信用证中写入另一单据要求，要求出口商对接受或拒绝改证进行确认。

第十二节　信用证的特点、优点和缺点

1. 信用证的特点

（1）信用证是建立在银行信用基础上的支付方式，开证行应进口商请求，给予出口商付款承诺。因此，与汇款与托收相比，银行在信用证中的介入程度最深。

（2）银行在信用证业务中须运作单据。但需要注意的是，银行在信用证业务中运作的只是单据而非单据涉及的实物货物、服务或其他履约情况。

（3）银行进行付款遵守的是严格相符原则。一方面，提交的单据须与信用证条款单证相符；另一方面，单据之间须单单相符。

（4）即使运作单据，银行也享有以下免责条款：

①银行对提交的任何单据的格式、充分性、准确性、真实性、篡改或其法律效力不承担责任。银行只核实单据是否与信用证表面相符。

②银行对以这种或那种方式参与信用证运作的第三方的行为不承担责任，银行对其指示执行跟单信用证运作的代理行的行为也不承担责任。

③银行对其无法把控的信息传送的延迟不承担责任。

基于以上特点,信用证具有一定的利弊。

2. 信用证的优点

(1)对出口商的优点。

①信用证对出口商最大的优点是出口商无需承担进口商不付款的风险。只要出口商提交的单据符合信用证的条款,其便可以依赖开证行对其进行支付。除此之外,信用证要求进口商先行申请,出口商在收到以其为受益人的信用证后再行发货。因此,信用证对出口商比对进口商更有利。

②通过信用证下的多种融资方式,只要出口商提交的单据符合信用证的条款,出口商便可以在发货后从其银行立即获得支付,甚至还可以在发货前获得支付,加速其资金周转。

③出口商无需担心资金能否转入或其货物是否允许入境,因为在信用证开立前进口商已取得外汇许可证和进口许可证。

(2)对进口商的优点。

①一旦进口商进行了支付,无需承担出口商不交货的风险。因为在要求进口商付款前,货运单据已交至开证行手中,进口商只要付款,就能赎单。

②申请开证时,申请人会被要求向开证行缴纳信用证金额的一定比例作为开证押金,有时无需缴纳开证押金。这给进口商带来的好处是减少了进口商对己方资金的占用,从而获得了融资。

③进口商可通过信用证条款对货物的质量、数量以及交货时间等进行控制。例如,信用证规定的最后装船日期用以控制交货时间,信用证要求提交的检验单据用以控制所涉及货物的质量和数量。

(3)对开证行的优点。

①开证行可以通过开立信用证赚取佣金。信用证本身便是一种融资方式,对开证行的额外好处是从信用证开立之时至对提交汇票与单据进行偿付时,开证行只出借了其资信,并没有资金支出。

②进口商付款前,开证行持有物权单据,并通过物权单据对货物拥有所有权。如进口商不付款,开证行可以通过售卖货物挽回其损失。

(4)对其他银行的优点。

①议付行在议付信用证时已获得了开证行的明确的付款承诺,因此通常议付没有风险。议付行通过议付信用证下的汇票与单据,赚取单据审核费用和贴现费用。

②其他银行在信用证运作过程中的每一笔服务都收取费用,赚取利润。

3. 信用证的缺点

由于信用证业务强调单据与信用证的表面相符,因此契约各方,如进口商、出口商以及开证行等的资信至关重要，任何一方的失信都会使其他当事人遭受风险。

（1）对出口商的风险。尽管出口商在信用证情形下获得了银行的付款承诺，无需承担进口商不付款的风险，但出口商仍需依赖开证行的资信。如果信用证是伪造信用证或是由虚构银行开出，或者在出口商发货后但收款前开证行破产，出口商都会招致损失。此外，出口商可能面临的风险是进口商、开证行，或者这两方在信用证中设置软条款以及故意地、不诚信地对单据进行挑剔，拒绝付款。

（2）对进口商的风险。由于银行会运作单据，进口商无需承担出口商不交货的风险，但进口商可能收到"不对的"货物、以次充好的或与销售合同的描述不符的货物。产生这种风险的原因是在信用证情形下，银行运作的只是单据而不是单据涉及的实物货物、服务或其他履约情况。如果出口商不诚信，就可能发"不对的"货物，却蔽之以"正确的"单据。

（3）对开证行的风险。不诚信的进口商、出口商，或者这两方可能诱使开证行开出信用证，诱使开证行进行支付。出口商可能用"正确的"单据掩盖虚假交易，而进口商也可能在开证行凭"正确的"单据对出口商履行了付款承诺之后，不去付款赎单。

第九章　保理、备用信用证和保函

学习目标

◇学习保理的定义及其所提供的服务。

◇学习备用信用证的定义及用途。

◇学习保函的定义。

◇学习合约保函与见索即付保函、直接保函与间接保函的差别。

◇学习保函的内容及分类。

◇学习支付方式的选择及组合。

第一节　保理

1. 保理的定义

保理是指某一金融机构(保理商)从某一贸易实体(出口商)购买其向贸易债务人(进口商)所售货物或服务的债权。通常,保理商无追索权购买出口商的应收账款,控制其对进口商的授信,管理其记账并为其收取账款。

简言之,保理是指某一金融机构购买出口商销售货物或服务所产生的债权,以确保其获得进口商的支付。

保理是为国际贸易提供的一种新型的金融服务,通常可与赊销和承兑交单配合使用。

保理起源于英国和北美,随着国际贸易的发展出现了一些世界性的保理机构。成立于1968年的"国际保理商联合会"(FCI)是世界上规模最大的保理机构,由40多个国家的100多家保理机构组成。中国于1993年加入该联合会。FCI制定了《国际保理管理规则》,制约出口商与出口保理商之间的合约以及出口保理商与进口保理商之间的合约。

2. 国际保理当事人

国际保理的四个当事人如下：

（1）出口商。出口商是保理商的客户，按出售的货物或服务向进口商开立发票，出口保理商为其应收账款办理保理业务。发票代表出口商的应收账款，也是其对进口商所拥有的债权。

（2）进口商。进口商对其购买货物或服务所产生的应收账款负债。

（3）出口保理商。出口保理商应按保理合约对出口商的应收账款办理保理业务。出口保理商通常是出口商银行。

（4）进口保理商。进口保理商同意收取由出口商开立的并由出口保理商让渡的应收账款。其对转让的应收账款进行支付，承担信用风险。进口保理商通常是进口商银行。

3. 保理商提供的服务

保理商提供包括买方信用评估、出口贸易融资、销售分类账管理以及应收账款收取的一揽子金融服务。这些服务关联度高，能降低保理商在保理过程中的风险。

（1）买方信用评估。保理商对进口商的信用进行评估并完成信用评估预评报告书。保理商据此核定一定期限内的发货前核准授信额度。在此核准授信额度之内的交易额度被称为已核准应收账款，保理商对其承担付款责任。超过此核准授信额度的交易额度为未核准应收账款，将由出口商自己承担其坏账风险。保理商用此方法保护自己免受进口商不付款的风险。

（2）出口贸易融资。出口商选择是否向出口保理商申请出口贸易融资。如果出口商选择该项融资且交易金额在核准授信额度之内，出口保理商在发票到期前以无追索权的方式议付出口商应收账款，提前付款加速了出口商资金周转。当应收账款向保理商转让后，物权也随之转让给保理商。

（3）销售分类账管理。发票交由保理商后，保理商将在其电脑记录系统中为出口商开立相应的账户分类账。保理商将提供诸如簿记、计算以及缮制银行对账单等专业服务。

（4）应收账款收取。保理商在发票到期时向进口商收取款项。如果款项之前没有提前支付，通常在扣除发票金额1%~2%的保理费后，贷记出口商账户。如果进口商在到期日未能进行支付且保理商没有对出口商进行过提前支付，则由保理商进行支付并加上从到期日至付款日的利息。

4. 国际保理的程序

国际保理的程序如图 9.1 所示。

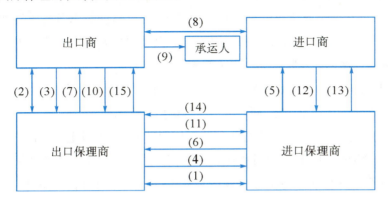

图 9.1　国际保理的程序

(1) 出口保理商与进口保理商签订代理协议。

(2) 出口商与出口保理商签订出口保理协议。

(3) 出口商申请核准授信额度。

(4) 出口保理商寄送核准授信额度申请书。

(5) 进口保理商对进口商进行信用评估并设定核准应收账款。

(6) 通知出口保理商核准应收账款。

(7) 通知出口商核准应收账款。

(8) 进口商、出口商在核准应收账款额度内签订以赊销或承兑交单为支付方式的销售合同。

(9) 出口商发货。

(10) 出口商填写"应收账款转让通知书"并签字,连同发票和其他单据提交出口保理商。出口商此时可申请出口贸易融资。

(11) 出口保理商将发票与其他单据寄送进口保理商。

(12) 进口保理商在发票到期日向进口商催收货款。

(13) 进口商向进口保理商付款,进口保理商向其交单。

(14) 进口保理商将款项汇至出口保理商。

(15) 出口保理商扣除保理费用后将款项贷记出口商账户。如果之前出口商获得融资,提前收到了部分款项,款项余额贷记出口商账户前应先扣除贴现费用。

5. 国际保理的优点

(1) 出口商在核定应收账款内能安全收款。保理是建立在银行资信下的支付方式,保理商承诺无追索权购买出口商在这一额度内的债权。

（2）只要出口商按时发货,出口商便能在到期日收到货款。出口商在向出口保理商提交发票和其他单据时,还可申请融资。

（3）由于保理商全权管理出口商的分类账,出口商可以节省管理和会计成本。出口商可以得到保理商的协助,得到其提供的从对海外进口商的资信评估到信用保护以及收款等一揽子服务。

（4）保理使出口商能以赊销或承兑交单的方式向国外客户进行销售,对国外供货商保有竞争优势,同时通过保理避免坏账风险。

（5）对于贸易商而言,保理的程序比信用证简单,费用比信用证低廉。保理使进口商免交开证费、开证押金以及可能产生的改证费用。信用证严格相符原则不适用于保理,如果出口商按时发货,就能得到保理商的支付。

第二节　备用信用证

1. 备用信用证的定义

根据 UCP 600 的规定,备用信用证是一种信用证或一种协议,无论名称或描述如何,代表开证行对受益人的责任,凭提交的与信用证条款相符的合规单据,对其：

（1）偿还申请人借贷的或预支给申请人的款项。

（2）支付应由申请人账户承担的任何债务。

（3）对申请人的违约进行支付。

在备用信用证情形下,银行只在申请人未能还款或违约的情况下才进行支付。换言之,如申请人履约,备用信用证便"备而不用"。因此,备用信用证的相关当事人通常并不希望出现交单的情况。备用信用证（致受益人的通知）如图 9.2 所示。

Name of issuing bank: The French Issuing Bank 38 rue FrancoisLer 75008 Paris , France	Irrevocable Documentary Credit Number 12345
Place and Date of Issue: Paris, 1 January 2023	Expiry Date and Place for Presentation of Documents Expiry Date: May 29, 2023 Place for Presentation: The American Advising Bank, Tampa
Applicant: The French ABC Co. 89 rue du Commerce Paris, France	Beneficiary: The American XYZ Co. Inc. 17 Main Street Tampa, Florida
Advising Bank: Reference No The American Advising Bank 456 Commerce Avenue Tampa, Florida	Amount: US $ 100 000. - one hundred thousand U.S. Dollars
Partial shipments ☒allowed ☐not allowed Transshipment ☒allowed ☐not allowed ☐ Insurance covered by buyers	Credit available with Nominated Bank: The American Advising Bank, Tampa ☒by payment ☐by acceptance of drafts at: ☐by negotiation
Shipment as defined in UCP 600 From: Tampa, Florida For transportation to: Paris, France Not later than: May 15, 2023	Against the documents detailed herein: ☒and Beneficiary's draft(s) at sight drawn on The American Advising Bank, Tampa

Singed statement of The American XYZ Co. Inc. that The French ABC Co. failed to perform its contractual obligations under the agreement concluded on Dec.17, 2022 between The French ABC Co. and The American XYZ Co. Inc. in which The French ABC Co. was the successful bidder.

Special Conditions:

It is agreed that we may be released from our liability under this Letter of Credit Prior to the expiry date, only if we receive notification from The American Advising Bank, Tampa by tested telex to the effect that The American Advising Bank, Tampa has been duly advised by The American XYZ Co. Inc that the above agreement has been completely performed by The French ABC Co. The American Advising Bank, Tampa to advise the beneficiary adding its confirmation. We herebyauthorize The American Advising Bank, Tampa to drawn on us by means of telex for the value of all drafts drawn under this credit, provided the telex states that all terms and conditions of the credit have been complied with.

We hereby issue the Irrevocable Documentary Credit in your favor. It is subjected to The International Standby Practices (ISP98) issued by International Chamber of Commerce, publication No. 590 in 1998.

The document consists of [2] signed page(s)

The French Issuing Bank

图 9.2 备用信用证(致受益人的通知)

从法律的角度看,备用信用证实质上是一种付款保证而非一种支付方式。作为一种信用证,UCP 600 的一些条款也适用于备用信用证。此外,备用信用证也受国际商会 1998 年第 590 号出版物《1998 年国际备用信用证惯例》(ISP 98)的制约。

2. 备用信用证与常规信用证的相似点

备用信用证与常规信用证的相似点如下：

（1）两种信用证都是独立于所涉合同之外的独立文件。

（2）两种信用证的付款承诺都由开证行给出，付款都凭提交与信用证条款相符的合规单据。

3. 备用信用证与常规信用证的不同点

（1）常规信用证的目的是服务国际贸易交易的货款结算，而备用信用证的目的是为贸易与非贸易合同的履约提供保证。

（2）常规信用证中开证行的责任在付款后终结，而备用信用证在申请人履约后对开证行无付款要求。

（3）常规信用证要求的单据是汇票和证明受益人履约的商业单据，而备用信用证要求的单据是汇票和证明申请人违约的文件。因此，备用信用证往往是光票信用证，通常不用于付款安排。

（4）常规信用证受所有 UCP 600 的条款制约，而 UCP 600 中的某些条款不适用于备用信用证。

第三节　保函

1. 保函的定义

保函（L/G）是指银行应其客户的要求，在委托人未能履行合约责任的情况下，凭规定的单据向受益人支付规定金额以内的书面承诺。它也被称为银行保函（bank guarantee）或保函（bond）。

保函涉及的契约责任可以是付款、交货、还贷或者是楼宇承建。在国际经济交易中，有时一方会坚持先开立一份以其为受益人的保函，再签订合同。

可以看出，不同的付款条件是信用证与银行保函中履行付款承诺的主要区别。在信用证情形下，银行凭受益人的履约进行付款；而在银行保函情形下，银行凭委托人的违约进行付款。在这一点上，银行保函与备用信用证的效果相似。

2. 保函的单据

下面的两种保函对单据的要求不同：

（1）合约保函。国际商会于 1978 年在其第 325 号出版物上出台了《合约保函统一规则》（URCG 325），对受益人从银行索取付款的条件做出了规定。

根据这一规则，要证明委托人违约，受益人须提交法庭判决书、仲裁书或委托人同意索赔书等证明文件。基于这一规则签发的保函称为合约保函。

合约保函要求受益人索赔时提交的证明文件对委托人提供了最大限度的保护。因此，受益人一般不愿意接受合约保函。

（2）见索即付保函。国际商会于 1992 年第 458 号出版物出台的《见索即付保函统一规则》（URDG 458）是制约保函运作的新规则。

在此新规则要求下，付款只凭受益人的书面要求便须"立即"支付，无论受益人所提要求是否合理，也无需提供第三方或委托人自己的证明文件。基于这一新规则签发的保函称为"见索即付"保函。

与合约保函相比，见索即付保函也被称为"无条件保函"，对受益人非常有利，也因此被银行和业界广泛接受。

3. 直接保函和间接保函

根据参与银行的个数，保函分为直接保函和间接保函。

（1）直接保函。直接保函是指由国外银行直接向受益人签发的保函。它通常有三个当事人：委托人/申请人、受益人和担保行。

①委托人/申请人。委托人是保函应其要求而开立的当事人。当其未能履行合约责任时，担保行在进行付款后将对委托人进行索赔。申请时，委托人须与担保行签订赔付契约。

②受益人。受益人是保函进行支付的当事人。当委托人违约时，受益人在提交保函规定的合规单据后得到支付。

③担保行。担保行是签发保函的银行，是在申请人国家的银行。其须签发与申请书内容一致的保函。当签发保函后，银行按保函条款承担对受益人的付款责任。银行有权向申请人索取偿付，补偿其向受益人支付的款项。

直接保函的程序如图 9.3 所示。

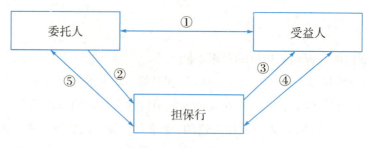

图 9.3　直接保函的程序

①双方签订合同。

②合同一方向其银行申请开立以国外合同另一方为受益人的保函。一方为保函申请人,另一方为受益人。保函基于担保行与申请人之间建立的赔付契约开立。

③担保行将保函寄送受益人。如果委托人履约,保函在保函到期日或到期事件到期后失效。失效保函退回担保行,担保行无需付款,保函程序完成。

④如果委托人违约,受益人凭规定单据向担保行索取付款。

⑤担保行对受益人进行支付后,凭赔付契约向委托人索取赔付。

（2）间接保函。在某些国家,特别是在中东国家,当地的法律和惯例不允许受益人直接接受由国外银行开立的保函。在这样的情形下,此国外银行将指示在受益人国家的另一家银行以此国外银行开出的赔付合约——反担保函开出保函。因此,由于另一家银行的介入,直接保函成为间接保函,涉及四个当事人和两个保函。其中,受益人的银行为担保行,而申请人的银行则为指示人。

间接保函涉及如下四个当事人:委托人/申请人、受益人、指示人和担保行。

①委托人/申请人。委托人是反保函应其要求而开立的当事人。当其未能履行合约责任时,指示人在进行付款后将对委托人进行索赔。申请时,委托人须与其银行签订赔付契约。

②受益人。受益人是保函进行支付的当事人。当委托人违约时,受益人在提交保函规定的合规单据后得到支付。

③指示人 。指示人是申请人银行,应申请人要求向国外银行开立反担保函。之所以称为反担保函,是因为保函凭此开立。

④担保行。担保行是受益人银行,基于反担保函开出担保行。在这种安排中,担保行扮演两种角色:保函的担保人和反担保函的受益人。

间接保函的程序如图9.4所示。

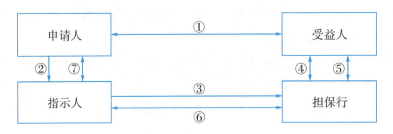

图 9.4　间接保函的程序

①双方签订合同。

②合同一方(申请人)向其银行申请开立以国外合同另一方为受益人的保函,凭银行与申请人的赔付契约开立。

③申请人银行开立以受益人国家的另一银行为受益人的保函,并据此保函指示后者代表其申请人开立指定当事人为受益人的新保函。原保函成为反担保函,并凭此开出新保函。申请人银行成为指示人,新保函凭其要求和指示开出。

④在指示人的要求下,受益人银行代表指示人的委托人向受益人开出保函并成为此保函的担保行。在委托人履约时,保函和反担保函在其到期日或到期事件到期后失效。失效的两份保函将退还其相应担保行,其相应担保行无需付款,程序结束。

⑤如果委托人违约,受益人凭保函规定单据向担保行索取付款。

⑥担保行凭反担保函向指示人索取偿付。

⑦指示人凭赔付契约向委托人索取赔付。

4. 保函的主要内容

保函的内容须清楚、具体和准确,避免涉及过多细节。保函应包括:

(1)受益人名称和签发日期。

(2)保函的类别和保函号。

(3)保函所涉交易的一般内容,如合同号码,合同双方当事人,合同签订日期,货物/服务/工程的相关数量、质量或履约要求。

(4)保函的金额及其币种。

(5)付款条件。保函应指明索取付款须提交的单据。如果付款条件依照国际商会第 325 号出版物,则保函为合约保函,对受益人不太有利。如果付款条件依照国际商会第 458 号出版物,则保函为见索即付保函,对受益人有利。

(6)保函的有效期。按照国际商会第 458 出版物的规定,保函须指明某一具体日期为到期日或指明到期事件。保函在到期日失效或在某一特定事件发生后的一段时期失效,如发货后 30 天。如果保函既注明了到期日期又注明了到期事件,则以先到的为准。

(7)对保函金额递减以及制约保函的法律法规及其所辖范围的规定。

(8)担保行名称及其签字。保函在到期日或到期事件,或者在保函对索赔进行支付后失效。无论是何种情形,失效后的保函正本须返还担保银行。

5. 保函的主要种类

根据《合约保函统一规则》的规定,保函的主要类别有投标保函、履约保函、进口保函、还款保函、补偿贸易保函、来料加工/来件装配保函和贷款保函等。

保函的种类繁多,以满足签约方在其经济活动中的不同目的。事实上,只要有保障权利与利益的需要,合同的一方都可以申请开立某种保函,获得来自银行的,而非来自合同另一方的履约承诺。

(1)投标保函。投标保函是担保行应投标人的要求开立以海外招标人为受益人的保函。如果委托人未能履行由于递交标书而应承担的各项责任时,担保行承诺在规定的时间内对受益人进行一定金额的货币赔偿。

投标保函的三个直接当事人如下:

①委托人。委托人是递交标书的投标人。

②受益人。受益人是招标人。

③担保行。担保行是在委托人未能履行由于递交标书而应承担的责任时进行支付的银行。

招标时,投标人的责任如下:

①投标人在开标前不得对标书进行修改或撤标。

②如果中标,投标人须与招标人签订合约。

③投标人签约后应申请开立履约保函或其他规定的保函以替换投标保函。

如果未中标,投标保函的到期日为开标日或开标日的几天后为止。如果中标,到期日顺延 3~6 个月,直至签订中标合同或开立履约保函或规定的其他保函。

投标保函的金额为承建工程合约金额的 1%~5%。投标保函的目的是保护受益人(招标人),以防委托人(投标人)不负责任的投标,造成违约。投标保函如图 9.5 所示。

TO：_____　　　　　　Issuing Date：_____

　　　　　　　　　　　　　　　　Bid security for Bid No. _____

　　　　　　　　　　　　　　　　For supply of _____

This guarantee is hereby issued to serve as a Bid Security of _____

(name of Bidder) (hereinafter called the "Bidder") for invitation for Bid (Bid No. _____) for supply of _____ (description of goods) to _____ (Name of the Buyer).

_____ (Name of issuing bank) hereby unconditionally and irrevocably guarantee and binds itself, its successors and assigns to pay you immediately without recourse, the sum of _____ upon receipt of your written notification stating any of the following：

a)The Bidder has withdrawn his bid after the time and date of the bid opening and before the expiration of its validity period；or

b)The Bidder has failed to enter into Contract with you within thirty calendar days after the notification of Contract award；or

c)The Bidder has failed to establish acceptable Performance security within thirty calendar days after receipt of the Notification Award.

It is fully understood that this guarantee takes effect from the date of the bid opening and shall remain valid for a period of _____ calendar days, and during the period of any extension thereof that may be agreed upon between you and the Bidder with notice to us, unless terminated and or released by you.

　　　　　　　　　　　　　　Issuing Bank _____

　　　　　　　　　　　　　　Signed by _____

　　　　　　　　　　　　　　　(printed name and designation of official authorized to sign on behalf issuing bank)

　　　　　　　　　　　　　　Official Seal _____

图 9.5　投标保函

（2）履约保函。履约保函是担保行应供货商或服务提供商或工程承包商的要求开立以买方或业主为受益人的保函。如果委托人未能履约，担保行承诺在规定的时间内对受益人进行一定金额的货币赔偿。

履约保函的三个直接当事人如下：

①委托人。委托人可以是销售合同中提供货物或服务的出口商，也可以是获得工程承建合同的承保商。委托人是投标保函下的投标人。

②受益人。受益人可以是销售合同中购买货物或服务的进口商，也可以是中标工程承建合同的业主。受益人是投标保函下的招标人。

③担保行。担保行在委托人违约时进行支付。

履约保函的目的是保证委托人履行合同。履约保函的有效期到货物或服务的交付或合同的完工为止。保函的金额一般是合同金额的 10%～15%。履约保函如图 9.6 所示。

To _____（Beneficiary）　Issuing Date _____
　　　　　　　　　　　　　　　　　　　Performance Bond No._____
　　　　　　　　　　　　　　　　　　　For the supply of _____
This Bond is hereby issued as the performance bond of _____（Applicant）（hereinafter called the supplier）for supply of _____（description of goods）under the Contract No. _____ to _____（the name of the beneficiary）.

The _____（name of the guarantor）hereby irrevocably guarantees itself, its successors and assigns to pay you up to the amount of _____（the amount of the guaranteed value）representing _____ percent of the contract price and accordingly covenants and agrees as follows:

a）On the supplier's failure of faithful performance of the contract（hereinafter called the failure of performance）, we shall immediately, on your demand in a written notification stating the effect of the failure of performance by the supplier, pay you such amount or amounts as required by you not exceeding _____（the guaranteed amount）in the manner specified in the said statement.

b）The covenants herein contained constitute irrevocable and direct obligations of the guarantor, no alternation in the terms of the contract to be performed thereunder and no allowance of time by you or any other act or omission by you, which but for this provision might exonerate or discharge the bank shall in any way release the guarantor from any liability hereunder.

c）The performance bond shill become effective from issuing date and shall remain valid until _____（the date of expiry）. Upon expiry, please return this bond for cancellation.

　　　　　　　　　　　　　　　　　　Issuing Bank _____
　　　　　　　　　　　　　　　　　　Signed by _____
　　　　　　　　　　　　　　　　　　　　（printed name and designation of official authorized to sign on behalf issuing bank）
　　　　　　　　　　　　　　　　　　Official Seal _____

图 9.6　履约保函

（3）进口保函／付款保函。进口保函/付款保函是担保行应进口商的要求开立以出口商为受益人的保函。如果委托人未能对其以赊销方式获得的货物进行支付,担保行承诺在规定的时间内对受益人进行一定金额的货币赔偿。

进口保函/付款保函的三个直接当事人如下:

①委托人。委托人是以赊销方式从出口商处获得货物的进口商。

②受益人。受益人是以赊销方式向进口商出售货物的出口商。

③担保行。担保行在委托人未能对出口商进行付款时进行支付。

进口保函/付款保函的目的是保证赊销方式下的付款。保函的应付金额为已交货货物的金额加上适当利息。

（4）还款保函／预付款保函。还款保函或预付款保函是担保行应出口商或承包商的要求开立以进口商或业主为受益人的保函。如果委托人违约,未对受益人向委托人支付或预付的金额进行偿还,担保行承诺在规定的时间内对受益人进行付款。

还款保函/预付款保函的三个直接当事人如下:

①委托人。委托人是收取了预付金的当事人。其可以是以预付货款方式

提供货物或服务的出口商,也可以是中标合同的承包商。

②受益人。受益人是向委托人预付款项的当事人。其可以是以预付货款方式购买货物或服务的进口商,也可以是对承包商预付款项的业主。

③担保行。担保行在委托人未能交付货物,或者服务或未能履行契约责任时,偿还预付金额。

还款保函/预付款保函的目的是担保货物或服务的交付或工程项目的履约。保函应付金额为预付金额且随每次发货或按工程完成进度自动规律递减。在国际贸易中,还款保函/预付款保函可以与预付货款结合使用以保护进口商。保函的有效期从委托人收到预付款开始至履约后的一个具体日期。

(5)补偿贸易保函。补偿贸易保函是担保行应资本货物的进口商的要求开立以资本货物出口商为受益人的保函。如果委托人未能保质保量按期交付该工厂的预期产品,担保行承诺在规定的时间内对受益人进行一定金额的货币赔偿。

补偿贸易保函的应付金额通常为资本货物金额加上利息。保函有效期为预期产品从进口国交付半个月后为止。

(6)来料加工/来件装配保函。来料加工/来件装配保函是担保行应原材料、配件或设备进口商的要求开立以出口商为受益人的保函。如果委托人未能履约,未能保质保量按时交付成品时,担保行承诺在规定的时间内对受益人进行一定金额的货币赔偿。

来料加工/来件装配保函的应付金额为原材料、配件或设备的价值加上利息。保函有效期为从进口国的交货日或交付成品日后半个月内为止。

(7)透支保函。当承包商在海外建立了一个完整的生产单位或获得一个基础设施工程时,其通常会在一家当地银行开立一个透支账户以获得融资。其在开立此透支账户前会要求先开立银行保函。

透支保函是担保行应承包商的要求开立以海外银行为受益人的保函。如果委托人未能履行对该账户透支金额的到期还款,担保行承诺在规定的时间内对受益人进行一定金额的货币赔偿。

透支保函的应付金额通常等于透支账户规定的透支限额。保函有效期在透支账户到期日后半个月内为止。

第四节　保函与信用证的相似点

保函与信用证的相似点如下:

(1)保函与信用证都建立在银行信用的基础上。这意味着开立保函或信用证的银行代表申请人/委托人向受益人做出付款承诺。

（2）保函和信用证在法律上均独立于所涉合同。银行只受保函或信用证的约束。

（3）在两种情形下，银行对提交单据的形式、充分性、准确性、真实性或单据伪造不承担责任。银行只需合理谨慎核查单据的表面真实性。

（4）银行仅凭提交合乎保函或信用证规定的合规单据进行支付。

第五节　保函与信用证的不同点

保函与信用证的不同点如下：

（1）适用范围。信用证只适用于贸易结算，开证行代表进口商对受益人做出付款承诺。

保函既适用于贸易交易也适用于非贸易交易，担保行对履约担保的付款承诺可以向合约的任何一方做出。

（2）付款承诺。信用证凭受益人的履约进行付款。因此，信用证开证行对受益人承担第一付款责任。跟单信用证要求提交能证明受益人履约的单据，如商业发票、提单、保单等。

保函凭委托人的违约进行付款。因此，银行对受益人承担第二付款责任。也就是说，一旦履约，保函无需进行付款。保函要求提交能证明委托人违约的证明，规定的单据可以是受益人开立的证明文件或是中立的第三方开立的证明文件。

（3）进行支付的银行个数。在信用证情形下，对受益人进行付款的银行不止一个，可以是开证行、保兑行、付款行、承兑行或议付行。因此，交单地点可以按信用证要求提交到上述任何一家银行的柜台。

对保函受益人进行支付的银行只有一个，在反担保函下为指示人，在保函下为担保行。无论是哪种情况，单据只能交到签发反担保函或保函的银行柜台。

（4）制约法规。信用证受《跟单信用证统一规则》（UCP 600）的制约，但UCP 600 只是一套规则，没有规定出现争端时所适用的管辖法规与管辖区域。

保函受《合约保函统一规则》或《见索即付保函统一规则》的制约。虽然这两者也只是规则，但它们指明争端出现时适用的管辖法规与管辖区域，保函在担保行所在地解决争端，反担保函在指示人所在地解决争端。

（5）可转让性。信用证可以转让，而保函不可以转让。

第六节　保函与备用信用证

1. 相似点

作为信用证的一种,备用信用证与保函的相似点如本章第四节所述。除此之外,备用信用证与保函最突出的相似点是在效果上,即开证行或担保行都须在申请人/委托人违约时对受益人进行支付。

2. 不同点

保函与备用信用证在以下方面有所不同:

(1)兑用方式。备用信用证的开证行、保兑行、付款行、承兑行或议付行可以进行即期付款、延期付款、承兑或议付。

但保函只能进行付款,只有保函的担保行和反担保函的指示人能进行付款。

(2)交单地点。备用信用证的交单地点可以是进行支付的银行地点。这意味着信用证可规定交单地点为开证行、保兑行、付款行、承兑行或议付行的柜台。这些银行可以是出口商银行,也可以是在进口国的海外银行。

在保函情形下,单据必须交给保函的担保行或反担保函的指示人的柜台。

第七节　支付方式总结

在国际贸易中,契约双方都在寻求既能规避对方违约带来的风险又能同时保持自己在国际市场中的竞争力的支付方式。

不同的支付方式对不付款和不交货的风险提供了不同程度的保护。对于一笔交易来说,贸易商可以只选择一种支付方式,也可以选择不同支付方式的组合来达到风险防范与保持竞争力之间的平衡。以下是实务中一些常用的选择与组合方式:

1. 预付货款与赊销组合

在这种组合中,双方同意进口商预付一定金额,余额通过赊销进行收取。金额的比例高低会在对市场情形、交易目的、货物状况、贸易伙伴的资信以及双方关系等进行综合考虑后设定。这种综合考虑也同样适用于下面 2、3、4 组合。

2. 汇款与托收组合

在这种组合中，双方同意进口商预付一定金额，余额通过托收进行收取。

3. 信用证与汇款组合

在这种组合中，双方同意用信用证结算大部分货款，余额通过汇款支付。这种方法常用于大宗商品，比如煤炭的交易中。大部分货物的货款通过信用证结算而在出口商将小部分余数发货后，向其电汇余款。

4. 信用证与托收组合

贸易商也可以在一张信用证下开立两张汇票：一张汇票通过光票信用证收取一定金额，另一张汇票通过即期付款交单或远期付款交单收取余额。

5. 托收与备用信用证或保函组合

当交易为承兑交单时，出口商可以要求进口商安排开立以出口商为受益人，金额为销售总金额，有效期为汇票到期日后一段时间的备用信用证或保函。如果进口商违约，出口商可凭备用信用证向开证行或凭银行保函向担保行索取赔付。

6. 赊销与进口保函组合

当交易为赊销时，出口商可要求进口商安排开立以出口商为受益人，金额为合约金额的进口保函。如果出口商发货后进口商不付款，担保行承诺对出口商进行赔付。

7. 预付货款与还款保函组合

当交易为预付货款时，进口商可要求出口商安排开立以进口商为受益人，金额为预支金额的还款保函。如果出口商在收到货款后不发货，担保行承诺对进口商进行还款。

第四部分　单据篇

第十章　商业发票、装箱单和保险单

学习目标

◇学习单据的分类和意义。

◇学习商业发票的定义和内容。

◇学习装箱单的定义和内容。

◇学习保险单的定义和内容。

◇学习风险种类和险别划分。

◇学习险别的选择原则。

◇学习保险单据的种类。

第一节　国际结算中的单据

1. 单据的分类

国际结算中的单据包括金融票据和商业单据，以便利款项的支付和货物的交付或服务的提供。金融票据主要包括汇票、本票和支票，已在第三章、第四章、第五章进行了介绍。从第十章开始的后续各章，将对商业单据进行介绍。

常用的商业单据有商业发票、装箱单、保险单、提单、检验证书和原产地证书等。这些商业单据可归类为基本单据和附属单据。

基本单据是指按照《国际贸易术语解释通则》的规定，如 CIF、CIP 或 FOB 等贸易术语的要求，出口商必须提交的单据，包括商业发票、保险单据和运输单据。

附属单据是指根据进口国法律法规或按进口商对货物情况的要求所必须提交的单据。它们主要有原产地证书、领事发票和海关发票、装箱单和重量单以及检验证书等。

2. 支付方式、价格术语和单据

支付方式可以是顺汇或逆汇，可以建立在商业信用上或银行信用上。不同销售合同的价格也选用不同的价格术语进行报价。所有这些都对单据的签发人、抬头或其他相关项目的缮制产生很大影响。这就意味着，在不同的支付方式和不同的价格术语下，交易中的金融票据和商业单据的具体细节各不相同。

特别是在信用证情形下，由于开证行承担极大的付款责任，开证行会在信用证的条款中对出口商须提交的单据做出规定，银行只凭严格相符原则履行其付款责任。因此，在信用证情形下的交易中，一方面，单据的开立者或签发者须确保单据符合信用证条款；另一方面，提交的单据须确保单单相符。

3. 单据的意义

支付方式以单据为中心，单据在现代国际结算中的意义从下列几点中得以体现：

（1）结算过程中运行的是单据。现代国际结算从现金结算发展到了非现金结算，金融单据已取代现金成为交换的媒介。在结算过程中，贸易商和银行处理的都是金融票据或商业单据而非现金和实物货物。因此，单据是在整个结算过程中运行。

（2）单据是销售合同的履约证明。正如第一章所介绍的，金融票据是收付款的命令，其目的是结清款项。一旦执行了命令，资金便从一个贸易商的账户转移至另一个贸易商的账户，从而结清款项。

销售合同对货物须满足的条件、运输、保险以及支付方式等责任都做出描述和规定。所有的这些责任都从相应的商业单据中得到反映。由于这一原因，商业单据种类各异，不同的商业单据分别表明贸易商是否承担交易中货物的生产、包装、发运以及保险等责任。提交某种商业单据，表示已承担了其相应的责任。因此，商业单据为货物的生产、包装、保险以及保质保量按时交付提供了单据证明。

（3）部分商业单据成为物权单据。正如第一章所介绍的，随着国际结算的发展，提单和保单这两种商业单据发展成为物权单据。

以提单为例，由于提单的持有人便是货主，因此出现了象征性交货。出口商提交物权单据便相当于交货，而进口商一旦收到物权单据便应该进行付款。当货物单据化以后，出现了凭单交货和凭单付款，而不是凭实物货物交货或付款的情况。

第二节　商业发票

1. 商业发票的定义

　　商业发票是由卖方按交付货物或提供服务的价值向买方开立的索取付款的会计凭证。商业发票主要列出了唛头和编号、货物描述、数量、单价和总价。在国际结算中，商业发票是催款的单据而非付款的凭证。

　　商业发票是基于销售合同而签发的，因此合同号码（S/C No.）应在商业发票中注明。如果用信用证结算，商业发票还须注明开证行名称、信用证号码以及信用证开证日期。

　　商业发票是基础单据，其他单据，如汇票、运输单据、保险单据和装箱单都基于商业发票开出。商业发票一般用卖方公司信头纸缮制并在其上清楚载明"商业发票"字样。商业发票如图 10.1 所示。

上海进出口贸易公司
SHANGHAI IMPORT & EXPORT TRADE CORPORATION
1123 ZHONGSHAN ROAD SHANGHAI, CHINA

COMMERCIAL INVOICE

TEL：021-65788866
FAX：021-65788867

INV. NO. : TX0053
DATE：FEB. 01, 2023
S/C NO. : TXT234
L/C NO. : TX0081

TO：
TKAMRA CORPORATION
302, KAWARA MACH OSAKA JAPAN
FROM SHANGHAI PORT　TO OSAKA PORT

MARKS & NO.	DESCRIPTIONS OF GOODS	QUANTITY	U/PRICE	AMOUNT
T.C TXT264 OSAKA C/NO.1-300	100%COTTON COLOUR WEAVE SHIRT 　TM 111 　TM 222 　TM 333 　TM 444 PACKED IN ONE CARTON OF 20 PIECES EACH	 2 000 PCS 2 000 PCS 1 000 PCS 1 000 PCS	CIFOSAKA USD 11.00 USD 10.00 USD 9.50 USD 8.50	 USD 22 000.00 USD 20 000.00 USD 9 500.00 USD 8 500.00

TOTAL AMOUNT: SAY US DOLLARS SIX THOUSAND ONLY.

WE HEREBY CERTIFY THAT THE CONTENTS OF INVOICE HEREIN ARE CORRECT.

DRAWN UNDER JAPANESE ISSUING BANK, OSAKA, IRREVOCABLE DOCUMENTARY CREDIT NUMBER TX0081 DATED JAN 15, 2023

Authorized Signature

图 10.1 商业发票

2. 商业发票的主要内容

商业发票主要包括以下项目：

（1）卖方名称和地址。卖方公司信头纸会预先印制其名称和地址。在信用证情形下，卖方的名称和地址应与受益人的名称和地址一致。

（2）买方名称和地址。在信用证情形下，发票应向信用证的申请人开出，其名称和地址应与信用证中所显示的信息保持一致。

（3）签发日期和发票号码。在实务中，商业发票的签发日期可以是所有单据中最早的日期。在信用证下，商业发票的签发日期也可以是介于信用证最后的装船日期和到期日之间的任何日期。发票号码是卖方给出的发票流水号。

（4）唛头。唛头的目的是方便承运人和收货人搬运与识别货物。它一般包含标志、卸货港/地、包装序号等。

发货如果没有使用唛头，"唛头号码"栏可注明"N.M.（无唛头）"字样或将此栏留空。但如果使用了唛头，商业发票中须载明唛头并在其他单据，如装箱单和提单中也载明同样的唛头。

（5）货物描述。商业发票在货物描述中载明货物的名称、包装和规格。在信用证情形下，货物描述应符合信用证的描述，虽然信用证只对货物做笼统描述。

（6）数量、单价与总价。卖方应细列单价并基于数量计算出总价，总价为进口商应付金额。价格应包含价格术语。在信用证情形下，发票金额通常为信用证金额。但银行不负责对计算进行核查。

（7）装货港/地和卸货港/地。装货港/地和卸货港/地须与价格术语一致。在信用证情形下，此信息还须与信用证相应条款一致。

（8）支付方式。商业发票应恰当指明选用支付方式的具体类别，如即期付款交单或见票后 30 天承兑交单等。在信用证情形下，开证行名称、信用证号码以及信用证开证日期应在商业发票中注明。

（9）卖方签字。根据 UCP 500 的规定，除信用证另有规定外，商业发票无需卖方签字。

第三节　装箱单／重量单

　　装箱单/重量单详细列出了货物的包装分类情况,如货物的净重、毛重以及体积尺寸,为商业发票的补充单据。装箱单使承运人、买方和海关更方便清点查验货物。

　　装箱单上的货物描述以及唛头要与商业发票保持一致。但商业发票中涉及单价和总价的部分不应在装箱单中出现。装箱单的签发日期可以与商业发票一致,也可以稍迟于商业发票,但不能早于商业发票。装箱单如图10.2所示。

上海进出口贸易公司
SHANGHAI IMPORT & EXPORT TRADE CORPARATION
1123 ZHONGSHAN ROAD SHANGHAI, CHINA

PACKING LIST

TEL: 021-65788866
FAX: 021-65788867

INVOICE NO. TX0053
DATE: FEB. 01, 2023
S/C NO. : TXT233

MARKS & NOS
T.C

TO:
TKAMARA CORPOATION
302, KAWARA MACH OSAKA
JAPAN
FROM SHANGHAI PORT　TO　OSAKA PORT

TXT233
OSAKA
C/NO. 1-300

GOODS DESCRIPTIPN & PACKING	QUANTITY	CTNS	G.W. (KGS)	N.W. (KGS)	MEAS (M³)
100% COTTON COLOUR WEAVE SHIRT	2 000 PCS	100	11/1 100	10/1 000	0. 22/22
TM 111	2 000 PCS	100	11/1 100	10/1 000	0. 22/22
TM 222	1 000 PCS	50	11/550	10/500	0. 22/11
TM 333	1 000 PCS	50	11/550	10/500	0. 22/11
TM 444					
PACKED IN ONE CARTION OF 20 PIECES EACH					
TOTAL	6 000 PCS	300	3 300	3 000	66

SAY TATAL THREE HUNDRED CARTONS ONLY

DRAWN UNDER JAPANESE ISSUING BANK, OSAKA, IRREVOCABLE DOCUMENTARY CREDIT NUMBER TX0081 DATED JAN 15, 2023

Authorized Signature

图 10.2　装箱单

第四节　保险单据

1. 保险单据的定义

　　保险单据是由保险人和投保人签订的,规定了保费、保额、承保险别、索赔程序以及其他适用条款的赔付契约,在承保险别出险时对投保人进行赔付的单据。保险单与提单同时发展成为物权单据。

　　货物在运输过程中面临风险,各方须对货物投保加以规范。货物的保险责任在《国际贸易术语解释通则》中已做出规定,货物在运输过程中的投保责任可由出口商或进口商承担。

　　各方在交易之初便应选定价格术语,并在销售合约中明确载明。价格术语是从出口商的角度而非进口商的角度进行责任描述。例如,如果价格术语为 CIF 或 CIP,那么出口商应对货物投保并与保险公司签订保险合同。如果价格术语为 FOB、FCA 或 CFR,与保险公司签订保险合同的责任应由进口商来承担。保险单如图 10.3 所示。

中 国 人 民 保 险 公 司
大连分公司
The People's Insurance Company of China
DALIAN BRANCH
总公司设于北京一九四九年创立

HEAD OFFICE：BEIJING ESTABLISHED IN 1949

地址：中国大连中山路 141 号　　　　　　　CABLE：42001 DALIAN

ADDRESS：141 ZHONGSHAN ROAD DALIAN CHINA　　FAX：336650 804558

TLX：86215 PICC CN

发票号次　　　　　　　　**保险单**　　保险单号次

INVOICE NO. 33563　　**INSURANCE POLICY**

POLICY NO. PYIE2003210206000002

中 国 人 民 保 险 公 司（以下简称"公司"）

THIS POLICY OF INSURANCE WITNESSES THAT THE PEOPLE'S INSURANCE COMPANY OF CHINA

根　据

(HEREINAFTER CALLED"THE COMPANY"), AT THE REQUEST OF 　　DALIAN I/E CO. LTD

（以下简称"被保险人"）的要求,由被保险人向本公司缴付

(HEREIN CALLED THE "INSURED") AND IN CONSIDERATION OF THE AGREED PREMIUM

PAYING TO

约 定 的 保 险 费,按 照 本 保 险 单 承 保 险 别

THE COMPANY BY THE INSURED, UNDERTAKES TO INSURE THE GOODS IN TRNASPORTATION

和背面所载条款与下列特款承保下列货物运输保险

SUBJECT TO THE CONDITIONS OF THE POLICY AS PER THE CLAUSES PRINTED OVERLEAF AND

特立保险单

SPECIAL CLAUSES ATTACHED HEREON.

标记 MARKS ANDNOS	包装及数量 PACKAGE & QUANTITY	货物描述 DESCRITION OF GOODS	保险金额 AMOUNT INSURED
N/M	4 CTNS	ART NO.42518	USD 1 700. 00

TOTAL AMOUNT INSURED 总保险金额：__US DOLLARS ONE THOUSAND SEVEN HUNDERD ONLY__

PREMIUM 保险费：__AS ARRANGED__   RATE 费率 __AS ARRANGED PER CONVEYANCE__ 装载运输工具：S.S. EASTWIND V.009E__ SLG. ON OR ABT 开航日期. __JULY 4, 2023__   FROM 自__ __DALIAN CHINA__ TO 至__BUSHAN PORT, KOREA__

CONDITIONS 承保险别：Covering All Risks as per Institute Cargo Clauses（1. 1. 1963）and Risk of War as per Institute War Cargo Clause（11. 3. 80）

所保货物,如遇出险,本公司凭此保险单及其他有关证件给付赔款。

CLAIMS, IF ANY, PAYABLE ON SURRENDER OF THIS POLICY TOGETHER WITH OTHER RELE-VANT

所保货物,如发生本保险单项下负责赔偿

DOCUMENTS. IN THE EVENT OF ACCIDENT WHEREBY LOSS OR DAMAGE MAY RESULT IN A CLAIM

的损失或事故,应立即通知本公司

UNDER THIS POLICY, IMMEDIATE NOTICE APPLYING FOR SURVEY MUST BE GIVEN TO THE

下述代理人查勘。

COMPANY'S AGENT AS MENTIONED HEREUNDER

NAME OF AGENTS：

CLAIM PAYABLE AT 赔付地点：__BUSHAN, KOREA__

　　DATE 日期：__JULY 4 2023　DALIAN__

中国人民保险公司

THE PEOPLE'S INSURANCE

COMPANY OF CHINA

大连分公司

DALIAN BRANCH

图 10.3　保险单

2. 保险单的内容

　　保险商预先印制空白标准保险单,由投保人在决定向此保险商投保时填入并签字。

　　(1)保险商名称及签字。保险商为保险公司、保险承销商或其代理。保险商依据保险单据对投保人进行赔付。由于保险单据通常印制在保险商公司信头纸上,保险单据一般已由保险商预签。

(2)投保人名称及签字。投保人是向保险商支付保费并在货物承保险别出险时向保险商索赔的当事人。在国际贸易中,投保人可为:

①出口商:当所选价格术语(如 CIF、CIP 等)规定货物投保责任由出口商承担时。

②进口商:当所选价格术语(如 FOB、CFR 等)暗示由进口商安排货物投保时。

(3)背书。背书虽然在保险单据的背面做出,但也是一个重要的项目。通过背书,保险单据的所有权被转让给被背书人,其在货物运输过程中承保险别出险时提出索赔。索赔通常在进口国发生,因此由进口商提出索赔较为方便。鉴于投保人不同,对背书的要求也有不同。

当投保人为进口商时,无需背书,因为进口商自己就是实际投保人。

当出口商是投保人时,其须在交单时对保险单据进行背书。在信用证情形下,通常信用证条款规定背书给开证行。开证行在进口商付款赎单时再将保险单据背书给进口商。但在其他支付方式下,出口商可以将单据背书给指定人或给发货人的指定人,或者直接背书给进口商使其成为实际投保人。出口商在未获得银行同意前不得将保险单背书给银行。

对保险单据的背书可以做成空白背书或记名背书。在信用证情形下,投保人须按信用证要求在交单时进行背书。

(4)货物描述。保险单据无需载明货物详细描述,可以只对货物进行笼统描述。但是,唛头、数量和包装等项目应与商业发票和其他单据的描述一致。

(5)投保金额。投保金额是投保人的索赔金额。金额须用数字和大写金额同时表示。通常,投保金额的币种须与商业发票的币种一致且为发票金额的 110%。

(6)保险费率和保费。保险商按货物的类别、承保险别、船只类别以及装运港和卸货港之间的距离等设定费率。在实务中,保险单据中的费率栏无需由出口商填写,通常显示为"按约定"。以"一切险"为例,欧美市场、亚洲市场和非洲市场的费率可分别为 0.5%、1.5% 和 3.5%。

保费是保险商向投保人、进口商或出口商收取的费用。保费按下列公式计算:

保费 = 保险金额×费率

由于单据中未具体列出费率,保费也以"按约定"字样显示。

(7)承保险别。承保险别是指为运输过程中的货物投保的险种,保险商只对承保险别的出险进行赔付。承保险别的完整信息包括险别种类、保险条款以及保险条款生效日期。

（8）运输信息。运输信息包括船名、装船日期、装运港和卸货港。运输信息的所有内容要与提单等运输单据保持一致。

（9）签发日期。保险单据的签发日期表示承保生效日期。该日期可以早于或与装运日期（如提单日期）相同，但不可晚于装运日期。如果保险单据的签发日期晚于装运日期，表示货物有一段时间脱保，这种情况通常不会被信用证开证行接受。

（10）索赔地点。保险单据应明确指明单据的索赔地点以及受理索赔的保险代理的名称和地址。

索赔一般在卸货地，即进口商的国家受理。如信用证有规定，索赔地应与信用证规定相符。

（11）全套。通常，全套保险单据包括一张正本和一张副本。

3. 损失

损失是指货物在运输过程中受到的损坏。按成因，损失分为海上风险导致的海上损失和外来风险导致的损失。

（1）海上损失。海上损失是指所有由于自然灾害和意外事故所引起的损失。当恶劣天气、风暴和雷电、地震、海啸以及洪水等造成事故，使船只或货物搁浅、沉没、烧毁等，这种损失就会发生。按货损程度划分，海上损失可以分为全部损失和部分损失。

全部损失是程度最为严重的损失，货物完全灭失或失去价值。全部损失又可分为：

①实际全损。实际全损是指货物完全损毁或不复存在。

②推定全损。推定全损是指货物的损毁程度虽然没有达到实际全损，但是货物的修理费用已超出货物原有的价值。

部分损失又称为"海损"，是指一部分货物已灭失或损毁，但货物还保有一定的价值或对货物的修复费用没有超过货物的原有价值。根据成因划分，部分损失可以分为：

①共同海损。共同海损是指在危急时刻，船长为了所有各方的共同利益，主动牺牲部分货物或有目的地支出某笔费用。共同海损须由相关的所有当事人共同承担。

②单独海损。单独海损是指部分货物由于意外灾害而产生的损失，不是某一方为了各方的共同利益而做出的有目的的行为而造成的。单独海损须由遭受损失的一方单独承担。

（2）外来风险。外来风险是指由海上损失以外的原因造成的风险，可以分为一般外来风险和特殊外来风险。

一般外来风险是指在货物运输过程中由于处理不当而带来的损失，分为

11 种。读者对这 11 种一般外来风险的名称和性质须有一般性的了解。

①TPND：偷窃、提货不着风险的简写，是指在运输过程中由于货物被盗、由于不当卸货、不当处理对货物造成的损毁，致使货物未能交货的风险。

②渗漏：由于容器破损致使流质货物渗漏流出的风险。

③破碎碰撞：易损物品遭受震动、碰撞、挤压而破裂的风险。

④钩损：在货物装卸过程中由于挂钩操作不当而导致的货物损失的风险。

⑤FWRD：货物由于淡水或雨淋而使货物受到玷污的风险。

⑥短量：货物由于外部包装破损而致使货物重量短缺的风险，但不包括货物在运输过程中正常的重量短缺。

⑦混杂玷污：由于货物混杂、相互污染而致使货物受损的风险。

⑧串味：由于货物受到其他物品气味的影响致使货物串味的风险。

⑨受热受潮：由于温度的突然变化或由于通风设备的失灵等致使货物受潮受热而导致货物损失的风险。

⑩锈损：因海水污染致使货物生锈而导致的货物损失的风险，但不包括货物自身生锈或因货物自身瑕疵而导致的货物损失。

⑪包装破裂：由于野蛮装卸使包装破裂而导致货物损失的风险。

特殊外来风险是指由于政治、军事、行政法规、行政程序以及这方面的改变等原因造成的风险与损失。特殊外来险有以下 9 种：

①战争险。

②罢工、暴动、内乱险（SRCC）。

③提货不着。

④拒收。

⑤黄曲霉素。

⑥舱面。

⑦进口关税。

⑧海关检验条款。

⑨码头检验条款。

4. 险别

制定不同的承保险别是为了承保不同的风险，险别界定了保险商的赔付责任范围。在保险单据中，"conditions"和"risks"也指承保的险别（coverage）。承保险别分为基本险险别和附加险险别。

（1）基本险险别。三种险别构成海洋保险基本险险别。"基本"是指这三种险别可以供单独选择一种进行承保，而且在选择其他附加险险别时须先选择基本险险别。

①平安险。平安险是指单独海损不赔，保险商的平安险的赔付范围只包

括全部损失和部分损失。与其他险别相比，平安险的承保范围最小。

②水渍险。水渍险又称为单独海损要赔，即承保所有的海上损失，不仅限于对单独海损的承保，其承保范围为平安险的范围加上单独海损。

如果水渍险不承保小额损失，通常会指明承保损失的百分比。承保损失的最小百分比称为免赔额（率）。此百分比可以是保险金额的 3% 或 5%。但现行的趋势是保单不再指明免赔率。"IOP"的意思是无免赔率，即保险商无论损失的金额多少，对水渍险导致的货物损失都进行承保。

③一切险。一切险的承保范围为海上风险和一般外来风险所引起的货物损失，但不包括特殊外来风险。因此，一切险的承保范围并没有涵盖运输过程中所有的风险损失。

（2）附加险险别。附加险险别是针对 11 种一般外来风险和 9 种特殊外来风险而设置的险别，投保人对这些风险可以进行分选。之所以称为附加险险别，是因为它们不可以单独承保。投保人只有在选择了基本险险别之后才能对附加险险别进行选择。

在对险别进行选择时，投保人应遵循以下原则：

①投保人在同一份保险单据中不能同时选择平安险、水渍险和一切险，因为其承保范围相互交叉。

②投保人选择了平安险或水渍险后，还可以从一般附加险险别和特别附加险险别中进行选择。

③投保人选择了一切险后，只能从特别附加险险别中进行选择。

以上原则如图 10.4 所示。

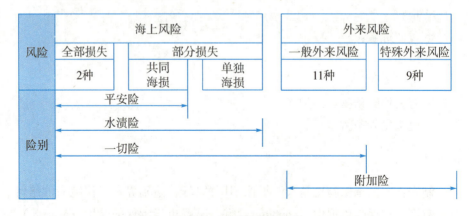

图 10.4　险别的选择原则

5. 保险条款

在国际保险市场，不同的海运协会对风险和险别制定了自己的保险条款。

（1）伦敦协会货物条款。伦敦协会货物条款（ICC）是由伦敦保险人协会于 1912 年制定并于 1982 年进行修改的保险条款。伦敦协会货物条款在中国乃至世界的保险市场都被广泛应用。伦敦保险人协会将险别分为海上险和战争暴动险。

①海上险。

协会货物条款 A[ICC(A)]:承保一切险。

协会货物条款 B[ICC(B)]:承保水渍险。

协会货物条款 C[ICC(C)]:承保平安险。

②战争暴动险。

协会战争险条款(货物)。

协会罢工险条款(货物)。

恶意损害险条款。

(2)中国人民保险公司海洋货物运输条款(PICC)。中国人民保险公司海洋货物运输保险条款是在 1972 年制定的,并在 1976 年、1981 年和 1991 年进行了修订。其主要条款如下:

①海洋货物运输险,包括平安险、水渍险和一切险。

②海洋运输"冷藏货物"险。

③海洋运输"散装桐油"险。

④海洋运输战争险。

⑤陆上运输火车、卡车货物险,包括陆运险和陆运一切险。

⑥陆上运输"冷藏货物"险。

⑦航空运输货物险,包括航空运输险和航空运输一切险。

⑧航空运输货物战争险。

⑨邮政包裹险,包括邮包险和邮包一切险。

⑩邮包战争险。

⑪活牲畜、家禽险(包括海上、陆上和航空运输)。

伦敦协会货物保险条款(ICC)和中国人民保险公司海洋货物运输条款(PICC)的险别责任范围基本上都是仓至仓条款,为投保货物提供自启运地发货人仓库开始,直至到达收货人仓库或储存所为止的整个运输过程的保险。

6. 保险单据的种类

(1)保险单。保险单是保险公司(保险商)和贸易商(投保人)签订的书面合约,包含了合约的所有条款以及投保险别的全部具体情况。合约双方的责任和权利的条款在保险单的背面载明。

保险单是保险合约的法律证明,是在实务中使用最广泛的一种保险单据。

(2)保险凭证。保险凭证除背面没有列入详细的保险条款外,其余内容与保险单相同。保险单的条款同样适用保险凭证。

保险凭证与保险单具有同等的法律效力。但在有些国家，投保人在起诉保险商时必须凭保险单。这就是说，只凭保险凭证不足以起诉保险商。

（3）联合凭证。联合凭证将保险凭证与商业发票合二为一，即在商业发票正面加注险别、保险金额以及保险编号。

（4）预约保单。出口商如果定期规律发货，一般会安排预约保单，又称为统保单或开口保单，即按约定的条款对在一定时间期限内的所有出口货物进行承保。每一次发货后，投保人（出口商/进口商）向保险商申报有关出运细节并支付保费。出口商在保险凭证上签字并将副本寄交保险公司存档记录。

预约保单的好处是避免了每次发货都需与保险商协商保险条件的麻烦。除此之外，出口商/进口商若因疏漏未向保险商发出通知的，只要不是出于恶意，保险商应予补办保险。补办时货物若已出险受损，保险公司仍予以赔偿。

但出口商售出如果是一次性的，没有必要安排预约保单。在这种情形下，出口商须与保险商协商保险条件，保险商签发保险单或保险凭证。根据 UCP 600 的规定，银行不接受预约保单，除非信用证另有规定。

第十一章　运输单据

学习目标

◇学习运输单据的主要类别。

◇学习海运提单的定义、作用、内容及分类。

◇学习海运运单的定义及作用。

◇学习空运运单的定义、作用及内容。

◇学习提单与运单的区别。

运输单据包括海运提单，海运运单、空运运单，公路、铁路、内陆水运单据，邮政收据、快递收据和投邮证明。

第一节　海运提单

当货物经海洋运输时，海运提单是最重要的运输单据。

1. 海运提单的定义

海运提单或提单(B/L)是由承运人、船运公司或其代理与发货人签订的，由承运人签发的，证明已收到发运至某具体目的地的货物并载明货物运输条款的运输单据。海运提单如图 11.1 所示。

Shipper SHANGHAI IMPORT & EXPORT TRADE CORPARATION 1123 ZHONGSHAN ROAD SHANGHAI CHINA		B/L NO. HJSHBI 142939 *ORIGINAL* 中国对外贸易运输总公司 CHINA NATIONAL FOREIGN TRADE TRANSPORT CORPORATION 直运或转船提单 BILL OF LADING DIRECT OR WITH TRANSSHIPMENT		
Consignee or order TO THE ORDER OF SHIPPER		SHIPPED on board in apparent good order and condition (unless otherwise indicated) the goods or packages specified herein and to be discharged or the mentioned port of discharge of as near there as the vessel may safely get and be always afloat.		
Notify party TKAMRA CORPORATION 302 KAWARA MACH OSAKA JAPAN		THE WEIGHT, measure, marks and numbers, quality, contents and value, being particulars furnished by the Shipper, are not checked by the Carrier on loading.		
Pre-carriage by	Port of loading SHANGHAI	THE SHIPPER, Consignee and the Holder of this Bill of Lading hereby expressly accept and agree to all printed , written or stamped provisions , exceptions and conditions ofthis Bill of Loading , including those on the back hereof.		
Vessel PUDONG V.503	Port of trans-shipment	IN WITNESS where of the number of original Bill of Lading stated below have been signed, one of which being accomplished, the other (s) to be void.		
Port of discharge OSAKA	Final destination			
Container Seal No. or marks and Nos.	Number and kind of packages Designation of goods		Gross weight (kgs)	Measurement(m^3)
GATU0506118 T.C TXT233 OSAKA C/NO.1-300	100% COTTON COLOUR WEAVE-SHIRT SAY THREE HUNDRED(300) CARTONS ONLY TOTAL ONE 40'CONTAINER CY TO CY FREIGHT PREPAID		3 300 KGS ⌈ON BOARD⌉	66 CBM
DRAWN UNDER JAPANESE ISSUING BANK, OSAKA, IRREVOCABLE DOCUMENTARY CREDIT NUMBER TX0081 DATED JAN 15, 2023				
REGARDING TRANSSHIPMENT INFORMATION PLEASE CONTACT			Freight and charge FREIGHT PREPAID	
Ex. rate	Prepaid at	Freight payable at SHANGHAI	Place and date of issue SHANGHAI FEB. 18, 2023	
	Total prepaid	Number of original Bs/L THREE	Signed for or on behalf of the Master as Agent	

图 11.1 海运提单

2. 海运提单的作用

海运提单具有以下四个作用：

（1）货物收据。海运提单是发运货物的收据，表明承运人已收到所述质量、数量且表面完好的货物备运。承运人负责向海运提单收货人交货。

（2）运输契约。海运提单是承运人和发货人之间签订的运输契约。海运提单背面详细载明双方的责任与权利。承运人的责任是通过海洋运输货物并将其交付收货人，发货人的责任是确保发运的货物表面完好且符合运输包装规定。

（3）物权凭证。海运提单是物权凭证。海运提单的合法持有人是货物的合法货主。承运人凭正本海运提单交货。正本海运提单成套开出，并注明正本份数。

由于一份正本海运提单可使持有人获得货物，因此拥有全套正本海运提单才能确保对货物的物权。出口商提交海运提单视作交货，海运提单成为物权单据是象征性交货的基础。

（4）可流通单据。作为物权单据，海运提单可以流通，即可以转让所有权。当海运提单被转让后，货物的所有权随之被转让。任何通过支付对价获得背书海运提单的受让人拥有海运提单物权。

3. 提单的内容

（1）承运人名称。承运人为船运公司，可以是船东或租船方。当运输合同是通过船运公司的代理商签订时，承运人应是船运公司而非代理商。签订运输合同的须是船运公司与发货人。

（2）发货人名称。发货人将货物交付承运人，可以是出口商或出口商的代理。在信用证情形下，发货人是信用证受益人。

（3）收货人名称。收货人是有权在指定目的地提货的当事人。收货人的不同写法使提单有不同的抬头。

①指示性抬头。指示性抬头的提单可以背书和交付转让。

第一，"给指定人"和"给发货人的指定人"。"给指定人"表明货物的所有权属于出口商发货人，其效果与"给发货人的指定人"一样。这种抬头的提单一般用于信用证和托收中。

在信用证情形下，出口商在交单时根据信用证条款将提单背书给银行，银行再凭进口商的付款背书给进口商。提单所有权经此转让后，进口商最终得到物权，获得货物。在实务中，信用证可要求提单做成空白抬头、空白背书。

在托收情形下，出口商在交单时将特别背书给进口商，银行凭进口商的付款（付款交单情形下）或进口商的承兑（承兑交单情形下）向其交单。

第二，"给开证行的指定人"。在信用证情形下，信用证可要求提单收货人为开证行的指定人，这样的提单表示银行对提单拥有所有权。银行凭进口商的付款向其特别背书提单，转让提单所有权，使其得到货物。

这种提单通常只用于信用证。在托收情形下，除银行明确表示同意外，提单收货人不能写成银行指定人。

第三，"给进口商的指定人"。当提单收货人为进口商指定人时，无需背书仅凭正本提单，进口商便可从承运人处提货。

这种提单通常用于赊销或预付货款。这种提单不可用于信用证，由于银行对提单无所有权，因此银行不愿意接受这种提单。

因为出口商对这样的提单也无所有权,所以这种提单不应用于托收中。

②限制性抬头。当提单收货人为指定收货人时,提单为限制性抬头。该指定收货人为进口商。在这种提单情形下,进口商在身份得到确实后,出示正本提单就可以获取货物。

这种提单用于赊销和预付货款中,进口商以简便的手续便可获得货物。但这种提单不用于信用证,也不用于托收。

(4)通知人。通知人是货物抵达后船运公司通知提货的当事人,其通常是进口商或其代理。当收货人栏未显示进口商名字时,其信息须在通知人栏给出。

当提单收货人为"给指定人""给发货人的指定人""给开证行的指定人"时,进口商名称和地址须在收货人处给出。但当提单收货人为"给进口商的指定人"或"给指定收货人(进口商)"时,通知人栏留空不填。

(5)船名和航程号。提单应提供船名,"V"是航程的缩写。

(6)装运港和目的港。装运港又称为装货港,目的港又称为卸货港。

当提单只涉及海洋运输时,提单只需写明两个港口的名称。但在其他情形下,提单也可用于提供门到门的联合运输方式。此时,在两个港口外还须注明收货地点和最终交货地点。

(7)唛头和序号。唛头和序号应该与商业发票和装箱单等单据上的一致。同样的唛头应印刷在货物的包装箱或包装盒上,显示货物为同一提单下的货物。

(8)货物描述。提单上只需提供货物的笼统描述。如果交易是在信用证情形下,提单须载明信用证号码、开证行名称以及信用证开立日期。

(9)总件数。提单须指明货物包装盒/箱的总件数。

(10)运费。运费有预付和到付两种。运费预付是指运费已由出口商支付,一般用于《国际贸易术语解释通则》中的 C&F 或 CIF 术语。运费到付是指应收运费在目的地向进口商收取,如用在《国际贸易术语解释通则》中的 FOB 术语。

(11)正本提单份数及承运人签字。该栏指明整套提单的正本份数。在实务中,正本提单份数可以为 2 份、3 份或 4 份。

正本提单须由船运公司或其代理签字。如为正本,提单上印有"正本"字样以便与副本区别。船运公司通常为存档目的签发无签字副本。副本不是物权凭证。

(12)提单签发日期。提单签发日期是船运公司收到货物备运或将货物装船的日期。

在信用证情形下,提单签发日须与信用证规定相符,通常介于发票日期和最后的船期之间。

4. 海运提单的主要类别

（1）按货物是否装船划分。

①已装船提单。已装船提单载有"已装上表面完好的货物"字句,确认出口商已将货物装在装运港的船上。

已装船提单的签发日期为运输日期,已装船提单有利于发货人早日收到货款。

②备运提单。备运提单载有"收到表面完好的货物"字句,只表示货物交给了承运人并置于其监管之下。

除信用证另有规定外,未载明"已装船"字样的提单不被银行接受进行结算。因此,备运提单须通过加注载有载货船名以及装船日期的已装船批注,改为已装船提单。备运提单上的运输日期是已装船批注日期,而不是备运提单的签发日期。

（2）按货物状况划分。

①清洁提单。当承运人未对"已装船/已收到表面完好的货物"字句做出修改,提单为清洁提单。

当承运人未发现货物或其包装有破损时,其将签发清洁提单。清洁的已装船提单在信用证情形下最易被银行接受。

②不清洁提单。如果承运人对"已装船/已收到表面完好的货物"字句有异议,其将对货物及其包装的受损情况在提单上加以注明。这样的加注使提单成为不清洁提单。在信用证情形下,银行不接收不清洁提单。

（3）按提单的抬头划分。

①可流通提单。可流通提单为指示性抬头提单,其收货人可以是指定人、发货人的指定人、开证行的指定人或进口商的指定人。

指示性抬头提单凭背书和交付可转让。可流通提单在支付方式中被广泛使用。

②不可流通提单。不可流通提单是指收货人为指定收货人,即进口商的提单。不可流通提单称为直交提单。

不可流通提单通常在赊销或预付货款中使用,有时也用于非商业目的的交易中。

（4）按是否转船划分。

①直运提单。直运提单是指货物由一艘货轮从装运港直运目的港,中途不转船运输的提单。

在信用证情形下,信用证规定"不允许转船时",须提交直运提单。

②转船提单。当装运港和目的港之间没有直运服务,须用两艘货轮运输,承运人须签发转船提单。货物在转运港从一艘货轮转入另一艘货轮。

在信用证情形下，信用证规定"允许转船时"，银行将接受承运人签发的转船提单。

（5）按是否载有运输合同细则划分。

①全式提单。全式提单在提单背面详细列出运输合同条款细则。

②简式提单。简式提单也是常规提单，只是未列出运输合同的条款细则。全式提单中的条款同样适用于简式提单。除在信用证中有相反规定外，银行接受简式提单。

（6）班轮提单。当货物由有固定航线的船只按固定的航程并在目的港有固定的泊位运输时，承运人签发的提单为班轮提单。

班轮提单最大的优点是承运人在航程开始前或刚开始后，能够向发货人发出预计的开船日期（ETD）和预计的抵达日期（ETA），进口商因此也可获知货物已发运，并将于某固定日期到达。大部分提单都为班轮提单。

（7）集装箱提单。随着集装箱货运业务的开展，集装箱可拖运至进口商、出口商的所在地，以便出口商装货和进口商卸货。

集装箱提单的货物可为拼箱货或整箱货，承运人提供从出口国集装箱堆场到进口国集装箱堆场的运输服务。

集装箱提单可以为传统的港到港运输签发，也可以为多式联运的门到门服务签发。

（8）多式联运单据（MTD）。根据 UCP 600 的规定，多式联运单据（MTD）是一种从出发地到最终目的地的，至少涉及海运、内陆河道、空运、铁路或公路运输的两种运输方式的新型运输单据。

在单一运输方式下，海运提单承运人仅提供港到港服务；而多式联运单据（MTD）的承运人能提供门到门服务。从 20 世纪 80 年代起，海运提单已发展成为既可适用于港到港的海洋运输，又可适用于门到门运输的多式联运。

多式联运单据的当事人如下：

①多式联运经营人（MTO）。多式联运经营人签发多式联运单据并对整个运输过程负责，无论是否实际安排整个运输过程或只是安排其中的一段行程。多式联运经营人相当于海运提单的承运人。

②发货人。多式联运单据的发货人将货物交至多式联运经营人并与之签订多式联运单据。多式联运单据的发货人相当于海运提单的发货人。

③收货人。多式联运收货人有权在目的地提货。与海运提单的收货人一样，多式联运单据的收货人也可做出指示性抬头或限制性抬头。多式联运单据（MTD）收货人及其流通性如表 11.1 所示。

表 11.1　多式联运单据(MTD)收货人及其流通性

项目	收货人	流通性	流通方式
指示性抬头	给指定人	可流通	须背书
	给发货人的指定人		
	给×××银行的指定人		
	给×××公司的指定人		
限制性抬头	给×××公司	不可流通	不适合

如表 11.1 所示,当收货人为指示性抬头时,多式联运单据可流通;而当收货人为限制性抬头时,多式联运单据不可流通。在信用证情形下,背书须符合信用证的规定。

多式联运单据与海运提单的区别如表 11.2 所示。

表 11.2　多式联运单据与海运提单的区别

海运提单 （B/L）	多式联运单据 （MTD）
签发人必须是承运人,即船运公司	签发人是多式联运单据经营人(MTO),可以是承运人,也可以是整个运输的经营人
承运人提供港到港单一海洋运输	MTO 提供至少有两种运输方式的门到门运输
承运人的责任从装运港收到货物或将货物装上船时起至货物在目的港卸下货轮时为止	MTO 承担从接收地收到货物置于其管控之下起直至将货物交到最终目的地时为止
承运人对在目的港收到货物或装船之前以及货物在目的港卸下货轮之后对货物的货损灭失不再承担责任	MTO 对货物在整个运输过程中无论何时与何地货物发生的货损灭失负责

(9)联运提单。联运提单与多式联运单据非常相似,联运提单由第一承运人签发,并且只为其安排的这段航程负责。

提单的各种分类并非是非此即彼的,一份提单可以是不同种类的组合。

第二节　海运运单

海运运单是由船运公司签发的运输单据,是提单之外的另一种海运单据。

海运运单只具有提单的两个作用:货物收据和运输契约。与提单不同,海运运单不是物权凭证也不可流通转让。因此,海运运单的收货人只能是指定收货人——进口商。

当出口商同意以赊销、预付货款方式或以非商业目的销售货物时,出口商可以要求船运公司签发海运运单而不是海运提单,以使进口商能以最少的程序,在最短的时间内获取货物。运单能实现这一目的是因为承运人可仅凭身份证明和海运运单的传真件就能将货物交付指定收货人（进口商）,而不要求其提交正本运单。

与直交提单相比,虽然两种单据的收货人都为指定收货人——进口商,但区别在于直交提单是物权单据,交货须凭正本提单;海运运单不是物权单据,承运人无需凭正本运单就可交货。

第三节　空运运单

1. 空运运单的定义和作用

当货物采用航空运输时,航空公司签发空运运单（AWB）是承运人（航空公司）与发货人之间的运输单据。

与海运运单相似,空运运单仅具有两个作用:货物收据和运输契约。航空运单不是物权凭证也不可以流通转让。当货物抵达目的机场后,航空公司凭身份证明和空运运单传真件就可以向收货人交货,而不要求其提交正本空运运单。空运运单如图 11.2 所示。

2. 空运运单的内容

（1）承运人名称。承运人为航空公司,是空运运单的签发人,与发货人签订运输契约。

空运运单上载明的"不可流通"字样,表示空运运单不是物权凭证。

（2）发货人名称和地址。发货人通常是出口商。

（3）收货人名称和地址

收货人可以是下列三种之一:

①进口商,主要用于赊销和预付货款。

②开证行,通常在信用证情形下。在托收情形下,只有在获得银行的同意和许可后,空运运单的收货人才可以是银行。

③出口商代理,通常用于托收。

当收货人为后两种时,开证行或出口商的代理有权向进口商催交货款。进口商付款后,银行或出口商代理将指示航空公司向进口商交货。

（4）承运人代理。为使在不同国家与地区的业务更为便捷,承运人在各地设有代理,其名称、代码以及账号在空运运单上指明。

Shipper's Name and Address	shipper's Account Number		Not Negotiable Air Waybill
SPEIRS AND WILLIAMS LTD., SHANGHAI BRANCH 320 ZHONGSHAN ROAD, SHANGHAI,CHINA			中国民航　✈ CAAC ISSUED BY THE CIVIL AVIATION ADMINISTRATION OF CHINA Beijing, China

Copies 1, 2 and 3 of this Air Waybill are originals and have the same validity

Consignee's Name and Address	Consignee's Account Number
BANK OF CHINA, HONG KONG WAICHAI BRANCH L/C NO. 01-192545	It is agreed that the goods described herein are accepted in apparent good order and condition (except as noted) for carriage SUBJECT TO THE CONTIDITIONS OF CONTRCT ON THE REVERSE HEREOF. ALL GOODS MAY BE CARRIED BY ANY OTHER MEANS INCLUDING ROAD OR ANY OTHER CARRIER UNLESS SPECIFIC CONTRARY INSTRUCTIONS ARE GIVEN HEREON BY THE SHIPPER. THE SHIPPER'S ATTENTION IS DRAWN TO THE NOTICE CONCERNING CARRIER'S LIMITATION OF LIABILITY. Shipper may increase such limitation of liability by declaring a higher value for carriage and paying a supplemental charge if required.

Issuing Carrier's Agent Name and City	Accounting Information
RTW SHIPPING, SHANGHAI	02100 8843 2

Agent's IATA Code	Account No.
93-5-3386	CS 123678

Airport of Departure (Addr. Of First Carrier) and Requested Routing
SHANGHAI

To	By First Carrier	Routing and Destination	to	by	to	by	Currency	WT/VAL		Other		Declared value for carriage	Declared Value for Customs
								PRD	COLL	PRD	COLL		
HK	CA						CNY	X		X		NVD	

Airport Destination	Flight/Date	For Carrier Use Only	Flight/Date	Amount of insurance	Insurance: —If carrier offers insurance and such insurance is requested in accordance with the conditions thereof, indicate amount to be insured in figures in box marked "amount of insurance"
HONGKONG		CA509/	16 OCT	NIL	

Handling Information

13 CTNS. NOTIFYING: PHILMEN INT. CO. E2, 3/F HANG FUNG IND. BLDG., PHASE-22G HOK YUEN ST. KLN

No. of Pieces RCP	Gross Weight	Kg lb	Rate Class Commodity Item No.	Chargeable weight	Rate Charge	Total	Name and quantity of Goods (incl. Dimensions or Volume)
13	390	K	4401	398.5	2.89	1 151.67	13 WOODEN CASES CONTAINING 26 CEMENT SPARY GUNS MODEL 435 SWG HONGKONG NO.435 C/NO. 1-13

Prepaid	Weight Charges	Collect	Other Charges
1 151.67			
	Valuation Charge		
	Tax		
Total Other Charges Due Agent			Shipper certifies that the particulars on the face hereof are correct and that insofar as any part of the consignment contains dangerous goods, such part is properly described by nam3e and is in proper condit ion for carriage by air according to the applicable Dangerous Goods Regulations.
Total Other Charges Due Carrier			
49.85			SPEIRS AND WILLIAMS LTD., SHANGHAI BRANCH
			Signature of Shipper or his agent
Total Prepaid	Total Collect		
1 201.52			
Currency Conversion Rate	CC Charges in Dest. Currency		2023-10-16　　　　SHANGHAI　　　　RTW SHIPPING, SHANGHAI
			Executed on (date)　　of (place)　　Signature of Issuing Carrier or his Agent
For Carrier's Use Only at destination	Charges at Destination	Total Collect Charges	
			999-1950 3022

图 11.2　空运运单

（5）机场名称。空运运单须指明起飞机场和目的机场的名称及航班号。

（6）海关货物价值申报。当货物无需向海关进行申报时，空运运单须注明"NVD"，意为无申报价值。

（7）运作信息。运作信息栏相当于提单通知人栏。当收货人栏未显示为进口商时，进口商名称和地址在运作信息栏中填入，否则留空。

（8）唛头。与海运提单中的唛头的作用一样，空运运单货物包装盒/箱上应刷制相同唛头，与其他相关单据上的唛头也应保持一致。

（9）货物简要描述。空运运单通常须注明货物的材质和数量以及货物的重量、规格和体积。

（10）航空运费。与海运提单的运费相似，航空运费分为预付和到付。预付表示出口商已预先进行了支付，到付表示将在目的机场由进口商支付。空运运单通常会注明运费金额。预付或到付须与所选的价格术语保持一致。

（11）发货人或其代理签字。发货人应保证空运运单上所填细节正确，如货物有危险品部分，须对该部分名称进行恰当描述，保证符合空运条件要求且符合适用的《危险品惯例条例》的要求。

（12）签发日期。签发日期为航空承运人收到货物并将货物置于其监管之下的日期。通常，这也是起飞日期。

（13）承运人或其代理签字。航运运单可由承运人或其代理签字。代理的签字须指明是代表承运人签字。

（14）全套。全套空运运单通常有 3 份正本、6 份副本和 3 份额外副本。正本一式三份。承运人持第一份正本，第二份正本和第三方正本分别交收货人和发货人。

在信用证情形下，根据 UCP 600 的规定，发货人可只提交第三份正本，即使某信用证规定提交全套正本。

第四节　其他运输单据

其他运输单据包括公路、铁路、内陆水运单据，邮政收据、快递收据和投邮证明。这些运输单据仅能行使两个作用——货物收据和运输契约，但不是物权单据，不能流通转让。

1. 公路、铁路、内陆水运单据

如果货物由卡车运送，则签发公路运单。《国际公路货运公约》（CMR）于 1956 年在日内瓦由 17 个欧洲国家签订颁发。中国不是 CMR 签约国。因此，虽然 CMR 托运单为陆上运输单据，但在承运人为中国公司的情况下，因其不能签发 CMR 托运单,如果来证要求提交 CMR 托运单,中国出口商须要求对方改证。

如果货物由内陆水道运送,则签发内陆水运运单。

如果货物由铁路运输,则开立铁路运单。铁路运单须依照《国际铁路货物运输公约》(CIM)的规定。该公约于 1893 年成形,于 1970 年颁布增加的协议,并不时修改以满足国际贸易的需要。

以上运输单据,无论名称如何,包括以下主要内容:

(1)签发日期。根据 UCP 600 的规定,除运单指明有另一收货日期,或者印戳、记载指明有另一收货日期或发货日期外,运输单据的签发日期为发货日期。

(2)发货人、收货人名称和地址。除信用证另有规定外,运单抬头为记名收货人,抬头不能为给指定人、给发货人的指定人、给×××银行的指定人或给×××公司的指定人。

(3)货物接受地点与交货地点。根据 UCP 600 的规定,运单须载明信用证规定的货物接受地点与交货地点。

(4)货物描述。货物描述要求对货物进行一般描述,说明货物数量、重量以及规格,载明信用证号码、信用证开证行名称以及信用证开证日期。

(5)唛头及序号。唛头及序号须与其他单据上的唛头及序号一致,同一唛头及序号刷印在货物的包装盒和包装箱上。

(6)运费。运输单据须指明运费是由发货人或收货人承担。

(7)对办理海关及其他手续所必要的指示。发货人须提供办理货物通关及办理其他手续的信息。

(8)正本。根据 UCP 600 的规定,运输单据必须看似为托运人或发货人开出的正本单据,或者没有任何标记表明单据开给何人。注明"第二联"的铁路运单将被作为正本接受。无论是否注明正本字样,铁路或内陆运输运单都被作为正本接受。如果运输单据上未注明签发的正本份数,提交的份数即视为全套正本。

(9)运输单据的签字。根据 UCP 600,运输单据必须看似指明承运人名称,并且由承运人或其具名代理人签署,或者由承运人或其具名代理人以签字、印戳或批注表明货物收讫。

承运人或其具名代理人的收货签字、印戳或批注必须标明其承运人或代理人的身份。

代理人的收货签字、印戳或批注必须标明代理人系代表承运人签字或行事。

如果铁路运输单据没有指明承运人。铁路运输公司的任何签字或印戳作为承运人签署单据的证据。

2. 邮政收据、快递收据和投邮证明

货物由邮局、快递或速递服务寄送将签发邮政收据、快递收据或投邮证明。近年来，随着电子商务的快速发展，小额在线交易在国际贸易中愈加普遍。

世界著名的快递服务公司有 EMS、DHL、UPS 和联邦快递。使用这种运输方式的货物通常价值高或数量少，如货物样本之类，要求送货时间及时。快邮服务和速递邮政服务提供桌到桌服务。

根据 UCP 600 的规定，证明货物收讫待运的快递收据，无论名称如何，必须看似：

（1）表明快递机构的名称，并在信用证规定的货物发运地点由该具名快递机构盖章或签字，表明取件或收件的日期或类似词句。该日期将被视为装运日期。

（2）如果要求显示快递费用付讫或预付，快递机构可出具表明快递费由收货人以外的一方支付的运输单据。

证明货物收讫待运的邮政收据或投邮证明，无论名称如何，必须看似在信用证规定的货物发运地点盖章或签署并注明日期。该日期将被视为装运日期。

第十二章　原产地证书、检验证书及单据审核

学习目标

◇学习原产地证书的定义及主要类别。

◇学习普惠制产地证书的主要内容。

◇学习检验证书的定义、类别以及内容。

◇学习领事发票、海关发票以及形式发票的定义及作用。

◇学习信用证情形下单据审核原则。

第一节　原产地证书

1. 原产地证书的定义

原产地证书是一种证明货物为某一国家所生产的单据,作为征收差别关税、征收配额和进口管控的依据,以确保进口商品达到原产地国的要求且符合进口国的卫生标准。

一些国家要求货物进口前须提供原产地证书。原产地证书由出口商填写证明细节,可由检验机构或商会等独立机构签发。在中国,原产地证书由中华人民共和国海关总署或由中国国际贸易促进委员会签发。中国国际贸易促进委员会签发的原产地证书如图 12.1 所示。

1. Exporter (full name and address) TIANJIN ANIMAL BY-PRODUCT IMP & EXP CORP 80 YANTAI STR., TIANJIN CHINA	CERTIFICATION NO： A2-489C
2. Consignee (full name, address, country) CRISTAL WILLIAMS LTD., 1445 BROADWAY, #0803 NEW YORK, N.Y. 10018 USA	CERTIFICATE OF ORIGIN OF THE PEOPLE'S REPUBLIC OF CHINA
3. Means of transport and route FROM TIANJIN TO NEW YORK BY SEA	5. For Certifying authority use only
4. County / region of destination U.S.A.	

6. Marks and numbers	7. Number and kind of packages; description of goods	8. H.S. Code	9. Quantity	10. Number and date of invoices
CR 612 WILLIAMS C/NO. 1-9	NINE BALES WHITE DEHAIRED COATWOOL	51. 05	953 NET	CR013073061 NOV. 10th2023

11. Declaration by the exporter The undersigned hereby declares that the above details and documents are correct; that all the goods were produced in China and that they comply with the Rules of Origin of the People's Republic of China TIANJIN ANIMAL BY-PRODUCT IMP & EXP CORP 80 YANTAI STR., TIANJIN CHINA	12. Certification It is hereby certified that the declaration by the exporter is correct CHINA COUNCIL FOR THE PROMOTION OF INTERNATIONAL TRADE, SHANGHAI, NOV. 10th 2023
Place and date, signature and stamp of authorized signatory	Place and date, signature and stamp of certifying authority

图 12.1　中国国际贸易促进委员会签发的原产地证书

　　如信用证对签发人未作规定，原产地证书可由出口商或生产企业自行签发，或者与商业发票合并。出口商在商业发票上载明，"我方（出口商）在此证明所发货物原产地为中国"或类似字句。出口商签发的原产地证书如图 12.2 所示。

```
                        CERTIFICATE OF ORIGIN
DATE _____
1. THE NAME OF EXPORTER _____
ADDRESS _____
2. NAME OF IMPORTER OR CONSIGNEE _____
ADDRESS _____
3. THIS IS TO CERTIFY THAT THE MERCHANDISE DESCRIBED IS GROWN/PRO-
CESSED/MANUFACTURED IN _____ (COUNTRY, PALCE)
```

MARKS & NOS	DESCRITION OF GOODS	QUANTITY	REMARKS

```
THE ABOVE DESCRIBED MERCHANDISE HAS BEEN LOAD _____ (NAME OF
CARRIER) ON/ABOUT _____ (DATE) DESTINED FOR _____ PORT.
4. THIS CERTIFICATE SHALL INVALID IN CASE OF ANY UNAUTHORIZED ALTERAT-
TION.


                                        ISSUED BY _____
```

图 12. 2　出口商签发的原产地证书

信用证通常要求由一独立的第三方签发原产地证书。在这种情形下,签发者在其公司信头纸上缮制独立的原产地证书。该证书不可与其他任何单据进行合并。

2. 普惠制产地证书（GSP）

（1）普惠制产地证书的定义和特点。普惠制（GSP）产地证书是一种常用的原产地证书。普惠制是发达国家给予发展中国家的关税优惠制度,以增加发展中国家的出口税收,加速其工业化进程与经济发展。它具有以下特点:

①普遍的:这种优惠制度惠及所有的发展中国家。

②非差别化的:这种优惠制度建立在无差别对待的基础上。

③非互惠的:这种优惠制度是发达国家对发展中国家给予的优惠,不要求发展中国家给予同样的优惠。发展中国家的出口商须填写普惠制产地证书以获得这种优惠。

普惠制原产地证书采用国际统一的标准格式,须由出口国授权机构签发。

普惠制原产地证书如图 12.3 所示。

1. Goods consigned from（Exporter business name, address, country） SHANGHAI XIAGUANG IMPORT AND EXPORT CORPORATION 1123 ZHONGSHANROAD, SHANGHA,CHINA	Reference NO. GENERALIZED SYSTEM OF PREFERENCES CERTIFICATE OF ORIGIN （Combined declaration andcertificate） FORM A
2. Goods consigned to（Consignee's name, address, country） YABAHARA TRADE CORPORTAION 302 KAWARA MACH, OSAKA, JAPAN	Issued in：THE PEOPLE'S REPUBLIC OF CHINA - （country） See Notes overleaf
3. Means of transport and route（as far as known） FROM SHANGHAI TO OSAKA BY S.S	4. Forcertifying authority use only

5. Item number	6. Marks and Numbers of packages	7. Number and Kind of packages；description of goods	8. Origin criterion（see Notes overleaf）	9. Gross weight or other quantity	10. Number and date of invoices
1	YTC 50053 OSAKA C/NO. 1-300 （in triangle）	LADIES SILK SHIRT SAY TOTAL TRHEE HUNDRED CARTONS ONLY * * * * * * * * * * * * * * *	"P"	G.W. 3 300 KGS	YTC50053 FEB.01,2023

| 11. Certification
    It is hereby certified, on the basis of control carried out, that the declaration by the exporter is correct.
ENTRY-EXIT INSPECTION AND QUARANTINE OF THE PEOPLE'S REPUBLIC OF CHINA, SHANGHAI
（company stamp）

SHANGHAI JUNE 05,2023（signature）
- -
Place and date, signature and stamp of certifying authority | 12. Declaration by the exporter
    The undersigned hereby declares that the above details and statements are correct; that all the goods were produced in

CHINA
- -
（county）
and that they comply with the origin requirementsspecified for those goods in the Generalized System of Preferences for goods exported to

JAPAN
- -
（importing country）
SHANGHAI XIAGUANG IMPORT AND EXPORT CORPOARATION, SHANHAI（company stamp）
SHANGHAI JUNE 04, 2023（signature）
- -
Place and date, signature of authorized signatory |

NOTES
Ⅰ. Countries which accept Form A for the purposes of the generalized system of preferences（GSP）:

		European Economic Community	
Australia	New Zealand		
Austria	Norway	Belgium	Ireland
Bulgaria	Poland	Denmark	Italy
Canada	Sweden	France	Luxembourg
Czechoslovakia	Switzerland	Germany	Netherlands
Finland	Soviet Union	Greece	United kingdom
Hungary	United states	Spain	Portugal
Japan			

Full details of the conditions covering admission to the GSP in these countries and obtainable from the designated authorities in the exporting preference-receiving countries or from the customs authorities of the preference-giving countries listed above. An information note is also obtainable from the UNCTAD secretariat.

Ⅱ. General conditions：

To qualify for preference, products must：

（a）fall within a description of products eligible for preference in the country of destination.The description entered on the form must be sufficiently detailed to enable the products to be identified by the customs officers examining them.

（b）Comply with the rules of origin of the country of destination. Each article in a consignment must qualify separately in its own right； and

（c）Comply with the consignment conditions specified by the country of destination. In general, products must be consigned direct from the country of exportation to the country of destination but most preference-giving countries accept passage through intermediate countries subject to certain conditions. (for Australia, direct consignment is not necessary.)

Ⅲ. Entries to be made in Box 8

Preference products must either by wholly obtained in accordance with the rules of the country of destination or sufficiently worked or processed to fulfill the requirements of that country's origin rules.

（a）Products sufficiently obtained：for single country shipments, enter the letter-P—in Box 8 (for Australia or New Zealand Box 8 may be left blank).

（b）Products sufficient worked or processed：for export to the countries specified below, the entry in Box 8 should be as follows：

（1）United States of America：for single country shipments, enter the letter -Y—in Box 8, for shipments from recognized associations of countries, enter the letter -Z— followed by the sum of the cost or value of the domestic materials and the direct cost of processing, expressed as a percentage of the ex-factory price of the exported products；(example -Y—35% or -Z—35%)　.

（2）Canada：for products which meet origin criteria from working or processing in more than one eligible least developed country, enter letter -G—in Box 8； otherwise -F—

（3）Austria, Finland, Japan, Norway, Sweden, Switzerland and the European Economic Community：enter the letter -W—in Box 8 followed by the Customs Co-operation Council Nomenclature tariff heading of the exported product. (example -W—98. 02.)

（4）Bulgaria, Czechoslovakia, Hungary, Poland and the USSR：for products which include value added in the exporting preference-receiving country, enter the letter-Y—in Box 8 followed by the value of imported materials and components expressed as a percentage of the f.o.b. price of the exported products (example -Y—45%)； for products obtained in a preference-receiving country and worked or processed in one or more than such countries, enter -PK—

（5）Austria and New Zealand：completion of Box 8 is not required.It is sufficient that a declaration be properly made in Box 12.

＊ For Australia, the main requirement is the exporter's declaration on the normal commercial invoice Form A, accompanied by the normal commercial invoice, is an acceptable alternative, but official certification is required.

图 12.3　普惠制产地证书

（2）普惠制产地证书的内容。普惠制产地证书格式 A 适用于大多数的贸易出口。但对纺织品或手工制纺织品等商品,信用证可能要求提交纺织品产地证或手工制纺织品产地证代替普惠制产地证书格式 A。

普惠制产地证书格式 A 第 4 条和第 11 条由签发机构填写,其他条目由出口商填写。

普惠制产地证书右上角框"Reference No."填写开证机构所编的证书流水号。"Issued in"填写普惠制产地证书格式 A 的签发国家。注意:此处须填写国家名称的英文全称,如"THE PEOPLE'S REPUBLIC OF CHINA"。

①货物来自(出口商名称、地址、国家)。普惠制产地证书格式 A 须填写产地国信息。中国出口商地址用汉语拼音填写。

若经其他转口商买卖,出口商后面应缮制"VIA",之后再填写转口商名称、地址和国家(地区)。

②货物运至(收货人名称、地址、国家)。普惠制证书要求填写进口国国家全称。收货人是货物的最终收货人或提单的通知人。如果运输单据的收货

人未指明,商业发票的抬头人为收货方。银行一般接受开证申请人、提单通知人、发票抬头人作为收货人。如果信用证规定运输单据不显示收货人名称,银行一般也接受收货人表述为"to whom it may concern"或"to order"。

注意:此处不可将中间商的名称填入此栏,收货人应是给惠国。

③运输方式和路线(就所知而言)。填写与证书有关的运输细节,包括提单或其他运输单据的签发日期,海运、陆运或空运运输方式,启运地、转运地和最终目的地。

货物出口至瑞士或奥地利等无海岸的国家须指明经第三国转运。例如,"2023年10月6日,从上海港经汉堡港转运至瑞士"。

④供官方使用栏由发证机构填写。

⑤商品顺序号。对于单项商品而言,填写"1"或留空。对于多项产品而言,按不同品类,分别填写"1""2""3"等。

⑥唛头和包装编号。唛头须包括文字、图案以及包装编号的全部信息,不能只写为"按发票号"或"按提单号"。中国出口商品的唛头不得显示货物在中华人民共和国之外的地方生产。

⑦包装的件数及种类、货物描述。包装件数用阿拉伯数字和英文同时显示。例如,"ONE HUNDERED AND TWENTY（120）CARTONS OF WORKING GLOVES"。如果商品有包装,须指明包装的种类。如果商品无包装,须指明"裸装货""散装货"或"挂装"。

商品描述中的商品名称必须具体,其详细程度应可以在商品编码(HS)的8位数中准确找到。与商品名称有关的品牌或货号无需显示,因为这些与商品编码和海关税则无关。

⑧原产地标准(见背面说明)。此栏为国外海关审查的核心栏目。不同的字面表示货物是否为全部国产。例如,字母"P"表示100%当地生产;字母"W"表示产品含国外原料或组件,但其价值低于产品FOB价的50%;字母"F"表示国外成分的价值低于产品出厂价的40%。

出口到澳大利亚、新西兰的产品,此栏可留空。

⑨毛重或其他数量。此栏应以商品的正常计量单位填写,如件(pieces/pcs)、打(dozen/doz)、台(set)等。以重量计算的则填毛重(G.W.),如只计净重,则须标上"N.W."。

⑩发票号码及日期。月份必须用英文全称或缩写格式。日期须与商业发票日期一致,不得迟于出货日期。

⑪签证机构证明。签证机构对出口商所填项目核查后,在此证明出口商的声明属实,并填写签署地点、日期、手签及加盖印章。手签与公章的位置不得重合。

此栏的签发日期不得早于第10栏的发票日期和第12栏的出口商申报日

期,且不能迟于提单日期。

⑫出口商申明。对于中国出口商品而言,生产国横线上填英文的"CHINA"。进口国横线上所填国家与第 3 栏的信息一致。日期可以与第 10 栏的发票日期同日,但不得早于发票日期。

普惠制产地证书要求出口商在签发人的声明之外再进行独立声明。出口商须证明商品在该国家种植、加工、生产。

第二节　检验证书

1. 检验证书的定义

检验证书是由检验商品的独立机构签发的以确保出口商品的质量、数量、包装以及其他情况的说明。检验证书应进口国、出口国当局的法规要求,或者应出口商、进口商、承运人或公证签发机构的要求签发。

在国际货物交易中,为履行合同,出口商、进口商、第三方检验机构或政府商检局都可对货物进行检验。检验机构的名称各异,如公证行、实验室等,其性质可以是官方的、半官方的或非官方的。美国的食品与药物管理局(FDA)、瑞士日内瓦的通用公证行(SGS)以及英国的劳氏公证行都是世界著名的检验机构。在中国,检验证书通常由国家质量监督检验总局(AQSIQ)、原中国出入境检验检疫局(CIQ)签发。

法定检验是依照进口国、出口国当局的法规要求对商品进行的强制检验,由进口国、出口国当局授权的官方机构或第三方独立机构进行检验。

2. 检验证书的作用和种类

检验检疫证书是国际贸易交易的重要一环。检验检疫证书具有如下作用:第一,它是海关检查、通关、征税以及关税优惠的依据。第二,及时报关报检是货物履行合同、保质保量、按时发货的保证。第三,它是信用证规定的提交银行进行结算的单据之一。此外,它是进口商退货以及向出口商、承运人或保险公司等相关责任人进行索赔的依据。

按对出口商品不同方面的检验要求,商品检验证书有不同的种类。其主要的类别如下:

(1)质量检验证书。

(2)数量检验证书。

(3)重量检验证书。

(4)健康检验证书。

（5）兽医检验证书。

（6）价值检验证书。

（7）植物检验检疫证书。

（8）消毒检验证书。

（9）卫生检验证书。

（10）熏蒸检验证书。

（11）公量检验证书。

3. 检验证书的内容

检验证书须在其公司信头纸上缮制。质量检验证书如图 12.4 所示。

中华人民共和国出入境检验检疫
ENTRY-EXIT INSPECTION AND QUARANTINE
OF THE PEOPLE'S REPUBLIC OF CHINA

共一页 第 1 页 Page 1 of 1
编号 No. : 210100223013678

CERTIFICATE OF QUALITY 品质证书

发货人
Consignor HONG YUN GROUP COMPANY LIMITED
收货人
Consignee　＊＊＊
品名　CHINESE LIGHT SPECKLED KIDNEY BEANS
Description of Goods 2009 CROP.(INNER MONGOLIA ORIGIN)

报检数量/重量
Quantity/Weight Declared　　-108. 575 - M/T
包装种类及数量
Number and Type of Packages　-2 150- GUNNY BAGS
运输工具
Means of Conveyance　VICTORY V. 146E

标记及号码
Mark & No.
N/M

This is to certify that we, did, at the request of consignor, attend at the warehouse of commodity on 17 Nov, 2023. The representative sample was drawn at random for inspection according to the stipulations of the L/C, the results were as follows:

Moisture 14.0 PCT

Admixture 0.1 PCT

Imperfectgrains, other color beans and water stain beans 4.8 PCT

Conclusion: The quality of the above commodity conform with the stipulations of the L/C No. 1201N10028

* *

印章　签证地点 Place of Issue　DALIAN, CHINA　签证日期 Date of Issue 18 Nov, 2023

Official Stamp

授权签字人 Authorized Officer Wang Xiaoyan　签名　Signature

我们已尽最大能力实施上述检验,不能因为我们签发本证书而免除卖方或其他方面根据合同和法律所承担的产品质量和其他责任。All inspections are carried out conscientiously to the best of our knowledge and ability. This certificate does not in any respect absolve the seller and other related parties from his contractual and legal obligations especially when product quality is concerned.

图 12.4　质量检验证书

(1)证书类别和编号。检验证书的类别按信用证要求,如品质证书。15位编号由商检签发机构提供,前 6 位为检验检疫机构代码。第 7 位为报检类代码,如出口货物代码为"2",第 8~9 位为年代代码。第 10~15 位为流水号。

(2)发货人。发货人应该为提单托运人。由于发货人通常为出口商、受益人,因此发货人通常为出口商。

(3)收货人。收货人一般写为"to whom it may concern"或"to order",收货人栏也可写成"＊＊＊",进口商不显示为收货人。原因之一是检验证书是公证证明,对任何持有人具有法律效力。再有,当提单做成空白抬头时,检验证书这样做与提单是保持一致的。

在信用证情形下,除信用证另有规定外,收货人栏也可以填入进口商的名字。

(4)货物描述。此栏按信用证规定的品名及商业发票的品名填制,可对货物做笼统描述。

(5)唛头及号码。唛头及号码须与信用证的规定和其他商业单据的唛头及号码一致。如无唛头,此栏填入"N/M"。

(6)报检数量/质量。此栏按运输单据、发票上的信息填写。如货物以净重计价,此栏的重量则填净重。如货物以毛重计价,此栏的重量则填毛重。

(7)包装种类及数量。此栏按运输单据、发票上的信息填写。如散装货无件数,此栏可填"in bulk",然后再加重量。

(8)运输方式。此栏填写运输工具的名称。

（9）检验结果。此栏是证书的核心内容。检验证书按要求对货物的重量、质量、数量等进行检验并载明结果。检验证书由检验机构对货物进行检验后填写，检验结果要与信用证规定保持一致。如果信用证规定检验证书必须指明出口商品的生产月份，出单人必须照办。

受益人应将信用证的要求告诉商检机构，商检机构按照信用证的要求缮制各种检验证书。检验证书不要加注信用证不要求提供的内容或证明文句。如果信用证的要求商检机构办不到，则应修改信用证。

证书结束时打上结束符号"＊＊＊＊＊＊＊＊＊"。

（10）签发地点。此栏填写签发证书的检验检疫机构所在地。

（11）签发日期。签发日期为检验机构基于检验日期的发证日期。一方面，检验证书的签发日期不能迟于提单日期；另一方面，检验证书的签发日期也不宜过早，以免检验证书在交单前过期。

有的信用证规定："检验证书须注明检验是在货物临近装船前进行。"在实务中，证书签发日期可与发货日期在同一天或稍早于发货日期。

（12）盖章签字。证书由主检验员签字并由出证机构盖章。如果信用证规定某具体检验机构进行检验，证书须由该检验机构签发。如果信用证无此规定，证书可以由任何一家经授权有资质的检验机构签发。

第三节　其他商业单据

1. 领事发票

领事发票是一种特殊发票，由驻出口国的进口国大使馆或领事馆签发。一些国家可能要求以领事发票为基础提交单据。领事发票既可以增加领事馆的收入，也可以发挥原产地证书的作用，作为向不同国家征收差别关税的基础，防止国外商品的倾销。领事发票还可以视作进口许可证，对不提交领事发票的货物征收高额关税，甚至对其禁运。

领事发票和商业发票是平行的单据，领事发票是一种官方的单据，有些国家规定了领事发票的固定格式，这种格式可以从领事馆获得。在实务中，比较常见的情况是有些国家来证规定由其领事在商业发票上做出认证声明，以证实商品的产地，向出口商收取认证费。对此，在计算出口价格时，出口商应当将这笔费用考虑进去。

对于出口商而言，申请领事发票可能费时费力，特别是当出口商所在地并无领事馆时。因此，出口商，比如在中国的出口商，可以要求改由中国贸易促进委员会签发领事发票。

2. 海关发票

海关发票是由进口国海关印制的,由出口商按进口国海关特定格式要求填入后签发的特殊发票。海关发票有以下三种格式:

第一,海关发票。

第二,价值及原产地联合证明。

第三,按某国海关规定的认证发票。

各国的海关发票格式不同,但内容须与商业发票的内容一致。目前,除经常使用的加拿大海关发票外,其他的海关发票已不多见。

与领事发票相似,海关发票具有以下职能:

(1)证实货物产地作为进口国海关征收差别关税的基础。

(2)确保进口货物的价格不低于其在国内销售的价格以防止倾销。

为达到以上目的,尽管海关发票因进口国海关规定的不同而有不同的格式,但都强调货物产地并要求细列价格组成。例如,如果所用价格术语为FOB,则报出的 FOB 价应明示扣除的包装费用、内陆运输费用以及其他相关费用得出的出口净价。如果所用价格术语为 CIF,则得出的出口净价还须继续明示扣除的运费和保费。需要注意的是,国内销售价格须低于出口净价。

海关发票与领事发票的区别在于手续上而不在于效果上。海关发票可以在符合进口国原格式的情况下在出口国印制,但领事发票须由进口国大使馆或领事馆印制。这就意味着出口商不需为领取海关发票缴费但须为领取领事发票缴费。

3. 形式发票

形式发票又称为预开发票或估价发票,在进口商、出口商签订销售合同之前开出。除清晰标明"形式"之外,形式发票与商业发票的格式和条目都一样。形式发票如图 12.5 所示。

ABC IMPORT & EXPORT CORPORATION, CHENGDU

12 SHAWAN STREET, JINGNIU DISTRICT, CHENGDU, CHINA

TEL: 028-87873456　　FAX: 028-87873457

PRO-FORMA INVOICE

TO:
CUDA TEXTILES TRADING
BLK43,05-06,
MARSILING RISE
733180 SINGAPORE

PRO FORMA INVOICE NO.: P2023AE0930-8
PURCHASE ORDER NO.:
DATE: 9 MAY 2023

FROM： SHANGHAI PORT			TO： SINGAPORE PORT	
ART NO.	COMMODITY & DESCRIPTION	QUANTITY	UNIT PRICE & TERMS	AMOUNT
			FOB SHANGHAI	
1652	WOMENS SILK SHIRT	2 311 PCS	USD 2. 850/PC	USD 6 586. 35
1750	WOMENS SILK SHIRT	2 517 PCS	USD 3. 100/PC	USD 7 802. 70
		4 828 PCS		USD 14 389. 05 ==========

TOTAL VALUE：SAY US DOLLARS：FOURTEEN THOUSAND THREE HUNDERED AND EIGHTY NINE AND CENTS FIVE ONLY

TERMS AND CONDITONS：
● TERMS OF PAYMENT：L/C AT SIGHT
● PACKING：TO BE PACKED IN CARTTON 23CM × 30CM × 45CM
● DATE OF SHIPMENT：ON OR BEFORE 30 AUG. 2023
● TOLERANCE：5% MORE OR LESS ALLOWED

CONFIRMED AND ACCPTED BY（BUYER）	SELLER：
---	---
SIGNATUE DATE	SIGNATURE

图 12.5　形式发票

形式发票的功能如下：

（1）形式发票可用作出口商向进口商的发盘。双方由此就价格和销售条款进行磋商，一旦进口商接受条款，将依据形式发票内容签订销售合同，并随后缮制商业发票。在实务中，出口商会被要求在商业发票中注明如下证实词句："货物符合形式发票号……的描述。"

（2）由于信用证开立时间一般早于商业发票签发时间，进口商将要求签发形式发票以申请进口许可证和外汇许可证。信用证通常也可基于形式发票，而非商业发票开出。在实务中，信用证会载明"按……日期的形式发票号……"。在这种情况下，商业发票上也要注明相同字句。

（3）在预付货款情形下，发货前须下先付款。因此，出口商为预付款项将签发形式发票而非商业发票。

（4）在寄售情形下，货物置于中间商手中，形式发票可用作中间商向潜在客户报价的参考。在落实潜在客户后，商业发票才签发。

（5）在国际招标中，招标人将要求投标人提交形式发票。招标人对不同投标人提交的形式发票进行比较，以确定与最具竞争力的投标人签订合约。

虽然与商业发票关系紧密，但形式发票不是正式发票，不能用于结算。形式发票只是一种报价，对买卖双方没有法律约束力。销售合同签订后，出口商应开立商业发票替换形式发票。

4. 厂商发票

厂商发票是厂方出具给出口商的销售货物的凭证,以本国货币显示货物在出口国国内市场的出厂价格。

来证要求提供厂商发票,其目的是检查是否有削价倾销的行为,以便确定应否征收"反倾销税"。厂商发票的基本内容要求如下:

(1)单据上部要印有醒目粗体字"厂商发票"字样。

(2)抬头人为出口商。

(3)厂商发票出票日期应早于商业发票日期。

(4)货物名称、规格、数量、件数必须与商业发票一致。

(5)以出口国货币报价,厂商发票价格须低于其相关商业发票价格,如按FOB价打九折或八五折。

(6)货物出厂时,除来证另有规定外,厂商发票和出厂货物不必缮打唛头。

(7)厂方为出单人,由厂方负责人签字盖章

5. 装运通知

货物装载后,外贸企业应及时向国外买方发出装船通知,以便对方准备付款、赎单以及办理进口报关和接货手续。

特别是在CFR/CPT合同中,卖方负责签订运输合同支付运费,而买方需自行办理货物运输保险。一旦货物装船或交给承运人,风险便从卖方转移至买方。因此,卖方应及时向买方发出充分详细的通知,以便买方及时为货物购买保险,否则出口商将对因此引起的货物损毁担责。

装运通知的内容一般包括订单号或合同号、信用证号、提单号、货物名称、数量、总金额、唛头、装运港/地、船名/运载工具名、预计启运日期和预计抵达日期等。装运通知如图12.6所示。

```
┌─────────────────────────────────────────────────────────────────┐
│              ABC IMPORT & EXPORT CORPORATION, CHENGDU             │
│      12 SHAWAN STREET, JINGNIU DISTRICT, CHENGDU, CHINA           │
│          TEL：028-87873456      FAX：028-87873457                 │
│                                                                   │
│                         SHIPPING ADVICE                           │
│                                                                   │
│  To：                           No.：                             │
│                                 Date：                            │
│                                 L/C No.：                         │
│                                 Insurance Cover Note No.：        │
│                                 Port of Shipment：               │
│                                 Port of Destination：            │
│                                 Date of Shipment：               │
│                                 Vessel Name：                    │
├───────────────────────────────────────────────────────────────────┤
│  SHIPPING MARK      DESCRIPTION OF GOODS      QUANTITY/WEIGHT      │
│                                                                   │
│                                                                   │
│                                                                   │
├───────────────────────────────────────────────────────────────────┤
│  SPECIAL CONDITIONS IN SHIPPING ADVICE                            │
│                                                                   │
│                                                                   │
│                                       SIGNATURE AND STAMP         │
└───────────────────────────────────────────────────────────────────┘
```

图 12.6　装运通知

6. 受益人证明

受益人证明是指出口商/受益人开出的证明,证明其按信用证要求完成了某项任务。例如,出口商/受益人向进口商提供了船运单据副本,向开证行拍发开船电报,证实货物符合合同规定等。

通常,受益人证明附带 EMS、DHL、FedEx 和 UPS 签发的邮政挂号收据、快递收据以资佐证。受益人证明由出口商出具并盖章,其签发日期不能迟于信用证规定的日期,也不能晚于启运日期,但可接受与启运日期相同的签发日期。受益人证明如图 12.7 所示。

ABC IMPORT & EXPORT CORPORATION, CHENGDU
12 SHAWAN STREET, JINGNIU DISTRICT, CHENGDU, CHINA
TEL：028-87873456　　　FAX：028-87873457

BENEFICIARY'S CERTIFICATE

INVOICE NO.：　　　　　　　　　　　　　NO.：
　　　　　　　　　　　　　　　　　　　　DATE：

BUYER：
L/C NO.：

THIS IS TO CERTIFY THAT THE GOODS ARE SHIPPED FROM SHANGHAI AND THECOLOR AND PATTERN ARE IN COMFORMITY WITH THE SELLER'S CATALOGUE NO. 3-B-948 STATED IN THE SALES CONTRACT NO. SC-OH0223-10.

………………………………
Authorized Signature

图 12.7　受益人证明

受益人证明无固定格式,但应显示信用证号码和发票号码。通常,除人称、动词时态需改动外,受益人证明的其他证实文句应照抄信用证上原文。

第四节　信用证情形下的单据审核

在国际结算中,单据由出口商提交。但是,不同的支付方式对不同单据的缮制、提交对象(如提交给进口商、进口商银行或出口商银行),都有不同的要求,不同的相关当事人对单据进行审核。读者对信用证以外的其他支付方式需参见前面章节以达到对制单要求、交单要求以及背后成因的理解。本章的重点是介绍信用证下的单据制作与单据审核。

1. 审单原则

(1)独立原则。独立原则表明,信用证独立于销售合同、独立于信用证申请书,虽然信用证是基于这两个文件开立的。这也表明银行只受信用证的法律约束。

(2)严格相符原则。在信用证情形下,单据按照信用证的条款规定制作。单据制作和单据审核应依据国际商会制定的严格相符原则。这一原则主要包括以下两个方面:

①单证相符。单据内容要与信用证条款相符。

②单单相符。不同单据的内容要相互一致。

任何不能符合这两方面的要求都会导致"不符点"，阻碍出口商获得银行的付款。

在单据相符的情况下，开证行接受单据，对已向出口商进行付款、承兑或议付的银行进行偿付。

如果发现单据存在不符点，银行将拒收单据，并在单据送达七天内以电子方式发出通知，列明所有不符点。

（3）银行仅运作单据。在信用证情形下，银行运作单据而非实物货物。银行不卷入贸易商就货物情况出现的合同争端，银行只需确认其收到的单据符合信用证条款。

开证行凭收到的合规单据付款，无论货物是否与合同相符。出现任何有关货物品质、数量的争议，进口方应直接向出口方索赔。

但是，银行不审核信用证未做规定的单据。如收到这样的单据，银行可退回提交人或转递单据，但不承担责任。

（4）银行免责条款。

①银行应对单据进行合理谨慎的审核，但对单据的真实性、格式或有效性不承担责任。"合理谨慎"是指银行基于其专业知识，确保提交的单据与信用证条款表面相符。此外，银行对提交的伪造单据不承担责任。

②银行对运作信用证业务的第三方的行为不负责。第三方可以是原银行，即开证行指示的另一银行为其代理银行，对信用证进行通知、承兑或议付，但其行为不为原开证行所控。

（5）合理的时间。开证行、保兑行或指定银行应给与合理时间审核单据。根据UCP 600的规定，拒付通知必须以电讯方式，如不可能，则以其他快捷方式，在不迟于交单之翌日起第五个银行工作日结束前发出。

2. 单据审核

所有单据须在信用证到期日前开出。银行审核各种单据的要点如下：

（1）审核商业发票。

①确保商业发票不能冠名为"形式发票"或"临时发票"。

②确保商业发票是由信用证受益人向信用证申请人开出。除信用证另有规定外，确保信用证不是向申请人外的第三方开出。

③确保货物描述与信用证描述一致。由于信用证中的货物描述仅为一般描述，确保发票中货物的详细描述不与信用证的要求相冲突。

④确保发票包含信用证中提及的货物、价格术语以及价格细目等细节。

⑤确保没有将会对货物状况或价值引起怀疑的任何附加的、不利的对货物的描述。例如，货物包装注有"用过""旧货""重新装配"等字样。

⑥确保发票中提到的诸如唛头、序号、运输等信息与其他单据中的相关信

息一致。

⑦确保发票金额与信用证金额相符且不超过信用证可用余额。

⑧确保发票中的币种与信用证的币种一致。

⑨如果信用证允许分船装运,确保发票金额涵盖整个发货过程。

⑩如信用证要求对发票签字,确保对发票签字。

⑪确保提交正确份数的发票正本与副本。

（2）审核汇票。

①确保汇票载有出票条款指明汇票在信用证情形下开立。确保出票条款包括信用证号码、开证行名称以及信用证签发日期。

②确保汇票出票人名称与信用证受益人名称一致。

③确保汇票受票人为银行,可以是开证行、保兑行或其他指定为付款行和承兑行的银行。汇票不得向申请人开立。

④确保汇票签发日期为提单日后 14～21 天内,且不超过信用证有效期。确保汇票在最后的交单日期前提交。最后交单日期为上述两个日期中较早的那个日期。

⑤确保汇票的期限符合信用证的要求。

⑥确保汇票金额不超过信用证可用余额。汇票的大写和小写金额须一致。确保汇票金额与发票金额一致。

⑦确保汇票的背书正确且无限制性背书。

⑧除信用证另有规定外,否则不开立"无追索权"的汇票。

（3）审核提单。

①确保提单为"清洁"且"已装船"提单。银行不接收提单载有使其"不清洁"表述的提单。

②确保"备运"提单上载有"已装船"批注。

③除信用证另有规定外,确保提单不是"租船合约"运输单据。

④确保提单载有发货人或其代理人。

⑤确保收货人提单按信用证要求做出。如果进口商名称未显示为收货人,应按信用证要求将其填为被通知人。

⑥确保提单按信用证要求正确背书。

⑦确保货物的一般描述与信用证的描述一致。如果有唛头、序号以及其他规格描述,应与其他单据的相应描述一致。

⑧确保提单上的"运费预付"与"运费到付"按信用证条款正确注明。

⑨确保提交提单的全套正本,除信用证另有规定外。

⑩确保提单在发货日后 14～21 天内,且在信用证的有效期内提交。

（4）审核保险单据。

①确保保险单据类别为符合信用证要求的保险单、保险凭证或保险声明。

②确保保险单据是由保险公司、保险承销商或其代理签发。

③如保险单据是向信用证受益人开立，确保保险单据被正确背书以便物权能向信用证申请人转让。

④确保保险单据的日期不迟于提单日期、运输日期或货物置于承运人监管的日期。

⑤除信用证另有规定外，确保保险金额和币种与信用证要求的金额和币种一致。银行不接收保险金额不足的保险单据。

⑥确保保险单据中货物的一般描述与信用证一致，其他如唛头、序号等细节与其他单据一致。

⑦确保保险单据承保货物从指定装运港或接受地至目的港或交付地的保险。

⑧确保保险单据在目的地进行索赔。

⑨确保保险单据的险别选择正确并按信用证要求承保。

⑩确保签发全套保险单据，并按信用证的规定提交。

（5）审核原产地证书。

①确保指明的原产地国符合信用证的要求。

②如果信用证要求提交原产地证书，确保原产地证书是一独立单据，不与其他单据联合开出。

③确保原产地证书按信用证要求进行签发、签字并合法认证。

④确保签发和提交正确类别的原产地证书。

⑤确保货物描述与其他单据的货物描述一致。

⑥确保签发和提交正确份数的正本和副本。

（6）审核检验证书。

①确保检验证书按信用证要求的当事人进行签发和签字。

②确保检验证书是符合信用证检验要求的正确类别。

③确保货物描述和唛头与商业发票及其他单据的描述一致。确保单据中的受检货物为出口货物。

④确保检验证书的签发日期早于提单的运输日期。确保检验日期与信用证要求日期一致。

⑤确保检验证书中不含对货物、规格、质量、包装等的不利字句，除非得到信用证授权。

（7）审核装箱单/重量单。

①确保装箱单/重量单为一独立单据，不与其他单据联合开出。

②确保装箱单按信用证要求细列货物的包装、重量以及规格。

③确保装箱单的签发日期与发票及其他单据保持一致。

④如信用证要求签字，确保装箱单已签字。

（8）审核其他单据。根据 UCP 600 的规定,如果信用证要求提交除商业发票、运输单据和保险单据之外的单据,信用证应规定这类单据的签发人、措词以及内容数据。如果信用证没有做出规定,银行将接受提交的这类单据,除非单据所含内容数据与提交的其他规定的内容数据不一致。

（9）审核面函。当出口商向银行提交单据要求付款、承兑或议付时,通常会填写由银行印制的致银行的标准面函,用以涵盖信用证规定的单据及指明其正本与副本的份数。此标准面函将置于其他单据之上,单据须按面函的单据顺序排列。面函如图 12.8 所示。

To Malayan Banking Berhad　　　　　　　　　　　　　　　　　　　Bank's Copy

Date

Dear Sirs

We enclose draft/s and documents as listed, please follow the instructions marked ☒

☐PURCHASE/DISCOUNT/NEGOTIATE subject to that payment

☐PURCHASE/DISCOUNT/NEGOTIATE subject to final payment (without advance) and to credit our account only upon receipt of funds from the reimbursing/paying bank.

OR

☐Present to the issuing bank for payment

Our Ref. No.	Drawee & Address	Tenor	Bill Amount

Documents attached	Draft	B/L	Comm. Inv.	Ins. Cert.	Cert. Orgn.	Pkg List	Wt. List	Bene. Cert.	Shpg Co. Cert.	AWB	DO	
Number of copies												

Enclosed also: 1 copy of Invoice and 1 photocopy of the original transport document for your file.

Covering:

Drawn under L/C No. - - - - - - - - - - - - - - - - - - Issued by - - - - - - - - - - - - - - - -

Dated - - - - - - - - - - - - - - -

Please follow instruction marked ☒

☐Advise acceptance and maturity date by cable/telex

☐In case of dishonor advise us by cable/telex giving reasons

Please utilize against Forward Contract No.

Date　　　　　　　　　　　　　　For

Please credit our Current Account No.　　　　　　　　with you.

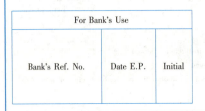

It is expressly agreed and we hereby undertake to repay or hold you harmless and fully indemnify you on demand the amount which you have paid us or will pay to us together with all costs and charges which you may have incurred. If payment is not made to you by the drawee of the draft and or the issuing bank of the letter of credit which has been discounted/purchased/negotiated or presented for payment by you for any reasons whatsoever including but not limited to any discrepancies in the documents.

We further agree that your bank assumes no responsibility for the authenticity or genuineness of documents delivered to your bank, nor for the quantity, quality, condition, genuineness, identity, title or delivery of the goods to which the documents relate.

For Bank's Use		
Bank's Ref. No.	Date E.P.	Initial

Yous faithfully

Authorized Signatures & Stamp

图 12.8　面函

银行审核面函的要点如下：

①确保面函的收件人为银行。

②确保面函为当下日期。

③确保面函引用的信用证号码正确。

④确保列举的随附单据的正本和副本份数正确，且单据中的金额、币种一致。

⑤确保寄送单据的银行为付款行、承兑行或议付行。

⑥确保付款指示清晰易懂。面函须清楚指明是否注意到有不符点，付款、承兑或议付是否是在保留追偿权的基础上做出。

3. 银行处理单据不符点的通常做法

（1）指定银行的做法。当提交单据出现单证不符或单单不符时，指定银行的做法如下：

①将所有单据或只将不符单据退还受益人/出口商进行修改，在信用证有效期和最后交单日期之前再次提交。

②在出口商要求下，向开证行或保兑行（如有）发电要求授权对不符单据进行付款、承兑或议付。

例如："在贵行信用证号码为＿＿＿＿＿，汇票金额为 ＿＿＿＿＿，我行编号为＿＿＿＿＿ 下提交的单据，除 ＿＿＿＿＿ 不符点外，其他内容与信用证条款相符。请电告我行是否议付单据。"

③要求受益人为其付款、承兑或议付开立赔付契约，表明如果开证行对不

符单据的付款、承兑或议付不做偿付,赔付契约开立人将退回包含利息和其他费用在内的款项。在这种情况下,指定银行在面函中将清楚载明:"我行对不符单据的付款/承兑/议付基于赔付契约。"

④依据实务经验以及与受益人的协议,以"保留追索权"的形式进行付款、承兑或议付,即如开证行对不符单据不做偿付,指定银行对受益人具有追索权。在这种情况下,指定银行在面函中将清楚载明:"我行对不符单据的支付保留追索权。"

⑤将所有单据退回受益人/出口商,由其直接向开证行寄单。

(2)开证行的做法。当受益人提交的单据或指定银行寄送的单据经审单后单证相符或单单相符,开证行须:

①接受单据。

②对受益人进行付款或对进行付款、承兑或议付的银行进行偿付。

但是,当单据为不符单据时,开证行将征询申请人的意见,如申请人同意接受不符点,开证行凭申请人按发票金额的付款对其交单,并对受益人或指定银行进行付款。如果申请人不接受不符点,开证行可行使拒付权。但是,在行使拒付权之前,开证行应遵循《跟单信用证统一惯例》的要求遵守如下规定:

①开证行是基于单据不符而非货物不符拒付。这是因为审核是对单据而非对其代表的货物进行审核。

②开证行须在不迟于收到单据次日起第五个银行工作日内发出拒付通知。银行可以自行做出拒付决定,或者在未能就是否接受不符点与申请人接洽而做出拒付决定。

③开证行须用 SWIFT、电报或电传等电子方式发出拒付通知。通知应载明拒付是由开证行而非进口商做出。例如,通知中包含任何诸如"买方拒绝……"或"我行客户拒绝……"的表述都是不当的,因为信用证是基于银行信用的。

④拒付通知须列出所有不符点,开证行不能用几个通知来提出不符点。根据《跟单信用证统一惯例》的规定,开证行不得在第一次通知中所列不符点不足以支持其拒付的情况下,在后续通知中进一步列出不符点。

⑤拒付通知还须指明单据在开证行手中等候交单人(出口商或指定银行)的处理,或者把单据交还交单人。开证行不得一边发出拒付通知,一边把单据向申请人交单。

4. 受益人处理单据不符点的通常做法

(1)判定开证行的拒付是否合理。在信用证情形下,开证行凭合规单据履行其对受益人的付款承诺。在实务中,不良开证行可能与不良申请人串通,用所谓的不符点拒绝付款。因此,在收到银行的拒付通知后,受益人应根据以下几点，判定开证行的通知是否合理、是否成立。

①拒付通知中所列不符点是否与 UCP 的相关规定冲突。

②银行是否要求受益人提交信用证未要求提交的单据。

如果开证行所提不符点不合理，受益人和指定银行应该立即电告开证行，催收款项，并对所致延迟付款的款项加收利息。在这种情况下，受益人与付款行、承兑行或议付行应该小心谨慎，配合行动，努力尽快收回款项。

（2）开证行拒付成立时的做法。如果开证行的拒付合理成立，受益人可以根据具体情况采取如下做法：

①立即修改单据，在信用证规定期限内提交正确单据。

②直接联系并请求申请人接受不符单据并进行付款。联系申请人很有必要，即使开证行对付款行、承兑行或议付行进行了偿付，开证行对其偿付可保有追索权。进口商如果不同意接受不符点，须退回偿付。

③对不符单据进行随证托收。虽然这不失为一种解决办法，但是把支付方式从信用证改成了托收，如果出口商不付款，开证行也不能进行付款。

正是由于任何不符点都能妨碍受益人得到支付，进出口贸易中的贸易商以及其他相关各方对银行审单方式的了解是正确缮制单据和正确提交单据的关键。

单据在国际结算中扮演着重要的角色。没有单据的参与，任何支付方式都不能单独存在。单据的使用促进了出口商的货款结算以及进口商的货物交接。单据在各种支付方式中运行。简言之，单据确保结算过程的顺利运行，并使国际贸易交易取得成功。

参考文献

[1]陈岩.国际商务制单[M].北京:对外经济贸易大学出版社,2011.

[2]傅泳.国际结算教程(英)[M].成都:西南财经大学出版社,2004.

[3]广东外语外贸大学国际经贸学院教材编写组.国际贸易实务[M].广州:广东高等教育出版社,2001.

[4]国际商会(ICC).国际贸易术语解释通则(2010)[M].北京:中国法制出版社,2011.

[5]国际商会中国国家委员会(ICC China).2000年国际贸易术语解释通则(Incoterms 2000)[M].曲鹏程,译.北京:中信出版社,2000.

[6]国际商会中国国家委员会(ICC China).ICC跟单信用证统一惯例UCP600[M].北京:中国民主法制出版社,2006.

[7]国际商会中国国家委员会(ICC China).国际商会托收统一规则[M].北京:中国民主法制出版社,2003.

[8]韩宝庆.轻松8步学外贸[M].北京:中国纺织出版社,2009.

[9]金融专业英语证书考试委员会.现代金融业务[M].北京:中国金融出版社,2006.

[10]黎孝先,石玉川,王健.国际贸易实务[M].北京:对外经济贸易大学出版社,2017.

[11]李贺,奚伟东.外贸单证实务[M].上海:上海财经大学出版社,2017.

[12]李雁玲,韩之怡,任丽明.国际贸易流程实验教程[M].北京:社会科学文献出版社,2010.

[13]刘崇仪.国际贸易[M].成都:西南财经大学出版社,1998.

[14]刘启萍,周树玲.外贸英文制单教程[M].北京:对外经济贸易大学出版社,2018.

[15]沈锦昶,徐秀琼,李宝华,等.国际支付与结算[M].上海:上海外语教育出版社,1996.

[16]帅建林,王红雨.案释国际贸易惯例[M].北京:中国商务出版社,2005.

[17]苏宗祥,徐捷.国际结算[M].北京:中国金融出版社,2020.

［18］苏宗祥.国际结算［M］.北京:中国金融出版社,2008.

［19］田运银.国际贸易实务疑难解答［M］.北京:中国海关出版社,2010.

［20］童宏祥,刘春娣.外贸跟单实务［M］.上海:上海财经大学出版社,2015.

［21］王红雨,傅泳,何康明.国际贸易实务(英文)［M］.重庆:重庆大学出版社,2015.

［22］王玉奇,罗丙志.新编国际结算［M］.广州:华南理工大学出版社,1999.

［23］余世明.国际贸易实务与案例分析［M］.广州:暨南大学出版社,2011.

［24］余心之,徐美容.新编外贸单证实务［M］.北京:对外经济贸易大学出版社,2016.

［25］张亚芬,李红.国际贸易实务与案例［M］.北京:高等教育出版社,2013.

［26］赵明霞.国际结算习题与案例［M］.北京:中国金融出版社,2010.

［27］中国国际商会.跟单信用证统一惯例:国际商会第500号出版物［M］.北京:中国对外经济贸易出版社,1994.